CW00922956

THE BORDER REGIMENT
IN THE GREAT WAR

Printed & bound by Antony Rowe Ltd, Eastbourne

[For Private Circulation only.]

THE BORDER REGIMENT IN THE GREAT WAR

BY

COLONEL H. C. WYLLY, C.B.

Printed and Published for the Regimental Committee by

GALE & POLDEN, LTD.

WELLINGTON WORKS, ALDERSHOT

ALSO AT LONDON AND PORTSMOUTH

PREFACE

THIS volume contains the history of the Regimental Depot and the thirteen Battalions into which " The Border Regiment " was expanded during the Great War of 1914-1918.

Our warmest thanks are due to the author, Colonel H. C. Wylly, C.B., for the skilful manner in which he has recorded the doings of the different Battalions in six separate theatres of war, and has merged them into one consecutive narrative—a task which at first sight appeared well nigh impossible.

Before commencing the work it was considered whether better results could not be obtained by keeping the history of each Battalion throughout the war separate ; but this idea was discarded, not only on account of the repetition which such an arrangement would have involved, but chiefly in order to bring out the important fact that The Border Regiment, both in peace and war, exists not as a collection of separate units, but as one large united family irrespective of the number of Battalions embodied in it. The two Regular and the two Territorial Army Battalions and the Regimental Depot are the permanent portions of the Regiment which exist to-day to bear the honours won by their comrades in the Service Battalions, now disbanded, and it is hoped that the personnel of those Service Battalions will always regard the existing four Battalions and the Depot as their living representatives.

The History of The Border Regiment has been compiled with a triple purpose in view.

Firstly, as a personal souvenir for those who fought with the Regiment to enable them to recall to mind the part which they and their comrades played in assisting to bring about the great victory.

Secondly, for the information of past members of the Regiment and the people of the counties of Cumberland and Westmorland.

Thirdly, for those who come after, in the hope that it will help to foster throughout the Regiment that feeling of *esprit de corps* on which the efficiency of our army so greatly depends.

Our thanks are also due to those officers who have prepared the sketch maps ; to Lieut.-Colonel H. W. Grubb, C.M.G., D.S.O., and the members of the Regimental Committee for their work in connection with the preparation of this History ; and to Mr. C. S. Seager, director of the publishers, for his valuable advice and assistance at all times so readily given.

P.G. Sinclair MacLagan
Major-General
Colonel Commanding The Border Regiment.

November, 1924.

CONTENTS

ILLUSTRATIONS

MAPS

The Border Regiment in the Great War

CHAPTER I

1914

THE OPENING OF THE WAR.

THE BATTLE OF YPRES.

THE statement has on many occasions been made that Great Britain was altogether unprepared for the war which broke out in August, 1914 : but this is only true in part. The country and the people were wholly unexpectant of a war of such magnitude as that which Germany forced upon the world, but the United Kingdom was probably actually more ready for war than ever before in its long history. The Regular Army had continued in the immediately preceding years to gather a very valuable experience in our constantly recurring Indian and Colonial campaigns and expeditions ; the war which some twelve years previously had been brought to an end in South Africa had put the British military forces to a rude if a very practical test ; the Regular Army, insufficient in numbers for the work there demanded of it, had been supplemented and reinforced by drafts from the Militia, Yeomanry and Volunteers and by large contingents from the forces of the Overseas Dominions and Colonies; and the military authorities had learnt in a hard school and with much expenditure of lives and treasure to realize the more serious of our defects of training and organization, and had done much to remedy them.

The South African War safely over, steps were taken to put our military house in order ; the office of Commander-in-Chief was abolished and an Army Council was set up, in the autumn of 1906 a General Staff was constituted, a reserve of officers for the Army was provided by converting certain Volunteer Corps into Officers Training Corps, while the Regular Army and the Army of the Second Line were equally reorganized for war on a scale larger than that ever before contemplated. The Regular Army was organized in an expeditionary force of six divisions of all arms, each of three infantry brigades, and one cavalry division, the total war establishment of each infantry division being 18,000 of all ranks with 76 guns and 24 machine guns ; the Yeomanry became the second line of cavalry, and was reorganized into 14 brigades ; while the Volunteers, who had for many years past represented a mere congeries of regiments, were converted into a local militia under the title of the Territorial Force and were grouped in 14 divisions and organized on the lines of the Regular Army. The old Militia was renamed the Special Reserve and was relegated to its ancient function of feeding the Regular Army in time of war.

Further, training was improved in every possible way, mobilization was regularly practised, and the result was that " in every respect the Expeditionary Force of 1914 was incomparably the best trained, best organized and best equipped British Army that ever went forth to war. Except in the matter of co-operation between aeroplanes and artillery, and use of machine guns, its training would stand comparison in all respects with that of the Germans. Where it fell short of our enemies was first and foremost in numbers ; so that, though not ' contemptible,' it was almost negligible in comparison with Continental armies even of the smaller States." [1]

The story of the events which led up to the war has been set down in books which abound, and there seems no need for its repetition in the pages of a regimental history of the war ; but certain dates may be recalled as showing their relation to the opening military events. On the 28th June the heir to the Austrian throne and his consort were assassinated at Serajevo, the capital of Bosnia ; on the 23rd July the Vienna Cabinet presented an ultimatum to the Serbian Government ; two days later Austria declared war ; on the 29th Russia ordered partial and on the 31st full mobilization of her forces ; on the 1st August Germany declared war against Russia and on the 3rd against France, having already on the 2nd August presented something of the nature of an ultimatum to the Belgian Government, setting forth that the German Government had certain intelligence of the intention of the French forces to march on the Meuse by way of Givet and Namur, and demanding unresisted passage for the German armies through Belgian territory. On the 2nd August the German troops crossed the Polish and French frontiers, and on the 4th that of Belgium, and on the same day Great Britain declared war on Germany.

On the 5th and 6th August meetings of the Cabinet were held in London and were attended by the chief Ministers, by Lord Kitchener, who became Secretary of State for War on the 6th, by Field-Marshal Sir John French, the Commander-in-Chief designate of the Expeditionary Force, and by the leading sailors and soldiers, and it was decided that *for the present* four infantry divisions only, and the cavalry division, should be embarked for France, embarkation commencing on the 9th ; that the regular garrisons of India and South Africa should be brought home, and that the British forces on arrival in France should be concentrated in the area about Le Cateau and Avesnes. The decision was further come to that the Expeditionary Force should be organized in three Army Corps, of which the nucleus of one had been kept up at Aldershot, but for the two others now formed the corps staff had to be improvised. The Army Corps were commanded, the Ist by Lieutenant-General Sir Douglas Haig, the IInd by Lieutenant-General Sir James Grierson and, later, on his death a few days after his arrival in France, by General Sir Horace Smith-Dorrien, the IIIrd by Lieutenant-General W. P. Pulteney, and the Cavalry Division by Major-General E. Allenby.

None of the battalions of The Border Regiment were included in either one of the above-named Army Corps. When the war commenced the Regiment

[1] *Official History of the War,* vol. i, pp. 10 and 11.

contained five battalions all told—2 Regular, 1 Special Reserve and 2 Territorial, and of these one battalion, the 1st, was stationed in Burma, the 2nd was quartered at Pembroke Dock, while the headquarters of the 3rd and 4th were at Carlisle and that of the 5th at Workington. As was the case with every other regiment of the British Army, The Border Regiment underwent very considerable expansion as the war progressed, and the war services of the different units, old and new, will be dealt with in the course of this record; but inasmuch as the 2nd and 5th Battalions were the only ones which proceeded to a theatre of war during the latter part of the year 1914, the earlier portion of this History is mainly concerned with these two battalions.

At the end of July the 2nd Battalion was engaged in battalion training at Rosebush Camp, some 27 miles distant from Pembroke Dock, when on the evening of the 29th orders were received to return to barracks with all possible expedition. A start was made that night and Pembroke Dock was reached at 6 a.m. on the 30th, when it was found that the " precautionary period prior to mobilization " had already set in. Next day several parties of varying strength were sent out to Invergordon in Scotland, to Grimsby, to the Severn Tunnel and to Swansea to furnish guards over docks and other important places, and on the 4th August orders were received for general mobilization. A conducting party then proceeded to Carlisle to fetch the reservists who were now coming in, while Lieutenant Lamb and Second-Lieutenant Clancey also left for Carlisle and there deposited the Colours in the Cathedral.

During the next few days several parties of reservists arrived from the Regimental Depot—92 on the 6th, 403 on the 7th and 153 on the 8th; on the 27th orders were received warning the Battalion to be prepared to move to Southampton at a very early date, and on the 29th the 2nd Battalion, 27 officers and 1,068 other ranks, with 62 horses, left Pembroke Dock in three trains, the last of these reaching Southampton at 7 p.m. that day. Here it was announced that the Battalion was to form part of the 20th Brigade, 7th Division, the other battalions of the Brigade being the 2nd Battalions of the Yorkshire and Wiltshire Regiments and of the Gordon Highlanders. On the 5th the Brigade moved by march route to a camp at Lyndhurst in the New Forest, and two or three days later the composition of the 20th Brigade was changed, when the 7th Division and its units were composed and commanded as under :—

Commander : Major-General T. Capper.
    20th Infantry Brigade : Brigadier-General H. G. Ruggles-Brise.
        1st Grenadier Guards.
        2nd Scots Guards.
        2nd Border Regiment.
        2nd Gordon Highlanders.
    21st Infantry Brigade : Brigadier-General H. E. Watts.
        2nd Bedfordshire Regiment.
        2nd Yorkshire Regiment.
        2nd Royal Scots Fusiliers.
        2nd Wiltshire Regiment.

22nd Infantry Brigade : Brigadier-General S. T. B. Lawford.
2nd The Queen's Royal West Surrey Regiment.
2nd Warwickshire Regiment.
1st Royal Welch Fusiliers.
1st South Staffordshire Regiment.

While camped at Lyndhurst 64 more reservists joined the 2nd Battalion The Border Regiment, and then on the afternoon of Sunday, 4th October, orders were issued that no one was to leave camp, and late in the afternoon part of the 7th Division began to set out for Southampton. About 10 o'clock that night the Battalion was ordered to march from Lyndhurst in two parties, the first party, Headquarters, " A " and " B " Companies and half the transport, under Lieutenant-Colonel L. I. Wood marched at 10.15 p.m. and the second party, consisting of the remainder of the Battalion under Major J. T. I. Bosanquet, half an hour later. On arrival at Southampton the men turned in for the rest of the night in sheds at the docks and embarked next day, the 5th, Colonel Wood's party in the *Turkoman*, and that under Major Bosanquet in the *Minneapolis*, which also carried the Headquarters of the 7th Division.

The strength of the 2nd Battalion The Border Regiment on embarkation was 30 officers, 1 warrant officer, 50 sergeants, 16 drummers and 910 rank and file.

The names of the officers accompanying the Battalion were : Lieutenant-Colonel L. I. Wood ; Majors J. T. I. Bosanquet and W. Lynn Allen, D.S.O. ; Captains G. E. Warren, L. E. H. Molyneux-Seel, R. N. Gordon, E. H. H. Lees, C. G. W. Andrews (adjutant), and C. A. J. Cholmondeley ; Lieutenants H. A. Askew, C. Lamb, P. J. Egerton, H. V. Gerrard, W. Watson and J. B. B. Warren ; Second-Lieutenants H. F. Chads, T. H. Beves, G. W. H. Hodgson, C. H. Evans, H. L. Chatfield, C. G. V. Surtees and T. J. Clancey ; Hon. Lieutenant F. W. Mitchell was quartermaster, and attached from the 3rd Battalion were Lieutenants H. P. O. Sleigh, E. C. Clegg, A. B. Johnson and M. S. N. Kennedy.

The fleet of some 14 huge transports got under weigh and steamed eastwards up the Channel, and it was tolerably soon evident that the reinforcements now leaving England were not intended to strengthen the original Expeditionary Force in Northern France.

What then had occurred to cause the diversion from the main war theatre of this very considerable force ?

The serious check which the German armies had sustained in the Battle of the Marne had drawn the attention of the Higher Command to the now increased importance of Antwerp as a place from whence a British force, backed by sea power and in conjunction with the Belgian armies, might strike at the flank and rear of the German invaders. " Antwerp was not only the sole stronghold of the Belgian nation ; it was also the true left flank of the Allied left front in the West. It guarded the whole line of the Channel ports. It threatened the flanks and rear of the German armies in France. It was the gateway from which a British army might emerge at any moment upon their sensitive and even vital communications." [1]

[1] *The World Crisis*, vol. i, p. 332.

The German failure at the Marne made the capture of Antwerp an urgent necessity for the invaders, and as early as 9th September the German Emperor gave orders that attempts be at once made for the reduction of the fortress, and on the 28th fire was opened upon the exterior forts with 17-inch howitzers. Some six divisions of Belgian troops were engaged in the defence of Antwerp, but the situation was very grave and the serious effect which its fall might have on the campaign was fully realized by the Allied Governments, so that when the Brussels Cabinet sent forth urgent appeals for help, both England and France gave serious thought to the manner in which such help could best be afforded, and on the 3rd October Field-Marshal Lord Kitchener was able to announce to the First Lord of the Admiralty, then in Antwerp, that the following reinforcements might early be expected :—

The 7th Division under General Capper, a Cavalry Division under General Byng, certain naval detachments, a French Territorial Division and a strong brigade of *Fusiliers Marins*—making some 53,000 men in all. Considering the heavy commitments of the Allies in the main theatre of war, these reinforcements were probably all that could at the time well be spared, the only question was whether Antwerp could resist the hostile attacks sufficiently long to allow of the French and British relieving forces arriving in time. The British infantry and cavalry began to disembark at Ostend and Zeebrügge early on the 6th October, while the French Division and the Marines were embarking at Havre or entraining for Dunkirk.

The left wing of the 2nd Battalion The Border Regiment in the *Minneapolis* was the first to arrive at Zeebrügge, and, disembarking, went at once by train to Bruges and marched from there to the suburb of St. André, where the officers and men were billeted. " We had to picquet the roads," writes an officer of the Battalion. " The Gordon Highlanders held an outpost line in front of us. Headquarters billeted at ' The Rosary.' The people very good to our men, but would take all their cap and collar badges, a great nuisance afterwards, as it was impossible to tell a man's unit when he fell out."

The troops remained all the 7th in St. André, and here about 5 p.m. the right wing and Headquarters of the Battalion which had landed at Ostend joined under Colonel Wood.

By this time the position of affairs in Antwerp had become very serious and General Rawlinson, the commander of the newly constituted IVth Corps, to which the 7th Division belonged, had visited the fortress on the previous day and had seen for himself how things were going, thereupon realizing that his plan of operations must undergo alteration. Could Antwerp have been saved from capture by the enemy, it had been intended that the Allied left should be so extended as to hold the line of the Scheldt from Antwerp through Tournai and Douai to Arras, thence menacing the German communications through Mons and Valenciennes. It being, however, now evident that Antwerp must fall, it was decided that the Belgian Army, covered by Rawlinson's corps, should retire by Bruges and Ghent to the line of the Yser, protecting the Allied left and preventing any German coastal attack. As a matter of fact, the evacuation of Antwerp by the Anglo-Belgian garrison commenced on the evening of the 8th October.

At 9.30 on the 8th October the 2nd Battalion, in pursuance of orders received, marched as rearguard to the Brigade via Leffinghem to Ostend and there entrained for Ghent, which was reached at 11 on the morning of the 10th ; here a halt was called until the afternoon, when the Battalion moved off again to Destelberghem, there taking up a line of outposts facing E.—" B," " C " and " D " Companies providing the outposts while " A " Company was in reserve in the village. The Battalion did not come under fire, but a body of French Marines, who occupied a position on the right of the 2nd Border Regiment facing S., was continuously engaged.

All through the night parties of refugees were streaming past from Antwerp, and these reported large German forces as moving north.

Up to this time the 7th Infantry Division and the cavalry under General Byng had formed an independent corps commanded by General Rawlinson and directed by orders issued from the War Office in London, but on the 9th Sir John French received a telegram placing Rawlinson under his command, and the commander of the IVth Corps was now told " to hold the line of the Lys if he could, but not to risk a big fight. If he could hold on to these positions I promised to connect up with him by the 13th or 14th. If, however, he were forced to retire, he was directed to do so in the direction of St. Omer, where the IIIrd Corps was now detraining." [1]

At 4 p.m. on the 11th The Border Regiment handed over the trenches they had made to the French Marines, and, later in the evening of the same day, proceeded by forced march, made all the longer and more tedious by reason of the guide losing his way, to Somerghem, which was reached early on the 12th ; and then leaving again after a few hours' rest, the march was resumed and the Battalion arrived at Thielt after dark and was accommodated in billets. Here, on the next morning a hostile aeroplane made its appearance and was shot down by fire from the Brigade. Marching on again through Roulers and Ypres, the Battalion was in Zillebecke shortly after midday on the 15th. During this march the enemy was for the first time met with, the Battalion scouts, under Lieutenant Lamb, coming upon a patrol of German Uhlans while searching a wood ; fire was opened at short range by both sides and 8 of the enemy were killed, while one officer and one man were wounded and taken prisoners. There were no casualties among the scouts.

At Zillebecke an outpost line was taken up and here an unfortunate incident occurred, Lieutenant Egerton losing his way in the fog while returning from inspecting an advanced post and being shot by his own sentries ; this officer, who had been for three years Adjutant of the 1st Battalion, died in Ypres a few hours later.

On the afternoon of the 16th the Brigade marched to Zandvoorde and the Battalion went into billets, but as hostile shell fire was expected entrenchments were dug, the 2nd Border Regiment being in support to the 2nd Battalion Scots Guards on the N. side of the village.

[1] *1914.* p. 201.

The orders received about this date by Rawlinson and under which he was acting are thus stated by the Commander of the British Expeditionary Force :— [1]

"Rawlinson was to move with his right on Courtrai, keeping generally level with the IIIrd Corps in the subsequent advance, should that prove possible ; his cavalry under Byng were to move to the N. of him.

"I had told Rawlinson that, whilst conforming to the general move E., he must keep an eye on the enemy's detachments known to be at Bruges and Roulers. I told him I would deal with these later by means of the Ist Corps, but for the moment his left required careful watching."

Two pages further on Sir John French writes that having good reasons to believe that Menin was very weakly occupied on the 17th, he issued orders to General Rawlinson to move on and attack that place on the 18th, but that General Rawlinson "did not march." This last remark is not, however, borne out by the war diary of The Border Regiment, wherein it is definitely stated : "18th October. The Battalion marched to Kruiseik and arrived 5 p.m. The Brigade outposts— 2nd Battalion Gordon Highlanders—came under shrapnel fire at about 6 p.m. The remainder of the day was quiet.

"19th.—The Brigade advanced in artillery formation on Menin, which was occupied by the enemy. On arrival at a village, America, the Brigade was subjected to a heavy shrapnel fire from enemy guns firing from direction of Menin. Two men of the Battalion were wounded. At 3 p.m. the Battalion fell back and entrenched on Kruiseik Hill leaving ' D ' Company at America as support."

As a matter of fact, in being ordered to advance and capture Menin, General Rawlinson was given an impossible task ; he was operating without material support on a front of 20 miles, and the abandonment of the advance was due to the sudden appearance of two new German army corps from the direction of Courtrai, the proximity of which was foreshadowed by the capture on the 18th by French cavalry, near Roulers, of some cyclists belonging to one of them.

On the morning of the 20th October " D " Company rejoined and the completion of the trenches on Kruiseik Hill was seriously taken in hand, but owing to the very great extent of frontage which the 2nd Border Regiment had to cover —some 2¼ miles—coupled with the nature of the country, companies, platoons and sections could not in all cases be connected by trenches. When completed the Battalion was thus distributed : " B " Company on the extreme left, " A " and " C " Companies in the centre and two platoons of " D " Company on the extreme right ; the remainder of " D " Company was in reserve some 600 yards in rear. About midday the Scots Guards reported that the Germans were advancing in considerable strength from the E. and were then only some 800 yards distant, and a patrol of " B " Company was nearly surprised in some houses S.E. of the village of Kruiseik and only with difficulty managed to get away.

By night the 20th Brigade was entrenched in the following order on the hill in a line resembling a half-circle or blunt salient : 1st Grenadier Guards, 2nd Scots Guards, 2nd Border Regiment, 2nd Gordon Highlanders, and orders were issued

[1] *1914*, p. 219.

that the " trenches were to be held at all costs." There were no supports or reserves to the Brigade, beyond the two platoons of The Border Regiment.

The other two brigades of the 7th Division were moved about during the operations of the next few days between Zandvoorde and Zonnebecke as occasion required, but the 20th Brigade did not move from Kruiseik Hill for upwards of a week. The battalions composing it had been directed to " hold on," and they did hold on, such of them as were spared, for each of the four battalions, Guardsmen and Linesmen, fought it out to a finish ; but in the early days of this fighting the 2nd Border Regiment probably suffered more severely than did any of the other three battalions, for their trenches, along the Zandvoorde Road where it cuts the Kruiseik–Wervicq Road, were commanded on three sides by the enemy's artillery and especially harassed by the German guns on the America Ridge about a mile to the S.E., where houses gave the German gunners good cover. It was impossible to leave the trenches by day and rations and supplies had to be brought up by night ; there was no telephonic communication and messages between the Head-quarters of the Battalion and the companies and to the rear had to be sent by runners ; further, the country was very close and the enemy snipers were able to advance at certain points undetected to within 300 yards of the trenches.

The enemy's bombardment of the trenches continued very heavy from the 21st to 24th, many of the trenches were blown in by the fire from the German heavy guns, while machine guns played upon the parapets, and many small attacks were launched and as often repulsed ; one officer, Second-Lieutenant Chatfield, had the curiosity to count the number of the German shells and estimated that during ten hours on the 24th they came over at the rate of 150 every hour ! On the night of the 24th–25th the Battalion machine-gun section was blown out of its trench, one gun being buried, and the detachment having to retire to a second position ; but next night, Lieutenant Watson, who with his men did splendid work throughout, returned, re-dug and reoccupied his first position, and early on the 26th, seeing the enemy advancing in large numbers, he advanced his machine gun to a position in a hedge running from the Headquarters trench to the village, and opening fire at 300 yards did satisfactory execution on the German infantry.

On the 25th some 200 of the enemy, who later were made prisoners by the Scots Guards, had broken through the line on the left of " B " Company of the Battalion, and then put up their hands in sign of surrender; but when Major Allen went forward with six men to bring them in he was at once shot dead with one of his party.

During the night of the 25th–26th the enemy had succeeded in making a con-siderable advance and was concentrated in large numbers in the plantations and broken ground in the British front ; he then launched an attack about 9 a.m. on the 26th and succeeded in capturing the front-line trenches occupied by " A " and " B " Companies, the few survivors of which—some 70 of all ranks—then retiring to the flanks and joining up in rear with the Scouts and the men of the Battalion Headquarters. The Germans continued to come on in masses, but eventually were held by the fire of the Scouts under Lieutenant Lamb, that of the machine guns under Lieutenant Watson, and the officers and men composing

Battalion Headquarters. At the same time " C " Company was brought up by Captain Molyneux-Seel to support " A " and " B " Companies, but no other reinforcements were forthcoming, and the orders from the Brigade were " hold on till nightfall, when you will be relieved."

At 6 p.m. Lieutenant-Colonel Wood was ordered to withdraw at dark and the Battalion then fell back on Zandvoorde, the 1st and 2nd Divisions, which had now at last come up, taking up the attack. The 2nd Battalion Border Regiment bivouacked for the night in a field near Zandvoorde, " C " Company marching in to Ypres and being there billeted, while next day, the 27th, the whole Battalion was concentrated at Zonnebecke.

In his despatch of the 20th November the Field-Marshal wrote as follows :—

" On the 27th October I went to the Headquarters of the Ist Corps at Hooge to personally investigate the condition of the 7th Division. Owing to constant marching and fighting, ever since its hasty disembarkation in aid of the Antwerp garrison, this division had suffered great losses and was becoming very weak, I therefore decided temporarily to break up the IVth Corps and place the 7th Division with the Ist Corps under the command of Sir Douglas Haig. The 3rd Cavalry Division was similarly detailed for service with the Ist Corps. . . . On receipt of orders, in accordance with the above arrangement, Sir Douglas Haig redistributed the line held by the Ist Corps as follows :—

(a) The 7th Division from the Chateau E. of Zandvoorde to the Menin Road
(b) The 1st Division from the Menin Road to a point immediately W. of Reytel village.
(c) The 2nd Division to near Moorslede–Zonnebecke Road."

Later in the same despatch Sir John French described the attack made by the enemy on the 29th against the centre of the Ist Corps, the equally heavy attack of the 30th in the direction of Zandvoorde and the consequent withdrawal to the Klein Zillebecke Ridge by the cavalry whereby the right of the 7th Division was exposed ; and finally gives it as his considered opinion that between 2 and 3 p.m. on Saturday the 31st October was the most critical moment in the whole of the Ypres Battle, when the 1st Division had fallen back from Gheluvelt to a line resting on the junction of the Frezenberg Road with the Ypres–Menin highway, while the 7th Division had been bent back to the Klein Zillebecke Ridge. During these days of strain the Kaiser was with his men, urging them on to repeated attacks by hysterical assurances that the winning of Ypres would decide the issue of the war. We may now see what part the 2nd Battalion Border Regiment played in these great and epoch-making operations.

Early on the morning of the 29th urgent orders were received for the Battalion —now only consisting of 12 officers and 538 other ranks—to at once reinforce the Gordon Highlanders who were being very heavily pressed, and the Battalion then advanced, deploying to its right with its left on the Ypres–Menin Road, and moved towards Kruiseik Hill ; but on arrival at the first of its ridges the Battalion came under an exceptionally heavy shell, machine-gun and rifle fire, and for the best part of an hour could make no further progress. When it was possible to resume the advance Lieutenant-Colonel Wood was almost at once hit, while Captain Molyneux-Seel was twice wounded by the fire from a machine gun concealed in a house which had been pointed out as one of the objectives of the advance ; and as Captain Warren had also been wounded the command of what was now left of the Battalion was assumed by Captain Askew.

"C" Company was on the right and "D" on the left with the machine-gun section, while "A" and "B," only 67 strong and temporarily amalgamated into one company, formed the reserve. "We advanced up the hill into Gheluvelt village," writes an officer who was present, " and held on to the top for over an hour before we were reinforced. The Colonel was hit early in the leg and got back safely. We then advanced on the N. slope of the hill through the village. I saw the German reinforcements coming along the Menin Road in fours about 1,200 yards away, so I got the machine guns across a ploughed field into some turnips and opened fire. One gun got hit almost at once and was *hors de combat*, but the other escaped owing to our changing our position every few minutes. The enemy broke off the road and lay in the ditch, which we opened on again until they were seen retiring and our ammunition supply was exhausted. We had no limber and could only carry about 12 boxes of ammunition. I got the guns back to a sunken road in rear and found Captain Warren and Lieutenant Simon Fraser of the Gordons sitting there. I was sitting between Fraser and a lance-corporal of ours when a shell burst killing them both instantaneously ; two of my team were wounded slightly. I then met Major Cator and the Brigadier, who told me to tell our companies in front to retire at dusk, as the Ist Corps were then once more in their own position."

On the 30th the Battalion received orders to move to the E. of Hooge to support the advance of the cavalry, and spent the day in some woods to the N.W. of a château near Zonnebecke, returning late at night to the cross-roads Hooge–Ypres–Menin and entrenching on the W. side of the road, a continuous line having been dug by morning. Throughout the whole of the 31st the Battalion was heavily shelled, but at night left its trenches and moved towards Klein Zillebecke and prepared a position between the 1st and 2nd Divisions, the Scots Guards being on the left and the Grenadier Guards and Gordons in reserve in rear. Again on the 1st November was the enemy bombardment very severe, but later The Border Regiment "got some of their own back." About 10 a.m. a German battalion in tolerably close formation was noticed crossing the open from one small wood to another, evidently in ignorance of the proximity of the British infantry in their entrenchments. Lieutenant Lamb with his scouts and Lieutenant Watson with his machine gun opened fire and did great execution, but naturally provoked retaliation, and by 1 p.m. the German fire had blown up the machine gun and killed several men, after which the enemy gunners began to search the wood and road with shells of all sizes. The machine gun had to be left for the time being while the team crawled away into safety, but at night the men went back and retrieved the gun.

Early on the morning of the 2nd November movements of the enemy on the right front of the position of the Battalion were noticed, and the left of "D"

Company was brought back so as to form a continuous line and connect with " C " Company ; the Battalion was now on the extreme right of the 20th Brigade. Then about 10 o'clock a very violent shelling began and continued for some five hours, a shell smashing the only gun of the Battalion remaining in action, killing one man and wounding five others of the machine-gun detachment, including Lieutenant Watson. On the gun-fire abating, bugles were heard sounding and the enemy attack came on, but the men of the Battalion held their fire until the Germans were almost on the top of them, and then opened with tremendous effect, the assailants being mown down in swathes. The enemy fell back to the shelter of the woods and then, after a brief interval the bugles sounded once more and the attack was again pressed, and again was there the same slaughter. This time, however, some of the troops on the right of the Battalion gave way, leaving that flank in the air and in danger of being turned, when Sergeant Booth, of the 2nd Border Regiment, seeing this, left his trench under heavy fire and with great gallantry brought up two sections from the reserve, reoccupied the vacated trenches and kept the line intact until three hours later reinforcements came up. That night the 2nd Battalion The Border Regiment was relieved by the Gordon Highlanders and retired to the woods near Ypres where it went into Brigade Reserve.

Here the Battalion remained until the 5th November, receiving its first reinforcement of 98 non-commissioned officers and men under Captain N. F. Jenkins, of the 3rd Battalion of the Regiment. On the night of the 5th the 20th Brigade marched by night to Locre, passing through Ypres, and happily, though the town was being heavily shelled and houses were falling on all sides, not a single man was hurt. Locre was reached about 5 a.m. on the 6th and all ranks lay down in a field till morning, when billets were told off.

" Day after day," writes the chronicler of the deeds of "the First Seven Divisions," [1] the same British battalions, jaded, depleted of officers, and gradually dwindling into mere skeletons, were called upon to withstand the attacks of fresh and fresh troops. It was not merely that the Germans had the superiority in numbers on each occasion when they attacked . . . but they had also the unspeakable advantage of being able at any time to direct a stream of fresh troops against any given part of our thin, weary, battered line. Thus, on 29th October the XXVIIth Reserve Corps attacked Kruiseik; on the 30th the XVth Army Corps attacked Zandvoorde; on 31st October and 1st November we had the XIIIth, XXIVth and IInd Bavarian Corps attacking the line from the Menin Road to Messines, to which on 2nd November must be added the XXVIth Army Corps. By this time, however, the 16th French Army Corps had come up."

During the hard fighting of these anxious days the 7th Division had been reduced from 400 officers and 12,000 non-commissioned officers and men to a strength of but little over 3,000 of all ranks, and the casualties in the 2nd Battalion The Border Regiment had been terribly heavy.

Between the 18th October and the 7th November 9 officers and 79 other ranks had been killed, 6 officers and 259 non-comissioned officers and men had been

[1] Hamilton, pp. 274, 275.

wounded, while 5 officers and 253 other ranks were missing, the majority of these last being either killed or wounded, a total casualty list of 611 all ranks ! The names of the officers, with the dates on which they became casualties, are as follows : *Killed or died of wounds :* Major W. Lynn Allen (25th October), Captains R. N. Gordon (23rd October), E. H. H. Lees (26th October), C. G. W. Andrews (26th October), and C. A. J. Cholmondeley (26th October), Lieutenants H. V. Gerrard (2nd November), J. B. B. Warren (25th October), and G. W. H. Hodgson (2nd November), and Second-Lieutenant T. J. Clancey (23rd October) ; *Wounded :* Lieutenant-Colonel L. I. Wood (29th October), Major J. T. I. Bosanquet (26th October), Captain G. E. Warren (2nd November), Lieutenants W. Watson (2nd November), T. H. Beves (26th October) and E. C. Clegg, 3rd Battalion (25th October) ; *Missing :* Captain L. E. H. Molyneux-Seel, Lieutenant H. P. O. Sleigh, Second-Lieutenants C. H. Evans, C. G. V. Surtees (killed) and T. H. Bowley, Leinster Regiment, attached (killed). Second-Lieutenant Evans was wounded and captured on the 26th October and was shot by the Germans after capture for trying to defend a man of the Regiment whom the enemy were ill-treating.

The conduct of the Battalion during these days did not pass unnoticed ; on the 3rd November the following message was sent to the Commanding Officer from the G.O.C. 7th Division : "*Stout action of The Border Regiment in maintaining its trenches throughout the day, although unsupported on its right, is much commended. Congratulate Border Regiment from me and tell them I am making a special report on their conduct through Corps Headquarters.*"

Then the following messages were received by the Brigadier from the Divisional Commander regarding the services of the 20th Brigade :—

"*The G.O.C. has had great pleasure in forwarding to Headquarters, IVth Army Corps, a despatch (of which this is a copy for your retention) testifying to the devoted conduct of the Officers and Men of the Brigade under your command during the recent operations near Ypres. He hopes you will take occasion to bring his remarks to the notice of the Officers Commanding Battalions concerned.*

"*20th Infantry Brigade. This Brigade had eventually the most difficult task to perform as it had to hold the exposed position of Kruiseik Hill. It was impossible to abandon this point without prejudicing not only the rest of the line, but also the pivot of all contemplated offensive action. In spite, therefore, of the natural unfavourable situation Kruiseik Hill had to be held. The 20th Brigade did this itself under constant violent artillery fire by day and often by night. The defence was by no means passive, but counter attacks were frequently and successfully made. Later on in the fighting this Brigade showed the same tenacity in defence and on one critical occasion (31st October) by its forward action was mainly instrumental in restoring the fight. The losses of this Brigade were very heavy.*

"*2nd Battalion Border Regiment. This Battalion held a portion of the Kruiseik position in front of Ypres during which it was exposed to particularly heavy shell fire for 3 days and nights. Many of the trenches were blown in, but no trench was given up by any portion of this Battalion. On 2nd November this Battalion formed the right of the Brigade at Veldhoek. Owing to troops on the right giving way the enemy was able to occupy some woods and so surround the right of The Border Regiment. Never-*

theless the Battalion held its line for some hours until the enemy could be driven from these woods by relieving troops. During the fighting this Battalion lost very heavily. The devoted and firm conduct of this Battalion repeatedly called forth the admiration of the Brigadier and of officers in other battalions in the same brigade ; and I, myself, can testify to its fortitude and determination to maintain its position at all costs ; a spirit which saved a difficult and critical situation.

" It is impossible to praise this Battalion too highly for its firmness and battle discipline."

Finally, General Rawlinson, the IVth Corps commander, wrote as follows :—

" After the deprivations and tension of being pursued day and night by an infinitely stronger force, the Division had to pass through the worst ordeal of all. It was left to a little force of 30,000 to keep the German army at bay while the other British corps were being brought up from the Aisne. Here they clung on like grim death, with almost every man in the trenches, holding a line which of necessity was a great deal too long— —a thin, exhausted line—against which the prime of the German first-line troops were hurling themselves with fury. The odds against them were about eight to one ; and when once the enemy found the range of a trench, the shells dropped into it from one end to the other with terrible effect. Yet the men stood firm and defended Ypres in such a manner that a German officer afterwards described their action as a brilliant feat of arms, and said that they were under the impression that there had been four British army corps against them at this point. When the Division was afterwards withdrawn from the firing line to refit, it was found that out of 400 officers who set out from England there were only 44 left, and out of 12,000 men only 2,336."

During the next ten days the 2nd Border Regiment made several moves, and there was not much leisure available for the reorganization and re-equipping made necessary by the disorder and loss occasioned by the recent fighting. On the 6th November the remnants of the Battalion—some 9 officers and 434 other ranks—marched from Locre to Meteren, and thence on the 17th to Sailly via Bac St. Maur, and owing to the depletion of its ranks it was for a short time formed into a composite battalion with the 2nd Gordon Highlanders, who had incurred almost equally severe losses in the long-enduring Battle of Ypres. On arrival at Sailly, however, several drafts of officers and men joined the service companies, and by the 1st December these amounted to 6 officers and 537 non-commissioned officers and men, so that the Battalion was then again at full war strength. The officers who came out were Lieutenant G. P. L. Drake-Brockman and Second-Lieutenants H. Owen, J. Horsley and C. R. Cooch,[1] with Captain R. F. Hanbury and Lieutenant G. P. Nunneley, both attached from the 4th Battalion Bedfordshire Regiment. On the 12th December Lieutenant Hatch-Barnwell brought out another draft of 20 men.

On the 1st December His Majesty the King inspected the 7th Division at Sailly and personally decorated Captain C. Lamb of the Battalion with the D.S.O. awarded for gallantry in action at Kruiseik in October.

On the 18th an abortive attack was attempted upon the portion of the German

---

[1] This young officer, the son of Major C. E. H. Cooch, also of the Regiment, was killed within a few days of his arrival in France during his very first tour of duty in the trenches.

trenches immediately in front of the Battalion whereby considerable loss was suffered. Towards midday Captain Warren received orders from the Brigadier that two companies of the Battalion, in conjunction with two companies of the Scots Guards, were to make an attack at 6.30 that night, and arrangements were accordingly made for the attack to be delivered at that hour by " A " and " C " Companies, the left being the road running S.E. of La Cordonnière Farm, while the left of the Scots Guards, who advanced on the right, was to be the Sailly–Fromelles road.

The advance commenced at 6.15 p.m., and though they were fired on throughout " A " and " C " Companies reached the enemy's trenches, suffering many casualties not only from the German fire, but also from that of our own guns. In consequence of this latter, the companies withdrew some fifty yards, lay down and waited for orders. These came after an interval of an hour that the advance was to be resumed. The attack, however, failed and the line again retiring lay down in front of The Border Regiment's trenches. Captain Warren now collected what remained of these companies and bringing up two platoons of " B " Company under Captain Jenkins again led the attacking line forward, but it was checked by the enemy's uncut barbed wire, and finally the men were withdrawn and the operations abandoned on receipt of orders from the Brigadier that " no further attack was to be attempted unless it could be done without heavy loss."

In these attacks the casualties were sufficiently numerous, two officers—Captains H. A. Askew and C. Lamb, D.S.O.—being killed (the former actually in the German trenches) or dying of wounds, while Lieutenant M. N. S. Kennedy and Second-Lieutenant N. Castle were wounded ; the losses among the other ranks totalled 110. " A " and " C " Companies returned to Sailly, the other two holding the line. Two men of the Battalion were awarded the Victoria Cross for gallantry under the circumstances narrated in the *London Gazette* of the 18th February, 1915, as follows :—

> " 10694 *Private Abraham Acton, 2nd Battalion The Border Regiment.*
> 6423 *Private James Smith, 3rd Battalion The Border Regiment (attached 2nd Battalion).*
> " *For conspicuous bravery on 21st December, at Rouges Bancs, in voluntarily going from their trench and rescuing a wounded man who had been lying exposed against the enemy's trenches for 75 hours, and on the same day again leaving their trench voluntarily, under heavy fire, to bring into cover another wounded man.*
> " *They were under fire for 60 minutes whilst conveying the wounded men into safety."*

Lance-Corporal Brewer and Private Clarke also were awarded the Distinguished Conduct Medal for bringing in Captain Lamb under heavy fire. The Germans returned Captain Askew's cap and badge with a note saying they had buried him, and had erected a cross to the memory of " a very brave British officer."

On the 22nd December Captain G. E. Warren was sent to England sick and on the following day Captain S. H. Worrall, of the 1st Battalion of the Regiment, but who was serving at the depot when the war broke out, joined the Battalion and took over command on Christmas Day, when also Second-Lieutenant A. V. H. Wood arrived with a draft of 130 non-commissioned officers and men.

In the morning of this day the enemy holding the trenches in front of " A " and " B " Companies signalled that they wanted to speak to an officer, and on one going over an armistice was by them proposed and thereupon arranged until 4 in the afternoon, for the purpose of burying the dead who had been lying between the trenches since the 18th October.

On the 29th December Lieutenant C. W. Wilson and Second-Lieutenant H. R. Wight joined the Battalion, and so closed the first year of the Great War; the men at the front were not forgotten by their friends at home, many telegrams were received, every officer and man of the Army was the recipient of a card of good wishes from their Majesties the King and Queen and of a present from H.R.H. Princess Mary, while a Special Order of the Day conveyed the following words of greeting from the Commander of the British Expeditionary Force :—

" *In offering to the Army in France my earnest and most heartfelt good wishes for Christmas and the New Year, I am anxious once more to express the admiration I feel for the valour and endurance they have displayed throughout the campaign, and to assure them that to have commanded such magnificent troops in the field will be the proudest remembrance of my life.*"

CHAPTER II

1914

THE 1ST BATTALION.

THE WORK AT THE DEPOT, THE MOBILIZATION AND TRAINING OF THE EXISTING
BATTALIONS AND THE RAISING OF THE NEW UNITS.

It is time now to turn aside for a while from the main theatre of war and see what was being done during these early days by the other battalions of The Border Regiment, those which were already in existence as also those others which were raised so promptly in the counties when the call was sounded.

In the late summer of 1914 the 1st Battalion of The Border Regiment was stationed at Maymyo in Upper Burma, having arrived in India in October 1908

1st Battalion. from Gibraltar, whither it had gone in the summer of 1906. The Battalion had thus been fully eight years on foreign service, a time when a unit of British Infantry is probably at the very height of its military efficiency.

The British garrison of India and Burma then consisted of 52 infantry battalions, of which 17 were quartered in Bengal, 14 in the Punjab, 12 in Bombay, 6 in Madras and 3 only in Burma, these three being the 4th Battalion Worcestershire Regiment, the 1st Battalion The Border Regiment, and the 1st Battalion Royal Munster Fusiliers.

The *Indian Army List* for July, the month prior to the outbreak of the Great War, gives the following distribution of the officers at that time on the strength of the Battalion : Lieutenant-Colonel R. O. C. Hume (on leave out of India) ; Majors A. S. W. Moffat, C. D. Vaughan (S.S.O. Maymyo), G. C. Brooke and A. E. St. V. Pollard (officiating D.A.A.G. Burma Division) ; Captains H. Nelson, G. A. Morton (Mandalay), S. H. F. Muriel (Wellington), G. H. Harrison, S. Pershouse (Depot), S. H. Worrall (Depot) and A. J. Ellis (adjutant) ; Lieutenants F. H. S. Le Mesurier, P. J. Egerton (on leave out of India), R. H. H. Moore (Mandalay), J. Forbes-Robertson, H. E. Festing (Asst. Instructor, School of Musketry, Satara), R. Head, P. G. W. Diggle (Depot), R. B. Taylor, G. C. May, J. G. Heyder, D. A. James and J. B. B. Warren (leave out of India) ; Second-Lieutenants C. A. Cuningham (leave out of India), A. F. C. Rutherfoord (leave out of India), W. O. Lay and F. I. L. Perry ; Hon. Lieutenant W. Ennis was quartermaster.

In this month of July the whole world was at peace, and even those in India who had most closely followed the course of events in Europe had seen no reason to suppose that any cloud was likely to arise which could obscure the political horizon; and as late as the 17th of the month those British regiments whose tour of Indian service was that year closing and which were consequently expecting to return to England during the coming trooping season, had received instructions confirming the provisional orders as to their move westward which, earlier in the year, had emanated from Army Headquarters. In Europe the transition from peace to war came with extraordinary suddenness upon a bewildered world; to those serving in India events must have seemed to move with dramatic swiftness, for though the Austrian ultimatum to Serbia, following leisurely upon the murder at Serajevo of the Austrian Grand Duke, was only presented on the 23rd July, within little more than a week—on the 31st to be exact—those units garrisoning the seaport towns of India were placed upon a war footing, while at midnight on the 4th August a state of war between Great Britain and Germany came almost automatically into being.

From India the Empire's call to arms received an immediate and whole-hearted response; the Princes, within and without her borders, placed the whole of their resources in men and in treasure at the disposal of the King-Emperor; but acceptable as were all the offers which came in hourly from east, west, north and south, it was primarily to the British Army, and especially to that matured and admirably trained portion of it which was serving abroad in foreign garrisons, that the military authorities looked to stand in the breach and bar the way while our armies of the second line were perfecting their training, and while new levies could be raised, armed, equipped and made ready for the field. Those who at home were responsible for the conduct of the war and for designing the part which the army of Great and Greater Britain was to play in it, were at once concerned to bring to England as soon and as rapidly as possible all that could be spared of the British garrison of India, replacing them by units of the Second Line, the officers and men of which, it was confidently expected, would readily volunteer for foreign service at the time of national emergency. Before the end of September 10 battalions of British infantry had already left India, some of these proceeding to France direct with the two divisions composing the Indian Army Corps sent thither under General Willcocks, others journeying to England to join the 8th Division then getting ready for service on the Western Front; by the end of the year 15 more battalions had sailed to meet the enemy; and when the year 1915 opened scarcely a dozen battalions of British infantry were left in the country, while the places of those which had gone to the war were filled, almost automatically as it seemed, by fine, strong battalions of the Second Line sent out from home.

The 1st Battalion The Border Regiment remained in Burma until nearly the end of November, 1914, for it was not until the 29th of that month that, having been relieved by the 1st/4th Battalion of the Regiment, it sailed for Calcutta in the P. & O. steamship *Nevada*, and disembarking after a four-days' voyage, camped on the Maidan under the walls of " Old Fort William in Bengal." Here some days were spent, all ranks fearing that the war would be over long before any of them could take a hand in it.

About 9 a.m. on the 5th December the Battalion entrained for Bombay, which was reached after a journey of four days and four nights on the 9th December,

3

embarking in the *Corsican* later on the same day and proceeding almost immediately to sea in a large convoy of some 40 transports, escorted, for the first part of the voyage, by the *Northbrook* and the French cruiser *Suffren*, and during the latter portion by the *Eclipse*.

The following are the names of the officers who embarked at Bombay with the Battalion : Lieutenant-Colonel R. O. C. Hume ; Majors A. S. W. Moffat, C. D. Vaughan, D.S.O., and G. C. Brooke ; Captains H. Nelson, G. A. Morton, S. H. F. Muriel, G. H. Harrison, A. J. Ellis and F. H. S. Le Mesurier ; Lieutenants R. H. H. Moore, J. Forbes-Robertson, H. E. Festing, R. Head, R. B. Taylor, G. C. May, J. G. Heyder and W. O. Lay ; Second-Lieutenants F. I. L. Perry, J. H. Proctor, A. Wright, F. Keenan, W. Bartholomew and W. Clague, with Lieutenant and Quartermaster W. Ennis.

Calling *en route* at Aden, Suez, Port Said and Malta, a stay of five days was made at Gibraltar in order to collect transports coming from China, and the voyage was continued until Avonmouth was reached on the 10th January, 1915, where the Battalion disembarked and proceeded at once by train to Rugby. Here the men were accommodated in billets, and the 1st Battalion The Border Regiment was now included in the 87th Brigade of the 29th Division. The formation of this Division had been authorized in the previous November ; it was now commanded by Major-General F. C. Shaw, C.B., and contained the 86th, 87th and 88th Brigades. The 87th Brigade was commanded by Brigadier-General W. R. Marshall and was composed of the 2nd Battalion South Wales Borderers, 1st Battalion King's Own Scottish Borderers, 1st Battalion The Border Regiment and the 1st Battalion Royal Irish Fusiliers.

Here then we may for the present leave the 1st Battalion preparing to proceed to a new and distant theatre of war, while we see what the other battalions of the Regiment have been doing during the five months since war was declared.

The 5th August, 1914, found the Depot at Carlisle all excitement and full of work, for during the preceding night news was received that war had been declared

Depot.　　　　　　　　　against Germany, and already the Army Reservists of The Border
　　　　　　　　　　　　Regiment had commenced to report themselves for active service.
The officers serving at the Depot at this time were Majors G. F. Broadrick, Captains R. N. Gordon, G. E. Beaty-Pownall, S. Pershouse and S. H. Worrall, Lieutenants A. B. Clayton and P. G. W. Diggle, with Captain and Quartermaster F. W. Austin. These soon had things in good train, so that on the evening of the 5th it was possible to send 500 Reservists to Pembroke Dock to join the 2nd Battalion of the Regiment.

By the 7th August another 600 Army Reservists had come in and these, with about the same number of Special Reservists of the 3rd Battalion, proceeded to Shoeburyness, the war station of that Battalion, on the 8th. These departures, and those of the officers detailed to accompany the different parties, left the Depot empty, except for the greatly reduced staff allowed for a War Base Depot under the command of Major W. F. Nash, D.S.O., of the Reserve of Officers, The Border Regiment, with him being Lieutenant W. E. Mason, Special Reserve, and Captain and Quartermaster F. W. Brown. In the meantime also the following officers had been detailed to raise and train the first of the Service Battalions now beginning to be formed : Major G. F. Broadrick, Captains H. W. D. Adam, 3rd Battalion, T. W. H. du Boulay, Reserve of Officers, The Border Regiment, and S. Pershouse, Lieutenants M. Radcliffe, G. Darwell and P. G. W. Diggle, Second-Lieutenants C. A. Cuningham, A. F. C. Rutherfoord and R. S. Irwin, 3rd Battalion.

Later, on various dates, the undermentioned officers joined the Depot for duty : Major J. H. G. Fielden ; Captains A. P. Frankland, D.S.O., Reserve of Officers Lancashire Fusiliers ; A. R. S. Lyon-Campbell, Reserve of Officers, The Border Regiment ; and Captain A. Lyon, Reserve of Officers, King's Royal Rifle Corps ; Lieutenants C. R. B. Aked of the 6th, and W. L. Dyson of the 7th Service Battalion. Of these Captain Frankland eventually proceeded overseas as a Railway Transport Officer, Captain du Boulay was sent as adjutant to a Rest Camp in France, Captain Lyon-Campbell left to take up an appointment as adjutant to a battalion of the King's Own Yorkshire Light Infantry, while Captain Lyon was employed on the staff of the Lowland Brigade, Territorial Force.

Prior to the outbreak of the Great War, the training provided for the Territorial Force was sufficient only to furnish the nucleus of a Second Line Army. Fourteen days in camp every summer, a short and simple musketry course, and such drills as could be afforded during the evenings at the battalion headquarters, did not seem likely to make a soldier fit to meet fully trained troops, and that this was realized by Lord Haldane seems evidenced by the fact that his scheme provided for a period of six months' training at home for all Territorial soldiers, should war break out, *prior* to their despatch on active service. But under Section XIII of " the Territorial and Reserve Forces Act of 1907 " it was distinctly laid down that while " any part of the Territorial Force shall be liable to serve in any part of the United Kingdom, no part of the Territorial Force shall be carried or ordered to go out of the United Kingdom," so that primarily the Territorial Force was a body intended for purposes of Home Defence only. It had, however, always been confidently expected that at a time of national emergency a very large percentage of the officers and men of the Force would readily come forward and volunteer for service overseas ; already during the preceding years of peace it had been open to all ranks to accept such an Imperial obligation, but the opportunity had not been very freely taken up, and in August 1914 it is doubtful whether anything like 5 per cent. of the personnel of the Force was eligible for foreign, and still less for active, service in the field.

On the 10th August, however, Lord Kitchener, now Secretary of State for War, sent the following note [1] to the Director-General of the Territorial Force :—

" *Lord Kitchener desires to be informed as soon as possible which of the Territorial Battalions and other units :—*

    1. *Volunteer for service abroad.*
    2. *Partially volunteer ; if so, how many of each category, officers by ranks.*
    3. *Desire to form part of the Home Defence Force not leaving the country.*"

[1] The original document, in Lord Kitchener's handwriting and in pencil, may be seen in the Museum of the *Royal United Service Institution*, Whitehall.

On the 4th August Army Order 281 had been issued, decreeing, among other mobilization measures, the embodiment of the Territorial Force, and on the issue being plainly put before their subordinates by commanding officers of Territorial Corps, the response was immediate and hearty, and something like 80 per cent. of the officers and men volunteered for service in the theatre of war, and the training at once became both continuous and intensive.   It soon, however, became apparent that extra or reserve units would be required to take the place, when called upon, of the Imperial Service unit, if and when the latter was ordered abroad, and also to act as a feeder to replace wastage in such unit; and the result was that on the 21st September, 1914, County Associations were authorized in Army Order 399 to form a Home Service unit for each unit of the Territorial Force which had been accepted for Imperial Service.   Even this expansion of the Territorial Force was early found to be insufficient for the large scale upon which the operations of the war were to be conducted and in view of the abnormal wastage which might be expected, and on the 24th November instructions were issued from the War Office conveying the decision which had been come to that when an Imperial Service unit proceeded overseas and was replaced at home by its Reserve unit, a *second* Reserve unit should at once be raised at the depot or peace headquarters of the original unit.

The above is all that for the present need be said as to the expansion of the Territorial Force.

Lord Kitchener, on assuming control as Secretary of State for War, at once grasped the need for immediate and immense augmentation of the Army, but there remained no regular Army basis upon which to build, and three alternative courses presented themselves for consideration : (*a*) To expand the Special Reserve which was partially Regular owing to the inclusion of the regular depot establishments ; (*b*) to use the organization of the Territorial Force, which provided a framework of 14 mounted brigades and 14 infantry divisions ; and (*c*) to create entirely new formations.   The objections to the first course were that it would disorganize the Special Reserve of the Regular Force already engaged in the campaign, that the number of the Special Reserve units was too small, and that they consisted practically of nothing but infantry.   The main objection to the second course was the inadequacy of the framework upon which to construct the hundred divisions which Lord Kitchener had envisaged ; duplication and re-duplication of those small nuclei would eventually entail practically new formations ; their duplication and re-duplication for dilution by the untrained manhood of the country would render them immobile and temporarily disorganize them for any purpose whatever ; while Home Defence would thereby be paralysed, and the possibility of using any units already existing and organized for reinforcements would be neutralized.

Lord Kitchener therefore decided to create new divisions forthwith, retaining the Special Reserve for its maintenance functions and simultaneously fostering the training and recruiting, and eventual duplication, of the Territorial Force in order to relieve Regular Army units in overseas garrisons, and to supply immediate unit reinforcements to the field army ; and further, as soon as the Territorial divisions, not broken up for the above two purposes, were sufficiently trained, to put them into the field as complete divisions. The new divisions were to be created as armies each of 100,000 men—popularly termed " Kitchener Armies."

No part of Lord Kitchener's administration of the Army has been more severely criticized than his decision to create entirely new armies rather than to use the existing machinery of the Territorial Force Associations for providing an expansion of the formations controlled by them. The reasons for the course which the Field-Marshal took are set forth in the address which he made to the Members of the House of Commons on the 5th June, a few days before he left England on his last voyage. He said : " When I took over the office of Secretary of State for War, I found myself confronted with a complicated emergency. The pre-war theory worked out by the General Staff on instructions from the Government of the day had been that, in certain eventualities, we should despatch overseas an Expeditionary Force of six divisions in all, or, in round numbers, 150,000 men ; that the Territorial Force should take over the defence of these islands ; and that the Special Reserve should feed the Territorial Force. On this basis, the business of the War Office in event of war was to keep the Army in the field up to strength and to perfect the arrangements for Home Defence.

" My immediate decision was that, in face of the magnitude of the war, this policy would not suffice. Whether our armies advanced, retired, or held their ground, I was convinced that not only had we got to feed the existing Expeditionary Force, and maintain an adequate garrison here and in India, but, further, we had to produce a new army sufficiently large to count in a European war. In fact, although I did not see it in detail, I must ask gentlemen of the House of Commons to recognize that I had, rough hewn in my mind, the idea of creating such a force as would enable us continuously to reinforce our troops in the field by fresh divisions, and thus assist our Allies at the time when they were beginning to feel the strain of the war with its attendant casualties. By this means we planned to work on the up-grade while our Allies' forces decreased, so that at the conclusive period of the war we should have the maximum trained fighting army this country could produce. . . . I must point out here, that the building of these armies was only a part of the task. The Expeditionary Force had to be kept going, and the Territorial garrison of these islands had to be kept up to strength and given the training necessary to enable them to take the field against equal numbers of trained troops, and most splendidly have they realized our expectations." [1]

While, therefore, the existing Territorial units were preparing themselves for war, and in some cases relieving the overseas garrisons of Regular troops who were at once recalled to form the 7th, 8th, 29th and mixed Anglo-Indian Divisions, and while additional battalions of Territorial regiments were being called into being, side by side the creation of the New Armies proceeded with remarkable rapidity, and, taking all things into consideration, with wonderful smoothness.

On the 8th August, 1914, Lord Kitchener asked for 100,000 men, and within a fortnight he had them in camp ; on one single day the enlistments totalled over 30,000—indeed the men came in more quickly than equipment could be provided

[1] Arthur, *Life of Lord Kitchener*, vol. iii, pp. 328, 329.

for them. The Field-Marshal's appeal brought thousands of recruits to the Depot of The Border Regiment at Carlisle, and the formation of Service Battalions went on as fast as they could be organized. This entailed an enormous amount of never-ending work, but the small Depot Staff under Major Nash, augmented by re-enlisted non-commissioned officers and Civil Police Instructors, successfully grappled with the rush of recruits and speedily brought order out of chaos.

On the 5th September, one month after the outbreak of war, the 6th Service Battalion, 1,000 strong, proceeded to Belton Park, Grantham, for training under
6th and 7th Battalions. Lieutenant-Colonel G. F. Broadrick and the officers and non-commissioned officers sent from the 2nd Battalion for that purpose.
Next, the 7th Service Battalion was formed and was sent on the 13th September, 1,000 strong, to Wool in Dorsetshire, under Captain Adam, who had no other officers with him and but one non-commissioned officer, no more being at the time available owing to the need for replacing the casualties of the Great Retreat by all the Regular officers who could be got together.

The 8th Service Battalion was the next to be raised and was composed for the most part of Westmorland and Cumberland men, this being the first of the
8th Battalion. Border battalions to be formed under the "pal" movement, and the men of the different companies being drawn as much as possible from the same localities. This Battalion, at the same strength as those already raised, was sent for training to Codford, Salisbury Plain, on the 10th September.

Finally, a 9th Service Battalion was formed and proceeded to Lewes for training on the 13th September, the Depot thus sending away two battalions,
9th Battalion. each 1,000 strong, on one and the same day, *in addition* to 250 men who were sent on this day to reinforce the Inniskilling Fusiliers.

From this time onward drafts of recruits were sent daily to the 3rd Battalion at Shoeburyness, to the Service Battalions and to the Extra Reserve Battalion which had been formed from the 3rd, and which was stationed at Seaford.

In October, 1914, the first of the men returning from the Expeditionary Force began to report at the Depot : the case of one of these, No. 10332 Private Wells, was unique, he having missed the 2nd Battalion on its passage through Bruges where he hid until he could escape from the Germans, an attempt in which he succeeded by posing with the help of the Belgians as a Belgian refugee—and a queer figure he looked when he reported at the Depot !

We may now take the various battalions of The Border Regiment in order of precedence and endeavour to show what each was doing during the opening months of the war.

The 3rd (Special Reserve) Battalion The Border Regiment had originally been a Militia Battalion the cadre of which, prior to the outbreak of the war, served at
3rd Battalion (Special Reserve). the Regimental Depot at Carlisle. Mobilized on the 5th August, 1914, the Battalion, 850 strong, proceeded practically immediately to Shoeburyness, its war station, and was thereafter quartered at Conway, in North Wales, in 1915, at Barrow-in-Furness from the end of that year to early in 1917 when it was sent to Crosby near Liverpool, where

it saw the war out.   In February, 1919, it was at Blackdown, near Aldershot, where the personnel provided the nucleus of the post-war 1st Battalion and assisted materially in its re-formation for subsequent foreign service.   In April the Battalion was transferred to Claremorris, Ireland, where it was joined by the cadre of the 2nd Battalion, then commanded by Lieutenant-Colonel (now Major) G. Darwell, M.C., at a strength of 3 officers and 17 other ranks, from which was built up the 2nd Battalion.

The 3rd Battalion was a draft-finding unit during the whole period of the war, and trained and sent overseas to other battalions of the Regiment and to units of other corps some 600 officers and 47,000 other ranks.   It was commanded at various times by Colonel R. W. Woodburne, Lieutenant-Colonels H. A. V. Ravenscroft and A. E. St. V. Pollard, while its adjutants were Captains G. E. Beaty-Pownall (since killed), H. Chatfield, M.C., and W. Watson, D.S.O.

In July, 1919, the Battalion was reduced to cadre and then returned to Carlisle to form the post-war establishment of the regimental depot.

The 4th Battalion The Border Regiment, to be known, so soon as its Reserve unit was raised and thenceforth for the duration of the war, as the 1st/4th Battalion,
4th Battalion.   mobilized on the 4th August under the command of Lieutenant-Colonel W. N. Donald, V.D., and then proceeded from Carlisle to Walney Island, Barrow, but during the first week of September it was sent to Sittingbourne in Kent and there joined the Home Counties Division.   About the end of the month Lord Kitchener decided to send three divisions of Territorial troops to India in replacement of regular units which he wished to bring to Europe, and it is on record that to one at least of those divisional commanders he gave a definite promise that " at the end of six months he intended to bring them home from India and replace them by less well-trained troops."   " Tell them also," said the Field-Marshal, " that they will share in all the honours of the war just as if they had gone to France."

On the 29th October, 1914, the Battalion sailed from Southampton in the *Deseado* for Bombay, under the command of Lieutenant-Colonel J. F. Waterlow, D.S.O., V.D., and proceeded thence to Burma, arriving at Rangoon early in December and relieving at Maymyo the 1st Battalion of the Regiment.   The *Indian Army List* for January, 1915, shows the following officers as serving at that date with the 1st/4th Battalion The Border Regiment : Lieutenant-Colonel J. F. Waterlow, D.S.O., T.D., Major E. Bousfield ; Captains A. Davidson, G. H. Heelis, L. Lamonby, W. D. Crewdson, D. Maclaren, J. P. Errington, J. P. Hele and F. S. Chance ; Lieutenants W. M. Pratchitt, G. A. Story, T. M. Banks, L. S. Hoggarth, P. M. Hope and R. B. Neville ; Second-Lieutenants, M. H. Raikes, F. H. Bettison, H. Highet and J. M. Norman, with Hon. Major and Quartermaster C. E. Atkinson.

The 2nd/4th Border Regiment, or the 4th Border (Reserve) Regiment, as it was originally called, was raised under the Army Order, quoted on a previous page,
2nd/4th Battalion.   at Kendal on the 24th October, 1914, under the command of Lieutenant-Colonel J. F. Haswell, V.D., with Captain F. W. Halton, T.D., as adjutant, and Colour-Sergeant Instructor W. A. Price as sergeant-major.   The Battalion consisted of 350 men who had been recruited for the

Battalion and 193 non-commissioned officers and men, many of these last being recruits transferred from the 1st/4th Battalion on its departure from England. The detachment from Sittingbourne arrived at Kendal on the 27th October, 1914, and the whole of the Battalion was billeted in Kendal. The period during which the Battalion remained here was occupied in training, recruiting and, as far as possible, in equipping the new unit.

On the 7th December the Battalion—strength 13 officers and 791 other ranks—proceeded to Blackpool and was billeted at South Shore, the headquarters being established at the Grand Hotel; one officer and 10 non-commissioned officers and men remained at Kendal as a depot. While at Blackpool the Battalion was attached to the South Lancashire Brigade under Brigadier-General Campbell. Drill and manœuvre were sedulously practised, but both equipment and armament were very short and the dearth of rifles especially interfered with training in musketry.

During the stay of the 2nd/4th at Blackpool the activity of the German submarines off the mouth of the Mersey and in the Irish Channel called for frequent patrolling of the coast line, and during the long winter nights the Battalion was constantly employed on the South Shore picquet, patrolling the coast by night for three miles in the direction of St. Anne's, while it also found the guard on the South Shore pier.

In accordance with the instructions issued from the War Office, to which reference has already been made, a third battalion was raised for the 4th, and 2nd and 3rd battalions for the 5th (Territorial) Battalions of the Regiment. These were raised purely for training and draft-finding purposes at various times and endured for varying periods during the war, but as such none of them left the United Kingdom for any theatre of war, and they afterwards became absorbed in other battalions of the Regiment or were converted into Training Reserve Battalions.

When at 6 p.m. on the 4th August at Workington the order to mobilize was received at the headquarters of the 5th Battalion of The Border Regiment, the **5th Battalion.** following appear to have constituted its officer corps : Lieutenant-Colonel G. Dixon, T.D., Majors T. A. Millburn and A. C. Scoular ; Captains A. D. Soulsby, J. Parkin, A. F. B. Smith, J. Huck, H. J. Bewlay and F. H. Ballantine-Dykes ; Lieutenants E. H. Dodgson, E. A. Lowe, S. Rigg, W. F. Spedding, H. R. Potts, H. C. Webb, J. W. Robinson and W. Adair ; Second-Lieutenants F. P. Longmire, W. S. Sewell, E. A. Iredale, C. N. Jenkins, F. B. Spedding, C. Graham, G. G. Askew, J. N. Franks and H. P. Smith. Captain T. W. MacDonald was adjutant, Lieutenant W. Siddans was quartermaster, while there were three chaplains, the Rev. H. E. Campbell, the Rev. S. P. Curwen and the Rev. A. V. Hodges.

On the evening of the 5th the Battalion left for Barrow, its war station, and here on the 14th October it received orders to hold itself in readiness to proceed to the Continent. Nothing further transpired until the afternoon of the 23rd, when a telegram came ordering all ranks to prepare for embarkation, and on the 25th the Battalion entrained for Southampton and the same evening embarked in the s.s. *Manchester Engineer* at a strength of 30 officers and 878 non-commissioned officers and men. The following are the names of the officers who sailed for France with the 5th Battalion: Lieutenant-Colonel T. A. Millburn, Major A. C. Scoular ; Captains A. D. Soulsby, A. F. Broadley-Smith, H. J. Bewlay, R. R. Blair, A. D. Cowburn, S. Rigg, W. F. Spedding and H. R. Potts ; Lieutenants H. C. Webb, J. W. Robinson, W. Adair, E. A. Iredale, W. S. Sewell, R. J. Rice, F. B. Spedding and C. N. Jenkins ; Second-Lieutenants F. P. Longmire, C. Graham, G. G. Askew, J. N. Franks, H. P. Smith, J. B. McGhie, H. M. Humphreys and P. W. McLagan ; Captain and Adjutant T. W. MacDonald, Major and Quartermaster G. Pecker, Surgeon-Lieutenant W. Marley-Cass and Chaplain and Hon. Lieutenant-Colonel H. E. Campbell.

The Companies were commanded as under : " A," Captain Blair, " B," Captain Broadley-Smith, " C," Captain Spedding, " D," Captain Rigg, " E," Captain Potts, " F," Captain Soulsby, " G," Captain Bewlay and " H," Captain Cowburn.

The Battalion disembarked at Havre on the afternoon of the 26th October and remained for several days in No. 1 Rest Camp, finding guards and fatigues, and escorts for German prisoners of war coming down from the front *en route* to prison camps in England.

The 6th Battalion—the first of the Service battalions of The Border Regiment to be raised under Army Order No. 324 published on the 21st August, 1914, which

6th Battalion.
sanctioned the addition to the Army of six divisions and Army Troops—was raised with really remarkable expedition at Grantham. The following narrative of events in the early life of the new unit shows the beginnings of things and the spirit in which all difficulties were met and overcome :—

" At the outbreak of the war, in August, 1914, I felt a great longing to rejoin the Army, so I wrote to the Depot, Border Regiment, at Carlisle, offering my services. I had been discharged from this Depot about 14 months previously, after having served 21 years in the Army, retiring with the rank of Colour-Sergeant. My services were eagerly accepted, so I at once packed up my old—now very old— kit-bag and made tracks for Carlisle. On arrival at the Depot I met Colonel Broadrick, who of course knew me well. He informed me that he had been given command of the 6th Battalion, the first formed battalion of The Border Regiment in the New Army, that he would have me in his battalion and that I was not to allow anyone else to claim me. He had several appointments to fill and would consider what would suit me best ; in the meantime I was to go on drilling squads. Next morning I *did* take over a squad—and ye gods, what a squad ! There were at least 150 of them, and this number increased about every five minutes. Here were old men, young men, men of varying degrees of fatness, ex-soldiers, ex-militia men, ex-volunteers, tramps, and a sprinkling of sleek-looking individuals who looked like shopkeepers. However, they were all keen and attentive, and although many of them had never been in the Army before, they were all the stuff of which soldiers were made.

" The dear old Depot became very much overcrowded. Cumberland must have answered this first call splendidly, and we all felt like real comrades to each other. At this time I met many dear old friends of The Border Regiment. We used to love to stand at the barrack gate to see who ' rolled up,' but whoever came our remarks were usually complimentary and full of welcome. The training was intensive, and between drilling, taking men to the doctor, getting them to sign attestation papers, taking them to meals in relays, and finding a place where they might rest their weary heads at nightfall, we ex-soldiers who had returned to the fold certainly worked very hard. However, the 1914 spirit was strong within us, and we soon learned to love these new-comers and to let them have the advantage of our experience. . . .

"Quartermaster White and I were ordered to Grantham with an advance party to prepare a camp for the Battalion which was to train there. I think I shall always remember the day we arrived at Grantham ; fortunately the weather was fine, but how hopeless it all seemed. There was only a very large field with neither tents, nor blankets, nor food, so we eat our haversack rations and rolled ourselves up in our overcoats and went to sleep, for we were all very tired, having had a long journey and a long march. We were awakened by the noise of a motor lorry which had arrived with a few tents, blankets, rations, some fuel and two 'dixies.' Needless to say, we at once started a fire, cooked a meal for ourselves and pitched our tents. . . .

"Next day stores and rations began to arrive and we got on merrily with the work. After three more days the Battalion arrived. I stood at the entrance to the camp to direct the companies to the various lines, but what a funny spectacle they presented ! Some were in khaki and some in plain clothes—and some in very plain clothes indeed ! However, Colonel Broadrick at the head looked very proud and capable and everyone was in good spirits.

"After this we settled down to that hard training and that up-hill fight to obtain arms, equipment and clothing that could only be conquered by the stout 1914 heart. Gradually we got clothing and equipment of sorts, emergency blue suits, emergency equipment, long worn-out rifles, civilian boots and overcoats of various patterns, and, most grotesque of all, emergency water-bottles made of tin and tied on with string ! These men did their training in these strange garments and did it well, and however curious they looked at the time, later, when we managed to rig them up properly, they did, indeed, present a fine appearance.

"At this stage our officers were :—

Lieutenant-Colonel Broadrick, commanding.
Major Caulfeild, D.S.O., second in command and commanding 'D' Company.
Major Marsh, commanding 'C' Company.
Lieutenant Cuningham, commanding 'A' Company.
Lieutenant Rutherfoord, commanding 'B' Company.
Captain Darwell, adjutant.
Lieutenant White, quartermaster.

With the addition from time to time of many efficient young officers from the O.T.C. ; some of these greatly distinguished themselves later. Lieutenants Cuningham and Rutherfoord were soon promoted captains. Sergeant B. McAuley was Regimental Sergeant-Major, Colour-Sergeant H. Johnson was Regimental

Quartermaster-Sergeant, and all the remaining senior non-commissioned officers at least were either ex- or time-serving soldiers. Thus it will be seen that our 6th Battalion had a good start, a good deal better than the other Service Battalions of The Border Regiment.

" We remained in camp until close on Christmas 1914 ; the weather began to be dreadful after the middle of October and the camp became a sea of mud. But this trouble came to an end when we were ordered into huts at Belton Park, where we carried out our winter training more comfortably."

The 6th Battalion of The Border Regiment now formed part of the 33rd Brigade of the 11th (Northern) Division, the Brigade being commanded by Brigadier-General R. P. Maxwell, and the Division by Major-General F. Hammersley, C.B. The Division contained the 32nd, 33rd and 34th Brigades, all composed entirely of battalions of the New Armies, and in the 33rd Brigade were the 6th Battalion Lincolnshire Regiment, the 6th Battalion The Border Regiment, the 7th Battalion South Staffordshire Regiment and the 9th Battalion Sherwood Foresters (Nottinghamshire and Derbyshire Regiment).

The actual date of the raising of the 7th (Service) Battalion of The Border Regiment was the 7th September, 1914, and the officers first posted to the new **7th Battalion.** unit appear to have been Brevet-Colonel J. S. Pelly, D.S.O., late of the Regiment, Major W. J. Ferguson-Davie, Captain R. L. Norrington (adjutant), Lieutenant W. L. Dyson ; Second-Lieutenants F. R. H. Morgan, L. A. Newton, T. L. Crosse, H. C. MacMichael, A. G. R. Williams, J. W. Tailford, D. J. G. Dixon, M. MacDonald, A. G. Rigby, R. M. B. Welsh and C. G. Page, with Honorary Lieutenant S. Ashby as quartermaster.

The Battalion, as already stated, was in the first instance stationed at Wool in Dorsetshire, and was included in the 51st Brigade of the 17th (Northern) Division ; the Division was then commanded by Major-General W. R. Kenyon-Slaney, C.B., the Brigade by Brigadier-General W. S. Kays, and the 51st Brigade contained the following battalions : the 7th Battalion Lincolnshire Regiment, 7th Battalion The Border Regiment, 8th Battalion South Staffordshire Regiment and the 10th Battalion Sherwood Foresters (Nottinghamshire and Derbyshire Regiment).

The 8th Service Battalion was composed of men from Keswick, Kendal, Windermere and from the towns and villages of Cumberland and Westmorland, and they **8th Battalion.** joined not only by individuals, but in many instances in bands of good friends of sufficient strength to form whole platoons at a time. Early in the month of September the Battalion went to Codford in Wiltshire for training under the command of Colonel H. R. Brander, C.B., with Lieutenant-Colonel Sir Henry Lennard as second in command. One of the company commanders at this time was Major P. Strahan, and these three officers were speedily joined by others who came back to the Army from retirement or joined it from civil life, and among these were Captain Wilkinson (the first adjutant), Captains Satow, Miller and Lyell and Major Birt.

All ranks of the new unit settled to their work not only cheerfully but with enthusiasm ; they worked long hours and did honour to their Battalion and to the Regiment of which it formed part by their excellent behaviour.

From Codford the 8th moved on November 10th to winter quarters at Boscombe near Bournemouth, where it remained until early in the new year, and where the fine appearance of the men and their remarkably good behaviour won the hearts of the people among whom they lived. While at Boscombe the oddments of uniform and civilian clothing in which at first all the men of the New Armies had been disguised, were withdrawn, and in the khaki, which was now at last served out, all ranks began to feel they were really members of the great British Army, the story of whose deeds in the early days of the war was now beginning to filter home.

The 8th Battalion The Border Regiment was now included in the 75th Brigade of the 25th Division: this division contained the 74th, 75th and 76th Infantry Brigades and was commanded by Major-General F. Ventris; the Brigadier of the 75th Brigade was Brigadier-General J. A. H. Woodward, and brigaded with the 8th Battalion Border Regiment were the 8th Battalion Lancashire Regiment and the 10th and 11th Battalions of the Cheshire Regiment.

The 9th Service Battalion was raised at Carlisle and was sent from there to Lewes on the 14th September, without any officers, and it was only three days **9th Battalion.** later that a commanding officer made his appearance in the person of Major G. Browne, of the Reserve of Officers of The Border Regiment. At the end of ten days a move was made to Seaford, where all ranks lived the strenuous life, moving again some three weeks later to Eastbourne, where the Battalion acquired such a reputation for good trench work that it was later selected to become a Pioneer Battalion.

The 9th was one of the battalions of the 66th Brigade of the 22nd Division. The Brigade included the 14th Battalion of the Manchester Regiment, the 9th Battalion South Lancashire Regiment and the 8th Battalion the Shropshire Light Infantry, the Division being under Major-General R. A. Montgomery, C.V.O., C.B., while the commander of the 66th Brigade was Brigadier-General C. P. Ridley, C.B.

The 10th (Reserve) Battalion was raised in October, 1914, and appears to have at first been stationed at Southend and later on at Billericay; its first commanding **10th Battalion.** officer was Lieutenant-Colonel C. H. M. Hitchins, formerly of the Indian Army. In 1915 it was made into a Reserve Training Battalion and eventually became a Young Soldiers' Battalion under a different number.

Soon after the outbreak of the war it became evident to those directing the Cumberland and Westmorland Territorial Force Association, that many men of the Border Counties, though anxious to join the Army, hesitated to offer themselves for general service, being ignorant where or with whom they would go through their training, and if they would be allowed to serve with their own friends.

The Earl of Lonsdale thereupon submitted to the War Office a proposal to recruit a special local battalion for The Border Regiment, wholly composed of men from the hills and dales of Cumberland and Westmorland. The approval of the Army Council was given, and an Executive Council was formed, consisting of Lord Lonsdale, Colonel Weston, M.P., Major Binning, Captain Wakefield and Mr. Gerald Spring-Rice.

It was decided to raise three detachments for " the Lonsdale Battalion " in three different localities: " A " and " B " Companies, at Carlisle, from East and

North Cumberland; " C " Company, at Kendal, from Westmorland; and " D " Company, at Workington, from West Cumberland.

The command of the new battalion was taken over by Lieutenant-Colonel P. W. Machell, C.M.G., late of the Essex Regiment, and he made his headquarters first at Penrith, but on the 17th October these were moved to Blackhall Racecourse, Carlisle, and in a very short time the organization of the companies was in full swing. For the first two months, however, the C.O. had not only to see to, but to do everything personally, for he had no Regular Army company officers at all, and was even without an adjutant until early in December, when Captain P. G. W. Diggle was appointed.

During the month of November the weather was very bad; the carpenters employed to build the huts could not work, and the men could not drill; though Blackhall Racecourse stands high, the camp became a sea of mud, while water for all purposes had to be fetched from a considerable distance. When the weather grew cold, and neither blankets nor greatcoats could be obtained, Lord Lonsdale sent down a thousand of each from London, and also supplied an ambulance-wagon, a water-cart, and thirty transport mules. At first, since no khaki was procurable, the uniform worn was of dark grey cloth, but later on regulation khaki uniform was supplied.

On the 3rd December, 1914, the War Office announced that the number and name of the new battalion was to be " the 11th Service Battalion The Border Regiment (Lonsdale)." In this month the Battalion was brigaded with **11th Battalion.** the 124th Brigade — Brigadier-General W. A. Collings—of the 41st Division in the Fifth New Army, being under the Western Command in so far as the Lonsdale Battalion was concerned, while the other battalions of the Brigade were under the Northern Command.

The last of the battalions of The Border Regiment to be raised was the 12th, originally created to be a Reserve unit exclusively for the benefit of the 11th (Lonsdale) Battalion, and it was called into being in September, 1915, **12th Battalion.** its commanding officer being Lieutenant-Colonel G. Browne, from the 9th Battalion. In its early existence it was stationed at Prees Heath Camp, Shropshire, and at the end of the year was amalgamated with the 12th (Reserve) Battalion East Lancashire Regiment to form the 75th Reserve Training Battalion, becoming a Young Soldiers' Battalion in February 1918. In July of that year the Battalion left Prees Heath Camp, and was sent to camp near Lowestoft, where its number was changed to the 233rd. It was now a graduated battalion, viz., was composed of boys in companies graduated according to their ages, and continued to send companies to France up to the end of the war. From September 1917 it was commanded by Lieutenant-Colonel C. R. I. Brooke, D.S.O., of the King's Own Yorkshire Light Infantry.

Having now placed on record the early work and services of the existing battalions of The Border Regiment, and described the raising and training of the new battalions which came into being after the war broke out, it is time to turn to the various theatres of the World War and endeavour to show how all the many units of The Border Regiment comported themselves therein.

CHAPTER III

1914

THE SECOND AND FIFTH BATTALIONS IN FRANCE.

1915

THE FIRST BATTALION IN GALLIPOLI.

THE truce which had been mutually and unofficially established during Christmas between the British and the Germans endured, so far as concerned any operations

2nd Battalion. on the front of the 2nd Battalion The Border Regiment, until the end of the first week of the New Year, and then on the 8th January the troops fired volleys over the German trenches to indicate that fighting was about to recommence, while this somewhat broad hint was accompanied by a message to the same effect which was sent across. The usual sniping then recommenced, and both the Gordon Highlanders and The Border Regiment suffered some few casualties before the men could understand that it was no longer safe to walk about " on the top."

The weather continued to be deplorably wet, and it was found impossible to hold the whole line of the trenches owing to the depth of the water and the impossibility of adequately draining them. The River Lys was in flood, and the water could not be run off the flooded plains of Flanders. Pivot posts were held now at selected points in the trenches, the intervals being occupied by retrenched posts at the back of the parados, manned by night only; but trench inspection became a work of daily increasing difficulty, the water in places being waist-deep, while parapets were constantly falling in. " On the 13th January," writes an officer, " it took the Colonel and me five hours to get from one end to the other of the subsection, and then we did not stop more than a minute or two at any post."

Later in the month there was frost and a fall of snow, but the thaw then again set in and the weather was wet and miserable. Fifty pairs of gum boots were issued for the use of the men on sentry, and proved a great preventive of frost-bite. The German snipers continued busy, and the casualties in the Battalion, though few in number, were usually fatal, the men being for the most part hit in the head, for in those early days trench helmets were not yet issued.

On the 30th January the following officers were serving with the 2nd Battalion: Lieutenant-Colonel Wood; Major A. S. W. Moffat, who had joined on the 24th from the 1st Battalion; Captains S. H. Worrall and A. B. Clayton; Lieutenants G. P. L. Drake-Brockman and C. W. Wilson; Second-Lieutenants B. Hutton,

W. Kerr, A. V. H. Wood, H. L. Cholmeley, G. N. Fraser, T. L. Wilson, J. Horsley, H. R. Wight, R. F. Newdigate, D. S. Richardson, H. F. Sampson, F. J. Cuthbertson, H. Owen and H. P. D. Helm; Lieutenant and Quartermaster F. W. Mitchell and Lieutenant W. Ormsby, R.A.M.C.; while attached were Captain R. F. Hanbury and Lieutenant G. P. Nunneley, both of the 4th Battalion Bedfordshire Regiment. It will be seen from the above how few officers now remained of those who left England with the Battalion.

On the 7th February we find in an officer's diary : " The Colonel went round the trenches with the Brigadier, but they found the water as deep as ever and waders up to one's arm-pits the only things to go round in. The trench posts and retrenchments are not connected up, but this is being worked at. We have been trying new loopholes in some of the posts for sniping, and they seem to have been of considerable value. The moon rises late now, and the nights are very dark." Then next day Major Moffat reports : " Drake-Brockman and I went to make observations on the German lines this morning. We could see distinctly two lines of trenches, and, I think, a third line of trenches in rear. There was any quantity of wire in front of their first line of trenches. We had a good view of Fromelles and the village in front, making our observations from a ladder propped up against an old knocked-down farm."

On the 15th February a draft of 50 "other ranks" arrived to join the service companies.

In his despatch of the 5th April of this year the Field-Marshal commanding the British Army in France states that : "about the end of February many vital considerations induced me to believe that a vigorous offensive movement by the Forces under my command should be planned and carried out at the earliest possible moment." He then enumerates the principal reasons which had led him to form this decision, and states that the main attack was to be carried out by units of the First Army, supported by troops of the Second Army and the general reserve, the object of the main attack being the capture of the village of Neuve Chapelle and the enemy's position at that point, and the establishment of the British line as far forward as possible to the east of that place. In those operations the 7th Division, and the 2nd Battalion The Border Regiment, were very actively engaged, and the part played by the latter will now be described from the diaries and letters of some of those who served with it.

The following order was issued by the General Officer Commanding the IVth Army Corps prior to the action :—

" *The attack which we are about to undertake is of the first importance to the Allied Cause. The Army and the Nation are watching the result, and Sir John French is confident that every individual in the IVth Corps will do his duty and inflict a crushing defeat on the German VIIth Corps which is opposed to us.*"

The Battalion paraded about an hour before dawn on the 10th March in front of its billets in the main street of Estaires, whither it had moved two days previously, and marched thence to a field just outside the town where the 20th Brigade was now forming up, and about 8 o'clock moved up to some trenches which had been dug during the previous week. Here the Brigade remained all that day and night, being in Corps Reserve. At 4.15 a.m. on the 11th a further move was made to the old front line of British trenches just in front of the Rue du Bois, partly by road and partly along some wooden lines, originally laid for taking up stores. The trenches were reached very shortly before dawn and the men were only just under cover, when the enemy began a tolerably heavy bombardment, chiefly from howitzers, causing some ten casualties in The Border Regiment.

The attack by the 20th Brigade commenced between 7.30 and 8 a.m., the Gordon Highlanders and Grenadier Guards being in the first line, the Scots Guards and The Border Regiment in the second or supporting line, the Brigade objective being the line Du Piètre. In the Battalion, " A " Company led, followed by " B " Company by platoons, and as each platoon left the breastwork it doubled in extended order to the old front line of German trenches which had been taken the day before. The leading companies then moved on further and " D " and " C "—less 11 and 12 platoons, which remained in the old British trenches—then occupied those vacated by " A " and " B." During this advance they lost about half-a-dozen men, mostly killed by stray bullets. Bayonets were fixed before advancing and remained so for the remainder of the engagement. The Battalion remained here for the rest of the day and the night, and was under shell fire fairly often during the day, but the majority of the shells went overhead and struck the farm-houses in the Rue du Bois, where the Headquarters of the 20th and 21st Brigades were. During this day the Battalion was in reserve behind the 21st Brigade. " A " and " B " Companies lost several more men during the day from both rifle and shell fire, the casualties for the day being about 50, including the following officers—Hanbury, Clayton, Sampson, Ehrenborg, Cox, Cholmeley and Ormsby.

On the early morning of the 12th " C " and " D " Companies moved forward and took up positions in trenches dug during the night and in advance of " A " and " B " Companies; the Gordon Highlanders withdrew into reserve, while the Scots Guards were ordered to take up a position on the right of The Border Regiment. The attack had originally been ordered for 8.30—the objective pointed out being a line of breastworks and trenches some 600 yards to the N.E., but the advance was postponed until 10.30 owing to fog.

At the appointed hour " C " Company moved forward, coming immediately under heavy machine-gun and rifle fire, and having a company of the Scots Guards on their right. The attack progressed for some 15 minutes, but the casualties were so heavy in both the leading regiments that the officer commanding the attacking line ordered the advance to stop until strong artillery or covering fire had been brought to bear. At the same moment an order arrived from the Brigade that the attack was postponed until 12.30 p.m., but as it had now already started there was nothing to be done but for the troops to remain halted in the positions they had reached. At midday the British guns opened a heavy fire and half an hour later the Battalion resumed its advance—still enfiladed, pushing on and getting close up to the position, which was rushed as the guns ceased firing. The Germans came out from their trenches holding up their hands and waving handkerchiefs in sign of surrender, and the 2nd Border Regiment sent back some 400 prisoners and captured large numbers of rifles.

The companies were now hurriedly reorganized and the advance pushed on in the direction of a red house on the road; but coming again under heavy flank fire and the Battalion being now practically isolated, Colonel Wood decided to halt and fall back to the German trenches, which were occupied and strengthened against possible counter attack.

During the advance the machine guns were brought up by hand under Second-Lieutenant Wood and did very good work.

The 2nd Battalion The Border Regiment was ordered to remain in the trenches it was now occupying and to be held in reserve ready to move forward if necessary to support an attack by the Grenadier Guards and Gordon Highlanders, but for some reason this attack was not made. All that day, and throughout that which followed, The Border Regiment remained under heavy shell fire, but had few casualties, and at last at midnight on the 14th, on relief by the Worcester Regiment, they marched back—what remained of them—into billets near Estaires.

The casualties during the Battle of Neuve Chapelle had been heavy; of the 24 officers of the Battalion who went into action on the 10th March, 2 were killed and 13 were wounded, while of the non-commissioned officers and men 65 were killed or died of wounds, 180 were wounded and 41 were missing. The names of the officers are: *killed*, Lieutenant C. W. Wilson and Second-Lieutenant G. N. Fraser; *wounded*, Captains A. B. Clayton, S. H. Worrall and R. F. Hanbury, Lieutenants T. H. Beves, R. K. Ehrenborg and L. W. Sutherland, Second-Lieutenants A. Owen, G. C. A. Cox, W. W. Ewbank, R. F. Newdigate, T. L. Wilson, H. L. Cholmeley and H. F. Sampson.

Congratulatory Orders and messages now began to come in; from the Brigadier came the following: "*The Brigadier-General Commanding desires to congratulate all ranks of the Brigade on the part they have played in the successful operations of the last five days round Neuve Chapelle. The heroism and devotion to duty of the Regimental Officers, Non-Commissioned Officers and Men have been beyond all praise—where all have done well, it is difficult to pick out any one individual Battalion. Although deeply deploring the loss of many gallant comrades, the Brigadier knows that all ranks must feel elated at their victory over the Germans, and he feels certain that the troops will do as well in the future as they have done in the past.*"

The message from the G.O.C. 7th Division was more personal to the Battalion and ran:—

"*The Divisional General has now received all the reports on the fighting near Neuve Chapelle on the 10th–14th March. He desires to commend the conduct of the 2nd Border Regiment, who, owing to the non-arrival of the order postponing the attack on the 12th March, attempted to attack without artillery support. This attack was made in a gallant manner and in spite of losses thus occasioned the Battalion was able to successfully attack later on the same day.*

"*The Divisional General much regrets the loss sustained by the Battalion.*"

4

Then the following is an extract from the IVth Corps Orders of the 14th March :—

"*The brilliant success which the troops of the IVth Corps have achieved in the capture of Neuve Chapelle is of the first importance to the Allied cause, especially at this period of the war. The heroism and gallantry of the Regimental Officers and Men, and the assistance afforded them by the artillery units, is deserving of the highest praise, and the Corps Commander desires to congratulate them on the severe defeat they have inflicted on the enemy, whose losses amount to not less than 4,000 men in killed and prisoners alone. The magnificent behaviour of the infantry units is deserving of the highest commendation, and in deploring the loss of those gallant comrades who have given their lives for their King and Country, Sir Henry Rawlinson hopes that all Officers and Men fully realize that what they have accomplished, in breaking through the German line, is an achievement of which they should all feel justly proud.*"

Finally, on the 19th April Field-Marshal Sir John French inspected and addressed the 2nd Battalion The Border Regiment in a field immediately N. of Estaires and spoke as follows :—

"*Officers, Non-Commissioned Officers and Men of the 2nd Battalion The Border Regiment.*

"*I have come here this afternoon as your Commander-in-Chief to thank you from the bottom of my heart for the magnificent part you took in the recent Battle of Neuve Chapelle. The last occasion on which I had the honour of addressing you was after the exceptionally heavy and strenuous fighting at Ypres where you added fresh lustre to your already splendid records. In congratulating the Battalion I then said I was sure that in the future they would acquit themselves, should the occasion offer, as creditably as they had done in the past.*

"*At the Battle of Neuve Chapelle, by your gallantry you have gained still further laurels and added still further honours to your already magnificent records. I know the part you took in this battle—you stormed a very strong redoubt of which the enemy were in possession ; you came under a very heavy fire and your losses were enormous ; but you took the work and 300 German prisoners. In congratulating you I thank you as your Commander-in-Chief, and not only I, but your Country, is grateful to you for the magnificent part you have played all through the war.*

"*I also congratulate you on the splendid front you now show in spite of your recent strenuous work and great losses. I wish you all every success in the future.*"

As to the German prisoners captured by the Battalion, Regimental Sergeant-Major Davenport tells the following story in his diary : " Colonel Wood got a German colonel and led him about on ' the top ' by the ear. The German colonel could speak English and asked Colonel Wood to let him change his hat before he was shot and the Colonel simply held on to his ear, but on repeating his request the Colonel said : ' I don't want to shoot you, I want you to collect your men together.' After this was done Colonel Wood handed the officer over to me with orders to hand him to Lieutenant Kerr, who marched the prisoners back. That same morning Sergeant Jackson, 3rd Battalion, was binding a wounded German officer up, and when he had finished the officer suddenly drew a revolver and shot Jackson in the leg. Private Sharples smashed his face in with the butt of his rifle ! ''

After Neuve Chapelle the ordinary trench work was carried on until early in April, when the Battalion was withdrawn for a fortnight's rest, during which time three drafts came out of 74, 35 and 24 other ranks respectively, Lieutenant Owen, who had recovered from his wound, coming out in charge of the last of these.

At the beginning of May a move was made, the 2nd Border Regiment proceeding on the 5th to Laventie, and marching thence on the 9th with the 20th Brigade to Rouges Bancs, where it was in reserve to the 8th Division, which was engaged in an only partially successful attack. On the 10th the Brigade moved on to Bethune, where Second-Lieutenant R. M. Burmann joined and took over the duties of adjutant, and where a couple of days were spent before the Battalion again marched on by way of Hinges and went into the trenches at Festubert, arriving there late on the afternoon of the 15th May.

The 7th Division was now to take part in the Second Battle of Ypres which, commencing on the 22nd April, ended on the 24th May in the closing operations of the Battle of Festubert. The enemy had obtained a certain measure of success in the early days of the battle mainly due to his employment of poison gas, and the British counter attacks had been so generally unfruitful that, as stated in his despatch of the 15th June, 1915, Sir John French, on the evening of the 10th May, " sanctioned Sir Douglas Haig's proposal to concentrate all our available resources on the southern point of attack." To this end the 7th Division had been brought round from the IVth Corps area to support this attack, which was timed to commence on the night of the 15th, the 7th Division being placed on the right of the 2nd and advancing with it and the Indian Division against the German trenches extending from Richebourg l'Avouè in a S.W. direction.

In the above-quoted despatch the Field-Marshal wrote : " At daybreak (on the 16th) the 7th Division, on the right of the 2nd, advanced to the attack and by 7 a.m. had entrenched themselves on a line running nearly N. and S., half-way between their original trenches and La Quinque Rue, having cleared and captured several lines of the enemy's trenches, including a number of fortified posts. . . . Sir Douglas Haig directed the attack to be suspended at this point. . . . The remainder of the day was spent in securing and consolidating positions which had been won, and endeavouring to unite the inner flanks of the 7th and 2nd Divisions, which were separated by trenches and posts strongly held by the enemy."

The foregoing may now be supplemented and expanded by the account given in the Battalion diary and by such individual stories as have survived.

To the 20th Brigade was allotted the task of breaking the enemy's line at two points—the 2nd Border Regiment from a corner shown on the map as P.5, to Prince's Road, roughly 150 yards of front, and the 2nd Scots Guards from Prince's Road to a point 150 yards further to the right. At 3.15 a.m. on the 16th two platoons of " A " Company went over to the attack but were unfortunately checked by two of our own shells, from heavy howitzers, dropping amongst them, fired by some mistake after the hour appointed for the bombardment to cease. The Company advanced a second time after heavy loss, and gained the German trenches, the previous gun-fire having completely destroyed the enemy's wire, which offered no impediment whatever, while the ditch having been bridged the previous night there were no serious obstacles to be overcome. The leading platoons were now at once reinforced by the remainder of the Company, but the German trenches were so completely levelled by our shell fire that they afforded little or no cover and an attempt was at once made to progress further, but onward movement was now stopped by a ditch full of water and by heavy machine-gun fire from the left flank. The whole of " B " Company was then pushed over and occupied the German front-line trench with orders to hold P.5 at all costs, and 80 Brigade bombers were attached to assist, and by them attempts were made to bomb down the trench to the left where some of the enemy were still in possession. Some 200 yards of trench in this direction was made good, but the supply of bombs was meagre and the ground gained had eventually to be given up; these parties came under a heavy trench-mortar fire during those attempts and suffered heavily, but despite their losses P.5 was held until the Battalion was relieved, and the Battalion objective was made good.

The machine guns under Lieutenant Wood were sent out well in front of the old German line and took up a position in a small German communication trench, while " C " and " D " Companies of The Border Regiment advanced into the German trench and prolonged the line to the right.

The casualties in all ranks, and especially in officers, had been very numerous; of the deaths of the Colonel and Second in Command the Sergeant-Major wrote home as follows: " Major Moffat got safely across and the line advanced to the second line, and at about 8 a.m. took that after a very stubborn fight over P.5, but in spite of it they got the second line. Whilst lying in front of the trench Major Moffat was shot through the head and died about two hours after remaining unconscious all the time. The Colonel sent up " D " Company at 8.45 and warned the Grenadiers who had to support and reinforce us, then suddenly moved off to the German trenches with Lieutenant and Adjutant Burmann—having sent me with a message to the O.C. Grenadier Guards. When I got back I was told that the Colonel had gone and would return very shortly, but almost at once in came the Adjutant calling for me and saying that the Colonel was hit. I called Colman, his servant, and after taking off our equipment, away we went and found the Colonel hit in left elbow and centre of back. He had fallen into a 6-feet water trench, but Lieutenant Burmann had pulled him out. I gave him some whisky and we lay down with him in rather a warm corner—heavy machine-gun fire from P.5 coming across, for they knew we were there. But we sold them and got the Colonel in by crawling, put him on my back and went about 30 yards at a time, then giving him a rest, but I am sorry to say he died unconscious about ten minutes after in the trench."

During the night of the 16th–17th the Battalion, consequent on its heavy losses, was relieved by the Grenadier Guards, and moved back, first to the old British trench line, where it was reorganized by Captain O. M. Crackenthorpe, now senior officer, and then to billets at Rue l'Epinette, where it arrived late on the afternoon of the 17th.

The casualties incurred in these operations, known as the Battle of Festubert, amounted to: *killed*, 11 officers and 110 non-commissioned officers and men; *wounded*, 5 officers and 240 other ranks; while 35 men were missing. The names of the officer-casualties were: *killed*, Colonel L. I. Wood, C.M.G., Major A. S. W. Moffat, Second-Lieutenants D. S. Richardson, R. M. Goodman, H. Owen, W. R. C. Simpson, F. McCance, N. A. Krohn, J. Horsley, K. Bates and H. G. Byng; *wounded*, Lieutenant W. Kerr, Second-Lieutenants G. P. Lindsay, S. F. Johnson, G. E. H. Slater and D. H. Leck; this left the Battalion with only two Regular officers—Lieutenant Mitchell, the quartermaster, and Lieutenant Wood!

Among the killed—on the 16th—was Private Acton, V.C.

On the 20th the 2nd Battalion arrived in billets at Busnes via Hinges, and between that date and the end of the month it received two drafts of 146 and 170 other ranks, a new commanding officer—Lieutenant-Colonel E. I. de S. Thorpe, from the 2nd Battalion Bedfordshire Regiment—and 8 officers from various regiments, and at the beginning of June the Battalion was, as one of the two original officer-members remarks, "rather a mixed crowd," so far as its officer corps was concerned. This was now composed as follows:

> Lieutenant-Colonel E. I. de S. Thorpe, 2nd Battalion Bedfordshire Regiment.
> Captain O. M. Crackenthorpe, The Border Regiment.
> Captain C. B. Dove, The Border Regiment.
> Captain H. K. Eaton-Ostle, Artists Rifles.
> Captain R. B. Corser, 2nd Battalion Yorkshire Regiment.
> Lieutenant F. W. Mitchell, quartermaster, The Border Regiment.
> Lieutenant W. Kerr, The Border Regiment.
> Lieutenant A. V. H. Wood, The Border Regiment.
> Lieutenant M. Thwaites, 2nd Battalion Yorkshire Regiment.
> Second-Lieutenant G. M. Prynne, Artists Rifles.
> Second-Lieutenant H. J. J. Sheppard, Artists Rifles.
> Second-Lieutenant K. M. Bourne, 2nd Battalion South Lancashire Regiment.
> Second-Lieutenant R. G. Spalding, 2nd Battalion South Lancashire Regiment.
> Second-Lieutenant A. F. Ventris, 2nd Battalion South Lancashire Regiment.
> Second-Lieutenant K. Sheriff, 3rd Battalion Royal West Kent Regiment.
> Second-Lieutenant A. W. Gates, 2nd Battalion South Lancashire Regiment.
> Second-Lieutenant R. F. Baker, 3rd Battalion Wiltshire Regiment.
> Second-Lieutenant R. M. Burmann, Artists Rifles (adjutant).
> Second-Lieutenant M. T. Smith, 3rd Battalion Hampshire Regiment.

On the last day of the month of May the Battalion marched to billets at Gorre, remaining here for the best part of a week, and for nearly four months the 2nd Border Regiment was employed in no operations of any outstanding importance. The trench duty continued to be both heavy and continuous; every day the diary records so many killed and wounded by "shell fire" or by

" parapet blown in by a shell." The billeting areas seem to have been constantly changed. During June they were sometimes at Gorre; at others at Les Harisoirs, Marias, Locon, Beuvry and Cuinchy. Many small drafts arrived, and young officers were continually joining, some of these youngsters becoming casualties within a few hours of arrival. The greater part of July was spent about Busnes, Lestrem or La Couture, where the losses seem to have declined in number ; and then by the end of August the Battalion appears to have returned to the Locon area, and was there temporarily attached to the 2nd Brigade of the 1st Division, and on the last day of this month was sent to reserve trenches at Noyelle. In the same month the 20th Brigade was reconstituted, the 1st Battalion Grenadier Guards and the 2nd Battalion Scots Guards being transferred to a newly formed Guards Brigade, their places being taken by the 8th and 9th Battalions of the Devonshire Regiment.

In September the 2nd Battalion was again called to take part in a general action, the account of which must for the moment be postponed while we turn aside and examine into the part which other battalions of The Border Regiment had been or were taking in the war ; but we may here note the names of those officers who were serving with the 2nd Battalion on the 1st September. They were : Lieutenant-Colonel E. I. de S. Thorpe ; Captains A. P. Blackwood, H. K. Eaton-Ostle, W. Kerr, G. R. M. Dove and A. W. Sutcliffe ; Lieutenants A. V. H. Wood, E. R. Chetham-Strode and R. K. Ehrenborg; Second-Lieutenants R. Rawlinson, M. T. Smith, W. R. M. Woolf, W. W. Moser, V. H. Luscombe, F. D. Adamson, G. M. F. Prynne, II. J. J. Sheppard, J. Malkin, W. N. Beaumont, A. J. Todhunter, W. B. Hetherington, W. L. Day and T. G. Grinter ; Lieutenant R. M. Burmann, Adjutant ; Lieutenant F. W. Mitchell, Quartermaster ; and Lieutenant D. H. Russell, R.A.M.C., Medical Officer.

The 5th Battalion of the Regiment, on arrival at Havre on the 26th October, 1914, found that it formed part of the Army troops under General Stopford, and

5th Battalion.   here it remained for some considerable time, providing detach- ments at Rouen, Boulogne, Abbeville and Dieppe, and escorting some 2,000 German prisoners to England. At the end of March, 1915, however, orders were received that the Battalion was shortly to be relieved on the Lines of Communication by a battalion of the Cheshire Regiment, and that it was then to concentrate at Arques, about 2 miles south of St. Omer, for training. In accordance with these instructions, the 5th Battalion left Havre on the 4th April and spent a month at Arques, undergoing very intensive training—" getting ready," as the more grim humorists of the Battalion described it, " for the slaughter." The strength was now 30 officers and 973 other ranks. On the 5th May it left Arques and proceeded by motor-buses to Droglandt, there to join the 149th Infantry Brigade, commanded by Brigadier-General G. P. Fielding, D.S.O., of the 50th (Northumbrian) Division, under Major-General W. Lindsay.

From Droglandt the Battalion was sent, again by motor transport, to Brandhoek on the 10th May, " evidently in support of the French troops," and here all ranks had their first sight of bursting shells, and came on the following day under shell fire, but suffered no casualties. On the 13th the 149th Brigade marched to and bivouacked in a field between Vlamertinghe and Ypres, but moved in the evening into huts one mile to the W. of Ypres.

On the afternoon of the next day instructions were issued that the Brigade had been placed at the disposal of the G.O.C. 4th Division, and that its battalions were to be separately attached to different brigades therein—the 5th Battalion Border Regiment to the 10th Brigade, while the four companies [1] of the Battalion were told off to the Royal Warwickshires, the Seaforth Highlanders, the Argyll and Sutherland Highlanders, and the Royal Irish Fusiliers respectively. These companies were up in the trenches when, early on the morning of the 24th May, the enemy attacked under cover of a discharge of poison gas, but was repulsed, though the defence suffered severe loss. The Battalion was relieved on the 28th, when it was found that 1 officer and 18 other ranks had been killed, 3 officers and 113 non-commissioned officers and men had been wounded, 90 men were suffering more or less severely from gas poisoning, and one man was missing. The officers' names are: *killed*, Lieutenant C. Graham; *wounded*, Second-Lieutenants H. P. Smith. J. W. Adair and W. F. D. de la Touche.

For nearly a fortnight now the 5th Battalion remained out of the trenches, moving during this period to Busseboom; but the 11th June found it in occupation of the defences of Hooge, and while here severe fighting took place, the 149th Brigade of the 50th Division co-operating with the 3rd Division to the W. and S.W. of the Château of Hooge, where the German line formed something of a salient which it was considered desirable to flatten out. The British artillery bombarded the enemy line from 2.50 a.m. until 4.15 a.m. on the 16th, when the 3rd Division attacked, the 149th Brigade being directed to seize any opportunity that offered of taking the offensive and improving the situation about Hooge. The attack was successful, and a fine action was performed by an officer and a private soldier of the Battalion. An officer and a corporal of the Royal Engineers had occasion to go across some open ground in rear of the British lines when the enemy opened machine-gun fire upon them, and the officer was almost at once killed, while the corporal was wounded. Upon seeing this, Captain R. R. Blair and No. 1194 Private C. Mossop, of "A" Company, at once went out and brought them in to the cover of a ditch, being throughout exposed to the enemy's fire.

On the evening of the 16th the Battalion was withdrawn to Sanctuary Wood, and next day was placed with the 151st Brigade in Divisional Reserve, and retired to some 1½ miles S.W. of Ypres, and on the 19th to hutments W. of Vlamertinghe.

The casualties during the week from the 11th to the 18th June numbered 43, and were made up as follows: Major A. F. Broadley-Smith and 6 other ranks were killed or died of wounds, while Captain and Adjutant T. W. Macdonald, Second-Lieutenant I. H. M. Humphreys and 34 non-commissioned officers and men were wounded.

By the 21st June the Battalion was back with its old Brigade, and on this day the 50th Division was directed to form part of the IInd Army Corps,

[1] The four-company formation had only been adopted this year in the 5th Battalion.

commanded by General Sir Charles Fergusson. This corps lay at the time to the
S. of Hooge, its northern unit being the 5th Division, with next to it on the
S. the 28th, and on its right again the 50th Division. For some three weeks
or more now the Battalion remained in the Wulverghem area, engaged in the
usual trench routine work and suffering the usual casualties inseparable therefrom. Two officers—Lieutenant R. J. Rice and Second-Lieutenant G. G. Askew—
were wounded, the latter accidentally, and while here the following officers joined
from the 2nd/5th Battalion of the Regiment : Captain H. C. Webb, Second-
Lieutenants H. Bennett, P. B. C. Holdsworth, C. K. Montgomery, J. M. Main,
O. J. Feetham, W. B. Bennett, H. E. Wood, A. S. Wilson, D. W. Glass, R. B. Oliver
and J. R. Percy. Within a week of joining, the last-named officer was wounded.

From now onwards until the end of August the 5th Battalion remained in
tolerable quiet, first in these parts and later about Armentières ; and now, having
brought the record of this unit of the Regiment up into line with that of the
Regular Battalion on the Western Front, it would seem to be time to return to
the 1st Battalion, which we left landed in England from India, and record its
doings, hard fighting and heavy losses in another and more distant theatre of the
World War.

Early in 1915, and possibly even before that, it seemed that the time was
drawing near when the 29th Division was to sail for an overseas theatre of war ;
1st Battalion.   indeed, there was no real object, and rather a waste of invaluable
time and material, in retaining overlong at home so splendid a
Division as was this last of the Regular Divisions of the Army. With the exception
of one Territorial Battalion, the 5th Royal Scots, it was wholly composed of
Regular Battalions recalled from Indian or Colonial service ; the artillery had all
fought on the Western Front, and the staff and commanders were men who had
made their names in France. The Division represented about as fine a body of
men as had ever been collected together, but possessed the one disadvantage
that there had been little or no opportunity for combined training.

Baggage was now restricted to a field-service scale ; leave was only accorded
for very limited periods, and subject to immediate recall ; all ranks underwent
anti-typhoid inoculation ; and an order was issued that identity discs were
invariably to be worn on the person.

The fact that the 29th Division was ordered to be mobilized on the
18th January did not seem to bring departure from England very much nearer,
for things remained *in statu quo* until the 12th March, when the Battalion, at a
strength of 26 officers and 810 other ranks, was reviewed with the Division by the
King. On this day Major-General F. C. Shaw, who had been badly wounded in
France and was as yet hardly fit for active service, handed over command of the
29th Division to Major-General A. G. Hunter-Weston, C.B., D.S.O.

Immediately after this Royal inspection orders were received for the Division
to prepare to embark for an " unknown destination," but by this it was generally
known that its destination was the Dardanelles, and some account must now be
given why an Expeditionary Force was to be sent to this particular and hitherto
unexplored theatre of the war.

When Turkey definitely entered into an alliance with the Central Powers, the British Government at once began seriously to consider the project of forcing the passage of the Dardanelles, believing that success would bring about the collapse of the Ottoman resistance and would open a thoroughfare from the Mediterranean to the Black Sea. The initial efforts made in this direction were no more than half-hearted ; they consisted merely of a long-range naval bombardment of the western forts early in November, 1914, followed by a period of some 3½ months' inactivity, during which the Turks and their German allies worked desperately at effectively fortifying the Straits. It was not until the third week in February, 1915, that the naval bombardment was repeated, but so little had resulted from all that so far had been attempted, that when in the month of March the ships of war of the Western Powers attempted to move further in to attack the main fortifications, the mine danger was now found to be so acute that the fleets were withdrawn, and no further attempt to force the passage was made. It was now after much thought decided that military assistance on as large a scale as possible must be afforded, and on March 12th Field-Marshal Lord Kitchener sent for General Sir Ian Hamilton and informed him that " we are sending a military force to support the fleet now at the Dardanelles, and you are to have command," adding later : " I hope you will not have to land at all ; if you *do* have to land, why then the powerful fleet at your back will be the prime factor in your choice of time and place."

The following were the troops which were to compose this Expeditionary Force :—

The 29th Division.
The 42nd East Lancashire Division.
The Royal Naval Division.
An Australian Division.
A Division of Australians and New Zealanders.
Two French Divisions.
Some Indian troops.

Of these General Hamilton remarks in his diary : " The 29th Division are extras —*division de luxe.*" But the force did not represent the strength it should have, the whole numbering something less than 100,000 of all ranks.

The Commander of the Army left England with his Staff on March 13th for the purpose of conferring with the naval authorities on the spot, and was in time to witness an abortive naval attack which took place on the 18th ; and as a result of all that he then saw he cabled home that he would require every man of the troops placed under his command to assist the fleet effectively to force the Straits ; but, possibly as a consequence of his absence during embarkation, those responsible for shipping the troops did not know what the army was intended to do, what was the plan of operation, and as a result units were packed anyhow on the ships—gunners without their guns and ammunition, engineers without their stores, and infantry separate from their transport—so that the whole expedition required to be reorganized and sorted out before the idea of a landing on a hostile shore could be in any way considered.

The embarkation of the 29th Division took place at Avonmouth, where on the 17th March the 1st Battalion Border Regiment was placed on board the two ships in which the officers and other ranks were to be accommodated, 26 officers and 887 non-commissioned officers and men embarking in the *Andania*, while 1 officer and 115 other ranks found passage in the *Duke of Edinburgh*. The fleet of transports sailed at 5.30 p.m. The following are the names of the officers and senior warrant and non-commissioned officers who sailed with the Battalion for the Dardanelles :—

Battalion Staff :
> Lieutenant-Colonel R. O. C. Hume, Major C. D. Vaughan, D.S.O. ; Captains A. J. Ellis, adjutant ; J. Forbes-Robertson, transport officer ; Lieutenants W. Ennis, quartermaster ; J. G. Heyder, machine gun officer ; and K. G. Hearne, R.A.M.C. in medical charge ; R.S.M. W. G. Denereaz ; R.Q.M.S. R. Hase ; Armourer Q.M.S. H. Fermor ; Sergeant-Drummer J. F. Turnbull ; O.R. Sergeant W. E. Robins ; Sergeant-Master-cook C. Brown ; and Pioneer-Sergeant J. Starkie.

" A " Company : Major G. C. Brooke, Captain R. Head, Lieutenant J. T. B. Dinwiddie, Second-Lieutenant W. Clague ; C.S.M. C. Smith and C.Q.M.S. H. Botham.

" B " Company : Captains G. A. Morton and R. H. H. Moore ; Second-Lieutenants J. H. Proctor, A. Wright and C. S. Cay ; C.S.M.F. Thorpe and C.Q.M.S. J. Coleman.

" C " Company : Captains S. H. F. Muriel and G. H. Harrison ; Lieutenants G. C. May, D. A. James and F. I. L. Perry ; Second-Lieutenant J. S. Kennedy ; C.S.M. H. J. Sedgwick ; and C.Q.M.S. W. Pannett.

" D " Company : Captains H. Nelson, F. H. S. Le Mesurier and H. E. Festing ; Lieutenant R. B. Taylor ; Second-Lieutenant W. G. Bartholomew ; C.S.M. J. Ruddick ; and C.Q.M.S. J. Troughton.

Malta was reached on the 24th and left again on the 26th—9 men remaining there in hospital—and the transports arrived at Alexandria on the 28th ; and here, after spending two days in the ships, the troops were put on shore, and the 86th and 87th Brigades marched out to and camped at Mex, some 4 miles to the W. of the town, the other brigade of the Division occupying a camp at Mustapha, on the other side of Alexandria. While here the troops were exercised in field work and in practising landings from boats, and here too, on the 7th April, the Infantry Brigades camped at Mex were inspected by General Hamilton, who wrote of that inspection in his diary : " There was a strong wind blowing which tried to spoil the show, but could not—that infantry was too superb ! Alexander, Hannibal, Cæsar, Napoleon—not one of them had the handling of legionaries like these. . . . If we don't win, I won't be able to put it on the men."

Next day the Battalion marched to Alexandria and again embarked— 26 officers and 927 other ranks, including the interpreter, one John Cohen, in the

Andania; 1 officer, 38 men and 52 horses and mules in the *Duke of Edinburgh*; and 8 men and 16 transport animals in the *Mercian*. There were left at Alexandria, in the Base, 3rd Echelon, 29th Division, O.R.S. Robins and 4 men in hospital. The transports sailed at 6 p.m. on the 10th and anchored in Mudros Bay very early on the morning of the 12th.

For rather more than ten days the troops remained in Mudros Bay, days spent by the Commanders and Staffs in reconnoitring the coast and drawing up plans for putting the troops and their supplies on shore, and by the soldiers in practising getting up and down rope ladders and in rowing and landing from boats, and then on the 24th the Battalion sailed for the Dardanelles.

It may be as well here to consider briefly the topography of the portion of the theatre of operations with which the 29th Division was concerned.

The shore of the Gallipoli peninsula is mostly steep with abrupt sandy cliffs rising from the sea to a height of from 100 to 300 feet. At rare and irregular intervals these cliffs are broken by the ravines and gullies down which the winter rain escapes, and at the mouths of these gullies are generally strips of stony or sandy beaches. Inland the ground is much broken and roughly indented with gullies, clefts and irregular valleys, which later proved very useful as avenues of communication. The most important of these were the Gully Ravine, Krithia Nullah and the Kereves Dere. Five miles or so from Cape Helles is the bare and lonely hill of Achi Baba rising to 700 feet. This hill commands all the landing-places and the intervening country. To the W. on a prominent spur stood the village of Krithia. The Krithia–Achi Baba position was a strong one, naturally adapted for defence, while the village of Krithia was of importance from the fact that it was from this direction that the hill of Achi Baba could best be approached.

The 29th Division and some units of the Naval Division were to make good the landing at Helles, which was to take place at five different beaches, known as " S," " V," " W," " X " and " Y," the main landings being effected at " V," " W " and " X " Beaches. It was hoped that by nightfall on the 25th April the so-called " Covering Force " would have captured Achi Baba and Krithia.

The troops set out upon their tremendous enterprise heartened by the following gracious message from His Majesty the King :—

" *The King wishes you and your Army every success, and you are constantly in His Majesty's thoughts and prayers.*"

The following was the Divisional Commander's message to his troops : " The Major-General Commanding congratulates the Division on being selected for an enterprise the success of which will have a decisive effect on the war. The eyes of the world are upon us and your deeds will live in history.

" To us now is given an opportunity of avenging our friends and relatives who have fallen in France and Flanders. Our comrades there willingly gave their lives in thousands and tens of thousands for our King and Country, and by their glorious courage and dogged tenacity they defeated the invaders and broke the German offensive.

" We also must be prepared to suffer hardships, privations, thirst and heavy losses, by bullets, by shells, by mines, by drowning. But if each man feels, as is true, that on him individually, however small or however great his task, rests the success or failure of the expedition, and therefore the honour of the Empire and the welfare of his own folk at home, we are certain to win through to a glorious victory.

"In Nelson's time it was England, now it is the whole British Empire, which expects that each of us will do his duty."

The 1st Battalion The Border Regiment and the Royal Irish Fusiliers were detailed to land at "X" Beach, a strip of sand about 200 yards long at the foot of an escarpment some 50 feet high, and nowhere difficult to climb, well defiladed from fire from the Asian shore of the Straits, but exposed to fire from the direction of Krithia and open to heavy seas in the Gulf of Saros. The configuration of the ground here made the fire from the ships tolerably effective ; the enemy trenches, owing to the steepness of the escarpment, were along the crest, and this was kept under a very heavy fire from the naval guns. The covering party was provided by the 86th Infantry Brigade.

At 5 a.m. on the 25th April the flotilla arrived within 3 miles of Cape Helles, and as soon as it was sufficiently light the Navy opened a bombardment of the southern end of the Peninsula, after which the various covering parties were sent on shore. At "X" Beach the actual landing was effected without serious opposition, though fighting was seen to be in progress as soon as the leading troops debouched into the open from the top of the cliffs overlooking the beach.

It was now the turn of the two battalions detailed to follow the 86th Brigade, and at 7.15 disembarkation commenced from the *Andania*, carrying the greater part of The Border Regiment, into Mine Sweeper No. 6, from which the whole Battalion, less those in the *Duke of Edinburgh* and *Mercian*—total strength 950— was transferred to pinnaces and cutters and landed on the beach, where the companies at once formed up below the crest and awaited orders. These did not materialize until midday, when "B" Company, under Captain Morton, and 2 Maxim guns were ordered forward to support the attack by the Royal Fusiliers of the 86th Brigade on Hill 115. Half an hour later those remaining with the Battalion heard heavy firing to the N. and E., and it became apparent that the Royal Fusiliers were suffering severely. The volume of fire increased and unaimed fire began to sweep over the top of the cliff. It was impossible now for those who had first landed here to push on and join hands, as had been hoped, with the troops at "W" Beach, and presently the Royal Fusiliers were driven back to their landing-place, their retirement masking all fire from the cliff. "C" and part of "D" Companies of The Border Regiment, led by Captain Harrison, were ordered to charge the enemy, now no more than some 400 yards from the cliff edge, and this was most gallantly carried out, in the face of a very heavy fire, and the advance continued for some 600 yards in an easterly direction, the enemy falling back before the bayonets of the dalesmen; but in this advance Lieutenant James was killed, with Sergeants Gregson and Johnson and Lieutenant Bartholomew mortally wounded.

At the same time "A" Company was sent to help to ease the situation on a ridge to the N.E., and a well-organized and steady advance was made without much loss to a point some 1,000 yards to the N.E. of "X" Beach, and the three companies were ordered to dig in on the positions they had arrived at. The Battalion now—3 p.m.—held roughly the following line : "B" Company, with the Royal Fusiliers, was dug in on a line parallel to and varying from 100–500 yards from the cliff edge 900 yards S.W. of "X" Beach ; then came a gap of some 200 yards, where the line was continued by two platoons of "D" Company, under Captain Le Mesurier. Between these platoons and the remainder of "D" Company came another gap nearly 400 yards in extent, after which "D" and a platoon of "C" Company continued the line from here for 300 yards in a northerly direction, when it turned back at right angles to the W., the part from the bend in the line to the coast being held by the rest of "C," the whole of "A" Company and 2 machine guns. Just before dark the line was reorganized ; the gaps in the centre were filled by the Royal Irish Fusiliers from the two left platoons of "D" Company up to the right of "B," from whence the Royal Fusiliers continued the line to the sea. "B" Company of the Battalion on relief moved up two platoons to reinforce "A," keeping the two others in close support on the left, the men under Captain Le Mesurier being moved forward to strengthen the right of the line held by the Battalion.

At the time when, at noon, "B" Company had gone forward in support of the attack by the Royal Fusiliers on Hill 115, Lieutenant Heyder with a machine gun supported its left, but his gun was almost at once put out of action by a rifle bullet. The Royal Fusiliers at this time were occupying a very large extent of ground and were exposed to a heavy cross-fire, with "B" Company of the Battalion holding a support line parallel to the cliffs S.W. of "X" Beach. About 2 p.m. the Royal Fusiliers retired through "B" Company, but eventually took up a line on the right of "B" and slightly more forward, continuing it to the coast. "B" Company was exposed to a very heavy fire, and suffered serious loss.

The casualties this day in the 1st Border Regiment totalled 2 officers and 25 non-commissioned officers and men killed, 3 officers and 78 other ranks wounded. The officers killed were Major Vaughan and Lieutenant James, while the wounded were Captains Nelson and Harrison and Lieutenant Bartholomew, the last-named dying next morning of his wounds.

Such, so far as the Battalion was concerned, were the events of Sunday the 25th April, and when darkness fell the situation was roughly as follows : The landing at "V" Beach had failed, all attempts to effect there any further landings had been abandoned, and those troops which were to have followed the covering force on shore had been diverted to "W" Beach ; "W" Beach was held, but the situation of the partially entrenched troops on the high ground was somewhat precarious ; "X" Beach was tolerably secure ; at "Y" and "Z" Beaches the troops there thrown on shore were holding on desperately against persistent attacks and overpowering numbers ; while the French at Kum Kale had done what was required of them, but were under orders to withdraw.

Just before midnight the enemy attacked, and fighting continued until dawn, when the Turks drew off, having lost heavily themselves and inflicted some few casualties on the defenders.

During the 26th the Battalion was not seriously engaged, but the enemy snipers " got busy," skilfully concealed in the trees clothing the valley which ran up into the position from the E., and there were several casualties among the parties bringing up rations, caused by a desultory fire which seemed to come from a small hut at the bottom of the valley. The 27th April passed in like manner, but about midday it was seen that our infantry were upon the point of capturing Hill 138 and the Old Castle, and a little later these captures were effected while our guns opened on the Turks as they fell back on Achi Baba. Sniping now at once ceased, all pressure on our line was for a time at least relaxed, and our reconnoitring parties which were sent out found some 30 or 40 enemy dead in front of the line of the Brigade.

Towards dusk orders were received by the Battalion to attempt to establish a fresh line running due E. from the right of " A " Company through the Sniper's Hut, whence the Royal Inniskilling Fusiliers were to continue it to the main road, the 88th Brigade and the French prolonging the line from the road to Eski Hissarlik, on the other side of Morto Bay. These orders necessitated the digging of fresh trenches, and the officers and men being thoroughly worn out the work could only be slowly done, but the line was completed by midnight, and the rest of the night passed quietly.

At 2 a.m. on the 28th the following orders were issued from Brigade Head-quarters : " The Brigade will advance at 8 a.m. Objective, a line running from Square 176 F. through Point 472 to 184 R.8. The Royal Inniskilling Fusiliers will take up to 472 inclusive and The Border Regiment from 472 to 184 R.8."

The advance commenced at the appointed hour, " A " and " B " Companies of the Battalion finding the firing line and supports, " C " and " D " and the machine guns being in reserve ; but just prior to the advance beginning a tolerably accurate shell fire was opened on the British trenches, and as the troops went " over the top " this increased greatly in activity. The formation adopted was—lines of platoons at 100 yards intervals, and 300 yards distance between the firing line and supports and between the supports and the reserve. The nullah, Gully Ravine, 500 yards N. of the trenches, was crossed without opposi-tion from the enemy infantry, and the forward movement was continued as far as a spur running N.N.E. from 175 Y.

The Royal Inniskilling Fusiliers, advancing up the spur on the S.E. of the nullah, came under heavy rifle and machine-gun fire, and it became evident that if The Border Regiment was to be of any material assistance its advance must be continued for at least another mile. They moved on, therefore, and by 11 o'clock two platoons of " A " Company were established in the former K.O.S.B. trenches ; here they came under a galling fire from the Bluff to the N. and from the forward slopes of the ridge N.W. of Krithia village, but owing to the conformation of the ground no reply to this fire was possible. Accordingly the two platoons of " B " Company, under Captain Moore, worked round the cliff and progressed for some 300 yards, then forming a firing line

GALLIPOLI.

1. 1st Battalion on board Fleet Sweeper going ashore for landing, April 25th, 1915.
2. Trench dug from Gully Ravine to the sea by the 1st Battalion, night April 28th/29th, 1915.
3. Working parties moving off from Gully Beach.
4. Gully Ravine during the attack, June 28th, 1915.
5. Turkish Cemetery at head of Gully Ravine, captured June 28th, 1915.
6. New pier under construction, "W", Beach.
7 & 8. H.Q., 29th Division, Gully Ravine, July, 1915.

across the ridge overlooking the opposite valley. The two platoons of "A" with Captain Head conformed to this, moving by the edge of the nullah.

About this time the enemy was observed retiring over the ridge N.W. of the village of Krithia, and all available rifles were directed on him at 1,000 yards range. But practically simultaneously a terrific rifle and machine-gun fire was opened on the firing line of the Battalion by the enemy from well-concealed trenches on the other side of the valley which crossed the front at about 600 yards. Casualties at once occurred and soon became alarmingly high. Urgent requests were sent off for reinforcements, but the supports and reserves had been held up by heavy shell and machine-gun fire from the high ground above Krithia, and there was some unavoidable delay before replacements could straggle up, suffering casualties all the way. The bulk of the reserves had now moved forward up a small nullah some 200 yards S. of the first line of the K.O.S.B. trenches, and, the sides of the cliff and nullah being here impracticable as a possible line of advance, owing to the severity of the fire, these were collected just below the crest line and led forward at the charge into the firing line. The call was well responded to, and though the men were much exhausted by the rapid advance and the steep climb, wearing their packs, they came on with splendid dash.

At 1.20 p.m. the enemy, who were in vastly superior numbers, now started to come in to closer range under a heavy and accurate covering fire, and many casualties were caused among the officers—Major Brooke, Captains Head and Muriel and Lieutenant Taylor being all killed within a few hundred yards of one another, while Lieutenants Dinwiddie, May and Clague were wounded. Up to this Captains Morton and Moore, by their fine example of coolness and courage, had kept the firing line steady, but now the cry to "retire" was raised on the right, and a somewhat precipitate retreat set in, and it was with some difficulty, and chiefly through the gallant exertions of Colonel Hume, Captain Morton and other officers, that the line was rallied and a fresh defensive position taken up 200 yards S. of the K.O.S.B. trenches.

Much-needed support now arrived in the Royal Naval Division, and these fresh troops helped to restore the situation, while later a company of the South Wales Borderers from the E. side of the nullah was also moved forward; but Colonel Hume was here shot while conferring with the O.C. Naval Division, and was carried out of action. He died of his wounds on the 1st May, deeply regretted by all ranks.

At four in the afternoon an officer who had been sent to Brigade Headquarters came back with orders for the remnants of the Battalion to retire some 300 yards and assist to straighten the line held by the Brigade; but Captain Morton, who was now in command, judged it inexpedient to retire until after dark, when he withdrew the Battalion to a position in rear. The violence of the enemy attacks had now considerably abated, and the withdrawal was effected without loss, and the line, from the edge of the cliff to the nullah, was entrenched and strengthened.

The casualties in the Battalion on the 28th amounted to 4 officers and

26 other ranks killed, 5 officers and 131 non-commissioned officers and men wounded.

The night of the 28th–29th passed quietly, but on the 29th, during which the Naval Division was withdrawn and the Battalion held the position alone, there was a good deal of heavy shelling by the Turks. During this day Second-Lieutenant Cay and 88 men came up from " X " Beach ; apparently this party had been ordered up to reinforce the Battalion during the previous day's fighting, but, failing to find their unit, the officer and men had temporarily been attached to the Drake Battalion of the Royal Naval Division.

On the morning of the 30th April the 1st Border Regiment went back to " Y " Beach as Brigade Reserve, and spent some forty-eight hours in comparative quiet and safety, but very early on the morning of the 2nd May they were ordered " to advance by way of Sniper's Hut in the direction of Achi Baba Peak and reinforce the first portion of the firing line met with." This was done, the support trench of the Royal Fusiliers being occupied, and from now until dawn on the 3rd May the fire of all descriptions and from both sides was terrific, and it was evident that the Turks were making a desperate effort to break the thin British line.

Just before dawn on the 3rd the Battalion was ordered to leave the trench and form up ready to counter-attack, and at daylight it was moved forward between the left of the Royal Fusiliers and the right of the South Wales Borderers. Led by Captain Morton, all dashed forward under heavy fire as far as the fire trench, where great difficulties were encountered, as the trench was already much overcrowded and it was for some time impossible to stop the firing sufficiently to enable the Battalion to get on and in with the bayonet. Taking advantage, however, of a brief lull in the firing, Captain Morton led his men in a charge on the enemy trenches ; success seemed about to crown this effort when, within 5 yards of the objective, Captain Morton and Lieutenant Perry were killed, while Captain and Adjutant Ellis, who was bringing up supports from the rear, was wounded. A bare half-dozen non-commissioned officers and men now remained unwounded in a shallow trench within 10 yards of the Turkish rifle-muzzles, and these, after holding on here for over half an hour, managed to crawl back whence they had started, one man at a time. Later in the day the Battalion was ordered back to Gully Beach.

During the next five days the line was gradually advanced, not without casualties, particularly in " A " Company, in which, among others, Lieutenant Proctor and C.S.M. Botham were knocked over by enemy fire ; but on the night of the 8th the Battalion was again withdrawn from the immediate front, and spent the best part of the next three weeks in comparative quiet in Divisional Reserve near " X " Beach. During this period some officers rejoined who had been wounded at or after the landing—Captains Nelson, Le Mesurier and Harrison, while two drafts of 40 and 90 other ranks joined from home, as did the following officers : Captains J. P. G. Mostyn, Norfolk Regiment, and H. Millard, Northamptonshire Regiment ; Second-Lieutenants Wallace, N. Castle, H. R. Wight, T. L. Wilson, R. F. Millard, P. New, J. L. E. R. Lake, W. de H. Robinson, F. B. Goodall, P. de Soissons and B. Bradshaw. During the same time Lieutenant W. O. Lay, of the Battalion, was wounded while attached to the Cyclist Corps.

On the 4th June the Battalion moved out from Divisional Reserve to trenches near the White House, and here casualties at once recommenced, four subaltern officers—Lieutenant A. Wright, Second-Lieutenants Wilson, Robinson and Lake—being wounded within the next four or five days.

The Turks had lately been showing an increased activity, and on the 10th The Border Regiment was directed to find a party to capture the enemy's sap and communication trench up the ravine, while the South Wales Borderers were to attack a small enemy trench near the communication trench at the same time.

Volunteers were called for, and 30 of these were at once forthcoming, and the party, led by Second-Lieutenant Wallace, crawled out from under the parapet by two saps, and in spite of a heavy fire rushed the enemy sap, bayoneting and bombing all the Turks found there. Some 200 yards of the communication trench were seized and was held throughout the night by " D " Company, under Captain Le Mesurier, which had followed on the heels of the attacking party. Captain Harrison was this day wounded—for the second time.

Next day General Hunter-Weston sent a message to the Commanding Officer stating that " *the G.O.C. Division congratulates all ranks on the excellent work performed by them last night, and feels confident that they will hold the ground gained at all costs.*"

This day a much-needed reinforcement of 4 officers—Captain J. C. Hodgson, Lieutenants E. C. Lester, F. A. Rupp and J. H. Hodgson—and 228 other ranks joined the Battalion from England.

The night of the 11th–12th was one of many alarms : the Turks attacked with bombs at 1 a.m. and 3.30 a.m., and an hour later the enemy made a determined counter-attack on the communication trench captured on the 10th. Captain Le Mesurier was wounded, his men were for a time evicted and the post reoccupied by the enemy; but Captain Moore made a call upon his men and led a charge, recapturing the trench; Moore, however, who undoubtedly saved the situation, was shot in the head and killed, while Second-Lieutenants de Soissons and Bradshaw were wounded, the latter mortally. In all 2 officers were killed or died of wounds and 3 were wounded, while 12 other ranks were killed and 33 wounded.

On the 12th the Battalion was relieved and sent for the inside of a week to Gully Beach, where Captains Ellis and Forbes-Robertson rejoined from hospital in Egypt on recovery from their wounds, but on the 17th the Battalion was back at the front, where the shelling had again become very heavy. On the 18th Second-Lieutenant Goodall was wounded and the Battalion Headquarters hit full and blown up by a high-explosive shell, whereby the Signalling-Sergeant —Slater—and 3 men were killed, and 4 others, including the Regimental Sergeant-Major and Sergeant Bowden, were wounded ; fortunately for themselves, the C.O. and Adjutant were away inspecting the line at the time this happened. On the 19th, when the Turks developed a strong but unsuccessful attack, Lieutenant Castle was wounded, and between the 23rd and 26th June, while back at Gully Beach, Captain Tennant and Lieutenant Adair, both belonging to the 1st Bedfords, brought out from home a draft of 80 men for the Battalion.

The 27th saw the Battalion again up in the trenches, and this day orders were issued for an attack next morning upon the Turkish position. The 1st Border Regiment was to attack and capture a small work known as Boomerang Redoubt and the Turkish portion of Turkey Trench, the capture of the first-named being allotted to " B " Company, under Captain Forbes-Robertson, while Captain Mostyn with " A " Company was to assault Turkey Trench. At 9 a.m. on the 28th a powerful bombardment of the enemy lines commenced and continued until 11, when " A " and " B " Companies dashed forward simultaneously. " A " arrived at the Boomerang Redoubt with practically no loss, escaping notice by the Turks owing to the thick dust raised by the bombardment, and the men at once set to work to clear out the enemy with bomb, bayonet and butt. The supports following in rear of this company did not escape equally scathless, Lieutenant Dyer and several men being killed and others wounded, but there was no check or hesitation, and both parties were soon busy inside the redoubt.

" A " Company had more trouble with Turkey Trench, for they were throughout exposed to a particularly murderous fire from a hitherto unlocated enemy trench running from Turkey Trench to H.12, and every man of the assaulting party was either killed or wounded, Captain Hodgson, leading the attack, being bayoneted. " A " Company's supports fared little better and suffered much from shell and rifle fire, but reinforcements under Sergeant Wood were gradually pushed forward and joined up with " B " Company in Boomerang Redoubt, the garrison of which then surrendered, 64 Turks becoming prisoners and being sent to the rear. The whole operation was thoroughly well organized, and was carried through with the greatest boldness and dash.

General Hamilton thus described the attack by the 1st Borders : " At 10.45 a small Turkish advanced work in the Saghir Dere known as the Boomerang Redoubt was assaulted. This little fort, which was very strongly sited and protected by extra strong wire entanglements, has long been a source of trouble. After special bombardment by trench mortars, and while bombardment of surrounding trenches was at its height, part of The Border Regiment at the exact moment prescribed leapt from their trenches as one man, *like a pack of hounds, and, pouring out of cover, raced across* and took the work most brilliantly "—a very happy simile as applied to a Regiment the " march-past " of which is the old hunting-song, " John Peel " !

Equally good work had been done on the flanks of the Battalion, which now advanced and began to dig in on the reverse slope of the ridge under heavy fire, whereby Captain Harrison and Second-Lieutenant Rupp were wounded and several other casualties were sustained. A barricade was set up across the ravine and barbed wire put out ; and all these arrangements were barely completed when a large body of Turks came charging through the ravine, but these were mowed down by machine-gun and rifle fire, and the attack melted away. A continuous fire was kept up by the enemy until dark, and repeated and spasmodic attacks were made throughout the night, but all were successfully beaten back and severe loss inflicted on the Turks, daylight revealing some hundreds of their dead close up to the short section of line held by the Battalion on the E. of the ravine. Just before dawn an especially sustained attack was made, but few of those who started upon it returned whence they came.

The Battalion loss this day was: Captain Hodgson and Lieutenant Dyer, killed; Captains Harrison (third time) and May; Lieutenant and Quartermaster Ennis; Lieutenants Cay, Rupp (second time) and Adair; and Second-Lieutenant Millard, wounded; while the killed, wounded and missing in "other ranks" numbered 153.

The day's operations, so far as concerned the 29th Division, were wholly successful, and on June 29th General Sir Ian Hamilton published the following Special Force Order :—

"*The General Commanding feels that he voices the sentiments of every soldier serving with this Army when he congratulates the incomparable 29th Division upon yesterday's splendid attack, carried out, as it was, in a manner more than upholding the best traditions of the distinguished regiments of which it is composed.*

"*The 29th Division suffered cruel losses at the first landing. Since then they have never been made up to strength, and they have remained under fire every hour of the night and day for two months on end. Opposed to them were fresh troops holding line upon line of entrenchments flanked by redoubts and machine guns.*

"*But when yesterday the 29th Division was called upon to advance, they dashed forward as eagerly as if this were only their baptism of fire. Through the entanglements they swept northwards, clearing our left of the enemy for a full thousand yards. Heavily counter-attacked at night, they killed or captured every Turk who had penetrated their incomplete defences, and to-day stand possessed of every yard they had so hardly gained.*

"*Therefore it is that Sir Ian Hamilton is confident he carries with him all ranks of his force when he congratulates Generals Hunter-Weston and de Lisle, the Staff, and each officer, non-commissioned officer and man in this Division, whose sustained efforts have added fresh lustre to British arms all the world over.*"

On the 3rd July three young officers—Lieutenants Frink, Hamilton and Coggin, 10th Staffords—joined for duty, while another—Lieutenant Lester—was killed while in charge of a working party.

The 1st Battalion The Border Regiment was now at long last to have a much-needed rest. On the 7th July they returned to Gully Beach, and marched thence on the evening of the 11th to "V" Beach, there embarking—two companies and Battalion Headquarters in H.M.S. *Renard* and two in trawlers—and proceeded to camp at Mudros, where they remained a full ten days, and where Captain May, Lieutenants Lake and Wilson came back recovered of their wounds, and here a draft of 199 joined the service companies, with Major F. G. G. Morris, Second-Lieutenants Ampt, Chambers and O'Brien, Major Morris assuming command of the Battalion.

CHAPTER IV

1915

THE 1ST AND 6TH BATTALIONS IN GALLIPOLI.

THE 2ND, 5TH, 7TH, 8TH, 9TH AND 11TH BATTALIONS IN FRANCE.

WE left the 6th Battalion at Grantham busily engaged in training, and here it remained until the middle of April, when the whole of the 11th Division was **6th Battalion.** ordered to Frensham, near Aldershot. The work now became more strenuous than ever. The war was going on, and the first of the Service Battalions of The Border Regiment had so far taken no part in it, when, on the morning of the 30th June, orders were received to prepare for active service, and it was made known that the destination of General Hammersley's command was the Dardanelles, where the original Expeditionary Force was now being considerably reinforced. An Indian Brigade had joined it from Egypt early in May, followed a few days later by the arrival of the 42nd Division; and now the 10th, 11th and 13th Divisions were all under orders to proceed to the Gallipoli Peninsula.

No time was lost. On the evening of the same day the 6th Battalion marched to the railway station at Farnham by wings, and proceeded thence by train to Liverpool, where the Battalion embarked in the transport *Empress of Britain*. The Battalion did not embark at full strength, for, by reason of the very short and unexpected notice given, some 200 non-commissioned officers and men were on leave in the N. of England, and were unable to get back in time to sail with their comrades; but these joined other details of the Division at Witley Camp, and were later sent on to their Battalion at Imbros.

The transports sailed on the night of the 1st July, escorted by two torpedo boat destroyers until off Ushant. The Straits of Gibraltar were passed through by night, and Malta was reached on the afternoon of the 8th. Here three days were spent, and then the flotilla steamed on for Alexandria, where there was much to be done in the very few days passed there, for all the 1st Line transport, except cookers and water-carts, had to be landed and left behind, and much labour was necessarily expended on this owing to the faulty loading of the ship. From Alexandria the voyage was continued to Mudros Harbour, in the Island of Lemnos, which was reached soon after midday on the 18th, and here the remainder of the Division was found, as also the 1st Battalion of The Border Regiment, which was in rest camp at Mudros.

Soon after arrival instructions were issued that the 33rd Brigade was to go on to Helles and relieve some of the troops there which were greatly in need of a rest, and on the 20th the Battalion was transhipped to the *Whitley Castle* and *Partridge*, and, reaching Helles next day, landed there in three parties by the hulk of the *River Clyde*.   Just after the first party was on shore the other two had to put back, owing to the Turks opening a heavy shell fire, and these landed later under cover of darkness.

" When dawn broke " (on the 22nd), writes an officer of the Battalion, " we looked about and found ourselves on a flat plain about 3 miles from Achi Baba in some shallow dug-outs very much exposed to view.   Orders were at once issued to the men not to show themselves, but, like so many rabbits, first one and then another kept bobbing up ; they had not yet learnt what fire was like, nor had even some of the officers who had seen much service realized the power of modern artillery.   Two battalions of the Brigade had moved up into the trenches, but we remained where we were all day, finding some fatigue parties for carrying water and ammunition to the front-line trenches.   At about 4 p.m. some of the war stores began to arrive, and fatigue parties were sent down to the beach to load them up on the Indian transport carts. . . . We had at least about 50 Turkish shells all landing in an oblong about 100 yards long and 50 wide."

While at Helles the Brigade was attached to the Royal Naval Division, and on the evening of the 25th moved up to the Reserve Line known as the Eski Line, two days later relieving the 6th Lincolns on either side of the Achi Baba nullah, companies moving independently, while the machine guns were taken by Lieutenant Crewdson up to a strong post just behind the front-line trenches.   While in the front line the disposition of the companies was as follows, from left to right : " C " Major Marsh, " D " Captain McAuley, " A " Captain Cuningham, while " B " was in reserve under Captain Rutherfoord.   " A " Company held what was called " the Horse Shoe," and linked up with " D " three-quarters of the way down the right of the nullah bank, " D " held the nullah and as far as the Turkish sap head, while " C " occupied the trench beyond.   Battalion Headquarters was in an old Turkish strong post behind " C " Company.   All the companies were connected by telephone.

There was much work to be done on the trenches, especially in regard to wiring, and since there were only some 35 minutes of darkness between the last of the daylight and moonrise, while the opposing trenches were no more than 150 yards apart, this wiring was a delicate operation, and Major Marsh was wounded while superintending it.   Where " D " Company held the line there was much bombing ; " Lieutenant James," we are told, " was in charge here and spent many days cheerfully bombing."   Colonel Broadrick has something to say about this period of battalion activity : " We had an interesting bit of the line," he wrote in a letter home, " as for one thing it touched, within hand-bombing range, the advanced Turkish line, and for another it was the last line captured from the Turks and was in process of being what they called *consolidated*.   We had few casualties and our bombers had the Turkish ones well in hand, thanks mainly to a catapult which we got hold of and which was A1."

On the 30th July the Battalion was relieved and moved back into the so-called rest camp, learning next day that it would shortly embark for Imbros; this took place on the night of the 31st, and at Imbros the remainder of the Division was found and also some details of the Battalion which had been left behind when the troops left Mudros Harbour.

It was apparent that some big operation was in prospect, but nobody had any idea what was about to take place or for what particular purpose the Division had thus been concentrated.

With the troops now at his disposal and with those on their way to him, Sir Ian Hamilton should have had available for any contemplated operations a force of 13 Divisions and 5 Brigades, representing a force of no less strength than 160,000 men; but the units composing his force were permanently below establishment, and actually the commander never had more than 110,000 men. But General Hamilton had decided to reinforce the Australian and New Zealand Army Corps at Anzac, to effect a landing in Suvla Bay, and then to capture the hill known as Khoja Chemen Tepe, the culminating point of Sari Bair, and from there grip the narrow part of the Peninsula. In his despatch of the 11th December, 1915, General Hamilton thus puts his proposals : " (1) To break out with a rush from Anzac and cut off the bulk of the Turkish Army from land communication with Constantinople. (2) To gain such a command for my artillery as to cut off the bulk of the Turkish Army from sea traffic, whether with Constantinople or with Asia. (3) Incidentally, to secure Suvla Bay as a winter base for Anzac and all the troops operating in the northern theatre."

The operations in connection with this scheme were to commence on the 6th August, and on this day the army was distributed as under :—

> At Anzac.—The Australian and New Zealand Corps, the 13th Division, an Indian Brigade, and a Brigade of the 10th Division.
> At Helles.—The 29th, 42nd, 52nd and Royal Naval Divisions and two French Divisions.
> At Mitylene.—The 31st and half the 30th Brigades.
> At Lemnos.—The other half of the 30th Brigade.
> At Imbros.—The 11th Division.

The 53rd and 54th Divisions and the last of the promised reinforcements were then approaching Mudros, and had been intended to land there and remain available as a general reserve, but actually these on arrival off Mudros Harbour were hurried on to Suvla Bay without disembarking.

The following order was issued by the Commander to his troops :—

" *Soldiers of the Old Army and the New !*

" *Some of you have already won imperishable renown at our first landing, or have since built up our footholds upon the Peninsula, yard by yard, with deeds of heroism and endurance. Others have arrived just in time to take part in our next great fight against Germany and Turkey, the would-be oppressors of the rest of the human race.*

" *You, veterans, are about to add fresh lustre to your arms. Happen what may, so much at least is certain.*

" As to you, soldiers of the new formations, you are privileged indeed to have the chance vouchsafed you of playing a decisive part in events which may herald the birth of a new and happier world. You stand for the great cause of Freedom. In the hour of trial remember this, and the faith that is in you will bring you victoriously through."

The following is the list of officers of the 6th Battalion who were detailed to take part in this fresh enterprise : Lieutenant-Colonel G. F. Broadrick, Major A. M. Caulfeild, D.S.O., Captain and Adjutant G. Darwell, Lieutenant and Quarter-master E. O'B. White, Lieutenant L. Skene, R.A.M.C. and Second-Lieutenant R. P. Cowen, Signalling Officer.

> " A " Company.—Captain C. A. Cuningham, Lieutenant J. A. Dixon, Second-Lieutenants H. W. Hill and H. B. de Montmorency.
>
> " B " Company.—Captain A. F. C. Rutherfoord, Lieutenants R. P. Gilbanks and G. K. Leach.
>
> " C " Company.—Major F. C. Marsh, Captain H. Johnson, Lieutenant W. A. Welsh, Second-Lieutenants R. N. Carr and W. S. Ross.
>
> " D " Company.—Captains B. McAuley and F. C. Clegg, Lieutenant N. Oxland, Second-Lieutenants C. R. Darwell and G. A. Collingwood.

Lieutenant B. F. Crewdson was Machine Gun Officer, and the senior warrant officer with the Battalion was R.S.M. Duke, while Captain K. M. Chance and Lieutenant B. R. Durlacher were told off to remain behind in charge of details.

The Commanding Officers of the units of the 33rd Brigade were now taken out in a destroyer and shown generally where the new landing was to be effected, and then on the 6th August about 5 p.m. the Battalion embarked on lighters and was then transferred to destroyers—two companies of The Border Regiment with Battalion Headquarters being on board one destroyer with the Brigade Head-quarters, and two companies of the Lincolnshire Regiment, the remainder of The Border Regiment and Lincolns being in another destroyer. These two battalions appear to have embarked the last of the troops of the 11th Division, the other battalions of the Brigade, which were intended to act as covering troops for the landing, being in four lighters towed by destroyers.

The orders issued were simple enough. The 33rd Brigade was to land at a point marked C and the Staffords and Foresters were at once to dig in on a line from the Salt Lake to the sea. The Lincoln and Border Battalions were to be in divisional reserve and were to move by way of Lala Baba to the point where the road from Kemiliki crosses the Asma Nullah, marching behind the 32nd Brigade, which was to land at Suvla Point and then, moving N. of the Salt Lake, take Chocolate Hill (Yilghin Burnu) and then the high ground N. and E. of it The 34th Brigade was to land at the point marked " P.P.," moving on the left of the 32nd Brigade. At daybreak two brigades of the 10th Division were to land and push on behind these last two brigades.

We may take from one who was present the following account of all that now happened so far as the 6th Battalion of The Border Regiment was concerned, and so far as could be seen from the divisional reserve : " The 33rd Brigade landed nearer to Anzac than was intended ; the 32nd met with more resistance than was anticipated at Lala Baba and were just getting clear of the sand spit by dawn ; while the 34th were held up at Hill 10 but took it at dawn. We found ourselves, as dawn was breaking (on the 7th), going in file along a narrow path between the Salt Lake and Lala Baba, the 6th Lincolns just ahead, so we had to get into a ravine in the side of Lala Baba to avoid being shelled to pieces. The Lincolns got in the sand hills but lost a good many men. We only lost about 12.[1] It will be noticed that the firing line had not yet reached the point where the reserves were told to form up. At about 6 a.m. the two Irish Brigades began to disembark and the reserve battalions watched their advance over the plain to our left front or N. One Irish Brigade pushed on behind the 32nd Brigade with a view to taking Chocolate Hill, which according to the orders was to have been captured by dawn.

"At about 5 p.m. Chocolate Hill had not fallen, so the Reserves were ordered out. We followed the Lincolns, moved across the sand spit, got into artillery formation, and began to advance via the N. side of the Salt Lake. We pressed on, the Battalion being in eight lines on a frontage of two companies, and advanced in this manner for about 2½ miles, Headquarters being with the leading platoon of " B " Company. The order of the Battalion was " A " and " B,", followed by " C " and " D." When we reached a ditch marked " F " it was getting dark and by then we had lost about 60 men. Colonel Broadrick sent Second-Lieutenant de Montmorency on to find out at what point, if any, the Lincolns needed reinforcing, but de Montmorency was wounded before he could give his answer. At any rate the Colonel ordered " A " and " B " Companies to close up on the brow of the hill and to press on in a fairly close formation. This was done and these companies arrived in close support of the charge of the Lincolns up the hill which they took.

"Shortly after Chocolate Hill was taken I took the telephone up, and on reaching the top found three companies of the Lincolns, two companies of The Border Regiment under Captains Cuningham and Rutherfoord, with Dublin Fusiliers and Royal Irish Fusiliers. I at once reported to Brigade H.Q. and was shortly afterwards told that General Hill was on his way to take command of the troops on the hill and consolidate it. Captains Cuningham and Rutherfoord now pushed on scouts and we made ready for a further advance."

About 9 a.m. on the 8th, orders were received that the Lincolns and Border Regiment were to retire into divisional reserve to the beach behind Lala Baba, where all arrived safely soon after 10 a.m.

This day, the 6th Battalion had 4 men killed, 2 officers—Second-Lieutenants W. S. Ross and H. B. de Montmorency—and 51 other ranks wounded and 3 men were missing. "The men," writes an officer of the Battalion, "were wonderfully fresh on the top of Chocolate Hill, and were dreadfully depressed at being sent back to the beach." Another, and far more severe ordeal was, however, awaiting them.

Sunday the 8th was passed on the beach and in the evening orders were issued to take part in an attack next day on the Turkish position, from Ismail Oglu Tepe

[1] The Battalion Diary gives 1 killed and 22 wounded.

to the windmills just S. of Anafarta Sagir, the order of attack being the 6th Border Regiment on the right, the 7th South Staffords in the centre, and the 7th Lincolns on the left, the advance commencing at 5.15 a.m. from under Chocolate Hill.

Some difficulty was experienced in reaching the starting-point in the dark, but the advance began at the appointed hour, "C" Company of The Border Regiment on the right and "D" on the left finding the firing line and supports, and "A" and "B" Companies the Battalion reserves, while 3 machine guns under Major Bridges were attached.

The advance proceeded satisfactorily till 6.10 a.m., the firing line reaching the nullah near Ismail Oglu Tepe ; but now the left of the Brigade line was suddenly driven in by the enemy coming on to Hill 70 and other high ground whence the Turks were able to enfilade the left of the Battalion firing line. Every officer in "A" and "B" except one had by this time been killed, but Sergeant-Majors Vincall and Thompson brought forward the remnants of these companies and reinforced the firing line. The enemy machine-gun fire was now very heavy and the firing line became divided into isolated groups. No supports came up, and now a further retirement on the left caused Colonel Broadrick to collect as many men as he could along the road about Tordut Cheshme, and this line was held all day.

It was now about 11 a.m. and "we had here," writes an officer, "about 30 rifles capable of use and on the right were 2 machine guns out in the open but with no one serving them ; presently it appeared as if the Turks on our left front about 300 yards away were going to advance, so in company with Sergeant Matthews, late provost-sergeant 1st Battalion, I went to the machine guns and found there was ammunition in belts with them, so we opened on the Turks on our left front. After the first belt was got off, Matthews, who had already been wounded, was killed and his gun knocked out of action by a rifle bullet that jammed the recoiling action, while the other gun was shot through the water jacket. I did No. 2 to Matthews' No. 1, and the way he fought that gun was splendid.

"The Turks apparently did not like the idea of coming on up to us, and gradually their fire died down as long as we kept still behind the fence and no one crossed the field behind us. We lay here until 5 p.m., when the Colonel said he thought we had better withdraw to the less exposed position on the western edge of the field. This we did, the Colonel going first and choosing the position to stop in." Here those with Colonel Broadrick dug in and remained more or less on this line all the next day. The Turks did not attack, but fired on any parties sent out to bring in the wounded.

On calling the roll at dawn on the morning of the 10th, there were only 5 officers—Colonel Broadrick, Captain Darwell, Lieutenant and Quartermaster White, Lieutenant Skene, R.A.M.C., and Second-Lieutenant Cowen—with some 120 non-commissioned officers and men, for the losses incurred in the previous day's attack totalled 12 officers and 26 men killed, 5 officers and 241 men wounded, while 1 officer and 131 other ranks were missing. The Battalion had gone into action with 22 officers and 696 non-commissioned officers and men, and the losses among senior non-commissioned officers were very great, 2 out of 4 company sergeant-majors and nearly all the senior sergeants being killed.

Of the officers, Major Marsh, Captains Cuningham, Rutherfoord and McAuley, Lieutenants Dixon, Gilbanks, Leach and Oxland, Second-Lieutenants Hill, McCausland, Darwell and Collingwood were killed; Captain Johnson, Lieutenants Welsh and Crewdson, Second-Lieutenants May and Carr were wounded, while Major Caulfeild was missing. Nearly all these casualties occurred in the brief space of some 3½ hours, between 6 and 9.30 on the morning of the 9th August.

The 11th Division now remained quiescent for some days while General Hamilton was maturing his plans for a fresh attack upon the Turkish position in this part of the Peninsula, and on the evening of the 20th orders were issued: the 53rd and 54th Divisions to hold the enemy from Sulajek to Keretch Tepe Sirt, while the 11th and 29th Divisions stormed Ismail Oglu Tepe, two Brigades of the 10th Division and the Mounted Division being held in reserve. "My special object," wrote the General in his despatch, "was the hill which forms the S.W. corner of the Anafarta Sagir spur. Ismail Oglu Tepe, as it is called, forms a strong natural barrier against an invader from the Ægean who might wish to march direct against the Anafartas."

The part here played by the two battalions of The Border Regiment will be described in detail each in its place, but in his despatch accounting for the comparative failure of the enterprise, General Hamilton states that the two leading Brigades of the 11th Division lost direction, moving N.E. instead of E., while the 33rd, following in support, not only fell into the same error but became divided, with the result that the attack by the 29th Division on the left of the 11th, upon Scimitar Hill, failed in equal degree, and the whole was obliged to fall back under cover of darkness to the original line.

At 2 o'clock on the afternoon of the 21st the 33rd Brigade left its bivouac and formed up behind Lala Baba in reserve to the 32nd Brigade which had orders to attack Hill W on the east of Ismail Oglu Tepe, where if successful it was to dig in while the 33rd Brigade pushed through and captured Hill 101. "The 29th Division," so runs the entry in the Battalion Diary, "was to attack on our left, but we had no definite information as to who was on our right."

An officer who fought this day with the Battalion writes: "The advance started at about 3.15 p.m. in artillery formation, we following the Sherwood Foresters. The whole attack drifted in to the left too much and missed taking a Turkish redoubt in the centre of the valley." The Battalion advanced almost due E. and when about level with Chocolate Hill, "A" Company, coming under rifle fire, extended, the remaining companies extending in succession as they arrived at the same place; and as "D" Company was complying, a written message from Colonel Broadrick was brought by Major Kelly, Norfolk Regiment, to Captain Darwell, to the effect that "C" and "D" Companies were to file to the right and take the Turkish redoubt a few hundred yards away to the right. This was done, the Turks quitting the position as The Border Regiment arrived at it. The battalions of the two brigades were now much mingled together, but the 6th Battalion, extricating themselves, advanced with some 50 men of the South Staffords, but by this time Captain Darwell had been wounded and Second-Lieutenant Stalker killed—he had only joined the Battalion that morning—and of those who pushed on with Colonel Broadrick to the base of Green Hill, barely 40 men remained unhit.

About 7 p.m. the Colonel and Captain Clegg had been killed and Captain Romanes wounded, while a fierce fire had broken out on the slopes of the hill and the wounded were in great danger ; here C.Q.M.S. Prosser did fine work in bringing them down into safety, thereby saving many lives and winning the D.C.M.

The positions arrived at by the 6th Border Regiment were maintained throughout the 22nd, and then at nightfall they were relieved by a battalion of the Royal Munster Fusiliers and moved into reserve trenches near the sea. The Battalion had gone into action on the 21st at a strength of 483, and had lost 3 officers and 12 men killed, 2 officers and 56 other ranks wounded, while 32 men were missing. The officers killed were Lieutenant-Colonel G. F. Broadrick, Captain F. C. Clegg and Second-Lieutenant F. B. D. Stalker, while Captains G. Darwell and J. Romanes were wounded.

The 6th Battalion remained some few days in divisional reserve, and owing to its losses the Brigade was for a time converted into one of two battalions, The Border Regiment and Lincolns forming one, the Staffords and Sherwood Foresters the other, but as drafts came out—one a hundred strong joined the 6th Battalion on the 13th September—this arrangement was cancelled. The Battalion continued to take its share of trench duty, incurring the usual casualties inseparable therefrom—the Medical Officer, Lieutenant Skene, was wounded on the 9th—while on the 21st September Major D. Mathers, of the Inniskilling Fusiliers assumed temporary command. On the 11th October a big draft of 150 non-commissioned officers and men came out from home with 6 young officers—Lieutenants N. D. Williams and D. F. Ridley, Second-Lieutenants F. R. Poole, W. L. Beattie, T. W. Wood and H. F. Samson—and later commissions as temporary lieutenants were bestowed on R.Q.M.S. S. J. Pirie and C.Q.M.S. A. V. Prosser.

And so the trench warfare went on for several weeks more, heavy rainstorms alternating with a bout of very severe frost, when sickness greatly increased, until on the 18th December the Battalion was embarked in the s.s. *Huntsgreen*, which took them for another period of rest to the Island of Imbros. Here the 6th Battalion remained nearly six weeks until the arrangements, which will be detailed later, for the evacuation of the Gallipoli Peninsula were perfected, when on the 27th January, 1916, the Battalion sailed for Alexandria in the s.s. *Tunisian*, and arriving there on the 1st February marched to the railway station at Ramleh and proceeded by train to camp at Sidi Bishr.

The 1st Battalion of The Border Regiment, as we have seen, had gone to the Island of Lemnos for change and rest on the 7th July, and remained there exactly a fortnight, returning to the Peninsula on the 21st, when it went **1st Battalion.** back to bivouacs on " X " Beach for a few days, and at the end of a week was up again in the firing line.

During the next ten days or so two drafts of 96 and 100 other ranks joined from England, and several new officers came out either on first appointment or for attachment. These were Captain Kennedy (8th Wilts) ; Lieutenants Marsden

(7th West Riding), and Holland (10th Suffolks) ; Second-Lieutenants Steer (10th Norfolks), Price, Cranfield, Coe and Armstrong. But now the Battalion was required to join its comrades of the 1st Service Battalion in the prosecution of the operations which for some few days past had been carried on at Suvla Bay.

Here there was now gathered the greater part of four Infantry Divisions—the 10th, 11th, 53rd and 54th—but these did not number more than at most 30,000 bayonets, by reason of the casualties which they had sustained ; and Sir Ian Hamilton now called up the 29th Division and another just arrived from Egypt, placing the whole force at Suvla under the command of Major-General de Lisle. In his final despatch General Hamilton tells us that : " It was not until the 21st that I was ready to renew the attack. . . . I decided to mass every available man against Ismail Oglu Tepe. . . . The scheme for this attack was well planned by General de Lisle. The 53rd and 54th Divisions were to hold the enemy from Sulajik to Kiretch Tepe Sirt, while the 29th and 11th Divisions stormed Ismail Oglu Tepe. . . . I arranged that General Birdwood should co-operate by swinging forward his left flank to Susuk Kuju and Kaiajik Aghala."

General Hamilton has thus described the hill which was to be stormed by the 11th and 29th Divisions, containing respectively the 6th and 1st Battalions of The Border Regiment : " The hill rises 350 feet from the plain, with steep spurs jutting out to the W. and S.W., the whole of it covered with dense holly-oak scrub, so nearly impenetrable that it breaks up an advance and forces troops to move in single file along goat-tracks between the bushes."

On the 16th August the 1st Battalion The Border Regiment marched back to " X " Beach and there embarked in two parties from " V " Beach, 600 of the Battalion at 9 p.m. and 319 half an hour later, and disembarking in the early hours of the 17th at Suvla Bay went into bivouac at Punar. Here at six in the evening orders were received directing the Battalion to move two hours later and march to the headquarters of the 159th Brigade of the 53rd Division, while " A " Company was to join the 158th Brigade ; but on reaching its rendezvous the Commanding Officer learnt that, owing to the lateness of the hour, the G.O.C. had decided to make no attempt to advance his line as had been proposed, and the Battalion thereupon retired to Azmak Nullah and there bivouacked for the night, pushing forward patrols in front of the line and accounting for several Turkish snipers who had been giving trouble. Here the 1st Battalion of The Border Regiment remained all through the 18th, and next day orders came from the 87th Brigade Headquarters for it to fall back again at dusk and return to the reserve camp. This was accordingly done, and here the Battalion remained inactive on the 20th in readiness to move on the receipt of orders.

These arrived on the 21st and were as follows : " The Brigade will attack Hill 70 on a frontage of 400 yards from behind the line now held by the King's Own Scottish Borderers. The artillery bombardment will commence at 2.30 p.m., and at 3.30 p.m. a covering fire will be opened by the King's Own Scottish Borderers in which 2 machine guns 1st Border Regiment will assist. At 3.30 the Royal Innis-killing Fusiliers will pass this line held by the King's Own Scottish Borderers and make the assault. The 1st Borders will be in support of the Royal Inniskilling

Fusiliers and will move up into the trenches at present held by the Royal Innis-killing Fusiliers as soon as that regiment vacates them. The King's Own Scottish Borderers will remain in reserve in the present fire trench."

At 3.30 the Royal Inniskilling Fusiliers advanced to the attack supported by the 1st Border Regiment, but half an hour later, the attacking line being checked by enfilade fire from the left, " C " and " D " Companies of the Battalion moved forward with " A " supporting " C ," and guarding the left flank, the whole speeded by an urgent message from 87th Brigade Headquarters—" Hill 70 must be taken."

At 5 o'clock a message came to Battalion Headquarters from Lieutenant Clague that he was within 500 yards of his objective and was unable to advance further, but that he was putting up head cover and needed reinforcements. At the same time two reports were received from Second-Lieutenant Armstrong, now the only officer with " D " Company, that his advance had reached to within 50 yards of the summit of the hill on his right, but that he was not in touch with any troops on either flank ; he also asked for support.

A few minutes later the Brigade directed that " when the Mounted Troops advance again on Hill 112, the South Wales Borderers will come up in support and take Hill 70 and the knoll on the left of it " ; while just before 6 p.m the officer commanding " B " Company of the Battalion sent back word that the " attack on the right appeared to have come to a standstill in a small nullah just below the crest of the hill, while the attack on the left was still hung up by fire from Knoll 105 D.8." But the Artillery Forward Observation Officer reported, on the other hand, that " the enemy have apparently retired from Hill 70 in the direction of the ridge going from 112, though stragglers are still on the N. side of the hill."

Between 6 and 6.15 p.m. the advance of the Mounted Troops and South Wales Borderers commenced, but was met with very heavy shrapnel, machine-gun and rifle fire, especially from a knoll on the left of Hill 70. A small party of men of different units did gain a footing in the Turkish trench on the right of the hill, but was almost immediately driven out again by enfilading shrapnel fire from the right ; and it was at once apparent that in the 1st Battalion of The Border Regi-ment casualties were rapidly mounting up—of 15 officers in the firing line, Lieutenant Clague being now the only one unwounded.

At 8 p.m. Major Nelson and Second-Lieutenant Coe came up from the rear to reorganize the shattered companies and establish a continuous line below the crest of the hill, while water-carrying parties and stretcher bearers were told off to go out to the firing line. Major Nelson judged and reported that the situation appeared to be hopeless, and that while the hill might be held until daylight it would then become untenable since, owing to the very stony nature of the soil, cover from shell fire could not be improvised. In consequence of these and other representations Major Nelson was ordered to carry out the evacuation of the position before daylight.

Very early on the morning of the 22nd a message came in from Lieutenant Clague saying he was still holding the extreme left of the position, had received no orders to retire, and had now only 33 men left of his own company of the

Battalion and 50 or so of various corps. Orders were sent him to withdraw at once, and this he succeeded in doing without further very serious loss, despite heavy sniping from the enemy.

During these operations the 1st Battalion The Border Regiment had again suffered many casualties : 38 non-commissioned officers and men had been killed, while 14 officers and 274 other ranks were wounded and 64 men were missing. The officers wounded were : Captains G. C. May, J. A. Tennant,[1] and J. T. B. Dinwiddie ;[1] Lieutenants J. H. Hodgson, F. A. Rupp, J. J. Adair,[1] J. F. R. Lake,[1] W. H. F. Chambers and K. C. Hamilton ; Second-Lieutenants P. New, N. C. Ampt,[1] F. G. Goodall, A. P. J. Armstrong and E. C. Steer.

Early on the morning of the 22nd, Lieutenant-Colonel A. E. St. V. Pollard came up and assumed command of the Battalion, and late the same night it was relieved by the 5th Inniskilling Fusiliers and withdrew to a gully in rear, and here or hereabouts it was joined by two drafts of 74 and 99 from England with the following officers : Second-Lieutenants J. W. Farrell, J. R. Streeter, D. Cargill, M. Duff, H. P. Ledward, G. H. S. McDonald, C. R. Wise, A. W. Fraser, and R. S. Mackenzie.

Here the Battalion remained in tolerable quiet until the 24th September, when it embarked at Little West Beach in two lighters, transhipping again to the s.s. *Ermine*, in which it proceeded to Kephalos in the Island of Imbros and was accommodated in a rest camp ; here another draft 54 strong joined from England under Second-Lieutenant Hill of the 6th Lincolns. But the period of rest was on this occasion only a very brief one, for by the 2nd October the 1st Border Regiment was back again at Cape Helles : " everything very quiet here, very little firing from either side." The 87th Brigade was now temporarily detached from the 29th Division and attached to the 52nd, and all hands were for a few days employed busily in work on dug-outs for winter occupation. This was a quiet time for all at Helles ; there was a certain amount of shelling though little or no damage was done, but there was a good deal of sickness, principally dysentery, jaundice and septic sores. However, the Battalion was now at a reasonable strength again, for another draft of 150 rank and file came out from home, a considerable number of men who had gone down sick or wounded returned to duty, while 8 subalterns joined the service companies—Lieutenant J. W. Ewbank, Second-Lieutenants O. W. N. Rowsell, G. Burns, A. W. H. Barnes, S. C. Cheverton, R. G. Cullis, W. J. M. Taylor and J. G. Rowan.

By this time the military authorities in England had realized that the operations in Gallipoli were becoming increasingly costly ; that, having regard to the needs of the main theatre of war, the difficulties of providing reinforcements for General Hamilton were almost insuperable, and that it was desirable to " cut our losses " and evacuate the Peninsula. On the 11th October Lord Kitchener cabled to Sir Ian asking for an estimate of the possible losses which a complete withdrawal would involve ; and on receiving a reply that these might be as high as 50 per cent., Lord Kitchener, on the 16th, directed Sir Ian Hamilton to return home for consultation on the situation, and informed him that General Sir Charles Monro had

[1] These five officers died of their wounds.

been appointed to take his place. Next day General Hamilton issued the following farewell order :—

"*On handing over the command of the Mediterranean Expeditionary Force to General Sir C. C. Monro, the Commander-in-Chief wishes to say a few farewell words to the Allied troops with many of whom he has now for so long been associated. First he would like them to know his deep sense of the honour it has been to command so fine an Army in one of the most arduous and difficult campaigns which has ever been undertaken ; secondly, he must express to them his admiration of the noble response which they have invariably given to the calls he has made upon them. No risk has been too desperate, no sacrifice too great. Sir Ian Hamilton thanks all ranks, from generals to private soldiers, for the wonderful way they have seconded his efforts to lead them towards that decisive victory, which, under their new Chief, he has the most implicit confidence they will achieve.*"

General Monro arrived on the Peninsula on the 30th October and reported very strongly against any continuation of the enterprise and in favour of early and complete evacuation ; but before accepting his view the Cabinet commissioned Lord Kitchener to visit the Dardanelles and talk the matter over with the responsible naval and military officers on the spot. The Secretary of State for War finally and reluctantly decided in favour of withdrawal, and early in November the necessary orders were given.

Lord Kitchener was the bearer of a message from His Majesty the King, "*expressing to all ranks of the corps and troops attached, His Majesty the King's deep appreciation of the ceaseless and arduous work performed by them during the past three months in the face of a determined enemy.*"

The evacuation did not immediately take place, for there was very much to be done, many arrangements to be made, since to bring away so large an army from open beaches in the face of a resolute and resourceful enemy, appeared to be one involving risk of very serious loss, even of disaster. At Suvla and Anzac alone more than 83,000 men had to be embarked, with guns, horses, mules and carts, many days' supplies and stores of all kinds, while the Turks were nowhere more than 300 yards distant from the British front and at some points were no more than 20 yards away !

On the 8th November, when the 1st Battalion was up in the firing line, a very daring act was done by Sergeant J. Cooper, who was with the right company in the advanced trench. Suddenly directing men on his right and left to cease firing, he jumped on to the parapet and rushed over to the Turkish trench 120 yards distant, and, standing up on the enemy breastwork, emptied his magazine impartially among the occupants of the trench, shooting down five of the enemy. He then ran back to his own lines, his retreat covered by the fire of his comrades.

The weather now became deplorable ; there was a very heavy rainfall on the 17th November which caused the trenches to be flooded and the parapets to fall in, and this was succeeded a week later by a blizzard of terrible severity ; many men died of exposure at their posts in the trenches, and some 10,000 sick had to be removed from the Peninsula.

During December, Captain J. R. C. Meiklejohn, Second-Lieutenants F. R.

Jessup, W. R. Rettie, H. Palmer and C. Campbell, and 106 men joined, of whom 89 were men who had recovered from wounds or sickness; while in the last week of the month Second-Lieutenant A. J. M. Taylor was killed, and Second-Lieutenant A. C. Randall was wounded.

It had been arranged that Anzac and Suvla should first be evacuated, and at this latter place there were actually no fewer than five divisions; but by the 20th December all these had been withdrawn, and on the 28th, when final orders were received that the whole force was to leave the Peninsula, the troops at Helles consisted of the 29th, 42nd, 52nd and Naval Divisions, and some few French troops. Then on the 29th, the 13th Division from Imbros relieved the 42nd at Helles, and it was now settled that the 13th and 29th Divisions should be the last to leave Gallipoli.

As part of the evacuation arrangements the 1st Battalion Border Regiment was told off to the left sub-sector of the covering force under Brigadier-General Tufnell, and during the 8th January, 1916, it was gradually moved into dug-outs behind the position which it was to occupy during withdrawal. The night of the 8th–9th had been decided upon for the final evacuation, and by 6.30 p.m. the Battalion was in position for covering the embarkation on " W " Beach or Lancashire Landing. " A " Company, Second-Lieutenant Streater and 2 machine guns, were on the left from Bakery Gully near the Cemetery, with a post—1 officer and 10 men—on the road below the cliffs; " B " Company, Captain Ewbank, and 1 machine gun, were occupying the ground from the Cemetery to the right, covering both roads of approach; while " C " Company, Second-Lieutenant Farrell, with an officer and 40 men of the King's Own Scottish Borderers and 1 machine gun, were on Hunter-Weston Hill. " D " Company was in support under Lieutenant Millard.

At 1.40 a.m. on the 9th January the last troops of the 29th Division, with Engineers and Artillery demolition parties, had passed through the defences, and the O.C. Covering Force then gave orders for withdrawal, and the Battalion accordingly fell back in the following order: " C " Company first, then " A," " B " and " D," Second-Lieutenant Fraser and 25 men being left as a small covering force on both the approach roads. Battalion H.Q., with " A," " B " and " D " Companies were at once sent to No. 2 Pier, where they embarked in lighters, later transhipping to the destroyer *Staunch*. While this was taking place the ammunition magazine on " W " Beach was blown up and 5 men of the Battalion were injured by falling *débris*. The *Staunch* was found to be rather overladen for the rising wind and seas encountered, and 4 officers and 184 men of the 1st Border Regiment were transferred to the *Princess Irene*.

The Battalion finally reached Mudros Harbour in driblets—" C " Company, 4 officers and 130 other ranks in one party, 5 officers and 25 men who had got adrift in a lighter and were taken in tow by the destroyer *Scorpion* in another, and Second-Lieutenant Fraser and his party in a third, and, arrived at Mudros, the whole Battalion then went on board the *Minneapolis* and *Nestor* and sailed for Alexandria on the 11th and 14th, arriving there on the 14th and 16th.

From here the two parties entrained for Suez, where the Battalion concentrated and settled down to steady training and reorganization, being joined later by Lieutenant J. B. Sinclair, Second-Lieutenant G. B. Cargill and E. A. Barry and a draft of 343 non-commissioned officers and men.

A return must now be made to the main theatre of the war, and an account be given of the operations in which the four Battalions of The Border Regiment (2nd, 5th, 7th and 8th), assembled in France in the latter part of the year 1915, took their part. In September there occurred the Battle of Loos, and the reasons for the attacks then made by the British Army and the general results which they achieved are given as follows in the Commander-in-Chief's despatch of the 15th October, 1915: "It was arranged that we should make a combined attack from certain points of the Allied line during the last week in September. The reinforcements I had received enabled me to comply with several requests which General Joffre has made, that I should take over additional portions of the French line. In fulfilment of the rôle assigned to it in these operations, the Army under my command attacked the enemy on the morning of the 25th September. The main attack was delivered by the Ist and IVth Corps between the La Bassée Canal on the N. and a point of the enemy's line opposite the village of Grenay on the S. At the same time a secondary attack, designed with the object of distracting the enemy's attention and holding his troops to their ground, was made by the Vth Corps on Bellewaarde Farm, situated to the E. of Ypres. Subsidiary attacks with similar objects were delivered by the IIIrd and Indian Corps N. of the La Bassée Canal and along the whole front of the Second Army.

"The object of the subsidiary attack by the Vth Corps was most effectively achieved. . . . The attack was made at daybreak by the 3rd and 14th Divisions, and at first the greater part of the enemy's front line was taken, but . . . the troops were unable to retain the ground and had to return to their original trenches towards nightfall.

"The general plan of the main attack on the 25th September was as follows: In co-operation with an offensive movement by the 10th French Army on our right, the Ist and IVth Corps were to attack the enemy from a point opposite the little mining village of Grenay on the S. to the La Bassée Canal on the N. . . . The attacks of the Ist and IVth Corps were delivered at 6.30 a.m. and were successful all along the line, except just S. of the La Bassée Canal."

Let us take first the main attack in which the 2nd Battalion of The Border Regiment was concerned.

2nd Battalion. The 7th Division, of which it formed part, occupied the angle caused by the Lens–Hulluch and Vermelles–Hulluch Roads, having the 9th Division on its left and the 1st on its right, and immediately faced the gap between St. Elie and Hulluch.

On the 20th, the 20th Brigade was ordered to form up on the night of the 24th–25th September, on the front Vermelles–Hulluch Road–Sap 2 preparatory to an attack on the 25th. Information gleaned was that the enemy's defences consisted of two well-defined lines of trenches, the first running from Fosse 8 southwards to Loos, the second, 1,500 yards to the E., running through Haisnes–

Cité St. Elie–Hulluch. The task of the 20th Infantry Brigade was to clear the trenches in front and occupy Hulluch and Benefontaine, pushing on thence to Pont Vendin to seize the Canal crossings. At 10 p.m. on the 24th the Brigade began its concentration, and by 2.30 on the morning of the 25th all its units were formed up as follows : first line, 2nd Gordon Highlanders on the right and 8th Devons on the left, each in four lines ; second line, 6th Gordons in support on right and 2nd Border Regiment in support on left ; third line, 9th Devons.

The Battalion occupied the following position : first line, Old Support Trench from Chapel Alley to Frog Lane, 1 machine gun, " B " Company, " D " Company, and 1 machine gun on left of Fosse Way ; second line, Curly Crescent from Chapel Alley to 100 yards N. of Fosse Way, 1 machine gun, " C " Company, " A " Company, 1 machine gun, headquarters. The gas attack commenced at 5.50 a.m., and at 6.30 the first line of the Brigade left their trenches, advancing at walking pace to the German trenches, the garrison of which, some 200 men, at once threw their arms down and their hands up, shouting " Kamerad." These were immediately sent to the rear and their trenches occupied by the 2nd Battalion The Border Regiment and 6th Battalion Gordons. Thus, in 35 minutes from the " push off," the enemy trenches in front of the 20th Brigade had been captured, but with heavy loss. Flooding over the German lines the Brigade moved forward without a check until they reached the Quarries in front of Hulluch, distant some half mile of uphill ground without cover. During the advance more prisoners and 8 German field guns were taken.

Now, however, the 22nd Brigade on the left of the 20th was held up, and two sections of the Battalion bombers were sent to try and bomb down the obstructing trench, but were unable to make any headway. But by 9 a.m. the 8th Devons, still supported by the 2nd Border Regiment, had reached Puits 13 and began to dig themselves in ; but the 22nd Brigade, being still very stoutly opposed, " D " Company of the Battalion, under Captain Sutcliffe, was ordered to attack the enemy here and, advancing with great dash, supported by Captain Eaton-Ostle with half of " A " Company, broke down all resistance and captured some 70 prisoners, thus enabling the 22nd Brigade to come up in line with the rest of the Division.

The attack had now, however, come to a standstill for want of further backing, and the position was that a forward line E. of Hulluch cross-roads was held connecting up on the right with the 1st Division, but with the left rather in the air. In rear the trench with the 8 captured enemy guns was under heavy German shell fire.

About 11 o'clock two battalions of the 21st Brigade reinforced the 20th, and orders were received stating that the IVth Corps was to attack Hulluch. Nothing, however, came of this attack and the Germans continued to hold Hulluch and Cité St. Elie, into which reinforcements seemed to be arriving ; these places were already strongly held and were well wired. The Battalion was now occupying the trench containing the captured guns, and at 4.30 p.m. orders came from Divisional Headquarters to consolidate the positions gained, which so far as concerned the units of the 20th Brigade, were held approximately as follows : 2nd and 6th Gordons E. of the Lens–La Bassée Road, with some men of the 8th and 9th Devons ; these were ordered to dig in and make the cross-roads a strong point, aided by two 1½-inch trench mortars. The 2nd Border Regiment and some of the 8th and 9th Devons and details of the 21st Brigade were in Gun Trench, in touch on the right with the 1st Division and on the left with the 22nd Brigade, and these also were ordered to dig in while the Engineers put up wire in front.

Shortly before midnight on the 25th the Germans made a strong counter-attack on the advanced position near Hulluch cross-roads before it had been put in a state of defence, and the assault was pressed home with the evident intention of retaking the captured field guns. The front line gave way, some of its defenders falling back on Gun Trench and some retreating even further, but they were rallied and helped to defend Gun Trench, many of the German assailants being actually killed on the very parapet. The attack was beaten off, but the advanced position at the cross-roads was lost, although all the rest of the ground gained this day by the 20th Brigade was held and consolidated.

Early on the 26th the Germans captured the Quarries from the 22nd Brigade, and many attempts to retake it were unsuccessful ; and on this day Major-General Capper, commanding the 7th Division, was mortally wounded.

Later in the day the Battalion was relieved in Gun Trench and retired to Breslau Avenue, the former German communication trench, and on the 1st October fell back to billets at Cambrin.

During the Battle of Loos 3 officers of the 2nd Battalion The Border Regiment were killed or died of wounds, these being Second-Lieutenants R. Rawlinson, W. N. Beaumont and W. R. M. Woolf, while 5 officers were wounded ; these five were Captain H. K. Eaton-Ostle, Second-Lieutenants W. B. Hetherington, R. K. Ehrenborg, T. G. Grinter and W. L. Day.

While the 2nd Battalion of The Border Regiment was fighting at the Battle of Loos, the 5th Battalion was engaged further to the N. in operations which, if not actually part and parcel of the same action, were at least co-operative, in that they helped to hold the Germans in their front and prevented detachments being made to swell the enemy forces further to the south.

5th Battalion.

On the 24th September the 5th Battalion was occupying trenches in the Armentières area, when the rumours as to more active operations which for some days past had been flying about, seemed about to materialize in the publication of a Brigade order stating that " in the event of the wind not being favourable to-morrow morning, the bombardment will start at 5 a.m. without the smoke " ; while the same evening a message in the following terms came through to the troops from G.H.Q. : " Chief wishes troops to be informed that he feels confident they will realize how much our success in the following operations depends upon the individual efforts of each officer, non-commissioned officer and man. He wishes this to be conveyed to them verbally and in such a manner as not to disclose our intentions to the enemy."

The intention, then, was that the 50th Division should organize a demonstration in order to assist the operations designed to take place to the N. and S., and arrangements were made to produce a dense smoke all along the divisional front with the view of creating in the mind of the enemy a fear that an attack was about to be made under cover of gas, so as to induce the Germans to keep their trenches fully manned. At the same time a heavy artillery fire was to be opened, coupled with rifle and machine-gun fire from the trenches. With this end in view the night of the 24th–25th was occupied in arranging piles of straw in front of the trenches, some of it sprinkled with water and those piles nearer the trenches soaked with parafin, while smoke bombs were also to be used, this particular part of the programme being in the hands of Lieutenant Adair, the Battalion Bombing Officer.

The demonstration had originally been timed to begin at 4.56 a.m., but was postponed for one hour on account of the unfavourable direction of the wind. At 6 a.m.—four minutes after the amended hour of commencement—orders not to light up came from Brigade Headquarters, but these were too late as the garrisons of certain trenches had already lighted their straw, the smoke going well over the German lines some 450 yards distant. The Battalion trenches were commanded as under :—

Trench 75, Major Bewlay; Trench 76, Captain Webb; Trench 77, Captain Blair. Captain Cowburn was in command of the supports, Lieutenant Wood was machine-gun officer, Lieutenant Adair—as already stated—was Battalion bombing officer, while a few days previously Major W. R. P. Kemmis-Betty, of the 5th Battalion Berkshire Regiment, had assumed command of the Battalion.

In pursuance of orders to display all possible activity, patrols and bombing parties were sent out towards the German lines. One of these parties—under Captain Blair, with Lance-Sergeants Tiffen and Graham, Lance-Corporal Mossop, Privates Lofthouse, Ball, Coles, Walker, Harker, Rooney and Farish—went out to bomb an enemy listening post, met and ambushed a German patrol and practically annihilated it, bringing in one of the enemy dead for identification purposes. These activities continued for many days, and it was not until the 9th October that the Battalion was relieved in the front line and went back to billets at Armentières.

During the remainder of the year neither the 2nd nor the 5th Battalion of The Border Regiment was engaged in any major operations, and they spent the months of October to December for long periods of time in the trenches and for shorter periods in divisional or brigade reserve, or in rest or training areas further behind the front.

During October the 2nd Battalion remained chiefly about Bethune, where, on the 28th, with other units of the Ist Corps, it was inspected by H.M. the King;
2nd Battalion. and where it was joined by Major S. H. Worrall, Captain W. A. Manly, Lieutenant R. W. Chetham-Strode, Second-Lieutenants W. E. Kelly, G. E. Coningham and G. G. Sharp, and drafts amounting to 194 other ranks. In November the Battalion was generally about Le Quesnoy, and while here Second-Lieutenant F. D. Adamson was killed in the trenches E. of

Givenchy, while the only accessions appear to have been Lieutenant H. P. D. Helm and 44 non-commissioned officers and men. In the last month of the year the 2nd Battalion underwent several moves—to Le Hamel, Gonneham, Saleux and Breilly to the W. of Amiens; and in this month it was joined by 5 subalterns—Lieutenants R. F. Millard and P. R. Dowding, Second-Lieutenants W. L. Johnson, D. Strange and S. J. Russell, and 209 other ranks.

Of the 5th Battalion there is nothing special to record during October and November, but on the 20th December it was moved to huts at Dickebusch, conse-**5th Battalion.** quent on transfer to the 151st Brigade of the 50th Division, taking there the place of the 5th Battalion Loyal North Lancashire Regiment; here the Battalion took over trenches on the right of Hooge.

During the latter portion of the year 1915, four more battalions of The Border Regiment had arrived on the Western Front—the 7th, 8th, 9th and 11th. The **7th, 8th, 9th and 11th Battalions.** 7th left Winchester in the 51st Brigade of the 17th Division on the 12th and 14th July, and crossed over to France in two parties, the total embarking strength being 31 officers and 932 other ranks. The following are the names of the officers : Lieutenant-Colonel R. L. Norrington ; Majors W. R. Foran and R. S. Irwin ; Captains C. G. Page (adjutant), J. H. Grogan, **7th Battalion.** J. H. Bowe, L. A. Newton, A. P. Nasmith, J. W. Tailford, W. F. Richardson and T. L. Crosse ; Lieutenants M. MacDonald, J. A. Stirling, D. J. G. Dixon, A. Gordon, R. M. B. Welsh, H. C. MacMichael, F. R. K. Morgan and D. F. R. Webster (machine-gun officer) ; Second-Lieutenants A. G. Rigby (signalling officer), W. I. McKeand (transport officer), L. Birch, C. H. M. Whiteside, J. C. White, J. M. Lee, J. P. Edgar, T. D. Noble and T. S. Swan ; Hon. Lieutenant S. Ashby was quartermaster, Captain Q. V. B. Wallace (R.A.M.C.) was in medical charge of the Battalion, and the Rev. L. G. Mannering was chaplain. The Divisional Commander was Major-General T. D. Pilcher, C.B., while the Brigadier was Brigadier-General W. S. Kays.

The rest camp at Boulogne was reached early on the morning of the 15th, and from here the Battalion proceeded next day, by way of St. Omer, Wallon Cappel and Eecke, to Reninghelst, where the bulk of the Battalion was placed in the IInd Corps Reserve, while companies were sent up to the trenches in relays for instructional purposes. At the end of August the 7th Battalion was lent for a time to the 3rd Division and marched to Kruistraat, where it took over some trenches. Here casualties began and Captain Tailford distinguished himself by bringing in, during broad daylight, the body of Private Lonsdale, which was lying within ten yards of the German parapet.

On the 25th September the 7th Battalion took part with the 3rd and 14th Divisions in an attack on Hooge, and the area to the N.W. and S.E. of that town, the rôle assigned to the Battalion being the holding of the trenches occupied while affording all possible help to the right of the attack. The 7th was not actually engaged as a battalion, but when at one time the right seemed in danger of collapse, Second-Lieutenants Lee and White were sent up with a party of bombers and kept the enemy at bay. The attack failed, however, and the enemy managed to regain what ground had been captured.

The Battalion had 9 men killed and 17 wounded this day, Second-Lieutenant Lee being wounded and missing.

Towards the end of October Captain Tailford and Second-Lieutenant Birch were wounded, and by the end of the year casualties in the Ypres salient had reduced the strength of the 7th Battalion to 18 officers and 393 non-commissioned officers and men.

It was not until the 26th September, 1915, that the 8th Battalion, then at Aldershot, left England for France, arriving on the day following at Boulogne, **8th Battalion.** and being sent on almost at once by train to the Hazebrouck area ; they were established in billets at Le Bizet by the 29th, and platoons at once visited the trenches by turns. Later on the Battalion was moved to Ploegsteert, and casualties began to mount up almost immediately, the enemy's bombardment being at times very heavy and his snipers more than usually active. The parapets of the trenches needed constant work to keep them in good order, while the draining of the trenches themselves presented constant difficulties. About this time Colonel Brander returned to England, Lieutenant-Colonel C. E. Bond assuming command in his place, while Major P. Strahan became second in command of the Battalion.

In and about Ploegsteert, then, the 8th Battalion of The Border Regiment passed the first three months after arrival on the Western Front.

The 9th Battalion disembarked at Havre early on the morning of the 4th September—strength 30 officers and 935 other ranks—and was pushed on early **9th Battalion.** next morning in two trains for the Amiens area, was detrained in the middle of the night at Longueru, and marched to Flesselles, where was the headquarters of the 22nd Division. Here various contradictory orders were received, while many rumours as to probable moves were in circulation ; but on the 11th the Battalion left Flesselles and marched some 13 miles to La Neuville for attachment to the 18th Division, and here was employed on pioneer duties of all kinds. Here, too, the Battalion seems to have had its first casualty, Second-Lieutenant A. F. Sandeman being slightly wounded. Before the end of the month several moves had taken place—from La Neuville to Herleville, thence to Bayon-villers, where one man was wounded and Second-Lieutenant Ogilvie was killed by the accidental discharge of a rifle.

The 9th Battalion remained for some few weeks longer in these parts, but already events were shaping which were to call this unit of The Border Regiment to a new and distant theatre of the world war.

The isolation of Serbia and Montenegro, and the attitude of Bulgaria and Greece had caused the Allied Powers to decide to land forces at Salonika to open up communications thence with the Serbian Army. Already early in the autumn of 1915 three French divisions had been despatched thither under General Sarrail, and in October the 10th British Division, withdrawn from Suvla, had been ordered to and had landed at Salonika. The 22nd Division was now also directed to proceed thither from the Western Front, and was in due course followed by the 28th, 26th and 27th, in the order named. As a result of these arrangements the 9th Battalion proceeded to Longueru and there began entraining on the morning of the 26th

October and, leaving at once, reached Marseilles at midday on the 28th. Here 29 officers and 860 other ranks embarked in the *Egra* and steamed out of the harbour at noon on the 29th, leaving behind Captain Wilson, 62 non-commissioned officers and men, and all the transport animals to come on by a later boat.

The 11th (Lonsdale) Battalion of The Border Regiment had continued its training during the spring and summer of 1915 at various centres, and was stationed in the autumn at Salisbury Plain, when it was placed under orders to proceed to France ; and leaving at 1 a.m. on the 23rd November, it sailed some eight hours later from Folkestone to Boulogne in the *Princess Victoria*, at a strength of 31 officers, 2 warrant officers and 995 other ranks. The officers were : Lieutenant-Colonel P. W. Machell, C.M.G. ; Major P. G. W. Diggle ; Lieutenants M. Gordon (adjutant), J. F. Dawson (quartermaster), G. Spring-Rice (transport officer), C. W. Margerison (signalling officer), G. N. Kirkwood, R.A.M.C. (medical officer), Second-Lieutenant J. B. Lowthian (machine-gun officer), and the Rev. A. J. W. Crosse (chaplain).

11th Battalion.

> " A " Company.—Captains R. Smith and L. B. Hogarth ; Lieutenants R. A. M. Harris, T. H. Hodgkinson and M. McKerrow ; Second-Lieutenant G. P. Dunstan.
>
> " B " Company.—Captains C. H. Clart and B. C. Harrison ; Lieutenants C. H. Walker, R. R. Craig and J. W. Moore.
>
> " C " Company.—Captains G. Rivington and C. P. Moore ; Lieutenant C. S. Brown ; Second-Lieutenants J. Ross and T. S. Gordon.
>
> " D " Company.—Captains A. J. Dawson and A. E. Corbett ; Lieutenants W. A. Hobson and W. S. Barnes ; Second-Lieutenants A. G. Robinson and G. Twynam.
>
> Regimental Sergeant-Major W. O. Scott, and Regimental Quartermaster-Sergeant T. Kennedy.

The Battalion formed part of the 97th Infantry Brigade, commanded by Brigadier-General Jardine, D.S.O., in the 32nd Division under Major-General Rycroft, C.B., C.M.G.

On arrival in France the Battalion moved by train to Longpré, and then marched on until it reached the Albert area ; and when the year 1915 closed officers and men were fortunate enough to find themselves in billets in Aveluy, close behind the lines.

This account, then, of the services in the war of eight battalions of The Border Regiment up to the close of the year 1915, may perhaps fittingly conclude with the text of the gracious message which His Majesty the King sent at this season to his soldiers in France and other theatres of the war :—

" Another Christmas finds all the resources of the Empire still engaged in war, and I desire to convey on my own behalf and on behalf of the Queen, a heartfelt Christmas greeting and our good wishes for the New Year, to all whom, on Sea and Land, are upholding the honour of the British name. In the officers and men of my Navy, on whom the security of the Empire depends, I repose, in common with all my subjects, a trust that is absolute. On the officers and men of my Armies, whether

now in France, in the East, or in other fields, I rely with an equal faith, confident that their devotion, their valour, and their self-sacrifice will, under God's guidance, lead to Victory and an honourable Peace. There are many of their comrades, alas, in hospital, and to these brave fellows also, I desire, with the Queen, to express our deep gratitude and our earnest prayers for their recovery.

" Officers and men of the Navy and Army, another year is drawing to a close, as it began, in toil, bloodshed and suffering ; but I rejoice to know that the goal to which you are striving draws nearer into sight.

" May God bless you and all your undertakings."

CHAPTER V

1916

THE BATTLE OF THE SOMME.

THE FIRST PHASE.

IST–14TH JULY.

AT the end of the year that had just come to a close there had been a change in the command of the British Forces on the Western Front, Field-Marshal Sir John French having returned to England to take over charge of the Home Forces, his place being filled by General Sir Douglas Haig.

During the last few months things had not gone particularly well with the Allies; the Russians, inadequately armed and supplied, had been driven back until the whole of Poland was in the hands of the Germanic Powers; the British adventure in Gallipoli had failed with heavy losses and the forces there engaged had been withdrawn; Serbia and Montenegro had been overrun and Bulgaria had joined the league of our enemies; while finally in Mesopotamia our advance had been checked, General Townshend was besieged in Kut and later in the year 1916 was obliged to surrender with some 9,000 men, British and Indian.

By the end of the year 1915 the British Empire had raised for its armies the enormous number of five million volunteers, but the strain of the recruiting service was great and occupied the time of many who might have been more profitably employed, while it was felt that the burden ought in justice to be more equally distributed, and in January, 1916, a Military Service Bill was passed under which every citizen of Great Britain from 19 to 41 was liable to be called up for service.

The early months of 1916 were comparatively uneventful, that is to say there was no action on any great scale fought by our troops during that time, but the British were far from being either idle or inactive and there were many sharp local encounters. In his despatch of the 19th May of this year General Haig wrote: "Although there has been no great incident of historic importance to record on the British front during the period under review, a steady and continuous fight has gone on, day and night, above ground and below it. The comparative monotony of this struggle has been relieved at short intervals by sharp local actions, some of which, although individually almost insignificant in a war on such an immense scale, would have been thought worthy of a separate despatch under different conditions, while their cumulative effect, though difficult to appraise at its true value now, will doubtless prove hereafter to have been considerable."

On the 21st February the Germans commenced their long-drawn-out attacks upon the French at Verdun, where the fighting was very severe and cost the enemy very much in blood and in prestige ; during the earlier part of this struggle the British troops were held in readiness to co-operate as they might be needed, but at the moment all that our Allies asked was that the British should relieve the French on a portion of their defensive front and this request was cordially met and the necessary relief granted.

When the year 1916 opened there were, it will be remembered, no fewer than seven battalions of The Border Regiment serving in France and Flanders.

The 1st Battalion in the 29th Division had left Suez, where since landing from Gallipoli it had been engaged in training, on the 12th March for Alexandria,

1st Battalion. where it embarked for Marseilles in the transport *Marilda*, arrived at Pont Rémy on the 22nd and proceeded to billets at Gorenflos, where leave to England was opened ; at the end of March the 1st Battalion marched to Amplier, some 20 miles S.E. of Doullens. The 29th Division was still in the VIIIth Corps commanded by General Hunter-Weston, but the Corps had by this time been re-constituted and was now composed of two Regular Divisions, the 4th and 29th, with the 31st Division of the New Army and the 48th (South Midland) Territorial Division. It formed part of General Rawlinson's Fourth Army which held the line from Albert to the Somme, where the British line joined on to the left of the French—the VIIIth Corps in the S. with, in order northward, the Xth, XVth and XIIIth.

The 2nd Battalion remained in the Bethune area up to the end of 1915, moving in the New Year to Breilly some few miles W. of Amiens. In February

2nd Battalion. it was in the trenches near Meaulte, where there were many casualties, especially from shell fire, casualties which the small, if frequent, drafts which arrived at the front were hardly adequate to replace. The first week in April found the Battalion at Bray, where it came under the orders of the Brigadier-General commanding the 91st Brigade, and, going into the trenches on the 13th, experienced from then onwards a very trying time. From the first it was evident that the enemy guns were registering on the British trenches, so that an attack appeared to be imminent and all possible arrangements were made to meet it. On the evening of the 19th the Germans opened an especially violent bombardment on the sub-sector held by the Battalion ; the front, support and reserve lines were all impartially shelled, the fire being most intense on the front about Mansel Copse. An hour or so later the barrage was lifted and a party of the enemy approached the lines of The Border Regiment about Blood Alley, but was driven back by bombs. The enemy then moved off to a flank and managed to enter the front-line trench before he was finally ejected. In this fighting Second-Lieutenant W. L. Johnson and 18 men were killed, Lieutenant J. H. Hodgson, Second-Lieutenant G. P. Lindsay and 42 other ranks were wounded, while 9 men were missing ; the bodies of some 7 of these last were recovered later by the relieving battalion, but so terribly shattered by shell fire that identification was impossible. Lieutenant Hodgson died next day of his wounds.

On the evening of the 20th April the enemy bombardment recommenced with great violence on much the same front as before, but the fire was not continued for so long. A party of the enemy approached the Battalion front line at the head of Blood Alley and threw bombs into the trench, The Border Regiment replying with Mills bombs; after a short fight the enemy fell back and renewed the attack on another part of the line but was again beaten off, and the British artillery retaliating with great effect the German trenches were blown in in many places. Of this period R.S.M. Davenport relates as follows: "We were moved to Bray and went into trenches at Wellington Redoubt, being attached to the 91st Brigade; during all this time we had three raids made on us by the enemy, losing many men but gaining very great honour. On our last raid Captain Kerr, M.C., was discovered by General Minshull-Ford, G.O.C. 91st Brigade, on the parapet with a revolver in one hand and a Mills bomb in the other, singing 'John Peel,' encouraging the men to ignore the terrific shell fire thereby. The Regiment repelled the raiders and gave them a real good licking." On this second day the Battalion suffered seven casualties.

The sequel to this may be seen in the following letter from Brigadier-General Minshull-Ford, commanding 91st Brigade :—

"*I wish to bring to your notice the splendid behaviour of the officers and men of the 2nd Battalion Border Regiment and 20th Company Machine Gun Corps on the night of the 19th April, 1916.*

"*Although subjected to an intense and concentrated bombardment of 40 minutes, in bad trenches, and in spite of heavy losses, they repelled the enemy by their rifle fire, bombing and machine-gun fire. I consider that the Officer Commanding took every possible step, both in anticipation of, and after, the bombardment commenced to repel the enemy. I personally visited all parts of the line very shortly after the fight, and I can testify to the splendid bearing of both officers and men. The Lewis and machine guns were all firing.*

"*I trust that you will allow me to forward the names of several officers, n.c.o.'s and men for immediate reward. I was especially struck with the conduct of Captain Kerr and Captain Drake-Brockman.*"

Finally Brigadier-General Minshull-Ford sent the following personal letter to Colonel Thorpe :—

"DEAR THORPE,
"*I cannot let your Regiment leave without writing to tell you how splendidly I think they have done. You took over a very bad piece of the line, and held it under exceptionally trying circumstances. I consider all your arrangements for defence were excellent and worked as well as they possibly could and that nothing could have prevented the loss which occurred.*

"*From my own personal observation I know how bravely all ranks did their duty, and thank you and them for defending the line so well—and for all they did for England.*

"*I consider it a great honour to have had your fine Regiment under my Command, and I wish you and it the best of luck. I was personally subjected (as they say) to an intense bombardment in a very cramped area yesterday, as you know, and it made me most fully realize a little of what you and your brave officers and men had to put up with; my dose lasted 8 minutes, theirs an hour and a half.*

"I shall be very pleased to forward the names of your officers and men who have specially distinguished themselves. Among them I hope you will send in Kerr's and Drake-Brockman's, and I am writing officially to General Deverill to express my admiration of the conduct displayed by all ranks of your Regiment. I am very sorry indeed for the brave men who have gone—they died at their posts.

"Yours sincerely,

"(Signed) M. MINSHULL-FORD."

On relief the 2nd Battalion went back to rest billets about Vaux sur Somme, where, and in shelters in the Bois des Tailles, it remained almost up to the opening of the very protracted operations known as the Battle of the Somme. Drafts amounting to 242 joined the service companies with the following officers : Majors G. F. Green, 1st Devons, and G. E. Beaty-Pownall ; Lieutenants T. J. Wilson and G. W. O'Brien ; Second-Lieutenants G. Morrison, G. A. Gillespie, A. J. Croft, D. H. H. Logan, N. Ellis, H. J. B. Warren, H. J. Hayman-Joyce, J. H. Dothie and W. R. Robertson.

During the winter of 1915–16 the 1st/5th Battalion remained in the Dicke-busch area, doing much good work and incurring casualties which, though not **1st/5th Battalion.** heavy as compared with those sustained by units on other parts of the front, served to keep the strength of the Battalion very low in view of the few men who came out to it from England. In the spring the Battalion moved to La Clytte and was stationed hereabouts, occupying the trenches or shelters in rear, when in July the long-prepared-for battle broke out.

The 6th Battalion remained in Egypt employed upon the Canal defences for several months after arrival in that country from Gallipoli, and it was not until **6th Battalion.** quite the end of June that the Battalion proceeded to Alexandria by train in two parties and embarked for Marseilles in the steamer *Scotian,* sailing on the 30th June under an escort of destroyers. Marseilles was reached on the 6th July, when disembarkation was effected and the 11th Division then proceeded by train and march route to Arras, arriving there on the 17th.

We have seen that at the end of 1915 the 7th Border Regiment was stationed in the neighbourhood of Ypres, but in the beginning of January, 1916, it **7th Battalion.** moved by march and rail to St. Omer, where it spent a quiet and peaceful month. It left this rest area again on the 7th February and made its way to Poperinghe, where for some few days it was in divisional reserve. But on the 14th the Battalion was concerned in an unsuccessful attempt to dislodge the enemy in its front and had 21 non-commissioned officers and men killed or died of wounds, while 92 were wounded and 3 men were missing, among the wounded being two young officers, Second-Lieutenants T. D. Noble and A. M. Jenkins. Thereafter up to the opening of the fighting on the Somme there were many moves—from Poperinghe to Dickebusch, thence to Bailleul, where

Photo   *Imperial War Museum*

A WORKING PARTY

Photo   *Imperial War Museum*

A FRONT LINE TRENCH

the Division passed to the IInd Corps commanded by General Sir C. Fergusson, from there to Houplines in the Armentières area, then for some six weeks to a training area about Eperlecques, until the end of June found the 7th Border Regiment in billets about Merlancourt.

The 8th Battalion remained in the Ploegsteert area until after the New Year, moving on the 26th January, 1916, via La Crèche to Strazeele, where

8th Battalion. company training was very seriously entered upon, officers went into Bailleul to attend lectures, and sport was not overlooked, the Brigade cross-country race being won by " A " Company of the Battalion, Corporal Close taking the Gold Medal for the first man home. On the 10th March Strazeele was left again, the troops moving by way of Hazebrouck, Boesighem and Nédou to Bryas, which was reached on the 16th and where a few days later the Battalion was inspected by General Sir Julian Byng. Here the training was of a more advanced order and the attack was sedulously practised, while the commanding officer and second in command visited the front-line trenches which the Battalion was shortly to take over. At the end of the month the 8th Border Regiment moved to Monchy Breton and in April was occupying trenches in front of Neuville St. Vaast, and when out of the front line provided many working parties.

In the third week in June the 25th Division, which had been training for some time W. of St. Pol, moved S. to the Fourth Army, and when the great battle commenced it lay around Warly, about four miles behind the front line and, with the 12th Division, formed the Fourth Army Reserve.

The 11th Battalion of The Border Regiment remained for many weeks after arrival on the Western Front about Albert, the general routine being seven days

11th Battalion. in the trenches, seven in very close billets as support, then seven days trenches again and then another seven in brigade reserve. On the 26th March the 32nd Division moved into the Fourth Army under General Sir Henry Rawlinson, but early in April there was a severe outbreak of measles in the 11th Battalion and it was moved into an isolation camp in Contay Wood, where it remained for a month.

On the 1st June the Battalion was in Divisional Reserve at Bouzincourt and four days later the 11th Border Regiment carried out a raid on the German trenches opposite the Leipzig salient. Lieutenant Barnes was O.C. raid and he had with him Lieutenants M. McKerrow, C. W. Margerison and L. Machell, with 82 other ranks—all volunteers, and the object was to find out as much as possible of the German trenches and dispositions and to take prisoners. The party for the raid had been under training for three weeks under Lieutenant Barnes and " the success of the enterprise was due to the great care that he took in training the party, and his leadership up to the end was most splendid." Of the results Colonel Machell wrote : " Complete success last night, only unfortunately Barnes was killed just before they got back, with five others. We took 11 prisoners alive, about 25 others killed. Men did splendidly, and I have telegrams from the Division—Major-General Rycroft, Corps—Lieut.-General Sir T. Morland and Army—General Sir H. Rawlinson, to-day."

The 11th Battalion had 1 officer and 5 other ranks killed, 17 men wounded, and 1 sergeant missing. The Corps Commander inspected and congratulated the raiders next day.

Having now brought all the seven battalions of the Regiment at this time serving in France up in line in preparation for the great events about to transpire, something must now be stated about what led up to the battle and as to the results which it was hoped to obtain.

As stated in General Sir Douglas Haig's despatch of the 23rd December, 1916, the Allies had already early in this year decided, in principle, on an offensive campaign during the summer; the matter had been thoroughly discussed in all its bearings, and it had been arranged that the attack must be made by the British and French in combination, since neither army was sufficiently strong to take the offensive unaided on anything like a large scale. General Haig was anxious for several reasons that the attack should be postponed as long as possible; the munition factories under British control were now working at greatly increased pressure and the stocks of ammunition of all kinds were being daily added to; but while during the first six months of this year the strength of the British armies on the Western Front grew from 450,000 to 660,000, a very large proportion of the officers and men composing them were still far from being fully trained, and the longer the attack could be deferred the more efficient would they become.

The German attacks on Verdun, begun in the last week in February, had been continuous and the pressure was now becoming almost insupportable, while in the Italian theatre of war the Austrians in the middle of May gained some substantial successes against our Allies. All these considerations induced Generals Haig and Joffre to agree that the proposed offensive must not be delayed beyond the end of June.

There were many preliminary arrangements to be made; huge stocks of ammunition and food had to be brought up to and collected within convenient distance of the front, and to facilitate this many miles of rail had to be laid, roads made and improved. Trenches had to be dug, mining operations undertaken, and some 120 miles of water pipes laid down. All this work was carried out under very trying conditions, under constant interruption by the enemy and in weather which was almost continuously inclement.

" The position to be attacked was of a very formidable character, on high undulating ground some 500 feet above sea-level, forming the watershed between the Somme and the rivers of S.W. Belgium. On the S. face of this watershed, the general trend of which is from E.S.E. to W.N.W., the ground falls in a series of long irregular spurs and deep depressions to the valley of the Somme. Well down the forward slopes of this face the enemy's first system of defence, starting from the Somme near Curlu, ran at first N. for about 3,000 yards, then W. for 7,000 yards to near Fricourt, where it turned nearly due N., forming a great salient angle in the enemy's line. Some 10,000 yards N. of Fricourt the trenches crossed the River Ancre, a tributary of the Somme, and still running N. passed over the summit of the watershed, about Hébuterne and Gommecourt, and then down its N. spurs to Arras. On the 20,000 yards front between the Somme and the Ancre the enemy had a strong second system of defence, sited generally on or near the S. crest of the highest part of the watershed, at an average distance of from 3,000 to 5,000 yards behind his first system of trenches."[1] For many months past no pains had been spared to render these defences impregnable.

The attack had been originally planned for the 28th June, but the weather was so bad that it was put off until the 1st July, which broke calm and warm; the British bombardment commenced, however, on the 24th June, a very large number of guns having been brought into position for the purpose. The attack on the front from Maricourt to Serre was to be carried out by the Fourth Army with its five army corps, while a subsidiary attack, to be made on both sides of the salient at Gommecourt, was entrusted to the three divisions of the VIIth Corps of the Third Army.

The disposition of the British forces from S. to N. at the opening of the attack on the 1st July was as under:—

> XIIIth Corps.—30th and 18th Divisions in front line, 9th Division in support
> XVth Corps.—7th and 21st Divisions in front line, 17th Division in support (2nd and 7th Border Regiment).
> IIIrd Corps.—34th and 8th Divisions in front line, 19th Division in support.
> Xth Corps.—32nd and 36th Divisions in front line, 49th Division in support (11th Battalion).
> VIIIth Corps.—29th, 4th and 31st Divisions in front line, 48th Division in support (1st Battalion).
> VIIth Corps.—56th and 46th Divisions in front line, 37th Division in support.

While the 12th and 25th Divisions (8th Border Regiment) were in Fourth Army Reserve.

The Battle of the Somme lasted so great a length of time—from the 1st July to the 17th November—and so many battalions of The Border Regiment were engaged in it, that it is not an easy matter to tell the story of the battle as a whole, while endeavouring to do full justice to the individual units concerned in it. General Haig in his despatch divides the battle into three phases, but it will perhaps be more convenient to follow the arrangement drawn up in a publication[2] compiled by the Historical Section of the Committee of Imperial Defence, and tell the story in four phases—the first, commencing on the 1st July and ending on the 14th of that month; the second phase, commencing on the 23rd July and ending on the 9th September; the third, commencing on the 15th September and ending on the 9th November; and the fourth and last beginning on the 13th November and closing on the 17th. Further, in following the fortunes of the various battalions in one of the greatest battles of modern times, it is proposed to begin at the southern end of the British line, or rather with the southernmost division containing a battalion of The Border Regiment.

[1] Despatch of 23rd December, 1916.
[2] *Principal Events of the War*, Part II.

The XVth Corps, commanded by General Horne and containing the 7th, 17th and 21st Divisions, occupied a front extending from a point opposite the village of Fricourt to Bècourt in the N., with the 7th Division on the southern or right flank.

FIRST PHASE,
2nd Battalion.

The following operation orders were issued in the 7th Division on the 26th June :—

" In conjunction with the French, who are operating from Maricourt southwards, the Fourth Army is about to assume the offensive. The attack will be developed to the N. and S. of Fricourt Village and Fricourt Wood by the 21st and 7th Divisions respectively, with the object of isolating the triangle formed by these localities, which will afterwards be dealt with in a subsidiary operation. The task of the 7th Division is to clear the trenches in front and seize and occupy the spur from the track at S.25 to Willow Avenue at X.29. Immediately on the right of the 7th Division, the left brigade of the 18th Division will advance simultaneously and prolong the 7th Division line towards Montauban. On the left of the 7th Division, advancing on the N. side and clear of Fricourt Village and Wood, will be the 50th Infantry Brigade, attached 21st Division, with their right on Fricourt Farm. That brigade will join hands with the 7th Division at Willow Avenue and prolong the line N. through the Quadrangle to Contalmaison.

" The Division will be distributed as follows :—

> Right.—91st Infantry Brigade.
> Centre.—20th Infantry Brigade.
> Left.—22nd Infantry Brigade, less 2 battalions and
> M.G. Company.

" Main Attack : will be carried out by the 91st and 20th Infantry Brigades. Subsidiary Attack : will be carried out by the 22nd Infantry Brigade, which will clear the German trenches N. of Bois Français at an hour to be decided on later, when the main attack has reached its final objective. This operation will take place in conjunction with the 2 battalions of the 50th Brigade, who will clear Fricourt Village and Wood.

" The object of the 20th Infantry Brigade will be to form a defensive flank facing N.W. to cover the advance of the 91st Brigade. Its objective is the line from the bend of Bunny Trench (road inclusive), along Bunny Trench, thence along Sunken Road to the junction of Orchard Trench N. with Orchard Alley—Orchard Alley to junction with Apple Alley, then along Apple Alley to the small salient in our present line.

" The special objective of the 2nd Border Regiment is Apple Alley from the junction with Orchard Alley to the present German front line.

" For the assault the 20th Brigade will be formed up as follows :—

> Right.—2nd Gordons.
> Centre.—9th Devons.
> Left.—2nd Border.
> Reserve.—8th Devons."

The Battalion was directed to advance in four lines of four platoons each at 100 yards distance between lines: 1st and 2nd Lines, " A " Company on the right and " C " Company on the left; 3rd and 4th Lines, " B " on the right and " D " on the left.

The first Battalion objective was Danube Support Trench, the second, Shrine Alley–Kiel Lane, the final objective being Apple Alley.

On the opening day of the Somme battle the 2nd Battalion companies were commanded as follows: " A " Company, Lieutenant G. M. F. Prynne, " C " Company, Captain L. A. Newton, " B " Company, Lieutenant R. F. Millard, and " D," Lieutenant P. N. Fraser.

During the artillery bombardment of the enemy position the Battalion was subjected to heavy retaliation by the German guns, but little damage was done. At 7.27 a.m. on the 1st July the Battalion moved forward until it reached Danube Support Trench, its first objective, when it began to wheel to the left in the new direction. So far the casualties had been few in the first and second lines, and had for the most part been caused by two enemy machine guns firing from the right and left respectively. The wheel completed, the advance continued towards the second objective, which was reached by the first line about 8.30 a.m., the line having by this been broken up into a number of groups of fighting men, all busily engaged in bombing and bayoneting the enemy, who, on finding their position stormed, took up a fresh line in shell holes and communication trenches, whence for a time they checked the advance. On reaching Shrine Alley the Battalion came under heavy indirect machine-gun fire from Fricourt and enfilade fire from Mametz, but the leading lines being reinforced by the third line the advance was continued to Hidden Lane, where it was again held up for a time by fire from Hidden Wood and from the junction of Kiel Support and Bois Français Support. The hostile party at this last place was bombed out without much difficulty, but the others had to be attacked across the open, which was done with great dash and determination by a party organized and led by Second-Lieutenant Russell. The two leading lines now pushed on to Apple Alley while the third line consolidated Hidden Lane, the right of the fourth line moving up to Hidden Wood to strengthen that flank.

At 5 p.m. this day the Battalion situation was as follows: Apple Alley, the final objective, was occupied by " A " and " C " Company of the 2nd Border Regiment with a party of 8th Devons on the right; " B " and " D " Companies held Hidden Lane as a support line; and Battalion Headquarters was established in an old dug-out in Support Trench. This position was maintained until the morning of the 3rd July when the Battalion changed over to Bois Français Support, moving again the same evening into reserve, and on the 5th to billets at Ribemont.

The casualties sustained in this attack were not very heavy all things considered, mainly by reason of the thorough manner in which the enemy wire had been cut by the fire of our guns, and also because the advance followed very closely in rear of the barrage. The losses were: killed or died of wounds, 4 officers and 89 other ranks; wounded, 6 officers and 240 non-commis-

7

sioned officers and men; and missing, 4 men. The names of the officers who became casualties were: killed, Lieutenant P. N. Fraser, Second-Lieutenants W. R. Robertson, D. H. H. Logan and P. D. Lucas; wounded, Captain L. A. Newton, Lieutenants R. F. Millard and G. W. O'Brien, Second-Lieutenants G. G. Sharp, F. Argles and H. Ellis.

On the 13th orders for another attack were issued; this was to be directed against the German trenches S. of Bazentin-le-Grand Wood, the 20th Brigade having the 3rd Division on its right and the 21st on the left. On this occasion the Battalion was to be on the left of the assaulting line, the objective of the 2nd Border Regiment being, first, the junction of the road and trench near the N.W. angle of "the Snout"; second and third, special points indicated on the trench map in possession.

On the night of the 13th July the Battalion moved up from its bivouacs in rear to the position of deployment in Caterpillar Wood, reaching there at 1.15 p.m. on the 14th, being subjected on the march to a heavy shelling by enemy field guns and howitzers firing H.E. and shrapnel. At 2.20 a.m. the line moved up as follows: 1st and 2nd Lines, left, "D" Company under Captain Wright, right, "B" under Captain Newdigate, 2 platoons of each in line; 3rd Line, "A" Company, under Lieutenant Dowding, in line of platoons ready to support either of the front companies; and 4th Line, "C" Company, under Second-Lieutenant Holland, in reserve. The lines advanced at 150 yards interval.

The night, though moonlight, was cloudy, and the 1st Line was able to move straight on to the S. edge of Flatiron Copse covered by scouts, the other lines following to their allotted positions in rear, all being in place by 2.35 a.m. From here the Battalion crawled silently forward, as ordered, to some 30 yards from the enemy trenches, where they waited for the lift of the barrage which was timed for 3.25, at which hour the 2nd Border Regiment again advanced and captured the first German line. Here a second halt had to be made until the barrage lifted off the Wood, when the advance was resumed and by 4.40 a.m. on the 14th July the final objective was in the hands of the British. Just previous to the assault "A" Company had been absorbed into the general line, two platoons of the reserve company had been advanced up to Flatiron Copse so as to be at hand should reinforcements be needed, while the other two platoons of this company remained in their place in Caterpillar Wood together with Battalion Headquarters.

This day the 2nd Border Regiment had again suffered many casualties: 2 officers—Second-Lieutenants M. S. Lawson and W. R. Hinton—and 23 other ranks were killed, Captain A. Wright and 136 non-commissioned officers and men were wounded and 58 men were missing.

The Battalion remained during the night in the captured position, and on the afternoon of the 15th was withdrawn to Pommier Redoubt, where it remained until the 19th July.

Another Battalion of the Regiment, the 7th, also fought with the XVth Corps in the early stages of the first phase of the battle, but being in the 17th Division, which at the outset was in support, it was not until the 2nd July that it moved up from its billets in Merlancourt to the front of Fricourt Wood with Battalion Headquarters in Fricourt Château, receiving at 3 a.m. next morning orders to attack Bottom Wood, at 9 o'clock, in waves of platoons on a two-platoon frontage in line, with a squad of Battalion bombers between each of the first four waves.

7th Battalion.

The order of companies was " B," " D " and " A " with " C " in reserve in Willow Trench. After leaving Fricourt Wood the first trench to be taken was Railway Alley, and this was captured without any serious opposition being met with, although Captain T. L. Crosse and Second-Lieutenant A. H. Crompton— the latter carrying a Lewis gun on his shoulder—were both killed. " B " Company remained in rear to clean up Railway Alley, while " D " Company pushed on to attack Bottom Wood lying some 250 yards further up the slope. A good deal of resistance was here experienced, mainly in the capture of an unmarked trench 50 yards in rear of Railway Alley, but this was overcome, when " D " and " B " Companies, supported by " A," attacked Bottom Wood. A small party under Second-Lieutenants Sanger and Thompson got into the wood and found the enemy here in strength ; the Germans did not, however, apparently realize how few in number their assailants were and all attacks were beaten off, and the enemy having been driven from Shelter Wood by our guns and infantry, the latter were able to push on and occupy Bottom Wood, when the position reached was at once consolidated.

The enemy's resistance had now here wholly broken down and they either ran or surrendered. During the night the 7th Border Regiment was relieved and went back into German dug-outs in Fricourt Wood. In these operations Second-Lieutenant H. H. Linzell was killed, Captain H. C. MacMichael and Second-Lieutenant F. P. Joyce were wounded.

The Battalion took no further part in the July fighting.

Moving northwards along the British line the next corps containing a battalion of The Border Regiment was the Xth, composed of the 32nd, 36th and 49th Divisions, in the first-named of which the 11th Battalion (Lonsdales) was serving. After the battle had commenced, however, the 25th Division, containing the 8th Border Regiment, was brought up into this section of the front line and during the first week was split up, its brigades being attached to other front line divisions as the exigencies of the moment demanded.

11th Battalion.

Of General Morland's Xth Corps the 32nd and 36th Divisions were in the front line, holding the right and left of it respectively and covering a front from one mile N. of Hamel to one mile N. of Ovillers. In front of the 36th Division the River Ancre cut through the British line almost at right angles and then, bending southwards, flowed in rear of and almost parallel to the front of the corps.

From the British front line the ground sloped upwards to the strongly held village of Thiepval, with a ridge in rear of it whence the German guns could sweep the whole approach.

At 10 p.m. on the 30th June the Lonsdales moved from dug-outs at Crucifix Corner to assembly trenches, which had been specially dug for them in the thickest part of Authuille Wood, where it had not been so far much shelled, and in these the Battalion spent the remainder of the night incurring no casualties.

The task assigned to the 97th Brigade in general and to the 11th Border Regiment in particular was a very difficult one; the objective was Mouquet Farm, but in order to effect its capture the 97th Brigade on the right of the Division—the 96th Brigade being on the left and the 14th in support—had first to move N.E. and then to swing to the E., while the Lonsdale Battalion had to move N. out of Authuille Wood for some little distance and then swing *due* E.; this movement, moreover, had not only to be calculated exactly as to time, but had to be done under heavy fire. The companies moved out from the wood in " blob " formation—on a front of two men, each half-platoon being in a little column of its own, not immediately in rear of the one in front, but slightly to one flank, this being considered the best formation under distant shell fire. On leaving their trenches in the wood, even before arriving at the front British trench, the Battalion came under a terrific machine-gun fire—the shell fire was practically negligible while such musketry as came in its direction was too high. There was no question of flinching; the companies, men dropping every moment, moved steadily on, and, on leaving the advanced British trench, pushed on straight to their front for a time and then, as had been ordered, wheeled eastward. The attacking line, supported by the Lonsdales, was having a hard fight to try and reach the German trenches, but few were able to get so far since the enemy machine guns were taking a terrible toll, mowing down the men in scores and causing very heavy losses.

Colonel Machell, gallantly leading his men, was shot dead almost immediately after leaving the forward trench; his adjutant, Lieutenant Gordon, was severely wounded, as he stooped over his body; Major Diggle, the second in command, was already wounded, and within a very short time out of 28 officers and 800 other ranks who left the wood, 25 officers and some 500 non-commissioned officers and men were out of action. Men could do no more.

In the other battalions of the brigade, and in the other brigades of the division, the losses had been no less heavy, thus depriving the attack of the weight and momentum necessary to achieve success. Nevertheless, all through the 2nd July the line reached held firm, the remnants of the Battalion providing fatigue parties for carrying up stores from the dumps in Authuille. Then on the night of the 3rd–4th the Division was relieved by the 25th Division and withdrew to refit after its tragic but splendid exertions. The Battalion marched to Contay Wood, where it was reorganized in two companies commanded by Second-Lieutenants Ross and Welsh, and on the 15th Major A. C. Girdwood, D.S.O., Northumberland Fusiliers, was appointed to command the Battalion, with Major Chamberlayne, 1st Lancers, Indian Army, as second in command. The Lonsdales took no further part in the first phase of the Somme Battle.

The following were the officers who became casualties in this action : *killed* or died of wounds: Lieutenant-Colonel P. W. Machell, C.M.G., D.S.O. ; Captains R. G. Smith, A. E. Corbett and C. Brown, Lieutenant C. W. Margerison ;

Second-Lieutenants A. E. Monkhouse, J. C. Parker, G. Coe, G. P. Dunstan, W. S. Paton and F. A. Rupp; *wounded*: Major P. G. W. Diggle, Captains B. C. Harrison and C. P. Moore, Lieutenants W. A. Hobson, C. H. Walker, T. H. Hodgkinson, M. Gordon (adjutant), and M. McKerrow; Second-Lieutenants J. R. S. Borman, J. W. Moore, W. Green, G. Black, F. M. Ransom and L. Machell; of other ranks 100 were killed, 371 were wounded and 19 men were missing.

On the morning of the 1st July, about 11 o'clock, the 8th Battalion of The Border Regiment, serving in the 75th Brigade of the 25th Division, received sudden **8th Battalion.** orders to be ready to move at short notice, but it was not until exactly twenty-four hours later that the Battalion marched to Martinsart Wood, from where it was sent forward to its appointed place in the front-line trench S. of Thiepval preparatory to an attack; the 11th Cheshires were on the left and the 2nd South Lancashires on the right. This attack by the 75th Brigade on the Thiepval Ridge from the Authuille direction was planned in conjunction with one by the VIIIth Corps against the enemy's line N. of the Ancre, while the 49th Division was to attack the German line S. of that river as far as the Thiepval spur, the 12th Division assaulting Ovillers and the defences immediately N. of the village. During the night, however, the operations by the VIIIth Corps and 49th Division were cancelled, while the attack by the 12th Division was to commence at 3 a.m. on the 3rd, that by the 75th Brigade at 6; but owing to the non-cooperation of the other bodies and to the fact that the 12th Division failed to reach its objectives, the attack of the 75th Brigade could hardly be expected to succeed.

At 6 a.m. on the 3rd the 8th Border Regiment advanced in four waves, "D" and "A" Companies from the front line and "B" and "C" from the support line, each company with two platoons in line and covering a front of from 150 to 200 yards. The two leading lines went over punctually at the appointed hour, the two others being held back in the front line until it was seen how things were going and until reinforcements should be called for. Before long a message came back from the leading companies asking for support in men and for supplies of bombs, and these were sent up until all the supports were exhausted, nothing having arrived to replace them from the reserve. Of this attack the Divisional Record [1] states: "The four companies of the Cheshires, the 8th Borders with 'A,' 'B,' 'C' and 'D' Companies, commanded respectively by Captain Bishop, Major Birt, Captain Miller and Captain Coxon, and the 2nd South Lancs., suffered very heavy casualties, were met by heavy flanking machine-gun fire and never reached their objectives. In the centre the Borders were more successful, but were unable, owing to pressure on their flanks, to maintain themselves in the German front line for more than one and a half hours." The frontage in the German line actually occupied by the 8th Border Regiment was about 180 yards in length, but the trench had been much damaged by the British guns, and there was very little cover. The right flank of the Brigade gave way, the word "Retire" was raised and passed along from the right; there

[1] *The 25th Division in France and Flanders*, p. 11.

was no telephone communication with Battalion Headquarters, all messages had to be sent by runners, who were new to the trenches and could not find their way in the dark, and the resultant delay and confusion prevented the due organization of bombing parties for the clearing of the German communication trenches.

The Battalion war diary states that " the German rifle and machine-gun fire was not particularly severe," but the Divisional History records that " being badly enfiladed by machine guns and heavy shell fire from Thiepval and beyond, they " (the Battalion) " were forced to retire to their original line. The failure of the operation can be largely attributed to the lack of time for recon-naissance, previous preparation, and the lack of co-ordination between artillery and infantry plans."

During the night of the 3rd–4th July the 25th Division relieved the 32nd in the line with the 7th Brigade on the right and the 75th on the left, but on the following night the 75th Brigade, with the 8th Battalion The Border Regi-ment, was withdrawn to Aveluy Wood, the Battalion going into bivouac on the southern side and remaining there throughout the 5th and 6th. The fighting during the opening operations of the Somme Battle had caused the 8th Border Regiment serious losses, 4 officers being killed and 10 wounded, while the casualties in other ranks totalled 430 ; the names of the officers killed were Second-Lieutenants D. J. Gordon, G. H. Foss, A. E. Aldous and L. Curteis, while the following were wounded : Major C. W. H. Birt, Captains A. O. Bishop and P. H. Coxon, Lieutenants A. Wingate-Gray, G. C. Hutton and F. W. H. Renton, Second-Lieutenants J. E. K. Bell, S. O. Withers, J. P. Edgar and F. L. Clark.

The Brigades of the 25th Division now began to rejoin their unit and from the 9th July the Division worked as a whole ; it was not, however, until the 13th that the 8th Border Regiment, which had been in reserve trenches in the vicinity of Albert, was again ordered up to the front, being engaged with its own brigade and the 7th in attacking northwards towards Ovillers. " The 7th Brigade," so says the Divisional Record, " failed to reach their objectives, but the 75th Brigade was more successful. The Border Regiment formed up under cover of darkness and drove the enemy from the front line trench without much difficulty. The capture of the communication trenches was a more difficult matter and progress was slow. . . . Casualties were heavy."

The Battalion had been ordered to attack and capture two lines of trenches on the S. side of Ovillers with " A " and " B " Companies on the right and " C " and " D " on the left, and all gained their objectives without meeting with any very serious resistance, but unfortunately during this advance Captain W. G. Cassels, commanding " A " Company, was killed, and Second-Lieutenant G. K. Rhodes received wounds of which he afterwards died. During the night the 74th Brigade relieved the 7th, and on the next morning the attack was renewed and some further progress was effected, The Border Regiment advancing from their recently captured trench, but being met by exceedingly heavy and accurate machine-gun fire. " B " and " D " Companies under Lieutenants Thomson and Stewart managed to get within 50 yards of the enemy's new trench, but were

Photo   *Imperial War Museum*

MINE CRATER BLOWN UP ON 1st JULY, 1916, BEAUMONT HAMEL

Photo   *Imperial War Museum*

GERMAN BARBED WIRE AND SHELL-HOLES AFTER RAIN

forced eventually to retire ; the old German front line was, however, held, and here the Battalion remained until the 17th, when it marched to bivouacs at Senlis.

Neither Brigade had been wholly successful, but the ground was very difficult, the defences being composed of a perfect labyrinth of trenches, dug-outs and well-protected machine-gun emplacements which the garrison of Prussian Guard Fusiliers defended with the utmost determination, and the attack here at least drew off the enemy's attention from other parts of the line, where the British offensive had better results. So much for the 8th Battalion in the first phase of the battle.

We left the 29th Division—or at least that part of it which contained the 1st Battalion of The Border Regiment—about Amplier, but in April it moved to the Acheux district, and here it remained throughout that month and those of May and June, engaged in trench warfare and incurring all the casualties inseparable therefrom.

1st Battalion.

The opening day of the Somme Battle, as already elsewhere stated, was to have been the 28th June, a date which was postponed by reason of unfavourable weather, but the time was not wasted in the 29th Division, along the front of which several raids were carried out on the German trenches. Thus, a raiding party of the 1st Border Regiment, 50 strong under Lieutenant Bremner, marched from Acheux in the afternoon of the 27th June, and leaving a portion of the front-line trench, known by the home-like title of " Knightsbridge Barracks," at 10.45 p.m., reached " Shaftesbury Avenue " three-quarters of an hour later. Two Bangalore torpedoes were to have here met the raiding party, but those bringing these engines of war lost their way and did not arrive with them until just after midnight, when on examination it was found that the fuse holes of the torpedoes were choked with sand. The party now started out and reached safely and undetected the cut in the wire, which was found passable except for the last portion, which consisted of a thick mass of iron knife-rest trestles. While Lieutenant Bremner was doing his best to cut through this obstruction, another raid by the Division started on the flank, the enemy was disturbed and put on his guard, machine-gun and rifle fire was opened and " Very " lights were sent up. Seeing that further progress could now hardly be hoped for, Lieutenant Bremner withdrew his party to their trenches.

The order of battle of the VIIIth Corps for the operations commencing on the 1st July was as follows : The 29th Division was on the right, the 4th was opposite Beaumont Hamel in the centre, while the 31st faced Serre ; the 48th Division was in reserve. Beaumont Hamel, which it was intended that the troops should force, was an especially strong position, containing huge quarries and excavations in which large numbers of the enemy could remain in absolute safety until the last moment, and the heavy British bombardment had done but little damage to troops thus sheltered, either in *personnel*, *materiel* or *morale*.

For the attack the 29th Division had the 86th and 87th Brigades in the first line, with the 88th in support.

The account in the Battalion Diary is unfortunately very meagre ; it runs : the Battalion, less 10 per cent., advanced just S. of Beaumont Hamel, its objective being Behucourt Redoubt. The 2nd South Wales Borderers, whose objective was the first two German lines, were wiped out by machine-gun fire in our own wire. The 1st Battalion The Border Regiment then went " over the top " from the support line and over the British first line, but the passage over the front trench having been ranged by the German machine gunners the day previously, the 1st Border Regiment met with heavy loss while crossing this trench and passing through the gaps in the wire. The men were magnificently steady, forming up outside the wire according to orders, then, inclining to the right, advanced as directed at a slow walk into No Man's Land. The advance was continued until only little groups of some half-dozen men were left here and there, and at last these, seeing no reinforcements in sight, took cover in shell holes wherever they found them.

By 8 a.m. the advance had come to a standstill, and the assault had definitely failed. An attempt was later made to renew it, but when it was found that all the brigades of the " Incomparable 29th " were equally reduced in numbers it was recognized that only a defensive line could now be held, and on the morning of the 2nd July the 1st Border Regiment retired to just N. of the River Ancre, where they were busily engaged in repairing the trenches and in bringing in wounded and burying dead, all under continued enemy sniping. Then, on the 8th July, the Battalion moved back to rest camp at Acheux and for the present at any rate took no further part in the Somme battle.

On the 1st July the Battalion had gone into action with 23 officers and 809 other ranks, of whom they lost, killed, wounded and missing, 20 officers and 619 non-commissioned officers and men. The following officers were killed : Captains F. R. Jessup and T. H. Beves ; wounded, Lieutenant-Colonel A. T. Ellis, Captain J. G. Heyder, Lieutenants B. L. A. Kennett, T. B. Sinclair and H. F. Sampson, Second-Lieutenants G. W. N. Rowsell, F. M. Talbot, A. W. H. Barnes, D. Bremner, F. T. Wilkins, D. C. R. Stuart and D. Cargill ; missing, believed killed, Second-Lieutenants W. K. Sanderson, J. Y. Baxendine, H. W. Fraser and L. Jackson ; wounded and missing, Second-Lieutenants H. L. Chomeley and W. P. Rettie.

So ended the first phase of the Battle of the Somme, as to which Sir Douglas Haig wrote in his despatch in describing the results of the first five days : " On a front of over 6 miles, from the Briqueterie to La Boisselle, our troops had swept over the whole of the enemy's first and strongest system of defence, which he had done his best to render impregnable. They had driven him back over a distance of more than a mile, and had carried four elaborately fortified villages " ; and at the end of the first phase he said : " The enemy's second main system of defence had been captured on a front of over 3 miles. We had again forced him back more than a mile and had gained possession of the southern crest of the main ridge on a front of 6,000 yards. . . . Our line was definitely established from Maltz Horn Farm, where we met the French left, N. along the E. edge of Trônes Wood to Longueval, then W. past Bazentin-le-Grand to the N. corner of Bazentin-le-Petit and Bazentin-le-Petit Wood, and then W. again past the S. face of Pozières to the N. of Ovillers."

CHAPTER VI

1916

THE BATTLE OF THE SOMME.

THE SECOND AND THIRD PHASES.

IN remarking upon all that had been at the outset accomplished and what still remained to be done, the British Commander-in-Chief wrote as follows : " There was strong evidence that the enemy forces engaged on the battle front had been severely shaken by the repeated successes gained by ourselves and by our Allies ; but the great strength and depth of his defences had secured for him sufficient time to bring up fresh troops, and he had still many powerful fortifications, trenches, villages and woods, to which he could cling in our front and on our flanks. We had indeed secured a footing on the main ridge, but only on a front of 6,000 yards ; and desirous though I was to follow up quickly the successes we had won, it was necessary first to widen this front.

" West of Bazentin-le-Petit the villages of Pozières and Thiepval, together with the whole elaborate system of trenches round, between and on the main ridge behind them, had still to be carried. . . . On our right flank the situation called for stronger measures. At Delville Wood and Longueval our lines formed a sharp salient, from which our front ran on the one side W. to Pozières, and on the other S. to Maltz Horn Farm. At Maltz Horn Farm our lines joined the French, and the Allied front continued still southwards to the village of Hem on the Somme. This pronounced salient invited counter-attacks by the enemy."

Before the operations could be resumed, such success as had been obtained be fully exploited, a pause was necessary for the relief of exhausted troops, the improvement of communications and the digging of fresh trenches ; and this delay, brief as it was inevitable, was taken every advantage of by the enemy for digging and wiring fresh trenches, both in front of and behind his original lines. He had also brought up fresh troops—when the first phase of the battle came to an end he had 138 battalions engaged in and behind the line N. of the Somme, as compared with 62 at the commencement of the battle—and there was no possibility of again taking him by surprise.

During the operations described in the last chapter there had been a re-distribution of corps, the two northern corps of Sir Henry Rawlinson's Fourth Army, the VIIIth and Xth, having been placed under the command of General Gough and forming a Fifth [1] Army.

[1] Throughout this Chapter Gough's Army is thus described, although as a matter of fact it was known as " The Reserve Army " up to the 30th October of this year.

In the second phase of the Somme Battle but two battalions of The Border Regiment took any active part, although others unquestionably by their presence at other parts of the long line contributed to the successes of their comrades on either side of them ; these two battalions were the 2nd and 7th, but as the last-named was the earlier employed the work it performed will be recorded first.

During the days immediately preceding the entry or re-entry of these battalions into the battle considerable gains had been made by our troops, but progress was slow and bought only by hard fighting, for the enemy had recovered from the effect of our early successes and was himself attacking wherever such efforts seemed to promise to be effective.

On the 5th August the 7th Battalion was holding Delville Wood, which during the preceding ten days the Germans had made repeated attempts to recapture, **7th Battalion.** and on the 7th the Battalion received orders to attack at 4.30 p.m. that day. The order of attack was two platoons of " B " Company on the left and two of " C " on the right with " D " Company in support, but the enemy trench was no more than 70 yards distant, and before the assaulting platoons had got half-way they were received with so heavy and so well-directed a volume of machine-gun and rifle fire that the attack—over very difficult ground full of shell holes and covered with fallen trees—could not be expected to succeed, and the survivors were ordered to withdraw after dark and occupy their original position. The casualties were 9 killed ; 34, including Second-Lieutenants Sanger, Cope and Gascoigne-Roy, wounded ; 4 missing and 1 wounded and missing.

On the 9th the Battalion withdrew to close support in Montauban Alley, incurring additional casualties during the retirement, 4 men being killed, and Second-Lieutenants Thompson and Matthews and 17 other ranks wounded. Then on the 15th the 7th Battalion moved by rail and march route to Bienvillers, and on the 4th September was stationed at St. Amand.

The heavy losses which the 2nd Battalion of The Border Regiment had sustained during the first phase of the Somme Battle had been replaced with really remarkable **2nd Battalion.** dispatch, for before the month of July had come to an end drafts amounting to 423 non-commissioned officers and men had been hurried out with the following officers : Lieutenants R. K. Ehrenborg, R. G. Hennessy and D. Elliott, Second-Lieutenants J. A. Malkin, D. M. P. T. Slark, R. L. Beckh, S. Martindale, J. T. Beaty-Pownall, H. D. Lees, C. F. E. Ingledow, R. B. Wood, H. G. Montgomerie, S. B. Bendle, W. B. Start, and D. N. Hill, these being followed in August, which month was spent in Breilly and Buire, by two more young officers, Second-Lieutenants W. B. Butler and L. S. Willox.

Early in September the 20th Brigade had been ordered to hold itself in readiness for a move, and on the night of the 3rd the Battalion boarded motor-lorries and proceeded to Fricourt, marching thence to Montauban, which was reached at 2 a.m. on the 4th September. Here guides were told off to the 2nd Border Regiment and 9th Devons, which battalion preceded them, and the two corps moved on to Bernafay Wood, where entrenching tools were awaiting them. On arrival here, however, it was found that the guide had disappeared, but the onward movement was continued, the Battalion being now under a very heavy shell fire.

By about 5 a.m. the 2nd Battalion was in position as follows :—

"A" Company, Captain Dowding, 2 platoons in Stout Trench, 2 platoons
in Support Trench, N. of Ginchy Avenue.
"B" Company, Captain Newdigate, in Support Trench, N. of Ginchy
Avenue.
"C" Company, Second-Lieutenant Malkin, in Ginchy Avenue.
"D" Company, Lieutenant Ehrenborg, in a trench N. of York Alley,
believed at the time to be Longueval Avenue.

The Battalion Headquarters was at the end of York Alley. At 10 o'clock,
on an appeal for support from the 9th Devons in front, "A" Company was
ordered up to support this battalion and two extra platoons were moved up to
Stout Trench; but by the time this had been done a report was received that the
9th Devons were being forced back by shell and machine-gun fire, consequently
"A" Company remained in its former position, while owing to the Battalion being
under heavy shell fire, the position was later slightly prolonged. The enemy gun-
fire continued all day, but the men worked hard to deepen the trenches and increase
the amount of cover, and the actual casualties were few, though many men were
buried and had to be dug out. Captain R. F. Newdigate and Second-Lieutenant
J. A. Malkin were, however, killed this day, while Second-Lieutenant S. Martindale
was missing, believed killed.

Late on the evening of the 4th September orders were received for two companies to relieve the 12th King's Liverpool Regiment in the Guillemont area, and
"B" Company under Lieutenant Butler and "D" under Lieutenant Ehrenborg
moved thither under charge of Lieutenant-Colonel Thorpe, while the adjutant,
Lieutenant Strange, marched the other two companies back into reserve in
Montauban Redoubt, where he handed them over to Major Beaty-Pownall. On
relief of the 12th King's early on the 5th the two companies with Colonel Thorpe
were thus disposed: "D" in a trench N.W. of Guillemont opposite Ginchy, with
"B" in support in rear and Colonel Thorpe's headquarters in a dug-out in New
Trench; the 2nd Gordon Highlanders were on the left and on the right were the
Royal Munster Fusiliers.

On the 6th September the 2nd Gordons and 9th Devons made two
attempts to take Ginchy in front of the trenches held by the 2nd Border
Regiment, but although these two fine battalions got into the village, they were
unable to hold it against the hostile shell and machine-gun fire and were obliged
to fall back. The Lewis guns of The Border Regiment did all possible to assist
the attack by firing from advanced positions and continued doing so until put out
of action by being buried.

On the morning of the 7th the 2nd Battalion was relieved and moved back to
Montauban, whence the whole Battalion went back to a bivouac S. of Fricourt,
and after one or two further moves found itself on the 18th of the month at Nieppe.

In the operations above described the Battalion had experienced casualties
to the number of 83; Captain Newdigate and Second-Lieutenant Malkin
had been killed, Second-Lieutenant Martindale was missing, believed killed,

while Second-Lieutenant Willox was suffering from shell-shock ; of the other ranks 10 were killed, 52 were wounded, 3 were missing, while 11 others were suffering from shell-shock.

Before this second phase of the battle finally closed the attack was reopened along the whole of the Fourth Army front, Ginchy was captured, elsewhere a great advance was made and the weak salient in the Allied line had disappeared, thus affording the front necessary for future operations ; further, since the opening day of the battle no fewer than 17,000 of the enemy had been taken prisoners.

" Practically the whole of the forward crest of the main ridge, on a front of some 9,000 yards from Delville Wood to the road above Mouquet Farm, was now in our hands, and with it the advantage of observation over the slopes beyond. East of Delville Wood, for a further 3,000 yards to Leuze Wood, we were firmly established on the main ridge ; while further E. across the Combles Valley, the French were advancing victoriously on our right. But though the centre of our line was well placed, on our flanks there was still difficult ground to be won. From Ginchy the crest of the high ground runs N. for 2,000 yards, and then E. in a long spur, for nearly 4,000 yards. Near the E. extremity of this spur stands the village of Morval, commanding a wide field of view and fire in every direction. At Leuze Wood my right was still 2,000 yards from its objective at this village, and between lay a broad and deep branch of the main Combles Valley, completely commanded by the Morval spur and flanked not only from its head N.E. of Ginchy, but also from the high ground E. of the Combles Valley, which looks directly into it." [1]

Of the objects hoped to be achieved by the operations of the third phase of the Somme Battle, General Haig wrote in the same despatch : " The general plan of the combined Allied attack which was opened on the 15th September was to pivot on the high ground S. of the Ancre and N. of the Albert–Bapaume Road, while the Fourth Army devoted its whole effort to the rearmost of the enemy's original systems of defence between Morval and Le Sars. Should our success in this direction warrant it, I made arrangements to enable me to extend the left of the attack to embrace the villages of Martinpuich and Courcelette. As soon as our advance on this front had reached the Morval line, the time would have arrived to bring forward my left across the Thiepval Ridge. Meanwhile, on my right our Allies arranged to continue the line of advance, in close co-operation with me, from the Somme to the slopes above Combles ; but directing their main effort N. against the villages of Rancourt and Frégicourt, so as to complete the isolation of Combles and open the way for their attack upon Sailly-Saillisel."

The order of battle of the Fourth Army, from S. to N., was as follows :—

    XIVth Corps.—56th Division, 6th Division, Guards Division.
    XVth Corps.—14th Division, 41st Division, New Zealand Division.
    IIIrd Corps.—47th Division, 50th Division, 15th Division.

And of the Fifth Army :—

    Vth Corps.—39th Division, 2nd Division, 48th Division in reserve.
    IInd Corps.—11th Division, 49th Division, 18th Division in reserve.
    Canadian Corps.—2nd Division, 3rd Division, 1st Division in reserve.

[1] Despatch of the 23rd December, 1916.

Photo   *Imperial War Museum*

DELVILLE WOOD

Photo   *Imperial War Museum*

SAILLY-SAILLISEL

In the back Army area S. of Bernaville was the XIIIth Corps with the 25th Division.

The Southern Army boundary was just S. of the Albert–Bapaume road and that of the Northern Army was at Hébuterne.

We left the 5th Battalion The Border Regiment about La Clytte at the end of July of this year, where it suffered many casualties from the activities of the German snipers, while the enemy machine-gun and rifle fire was **THIRD PHASE, 5th Battalion.** also persistent and accurate. Here the Battalion suffered a very serious loss in the death of Captain R. C. R. Blair, D.S.O., who was killed just after returning from a raid upon the enemy trenches and while he was pointing out to his men some repairs needed to the wire. The Divisional General, Major-General Wilkinson, and Brigadier-General Clifford, commanding 149th Infantry Brigade, to which the Battalion was at the time attached, sent messages of condolence to Colonel Hedley; that from the Brigadier was as follows :—

" I cannot tell you how distressed I am to hear that Captain Blair has been killed. There never was a more gallant officer, and I know what the loss must be to you and your Battalion. Please convey to all ranks of your Battalion my deepest sympathy with them in their loss."

During July three drafts amounting to 369 " other ranks " reached the 5th Border Regiment. At the end of July the Battalion took over trenches about Locre and there was much excellent patrol work done by small parties led by young officers, but the enemy here was not especially enterprising, and it was surmised that a relief had probably taken place. Then about the end of the first week in August the 50th Division was relieved by the 19th, being under orders to move S., and accordingly on the morning of the 11th the Battalion marched to Godevarsvelde and there took train for Candas in Picardy, marching from there by easy stages and by way of Beaumetz, Vignacourt, Flesselles, Lillers Bocage, Rainneville, Montigny and Behencourt to Baizieux Wood, where the Battalion arrived on the 17th in heavy rain and erected shelters of various kinds. The Division was now in the IIIrd Corps and courses of instruction of all descriptions were the order of the day.

The Battalion was now to take part in the third phase of the Somme Battle and accordingly marched on the 10th September via Millencourt to Bécourt Wood, and during the two days following arrival here provided large working parties for burying cables near Railway Copse, moving finally at dusk on the 14th to Shelter Wood. From here on the next morning the 5th Border Regiment moved forward to Quadrangle Trench and thence to trenches at the S.E. corner of Mametz Wood, where orders were issued that the 151st Brigade was to move up that night, attack and capture the German trenches known as Star Fish Line and Prue Trench. Darkness had set in before the Quarries were passed where were the Brigade Headquarters and where guides were provided ; these, however, seemed almost at once to lose their direction, with the result that the Battalion did not reach the assembly position until some 30 minutes after the appointed time. At 11 p.m. the 5th Border Regiment was directed to push on to the objectives and get in touch with the

6th and 9th Battalions Durham Light Infantry, portions of which had already gone forward.

By reason of the darkness and general state of the ground the Battalion was unable to reach the objectives assigned to it, but advanced some 600–700 yards and as daylight was coming on the men then dug themselves in ; some of the Battalion managed to get almost up to the Star Fish Line in touch with some of the 6th Durhams, but were then driven back by machine-gun fire and fell back in line with their comrades, digging in between Bow and Crescent Alley.

During these operations Lieutenant G. H. Dawes, acting adjutant, and Second-Lieutenant R. P. Baxter were killed ; Captain Spedding, Second-Lieutenants Coombes, Lain, and Pursglove were wounded ; while the losses in other ranks totalled 100 ; Captain M. R. Inglis, R.A.M.C., was killed while attending to the wounded in the field during the night.

On the night of the 17th–18th " A " Company of the Battalion was withdrawn to Hook Trench, and during the night the 5th Border Regiment was ordered, in conjunction with the other units of the Brigade, to attack Star Fish Line at 5.50 a.m. The companies in the front line again advanced at the hour noted, but the same difficulties were met with as on the previous day—the ground was very sodden and the machine-gun fire exceptionally heavy—and the attack again failed, again with no inconsiderable loss, Captain D. W. Glass and Second-Lieutenant A. Feetham being killed, Lieutenant H. R. Smith wounded and Second-Lieutenant Hall shell-shocked ; some 60 other ranks also became casualties.

The companies, except " A " which remained out attached to the 8th Durhams, were withdrawn to Swansea Trench on the night of the 19th and next day to trenches at the S.W. corner of Mametz Wood.

The following letter was circulated to battalions by the O.C. 151st Infantry Brigade :—

"*I have been asked by the Divisional Commander to convey his warm thanks to the four battalions of the 151st Brigade for the whole-hearted efforts they have made during the strenuous operations of the last few days and for the success which they have achieved. He would have liked very much to have come round to see Battalion Commanders personally had he the time and opportunity to do so at present. For myself I should like to add that I am full of admiration at the soldierly spirit displayed by all ranks of the four battalions in the attack, and their endurance under very considerable hardships, privation and exertion lasting nearly a week.*"

In the middle of September the village of Flers had been captured by the 41st Division, but the front German line here bent away from the British position as it trended towards the N.W., so that although it had been made good over a large portion in the Battle of Flers, it was still intact opposite nearly the whole front of the IIIrd Corps. Orders to attack this portion were issued on the night of the 1st October, and the 5th Border Regiment was told off, with the 8th Durham L.I., to attack and capture the first and support line of German trenches. The Battalion had only three companies present at this time, " A " Company having recently been sent to an isolation camp by reason of a severe epidemic of dysentery.

The assault was to be made in four waves by three companies each on a platoon front, the first and second waves composed of the 5th Border Regiment, the third and fourth of the 8th Durhams, while it was timed to commence at 3.15 p.m. after a prolonged artillery bombardment. As the barrage lifted, the first wave of the Battalion left the assembly trench, followed by the remaining three waves at 50 yards intervals, and so rapid and determined was the advance that the objectives were in our hands before the enemy had realized what was happening, an enemy machine gun being captured just as it was coming into action. The position was consolidated and held until the night of October 2nd, when the Battalion was withdrawn, finally marching back by way of Albert to hutments at Henencourt Wood, and so ended the share taken by the 5th Battalion The Border Regiment in the Battle of the Somme.

The following order of the day was published on the 6th October by the G.O.C. Division :—

" *Nobody could be prouder than I am at commanding such troops as you of the 50th Division. Within a few days of landing in this country you made a name for yourselves at the Second Battle of Ypres. Since that battle you have gained a great reputation on account of your magnificent defence of a portion of the Ypres Salient during the worst months of the year. From the 15th September to October 3rd, you have had another chance of showing your qualities in attack, and it is not too much to say that no division in the British Army has, or could have, done better. You have advanced nearly two miles and have taken seven lines of German trenches.*

" *Your gallantry and determination on every occasion since you joined in the Battle of the Somme has been worthy of the highest traditions of the British Army.*

" *I deplore with you the loss of many of our intimate friends and comrades. I thank you all for the excellent and cheerful way in which you have undertaken every task put to you.*"

Early in September the 6th Battalion of The Border Regiment left the Arras area, where it had remained ever since its arrival on the Western Front from **6th Battalion.** the Dardanelles, finding itself by the 6th of the month in trenches about Ovillers, the 33rd Brigade being disposed with the 7th South Staffords on the left, the 9th Sherwood Foresters on the right, the 6th Border Regiment in support, with the Lincolns in Brigade Reserve at Bouzincourt. The Battalion came almost at once in contact with the enemy, losing on the 16th an officer of great promise, Second-Lieutenant Allured, whose death was regretted by all ranks of the 6th Border Regiment. Here a prisoner was captured, and from documents found upon him it appeared that the 213th Reserve Regiment was holding the Danube and Well Trenches opposite with a company 120 strong.

The IInd Corps, commanded by General Jacob, had been directed to effect the capture of Thiepval and the work was entrusted to the 11th and 18th Divisions of this corps. The position here had for some time past been something of a thorn in the side of the British, since not only was it very strongly held, but it was also flanked by formidable systems of trenches, while just above Thiepval Village itself was a long slope rising to a ridge on the summit of which was the Schwaben Redoubt.

The capture of this position would give the British armies command of all the ground held by the enemy N. of the Ancre, and the Germans, fully realizing this, had been ordered to hold the position at all costs and had been given some 400 guns to enable them effectively to resist all assaults. To attack the position here General Jacob's two divisions had been reinforced by the guns of the 25th and 49th Divisions.

For the attack the 18th Division was on the left immediately facing the château and village of Thiepval, while on the right was the 11th Division with two of its Brigades in the front line, the 33rd and 34th, on left and right respectively. In front of these brigades was first Joseph Trench, in rear of that Schwaben Trench, behind again was Zollern Trench, while crowning the hill was Schwaben Redoubt, the whole joined together by a network of communication and flanking trenches. In the 33rd Brigade the 6th Border Regiment and 9th Sherwood Foresters formed the assaulting line.

At 12.35 p.m. on the 26th September, " the waves," to quote the Battalion Diary, " left in grand style all along the line, Joseph and Schwaben Trenches being carried by 12.45 p.m., the attack of The Border Regiment being led by Captain Carr and Second-Lieutenant Fulton who, though both wounded before the objective was reached, ' carried on ' and saw their men established; the captures here amounted to 2 machine guns and 191 prisoners, while nearly one hundred of the enemy were killed.

" The night of the 26th–27th was spent by the 6th Battalion in Joseph and Schwaben Trenches, where they experienced some annoyance from a gun firing upon them from Schwaben Redoubt, and early on the morning of the 27th Captain Morris was sent forward with ' C ' Company to reinforce the 9th Sherwood Foresters, when the situation was as follows: The Foresters held part of Hessian Trench, but their flanks were rather in the air, as neither the 34th Brigade on the right nor the 18th Division on the left were as yet quite up in line, while the tanks attached to these troops had also failed to come up."

On the afternoon of the 27th, Headquarters and " A " Company pushed forward to Zollern Trench, and about an hour later orders were received to attack Hessian Trench with " C " Company (Captain Morris) in conjunction with the 34th Brigade, and this was at once carried, Captain Morris and Second-Lieutenant Barry being wounded; here 2 more machine guns and 60 prisoners were taken and one of the guns was reversed and turned on to the enemy, as the assailants entered the trench, by Sergeant Cannon, with most excellent effect. " A " Company was now sent up to reinforce " C " and the 9th Sherwood Foresters then withdrew. The night of the 27th–28th was an unpleasant one for those in Hessian Trench, as the shelling by the German guns was heavy and accurate, while in the earlier part of the evening the enemy attempted a counter-attack which was driven off by rifle fire. During the night the 6th Battalion was thus distributed: " A " and " C " Companies in Hessian Trench, " D " Company in Zollern and " B " in Schwaben Trench.

At midday on the 28th the 18th Division attacked and captured Schwaben Redoubt, while the 32nd Brigade advanced on the right of The Border Regiment and made an attempt to carry Stuff Redoubt, but this was unsuccessful, with the result that the Germans still held on to part of the crest line.

The Battalion remained in the trenches during another night of heavy shelling, and then on the 30th September was withdrawn, the 11th Division being relieved by the 25th and falling back to Hedauville ; the Battalion then proceeded by march and in motor-buses to Montigny-les-Jongleurs, where it remained until the end of October.

During the above operations the 11th Division had sustained losses amounting to 144 officers and 3,500 other ranks, but had taken prisoners 30 officers and 1,125 other ranks, with a great number of machine guns and trench mortars. In the 6th Battalion Border Regiment the casualties had been numerous ; in killed there were 1 officer and 43 other ranks ; wounded, 10 officers and 155 men, while 1 man was missing.

The following message was received on the 28th September by the Major-General commanding the 11th Division from General Sir Hubert Gough, commanding the Fifth Army :—

" *My best congratulations to you and your Division on their gallant fighting throughout the successful operations in which you have been engaged since the capture of the Wonder Work. You have all done splendid work.*"

The 7th Battalion of The Border Regiment underwent many moves during the months of September and October ; we left the Battalion arrived at St. Amand

7th Battalion.
early in September, a week later it was at Halloy, on the 18th at Sailly au Bois ; the opening days of October found it at Mezerolles, from where it went, in succession, back to Halloy, then to Souastre and Doullens, finally being on the 22nd October at Mericourt and Ville sur Ancre, the 17th Division having now been ordered up to relieve the 8th in the front line.

The attack which opened on the 3rd November, and which resulted in a further considerable pushing back of the German line, was carried out by the 50th and 51st Brigades of the 17th Division, great work being done by the last named of these brigades, the 7th Border Regiment and 7th Lincolns specially distinguishing themselves. These two battalions not only cleared up Zenith Trench, but upon the Germans countering they reserved their fire until the enemy was within 40 yards, and then mowed down several hundreds of them. Of the action and all that preceded it the Battalion War Diary speaks as follows :—

" *2nd November.*—During the night efforts were made to reconnoitre Zenith Trench under direction of Captain Nasmith. Very little information could be obtained except that it did not appear to be strongly held. Orders had already been issued to take Zenith Trench by surprise if it were at all possible. Patrols had not finished their work till about 4 a.m., and by the time arrangements were made tentatively for a company attack daylight had arrived and the attack could not be carried out.

" A report was rendered to the Brigade in which willingness was expressed to attempt a surprise attack on Zenith Trench about 5.30 in the evening. Permission to attack arrived about 2 p.m., and Major Irwin sent up to the front line and arranged with Captain Nasmith all details for the attack, orders were issued and the 10th West Yorks on the right and 9th Northumberland Fusiliers on the left warned. During the morning Second-Lieutenant Sanger was sent to the right of the trenches, then in the occupation of the 7th Lincolns, and arranged that if the attack was a success 3 Very lights would be fired in rapid succession from the right enemy bombing stop, which would be a signal to the Lincolns to close in to the left and take up the gap of about 120 yards which existed between the enemy bombing stop and that of the Lincolns. The attack was carried out by ' B ' Company and one platoon of ' D ' and the Battalion bombers under Second-Lieutenant Sanger, also 3 Lewis gun squads. Total amounted to 129 non-commissioned officers and men. ' D ' Company, less one platoon, was in close support and Captain Nasmith was in command with four officers.

" The attack started at 6 p.m. and was a complete success. In the dim moonlight our men got in on the left without being observed and got within 20 yards on the right without being seen. The left was taken without much opposition, but a sharp bombing attack ensued on the right in which some 20 or 30 of the enemy were killed. The Lincolns on the right could not believe that the trench had been taken and opened rapid fire and also bombed, with the result that the gap between the bombing stops could not be cleared. Zenith Trench was at once consolidated and advance patrols sent out. A post was established in Eclipse Trench—leading back towards the enemy—about 150 yards forward. About 8 p.m. the enemy counter-attacked in small numbers, but were easily repulsed.

" The Battalion was relieved about 10.30 p.m. by the 7th Lincolns, and during the relief about 30 of the enemy attempted to counter-attack up Eclipse Trench ; 4 of them were taken prisoners. Our casualties during the attack were only 1 officer (Second-Lieutenant Jackson) killed, 1 man killed and 8 wounded."

On relief the 7th Border Regiment went back to a camp at Montauban where the following order of the day was published by the G.O.C. 17th Division :—

" *The G.O.C. wishes to place on record his appreciation of the gallant manner in which Zenith Trench was captured and held against all counter-attacks by the 7th Border and 7th Lincolnshire Regiments. The fact that the 7th Border had already done 48 hours in close support and were completing their tour of 48 hours in the front line makes their performance all the finer. The G.O.C. is particularly pleased with the initiative displayed by the Battalion and Company Commanders concerned. The dash and determination displayed despite bad weather and most trying conditions reflect the greatest credit on all ranks concerned and will still further enhance the good name gained by the 17th Division in the Battle of the Somme.*"

We now turn to the 25th Division and the 8th Battalion of The Border Regiment.

At the close of the operations connected with the first phase of the Somme

8th Battalion. fighting the 25th Division was relieved by the 48th, and then moved to the neighbourhood of Beauval for a short period of rest. Following this the Division held—from the 23rd July to the 10th August—a sector of the line from the River Ancre northwards, taking no part in actual offensive operations, but offering a certain measure of assistance to the troops attacking S. of that river, while much useful work was done in digging new forward assembly trenches used later on in the attacks on Beaumont Hamel and the German defences S. of the Ancre. Here the brigades of the 25th Division came under a heavy fire from guns and trench mortars and suffered from a new type of German poison-gas shell then used for the first time.

Early in August there was a short period of rest and training about Bus en Artois, after which Divisional Headquarters moved to Hedauville, and the brigades served in the sector which included portions of the Leipzig Salient taken from the enemy in July. Following on this the Division was engaged in certain local attacks, and then early in September attacked N. up the Thiepval Spur in conjunction with an attack by the 29th Division N. of the Ancre, but the 8th Battalion took no part in these operations since at the time it was holding front-line trenches at the Leipzig Salient.

After this the 25th Division remained at rest for some three weeks, and finally, on the 25th September, commenced its forward move to the front in the Thiepval area, and early in October the 8th Border Regiment found itself in trenches about Ovillers, where a certain amount of training was carried on. From here it went up into the trenches on the right of Pozières in relief of the Canadians, and there at once casualties began to mount up, the C.S.M. of " D " Company being killed and 3 young officers, Second-Lieutenants Turner, Lewis and Wilson, wounded.

It was fully expected at this time that a further advance would shortly be attempted and work on communication trenches and forward dumps was pushed on. On the 16th October the 39th Division extended its front as far as Stuff Redoubt, two brigades of the 25th Division, the 74th and 75th, being aligned on its right, each brigade holding a front of about 1,000 yards, and a battalion of the 7th Brigade being attached to each for working parties. An attack was arranged for the 19th October on Stuff and Regina Redoubts, but heavy rain caused its postponement until the 21st, on which date at 12.6 p.m. the 25th Division attacked, having the 18th on its right and the 39th on the left. The distance from the advanced British trench to Stuff and Regina Redoubts varied from 200 to 500 yards,

All the enemy line of trenches, strong points and machine-gun emplacements were heavily bombarded and the shelling by the British guns was most effective.

The 74th Brigade was on the right and the 75th on the left, and the objective assigned to the 8th Border Regiment was a strip of Regina Trench some 350 yards in length, which they were to attack in conjunction with one company of the 11th Cheshires, starting from Hessian Trench, where they assembled at 6 a.m. on the 21st October; the Border was the right battalion of the brigade.

The Companies were this day commanded as follows: " A " Company, Lieutenant Slater; " B," Captain Watson-Thomas; " C," Captain Miller and " D," Captain Stewart, and advanced in four waves of half-company columns. The ground was not so much cut up by shell fire as had been expected, and being tolerably easy to advance over the attack was rather hurried, the result being that the leading wave arrived on the objective before the barrage lifted and suffered some loss, but the wire had been well cut and presented no obstacle, and within 10 minutes of the attack being launched, German prisoners were being sent back across No Man's Land, and the dug-outs in their support and front lines were being bombed and cleared.

As a matter of fact when the trench was reached on the left the men got in so easily that they did not realize they had gained their objective ; a gap was also left on the right owing to opposition from a machine gun in a large dug-out on this flank ; while from dug-outs and emplacements on the left of Stump Road Germans were seen to be emerging. Within a minute of reaching Regina Trench some officers and about 80 men, of whom 40 were Border men, left the trench and made straight across for them, but Captain Stewart recalled these men and got them to work on the trench ; finding that while he was in touch with the 8th South Lancashires on the left the right had been held up, he ordered a block to be made here until more men could be collected.

Lieutenant E. D. Birnie was now sent up with all the bombers remaining at Battalion Headquarters to try and get touch with Captain Stewart by bombing up the communication trench, but on arrival he found that the dug-out just beyond the block was ablaze and he was unable to get past, but under cover of the smoke he managed to get his squad, and 10 other bombers whom he had collected *en route*, man by man to Regina Trench, where was Captain Stewart, with only one casualty.   He now got to work in a very gallant manner, standing up on the parapet and firing on the enemy while his party worked up the trench.   Lieutenant Birnie accounted for about 8 of the enemy when the rest, some 80 in number, surrendered. The trench was cleared, touch gained and consolidation proceeded unhindered.

This day the 25th Division captured 731 of the enemy including 5 officers, as well as 3 field and 19 machine guns, but the casualties in the 8th Battalion numbered 162, Captains T. D. Miller, M.C., and W. P. Watson-Thomas and 18 other ranks being killed ; Lieutenant Le May and 111 men were wounded, while 30 men were missing.

The following day, and during the night of the 22nd–23rd October, the Division was relieved and marched back to the neighbourhood of Doullens ; but before it left the Fifth Army in which it had been fighting, with but short intervals, for four months, the units of the Division were inspected by the Commander-in-Chief, and the following appreciative message was received from the Army Commander :—

" *It is with great regret that the Commander of the Reserve Army bids farewell to Major-General Bainbridge and the 25th Division. This Division has the proud distinction of having served longer in the Somme Battle than any other in the Army. During the past four months it has been successful in many engagements, has taken many prisoners, and has inflicted very heavy losses on the enemy. These successes are due to good leadership and sound organization in the higher ranks, and to a spirit of cheerfulness, courage and resolution in the junior ranks, officers and men. It has every reason to be proud of these achievements and this spirit.*"

This then brings to a close the account of the part which the several battalions of The Border Regiment played in this stupendous battle ; but it must not be imagined that because the seven battalions of the Regiment were not continuously engaged during the whole four and a half months that the operations endured, they were not therefore taking their full share, when withdrawn from the immediate battle front, in contributing to the general success which was achieved. In his despatch of the 23rd December, 1916, General Sir Douglas Haig pays a tribute to the rôle of the troops holding other portions of the line, a rôle which he declares to have been neither light nor unimportant, since they were responsible for the security of the line held by them and for keeping the enemy in their front constantly on the alert. "Their rôle," he wrote, "was a very trying one, entailing heavy work on the troops and constant vigilance on the part of Commanders and Staffs. It was carried out to my entire satisfaction, and in an unfailing spirit of unselfish and broad-minded devotion to the general good, which is deserving of the highest commendation.

"Some idea of the thoroughness with which their duties were performed can be gathered from the fact that in the period of four and a half months from the 1st July some 360 raids were carried out, in the course of which the enemy suffered many casualties and some hundreds of prisoners were taken by us. . . . Our troops penetrated deeply into the enemy's defences, doing much damage to his works and inflicting severe losses upon him."

And the results of the long-continued struggle may be summed up in two lines : Verdun had been relieved ; the main German forces had been held on the Western Front ; and the enemy's strength had been very considerably worn down ; while of the soldiers by whom these results were gathered their Commander wrote : " among all the long roll of victories borne on the Colours of our regiments, there never has been a higher test of the endurance and resolution of our infantry. They have shown themselves worthy of the highest traditions of our race and of the proud records of former wars."

This chapter may fittingly close with a few words stating what the seven battalions were doing in France and Flanders during the months of November and December, and where the end of the year 1916 found them, and then we must turn, to another theatre of the war and see how the 9th Battalion was faring in Salonika.

The 1st Battalion spent the greater part of September in the Ypres sector, moving in the first ten days of October to Buire, then to Fricourt and later to Guédécourt, where it took over for a time the trenches known as **1st Battalion.** Grense and Gap Trenches, Sunken Road and Pilgrim's Way and where the casualties in one week amounted to 80. At the end of October the 1st Border Regiment proceeded via Mametz to Albert, stayed there a very few days and then moved on to Allery and thence back again to the neighbourhood of Buire. In December the Battalion made many moves, to Guillemont, Corbie, Condé and Picquigny and finally to Hangest, where it saw the old year out.

When the 2nd Battalion was withdrawn from the Somme fighting in the middle of September it went to billets at Nieppe near Bailleul, and here on the 12th took **2nd Battalion.** part in a raid on the German trenches, which did no little damage to the enemy and created much "alarm and despondency," but resulted in 13 casualties to the raiding party of the 2nd Border Regiment, Second-Lieutenant R. B. Wood and 3 men being killed, while Second-Lieutenant S. B. Bendle and 8 other ranks were wounded. In November the moves were many and frequent, but at the end of the month the Battalion was at Mailly Maillet. The middle of December found the 2nd Battalion about Beaumont Hamel suffering a good deal from the persistency and accuracy of the enemy's shell fire, but the Battalion patrols were very active and full of resource. On New Year's eve a patrol of three went out under Second-Lieutenant J. Hayton and came suddenly face to face with two of the enemy. Young Hayton's revolver had slipped round his belt and he was unable to draw it, but with ready presence of mind he " drew " his pipe instead and pointed it threateningly at the head of one of the enemy who murmured " Kamerad," put up his hands and was taken prisoner. The other German took the chance of the pipe " going off," turned and fled and got away in the darkness ! On the 31st December, 1916, the strength of the Battalion was only 26 officers and 726 other ranks as against 30 officers and 823 other ranks at the end of the month previous, but there had been a good deal of sickness due to the inclemency of the weather.

While stationed about Henencourt Wood whither the 5th Battalion had been withdrawn after the Somme, all ranks were very busily employed in making new

5th Battalion, roads and in improving existing ones, and when on the 1st December it moved via Albert and Millencourt to Warloy the following order appreciative of the work done was published by the G.O.C. IIIrd Corps :—

" *The Corps Commander wishes to place on record his great appreciation of the work done by the troops on the roads, railways and tramways during the last six weeks in the* IIIrd *Corps area under adverse weather conditions. He fully realizes the great amount of extra labour it has involved, but trusts that all ranks will realize how essential the work was in view of future operations and also for their own welfare.*"

At the end of the year the Battalion was in a camp N. of Mametz Wood.

From Montigny-les-Jongleurs the 6th Battalion proceeded early in October to Cramont where notification was received that the machine guns captured in

6th Battalion. action by the Battalion had been sent to the following towns of Cumberland and Westmorland : to Carlisle two and to Kendal, Workington and Wigan one each. Leaving Cramont on the 14th the Battalion marched by way of Bonneville and Contay to Varennes and then to the trenches about Beaucourt, where on the 25th an isolated post of The Border Regiment was heavily attacked by a company of the enemy, but thanks to the timely assistance afforded by two patrols on the right and left respectively, under Captain Price and Sergeant Gordon, the post was able to withdraw with the loss of two men only.

Here, too, on the 20th November a very fine piece of work was done, of which the following account is taken from the Brigade Intelligence Summary : " A patrol of the 6th Border Regiment, composed of Captain James, D.S.O., Lieutenant Ridley and No. 10998 Private J. Rooney went out in the mist yesterday morning and reconnoitred the ground E. and discovered there an abandoned 77 mm. gun. This was reported, and a party composed of 1 officer and 4 men of the R.F.A. and a party of The Border Regiment went out yesterday afternoon to bring the gun in. This party did extraordinarily well, and with great labour the gun was brought in ; the enemy having apparently in the meanwhile observed them, turned a machine gun on them hindering the work considerably. Great risk was attached to the undertaking, as was afterwards shown."

The 6th Battalion passed the closing days of the year in the line about Thiepval.

The 7th Battalion remained during November in the Montauban area, moving at the beginning of December into rest billets where training was carried on, but on the 12th it marched to Longpré and there entrained, proceeding via Corbie and Carnoy to Meaulte and then into brigade reserve at Guillemont, **7th Battalion,** where the Battalion was for a time attached to the 50th Infantry Brigade. " Weather wet, camp in bad state of mud and huts leaked," and hereabouts and under such conditions the Battalion appears to have spent the " festive season " of 1916.

On the 28th October and following days the 25th Division entrained for Caestre in the Second Army area, and three days later the Headquarters moved to Bailleul, **8th Battalion.** the three Brigades, among them the 75th containing the 8th Battalion The Border Regiment, taking over the Ploegsteert sector. With a frontage of about 6,000 yards the line extended from the River Lys on the right to Hill 63 on the left, when St. Ives became the northern boundary of the divisional front. This was a fairly quiet sector so far as the activities of the enemy were concerned, but the fatigues were many and kept all ranks busily employed up to and after Christmas.

When in the middle of July the 11th Battalion emerged from the fighting connected with the first phase of the Battle of the Somme, steps seem to have been at **11th Battalion.** once taken to fill up the gaps in the commissioned ranks and the following officers joined : Major E. Lake-Greere, Captains M. G. Nelson and C. B. Dove ; Second-Lieutenants D. W. Brady, C. W. McConnon, J. H. Simcock, H. N. Spence, G. G. Bickers, T. Story, S. W. Wilson, R. S. Jones, C. V. Holme-Parker, W. L. Allcroft, H. J. S. Stone and W. R. Gillespie. The Division was now in the First Army.

At the end of July the " Lonsdales " were at Noyelles, finding carrying parties for the 8th Division to which they were temporarily attached ; early in August they left for the Cambrin area with rest billets when out of the line in Bethune, moving again the first week in September for Quesnoy to take up a reserve position in the Cuinchy sector, and then returned to the Cambrin area and remained there until the middle of October. Thereafter there were frequent minor moves, but during November some time was spent training at Le Vicogne, and then about the 15th the Battalion was at Engelbelmer near Contay, and was now called up with the 32nd Division to take part in the final operations of the Battle of the Ancre, the Division being required to fill the gap between the right of the Fifth and the left of the Fourth Army and to advance in the direction of Pys. The position in front of the 32nd Division was composed of a powerful system of defences in two lines known as the Munich and Frankfort lines, set in ground which, by reason of the recent rains, had become particularly swampy.

It was on the 17th November, the day when the Somme Battle came officially to an end, that the 32nd Division took over the front-line trenches, relieving the 18th Division which moved further to the left, and the advance therefrom commenced on the morning of the 18th, the 14th Brigade being on the left and the 97th on the right ; but the battalions composing these started off very short of bombs, while the state of the ground was so awful that the rate of advance could not exceed one mile an hour.

To quote the War Diary of the 11th Border Regiment : " At zero time— 6.10 a.m.—the artillery barrage opened and the Battalion advanced in perfect order to attack. The companies got well away and it is certain that the leading platoons and several others got well over Munich Trench, but from this time it was difficult to ascertain the exact position of every company. The Germans put over a heavy bombardment and sent up several rockets which burst into four red stars ; there was considerable hostile machine-gun fire, apparently from guns well in rear of Frankfort Trench. Soon after daylight Captain Ross and Second-Lieutenant Greenhill with some men of The Border Regiment and K.O.Y.L.I. were held up by a strong point in a trench running from Wagon Road to Munich Trench : here sharp fighting ensued and bombing attacks were delivered. A bombing post, supported by 2 Lewis guns, was placed in the trench (the guns commanding both flanks), and fighting went on all through the day," but the Germans were as many as the stormers and better supplied with bombs, while the terribly *holding* nature of the ground forbade the rapid forwarding of reinforcements. Some men of The Border Regiment got up to and inside the German wire and occupied shell holes, but could get no further and struggled back after dark. During the day, and up till 10 p.m., the devoted stretcher-bearers were continuously going over the top attending to and bringing in the wounded.

When dusk fell those that were left of the Battalion were collected and reorganized and Wagon Road placed in a state of defence, and here the " Lonsdales " held on till a little after noon on the 19th, when they were relieved and went back to billets at Mailly-Maillet. There can be no doubt that some officers and men fought their way right through to the objective ; some, like Sergeant-Major Johnstone and Private Dixon, broke back again and rejoined after dark, but Captain Welch and others were cut off and held out until over-whelmed, though several rescue parties were sent out to try and discover their whereabouts and help them in.

During the whole of December the Battalion was in rest billets at Pushevillers ; it was a long and cheerless winter, with much to be done, gaps to be filled, men to be trained, and every preparation made for the battles still to come. On the 12th December the German Emperor had opened negotiations for peace, but nobody— probably not even the arch-*poseur* himself—regarded them as in any way serious.

At Christmas, 1916, His Majesty King George sent the following gracious message to his sailors and soldiers warring by land and sea :—

" I send you, my sailors and soldiers, hearty good wishes for Christmas and the New Year. My grateful thoughts are ever with you for victories gained, for hardships endured, and for your unfailing cheerfulness. Another Christmas has come round and we are still at war, but the Empire, confident in you, remains determined to win. May God bless and protect you !

" At this Christmastide the Queen and I are thinking more than ever of the sick and wounded among my sailors and soldiers. From our hearts we wish them strength to bear their sufferings, a speedy restoration to health, a peaceful Christmas, and many happier years to come.

" GEORGE R.I."

CHAPTER VII

1915 and 1916

THE 9TH BATTALION IN SALONIKA.

In dealing with the events of the year 1915 we left the 9th Battalion of The Border Regiment embarked at Marseilles and journeying with the other units of the 22nd Division for Salonika. The weather was fine, the sea calm **9th Battalion.** and the voyage uneventful, and on arrival at Alexandria on the 3rd November preparations were made for disembarkation. Orders were, however, almost immediately issued for the troops to stand fast, pending a probable change of destination; but on the 4th orders came for the voyage to be proceeded with, and the fleet steamed out of harbour again that afternoon, one man of the Battalion being left behind sick in hospital.

After leaving Alexandria special precautions were taken owing to the reported presence of submarines in the eastern waters of the Mediterranean; all lights were shielded during the night, and the men were directed to have their life-belts handy to slip on at all times.

Salonika was reached on the morning of the 7th November and disembarkation commenced shortly after noon, " B," " C " and " D " Companies being put on shore first, and marching under command of Major Wootten to a camp on the western bank of the River Galiko, some 8 miles distant. The camp was reached at dark—though actually there was nothing in the shape of a camp to be seen, no tents and only the bare side of a hill beaten by a cold wind. Here the three companies were met by the Commanding Officer and Adjutant, who had gone on ahead, and during the course of the following morning Major Morse turned up with " A " Company and the machine-gun section, these having remained on board to assist in and superintend the disembarkation of the Battalion stores. After the cold night spent in the open all hands were glad to start clearing the camp of stones, bringing in the stores and building reed shelters.

The 9th Battalion remained in this camp until the 19th November, busily employed in making roads and improving the water supply. By degrees the battalion transport was equipped with animals borrowed or commandeered, while bell-tents arrived sparingly in grudging instalments of two or three at a time. On the 13th Captain Wilson and 62 men of the transport, who had embarked later at Marseilles, rejoined the Battalion. In this camp the nights were cold, while the days were warm; the weather was fine and the health of the men continued excellent. The rations were good and plentiful, except that bread was hard to come by and there was a great dearth of tobacco and cigarettes. The signallers were now put under training, the Battalion scouts were got together, and all ranks were exercised—so far as the many fatigues permitted—in hill warfare.

On the 20th the Battalion moved to another camp some three miles to the E. and nearer to Salonika, and here the men were mainly employed in bridging the stream near camp. But on the 24th another move was made, and the Battalion was now camped with the artillery of the 22nd Division on the E. bank of the Galiko. Here the troops appear, for the first time, to have formed a perimeter camp with outpost picquets.

Towards the end of November the weather changed for the worse ; on the 27th snow began to fall in the early morning and ended in a blizzard, the cold was intense, and there was heavy frost at night with consequent difficulty in getting up supplies. " Rum," so the Diary would have us believe, " was issued late at night and *kept for the next day*," which seems to show unusual self-control on the part of the 9th Battalion of The Border Regiment !

On the 30th, when the weather showed signs of improvement, orders were received to be prepared to move N. at short notice, and all horses were now exchanged for mules and additional men indented for to complete the new scale of transport.

Marching into Salonika on the 1st December, the Battalion entrained for Doiran in three parties—at 8 p.m. and 11 p.m. on the 1st and at 2 a.m. on the 2nd, the transport, both mules and wagons, having been completed just prior to departure ; and the different parties arrived in the early hours of the morning at a camp about four hundred yards on the Greek side of the frontier between Doiran Station and Doiran Village. There were no tents, as these had all been left at Salonika, so bivouacs were put up.

The Battalion was now attached to the 10th Division.

On the 4th December the Left Half Battalion, under command of Major Wootten, moved out into camp about 2½ miles N. of Kilindir Village and commenced work on the road next day, when the remainder of the Battalion marched to another camp about a mile N. of Doiran Railway Station, and started work on another section of the same road.

It was now tolerably evident that some operations of a rather special character were in view, for the men's second blankets were ordered to be returned to Salonika, while all officers were directed to cut down their kits to a maximum weight of 15 lbs. ; and then on the 8th December emergency rations were issued, all excess baggage and battalion equipment which could be spared was sent to Doiran for conveyance to Salonika, and at 8 p.m. that evening orders were issued for Battalion Headquarters, three companies and the machine-gun section to move at once into reserve to the 29th Brigade of the 10th Division to a place S. of Hasanli. This was carried out, leaving all transport except machine-gun and ammunition wagons to follow on next morning. It was a very cold night, spent in the open with no more than one blanket per officer and man.

On the 10th December the 9th Border Regiment took over the trenches held up to this by the 29th Brigade, just N. of Pazarli, and immediately E. of Kara-Bail ; these were situated on high ground necessitating a stiff climb up a rugged, hilly track from Hasanli, and all blankets had to be carried up on pack-mules, while the men discarded their kits. Here the Battalion occupied a sub-section with the Royal Irish Rifles of the 29th Brigade on their right, and the 14th King's Liverpool Regiment of the 65th Brigade on their left. All wheeled transport was left at Hasanli, while " D " Company had remained behind at work on the Kilindir Road.

Every precaution had here to be taken and patrols were constantly moving out to the front, for reports had been received that the enemy were advancing in force over the hills to the N.; but nothing was seen of them on the front held by the Battalion. Nevertheless, about midnight orders were issued for the evacuation of the position, and the troops were withdrawn to Hasanli, all stores being brought away and Lieutenant Grace remaining behind with 20 scouts to cover the withdrawal. The rearguard of the Battalion left Pazarli about 5.30 a.m. on the 11th, arriving at Hasanli about an hour and a half later ; here a halt was made while all ranks got some food, and the retirement was then continued through Doiran Village to a camping ground just E. of Doiran Railway Station, which was reached at 1 p.m. The men came in splendidly, though some of them were carrying as much as 70 lbs. weight of stores which could not be brought away by the small number of pack-mules available.

As Lieutenant Grace and his scouts left the position, enemy scouts were seen to be coming down towards Hasanli.

The Battalion now left the 10th Division and returned to the 22nd, the head-quarters of which were in and about Doiran, joining the 65th Infantry Brigade and moving to Kilindir.

On the 13th the Battalion entrained at Kilindir and proceeded to Salonika, reoccupying its former camp on the E. bank of the Galiko River.

The 9th Battalion had not, however, been stationed here more than a very few days, when—on the 17th—Headquarters, " B," " C," and " D " Companies were ordered to entrain at 1 p.m. and move to the neighbourhood of Gradobor, with G.S. wagons horsed by the Royal Field Artillery ; and on arrival at their destination at 7 o'clock that evening the three companies moved to a camping ground N. of Gradobor, while " A " Company marched to Akbunar.

Just as the Battalion was entraining for this move, Lieutenant-Colonel Cooke received orders that he had been appointed to the command of the 67th Brigade and was to remain behind, handing over the Battalion to Major Wootten.

Here, then, or in a camp nearer to Pirnar, the 9th Border Regiment remained during what was left of the year 1915, busily engaged on pioneer work of all kinds, and enlivened during the last night of the year by enemy aircraft dropping bombs on the camp.

The operations in which, while attached to the 10th Division, the 9th Battalion had taken part, were the result of the decision which had early in the year been come to of sending Allied troops to the assistance of Serbia. The 10th British and two French divisions had accordingly penetrated into that country, but it was very soon evident that the power of resistance of the Serbian armies had temporarily been broken, and that the Allied forces thus belatedly arriving could offer them no material assistance ; while the position of the British troops was daily becoming more precarious, owing to the concentration of a large German-Bulgarian force in the Strumnitza Valley. The advanced troops were accordingly ordered to withdraw into Greek territory, while some of the British reinforcements now arriving—part of the 22nd Division among them—were sent up in support. The right of the 10th Division was attacked on the 6th, 7th and 8th December, but it repulsed the opposing Bulgarians and the final retreat to Salonika was not further interfered with.

The general situation at the beginning of 1916 was more or less as follows : On the right the districts of Seres and Drama were occupied by Greek troops, who held the pass through the mountains formed by the gorge of the Struma. At Stavros, on the Strymon Gulf, began the fortified lines of the British position, extending across the neck of the Chalkidike Peninsula N.W. to the Galiko River, and then to Lake Doiran. Here began the lines of the French, which were continued as far as the Vardar and covered its lower reaches on the west.

Here, then, the Allies set to work upon the creation of a protected base by the construction of the entrenched camp of Salonika ; and for the first three or four months of 1916 the building of what, from its landward side at least, grew by degrees into something of the nature of a first-class fortress, engrossed the energies of the Anglo-French Army. The nature of the ground about the town lent itself to the construction of a really strong defensive position. Eight miles to the N. of Salonika a high ridge runs E. and W., dominating the plain beyond ; and owing to the complete inaction of the enemy—latterly wholly Bulgarian, since the great attack on Verdun, which began in February of this year, drew away nearly all the German troops in the country—who had halted some 30 miles away, the work of fortifying and extending the Anglo-French position was carried on without any interference whatever, except for the occasional visits of German aircraft. When completed, the Allied position was practically impregnable; the eastern portion of it was very strong and rested on the sea, while in the western portion two sections only were open to possible attack—the 20 miles from Lake Langaza to the Vardar River, and the 18 miles of the Vardar Valley. But the position was throughout a commanding one, was heavily wired all along its front, and before it lay 7 miles of swampy plain over which an attacker must advance.

Before the New Year was more than a very few weeks old the British Army at Salonika consisted of the 10th, 22nd, 26th, 27th and 28th Infantry Divisions, to the command of which, early in May, Lieutenant-General G. F. Milne, C.B., D.S.O., was appointed.

The 9th Battalion The Border Regiment remained in the camp to which it had moved at the end of 1915, doing much excellent work as the Divisional Pioneer Battalion in making and improving roads all about the Salonika position, in preparing dug-outs for machine-gun and Headquarter battle positions, and making emplacements for heavy guns. The companies were detached a good deal in order to be near their work, much of which was quarrying out of the rock. On the 9th May orders were received for a move, and on the following day the Battalion proceeded to the neighbourhood of Kukus, where the same kind of work, especially on the roads, was at once taken in hand. On this date, so the Commander of the British Forces reported,[1] " the greater part of the Army was concentrated within the fortified lines of Salonika, extending from Stavros on the E. to near the Galiko River on the W.; a mixed force, consisting of a mounted brigade and a division, had been pushed forward to the N. of Kukus in order to support the French Army, which had advanced and was watching the right bank of the Struma River and the northern frontier of Greece. Further moves in this direction were contemplated, but, in order to keep the Army concentrated, I entered into an agreement with General Sarrail by which the British forces should become responsible for that portion of the Allied front which covered Salonika from the E. and N. By this arrangement a definite and independent area was allotted to the Army under my command."

It was on the 26th of this month that the Bulgarians, apparently alarmed at the transfer to Salonika of a large body of Serbian soldiers who had been training and recuperating in the island of Corfu, suddenly advanced on to Greek soil N. of Seres and Drama, and occupied, with the acquiescence of the Greek Government, Fort Rupel and one or two other works which commanded the line by which they seemed to fear that an Allied advance might possibly take place. The movement did not presage a Bulgarian offensive, as was at first imagined; it was merely a defensive movement and had no other purpose or meaning.

The end of June found the 9th Border Regiment making a fresh move, for on the 29th orders were issued to the G.O.C. 22nd Division of the XIIth Corps that his " Pioneer Battalion " was to be placed at the disposal of the XVIth Corps for work on the Salonika–Seres Road, and that it was to camp at Kilo. 27 and take over the maintenance of the road from Kilo. 22 to Kilo. 31 from the 39th Company R.E. In accordance with the above the Battalion marched on the evening of the 30th June, halted for the night at Ajvatli, and arrived at its destination on the night of the 1st–2nd July. Here the 9th Battalion was engaged in similar work to that which it had elsewhere performed, while it was also employed in laying Decauville railways. This continued up to the end of July, when it rejoined its own Division in the neighbourhood of Kukus.

The Allied army in Salonika had by this been strongly reinforced—some 70,000 Serbians having arrived from Corfu—and was now ready to take the offensive, and on the 10th August a combined attack was commenced " against the Bulgarian defences S. of the line Doiran–Hill 535. The French captured Hill 227 and La Tortue, while the British occupied in succession those features of the main 535 Ridge, now known as Kidney Hill and Horseshoe Hill, and, pushing forward, established a series of advanced posts in the line Doldzeli–Reselli."

In these operations the 9th Border Regiment took no active part, although there can be no doubt that the good work it had so long been doing in and to the front of the British position materially contributed to their success. Officers and men appear, however, to have been in a good position to see all that was going forward, the Battalion, on the opening of the Allied offensive, being disposed

[1] General Milne's despatch of the 8th October, 1916.

with Headquarters, " A " and " D " Companies at Yenikeui, and " B " and "C" at Rates Ravine.

On the 28th August orders were received to move into the XIIth Corps area near Armutchi to carry out some especially urgent work, and the Battalion accordingly marched off that evening in small parties independently via Cuguinci and Vergetor to Haidarli, the last party getting into camp just before midnight, and all commencing road work early next day.

On the day that the 9th Battalion made this move, Germany and Bulgaria declared war on Roumania, with the result that a total of fourteen nations was now engaged in what might with truth be described as " the World War."

As a result of the Allied operations which had been initiated early in August, it became possible materially to shorten the Allied line between Doiran Lake and the River Vardar, and on the 29th General Milne had extended his front as far as the left bank of that river so as to set free more troops for the further offensive proposed by General Sarrail ; and by the last day of this month the position held extended from Hill 420 to the Vardar River just N. of Smol, while in the Struma Valley a French mounted detachment was pushed forward to Seres. In the meantime, however, the Bulgarian forces had advanced into Eastern Macedonia southwards from Monastir, and in the second week of September the British, in order to assist the counter-movement which our Allies were making from the direction of Lake Ostrovo, began an attack on the Macukovo Salient close to the left bank of the Vardar River. " With this object in view," wrote General Milne in his despatch of the 8th October, 1916, " the whole of the enemy's entrenched position was subjected to a heavy bombardment from the 11th to 13th September, the S.W. corner of the salient, known as the Piton des Mitrailleuses, being specially selected for destruction."

It was in this area that the 9th Border Regiment had now for some weeks past been at work, and on the 13th there seemed some likelihood that it might be needed to lay aside spade and pick and take up rifle and bayonet, for orders were received that " no work was to be done but that we were to rest in view of standing by during the night in case assistance were required in the attack about to take place on the Piton des Mitrailleuses by the 65th Brigade. Very heavy bombardment all day, which was intensified at dusk. Attack time was 7.30 p.m." Then on the 14th the Battalion diary contains the entry : " not having been required, work as usual. Enemy trenches occupied." These had been captured " by a skilfully planned and gallant assault in which the King's Liverpool Regiment and Lancashire Fusiliers specially distinguished themselves."

Towards the end of September the several companies of the Battalion were distributed among the brigades as the exigencies of the work to be done demanded, and on the 29th " B " Company, while working under the C.R.E. on a line of defences some 3,000 yards N. of the mouth of the Selimli Ravine, was heavily shelled, but fortunately sustained no casualties, damage being done only to kits and equipment and explosives. The enemy artillery appeared to be searching for a battery, and having found it the rate of fire increased and the scrub on the hillside was set on fire. The Bulgar guns then put up a barrage some 500 yards behind the camp so as to prevent the approach of assistance.

Although the 9th Battalion of the Regiment was not actively engaged in the operations above alluded to, still it had done very much by the hard and continuous pioneer work it had carried out to ensure their successful conclusion, and the following message from the Army Commander to the G.O.C. 22nd Division may certainly be taken as including the 9th Border Regiment :—

" Please convey to General Gordon and all the troops responsible for the capture of the ground near Piton des Mitrailleuses my heartiest congratulations on their success in face of determined opposition by enemy and topographical difficulties. The attack seems to have been skilfully planned and admirably supported and carried out."

And so the 9th Battalion " carried on " during October and November, gaining golden opinions for the good work done and for the cheerful spirit in which all demands by the C.R.E. and other importunate persons were met. In October a draft arrived of 130 non-commissioned officers and men sent out by the 3rd Battalion, and almost entirely made up of men who had served in other battalions of The Border Regiment ; these were followed a few days later by 2 young officers, Second-Lieutenants G. Ibberson and E. P. H. Mitchell. In the third week in November leave was opened—the first which had been accorded since arrival in the country—and in this month another draft, 156 strong, arrived, while 4 new officers joined from the Westmorland and Cumberland Yeomanry—Second-Lieutenants W. Fielding, C. F. Pickworth, R. Logan and A. C. Stern.

The end of 1916 closed, for the 9th Battalion, very much as it had endured during the summer and autumn—plenty of hard work, with engineering difficulties of no mean kind to be overcome, constant moves, the Battalion, and even the companies, everlastingly split up in many small parties working under junior officers or even non-commissioned officers, under all possible vicissitudes of climate, upon the bleak, storm-swept hill-sides, or in the poisonous malaria-ridden valleys. " The winter season had now fully set in, and the frequent rains had rendered the soil of the Struma Valley wet and heavy. Problems of transport and communications became more difficult, and the main Seres Road was kept open only with the greatest difficulty. In the valley itself horse transport had to be abandoned N. of Orljak, and recourse had to light railways, while the sudden rises of the river rendered communication precarious, and necessitated considerable work in the construction of heavy bridges." [1]

During the winter months, since, that is to say, the end of November, 1916, the British forces occupied the front covering Salonika from the E. and N., and extending from the mouth of the River Struma along the Tahinos–Butkova–Doiran Lakes to the River Vardar, a distance of approximately 90 miles, while an infantry brigade was in addition stationed about Katerini on the western shores of the Gulf of Salonika.

[1] General Milne's despatch of the 14th November, 1917.

CHAPTER VIII

1917

THE IST, 2ND AND IITH BATTALIONS IN THE ANCRE OPERATIONS.

THE IST, 5TH AND 7TH BATTALIONS IN THE ARRAS BATTLES.

THE 2ND BATTALION IN THE OPERATIONS ABOUT BULLECOURT.

THE year 1916 had ended on the Western Front with the very considerable success of Beaumont Hamel, which gave the British the command of both sides of the Valley of the Ancre, while several of the attacks carried out during the winter months greatly improved the situation in the Beaucourt Valley ; and as soon as the improvement in the weather permitted further active operations to be undertaken, proceedings were commenced to drive the enemy from the remainder of the Beaumont Hamel spur. Early in January, however, in compliance with the wishes of General Joffre, a gradual extension southwards of the British front took place as far as a point opposite the town of Roye, and this was completed towards the end of February. The order of the British Corps thereafter, taken from S. to N., was as under :—

Rawlinson's Fourth Army, then the Fifth Army under Gough, the Third under Allenby, the First under Horne and the Second in the N. under Plumer.

In rear of the positions held by the enemy on our immediate front, he had prepared two strong systems of defence. The first of these—known as the Le Transloy–Loupart line—consisted of a double line of trenches heavily wired and running N.W. from Saillisel past Le Transloy to the Albert–Bapaume road, where it turned W. past Grévillers and Loupart Wood, and then N.W. again past Achiet-le-Petit to Bucquoy. Parallel to this line, but on the far side of the crest, was another defensive system on the line Rocquigny, Bapaume and Ablainzeville.

This year was not remarkable for any one great protracted battle, such as that of the Somme in 1916, but there was a succession of battles, continuous fighting throughout the year from January to November, and these operations may be divided as follows :—

(1) The operations on the Ancre from the 11th January to the 13th March.
(2) The German retreat to the so-called Hindenburg Line from the 14th March to the 5th April.
(3) The Arras offensive from the 9th April to the 15th May.
(4) The operations round Bullecourt from the 11th April to the 16th June.
(5) The operations towards Lens from the 3rd June to the 26th August.

(6) The Battle of Messines from the 7th to the 14th June.

(7) The Battle of Ypres from the 31st July to the 10th November.

(8) The Cambrai operations from the 20th November to the 3rd December.

The year's fighting began in January with a number of small operations, and " before the end of the month the whole of the high ground N. and E. of Beaumont Hamel was in our possession, we had pushed across the Beaucourt Valley 1,000 yards N. of Beaucourt Village, and had gained a footing on the southern slopes of the spur to the E." [1]

The operations which commenced early in January, and which had for their object the clearing of the Beaumont Hamel spur, were carried out by the 3rd, 7th and 11th Divisions ; but although the 2nd Border Regiment belonged to one of these and the 6th Battalion of the Regiment to another, the first named appears to have been the only one of the two which was engaged.

At the beginning of the year the 2nd Battalion was in billets in Mailly-Maillet in brigade reserve, when on the 7th February it was moved up to the front, and **2nd Battalion.** two days later was ordered to attack Leave Avenue and Muck Trench next day ; and by 11 p.m. on the 9th the Battalion was in occupation of its preliminary position and disposed as follows :—

" A " Company on the right in an assembly trench, its objective being a point in Leave Avenue, and with orders to make a block some 50 yards E. of Muck Trench and Leave Avenue.

" C " Company in the centre in Beaucourt Trench, its objective being another point in Leave Avenue.

" B " Company on the left in Beaucourt Trench, its objective being a third point in Leave Avenue, and its orders to make a block some 50 yards N. in Munich Trench.

Supporting troops of each company were in Hardwick Trench and " D " Company was in reserve. At 2 a.m., on the 10th February, the British field guns put a barrage on No Man's Land, by which time the attacking troops had formed up and commenced to move forward ; and half an hour later these had occupied the enemy positions, capturing 3 officers and 143 other ranks, 2 machine guns and an automatic rifle ; the captured position was at once consolidated. The going in No Man's Land was very heavy indeed, and several men stuck in the deep mud and had to be dug out.

The casualties in the 2nd Border Regiment were slight and occurred chiefly from our guns, due to the fact that the attackers followed up the barrage too closely ; on the other hand, their rapid advance prevented the enemy getting out of his dug-outs and using his machine guns on the barrage lifting. About 6 in the morning the enemy showed some inclination to counter-attack, but was driven back by the Battalion bombers, and the 2nd Battalion remained all day in the position, which was heavily shelled. On the night of the 10th–11th they marched back on relief by the 1st Battalion Royal Welch Fusiliers to billets in

[1] Despatch of the 31st May, 1917.

9

Mailly-Maillet. The casualties sustained on the 10th amounted to : killed, Captain S. F. Johnson and 6 other ranks ; wounded, Lieutenant R. K. Ehrenborg, Second-Lieutenant C. F. E. Ingledow and 44 other ranks, while 2 men were missing.

The Division stayed some days longer in occupation of the ground gained, the enemy infantry remaining comparatively inactive, while the British, on the other hand, patrolled vigorously to find out what the enemy was doing. Thus on the night of the 19th a patrol of The Border Regiment, under Second-Lieutenant Gronow, discovered that Frankfort Trench, reported held by the enemy, was unoccupied. On the 20th Second-Lieutenant Gronow and Sergeant Garwood carried out a skilful reconnaissance in broad daylight, and definitely established the fact of Frankfort Trench being unoccupied ; after examining all the enemy dug-outs they went still further forward and located the true German line, being heavily shelled when returning to their lines. No. 6183 Private Thompson also went out in broad daylight, as did No. 18347 Private Rooney, the former locating the German positions and bringing back most useful information, while Rooney not only examined Salford Trench—which he found unoccupied—but went some 50 yards further forward, when the Germans opened on him with shrapnel and he had to retire.

The Battalion was later relieved and, falling back by Bertrancourt and Beauval, was in billets at Pernois by the end of the month, having had Second-Lieutenants D. A. Gillespie and H. D. Lees and 3 more men wounded.

During February the Battalion had been strongly reinforced, drafts numbering altogether 222 coming out with the following officers : Major S. H. Worrall ; Captains C. E. Graham, S. F. Johnson (killed in action), and E. R. Chetham-Strode ; Second-Lieutenants J. J. Dedman, J. Harding, F. W. Keenan, R. Abram and A. Harper.

The Battalion remained in active training at Pernois until about the 20th March, when it went back again to Bertrancourt, coming there under the command of the Brigadier-General commanding the 91st Infantry Brigade and being placed at first in brigade reserve, but later—from the 25th to the 28th—being engaged in the operations which caused the German front line to cave in to a depth of 3 miles N. and S. of the Ancre, and the occupation by the infantry of Gough's Fifth Army of the towns of Serre, Puisieux, Pys, Miraumont, Eaucourt, Warlencourt, and all the ground for 11 miles from Gomiecourt in the N. to Gueudécourt in the S.

During these operations, which were continued until nearly the end of March, some wholly admirable battle patrol work was done by the officers and men of the 2nd Battalion The Border Regiment, in reconnoitring the villages and the ground leading thereto in order to discover whether the enemy was falling back, what positions he had evacuated, and which of those remaining in his hands were still held in strength. In all this very delicate and anxious work, the following leaders particularly distinguished themselves : Captains C. E. Graham and T. T. Beaty-Pownall ; Lieutenant R. Maxwell ; Second-Lieutenants E. R. L. Bishop, T. Gronow, D. D. Low, R. Abram, R. J. Cunningham, J. Moore, J. J. Dedman, W. G. Grahame, A. Harper and E. J. Peacock ; No. 10624 Sergeant H. Hurndall and others. These operations could not, of course, be carried out without risk and loss, and in the course of them Captain T. T. Beaty-Pownall and 22 other ranks were killed, Second-Lieutenants D. D. Low, R. J. Cunningham, T. Gronow, A. Harper, J. J. Dedman, and 63 non-commissioned officers and men were wounded, while 16 men were missing. Wastage from sickness was not inconsiderable, no fewer than 124 " other ranks " being evacuated sick during the months of February and March, and though many drafts arrived, mainly composed of men who had previously served, they were weak in strength—varying from 6 men to 13—and in the two months under review totalled no more than 71. On the other hand, a good many young officers had joined : in February, Lieutenant R. Maxwell, Second-Lieutenants G. S. Rutherford, J. B. R. Edwards, D. B. Dempster, R. Adamson, E. R. L. Bishop, E. J. H. Mettam, R. J. Cunningham, D. T. Holmes, J. B. Dunlop, D. D. Low, and C. B. Barr; and in March, Second-Lieutenants W. G. Grahame, W. Inkpen, E. J. Peacock and M. Seymour-Isaacs.

At the end of March the 2nd Battalion was occupying billets at Ervillers.

During much the same period as that during which the 2nd Battalion was engaged in the operations on the Ancre, the 1st Battalion was taking part in fighting
1st Battalion. further to the S., in the neighbourhood of the Somme, fighting which, if it is not usually included by historians among the leading events of this year's campaigns, yet, if one may judge by the casualties incurred by the Battalion and the very special remarks published by the Commanders under whom it served, was certainly not negligible and is of very considerable regimental interest.

When the year 1917 opened the 1st Battalion was engaged in training at Hangest, but on the morning of the 12th January it entrained, and after a four-hours' journey arrived at Mericourt, from where it marched to Bresle. After halting here for one day the Battalion marched on by Meaulte and Carnoy, and on the 7th was in the firing line about Guillemont, where ten days later it was told off, in company with the 1st Royal Inniskilling Fusiliers on the right, to attack a portion of the enemy position S. of Le Transloy, known as Landwehr Trench. The attack began at 5.30 in the morning of the 27th and met at once with really remarkable success. By 7 o'clock 117 German prisoners had been passed back, and reports reached Battalion Headquarters in Antelope Trench that the first and second objectives had been gained, while fifteen minutes later a written report was to hand from the right company of the Battalion confirming the capture of the first objective, and stating that so far casualties had been few ; this company alone sent back 45 prisoners. At 8.45 this company passed back another batch of 75 prisoners, and reported that consolidation of the captured position was very difficult owing to the frozen nature of the ground, that there was little shelling by the enemy, but a good deal of hostile sniping. A later report, however, stated that the enemy seemed alive to the situation, and that his shelling of the position was increasing in weight and volume.

At 12.45 p.m. a report came back that consolidation was proceeding slowly, a certain amount of wire had been put down round a strong point which was being dug, while Lewis-gun emplacements had been made across Sunken Road on the right flank of the strong point. By 2 in the afternoon all was secure, and the importance of the gains achieved may be judged by the congratulatory messages which from 4 p.m. onwards began to come in. From the Commander-in-Chief came :—

" ' *Congratulate the 29th Division warmly, and in particular the 1st Border Regiment and 1st Royal Inniskilling Fusiliers, on the success of their operations carried out this morning.' In forwarding this message the Army Commander wishes to add his congratulations to the 29th Division on their most successful enterprise.*"

Congratulations were also received from the XVth Corps Commander, Lieutenant-General the Earl of Cavan, from the Anzac and New Zealand Corps, the 20th Division, and the 4th and 5th Australian Divisions, while Lieutenant-General de Lisle, commanding the 29th Division, sent the following message to the Brigadier :—

" *I send you warmest congratulations on the fine attack of your Battalions.*"

The total prisoners for the day taken by the 1st Border Regiment and 1st Royal Inniskilling Fusiliers were 6 officers and 355 other ranks unwounded, and about 25 wounded, while 5 machine guns were captured, 3 of them by The Border Regiment, who also took 4 of the captured officers and 200 of the men. Sergeant E. J. Mott was awarded the first V.C. won by the 1st Battalion in the Great War for his action in capturing one of these machine guns. Although severely wounded in the eye, he rushed the gun, which was holding up his company, single-handed, and after a desperate struggle with the gunner, took him prisoner and captured the gun. A very useful map was also taken whereon were shown all the enemy " dumps," headquarters, railway lines and batteries—those also of the British were tolerably accurately given !

The Battalion now marched back to Carnoy, where the Divisional Commander paid a visit to the camp and personally congratulated the C.O. and officers on the splendid action of the 27th, afterwards entering each hut and thanking the men.

Losses had, of course, been sustained by the Battalion, and these totalled 137 : Lieutenants W. de H. Robinson, M.C., S. C. Cheverton and W. L. Beattie, and Second-Lieutenant A. M. Clark and 12 non-commissioned officers and men were killed, Second-Lieutenant H. T. Thompson and 87 other ranks were wounded, while 33 men were missing ; then in the course of the week following, when the Battalion returned to the line, 2 men were killed and 18 others, including Lieutenant Lindsay, were wounded.

During the greater part of February and March the 1st Border Regiment was in a training area about Bussy, and in the latter month received two small drafts totalling 82 non-commissioned officers and men ; and at the end of March it was at or near Vignacourt, waiting to be again called to take part in a larger operation.

The only other Battalion of The Border Regiment which had any share in the early operations undertaken by our far-flung battle line was the 11th, the Lonsdale **11th, the Lonsdale Battalion.** Battalion, which at the beginning of 1917 was stationed in the Mailly-Maillet area ; but early in February it was withdrawn to Lythan Camp near Beaussart, where the attack was practised over ground which had been carefully laid out so as to correspond in every detail with an attack which was shortly to be made on the enemy position. The whole of the 9th February was spent in making the necessary preparations, equipment and bombs were drawn, and the operation orders were read and discussed, and on the following afternoon the " Lonsdales " paraded and marched to Beaumont Hamel, the 97th Brigade being detailed to drive the enemy off the ridge and out of Ten Tree Alley on the night of the 10th–11th.

At 6 p.m. the first platoon of " D " Company moved off from the Quarry in Beaumont Hamel, where rifle and Lewis-gun ammunition had been issued, and as it marched off guides were dropped along the route to be followed up to the tape—Wagon Road–Walker Quarry–top of Walker Avenue and across it to Gough Road–Frankfort Post. The platoons in rear followed at intervals of 100 yards along this route, " C " Company (under Captain Ross) being the first to move, and taking up a position on the tape in four waves, viz. two platoons in front forming first and second waves, two sections of each platoon being in extended order in front and two in rear at 20 yards distance ; one platoon 40 yards in rear again extended right across the company front and formed the third wave ; one platoon 70 yards in rear, making the fourth wave, in sections in file. " B " Company (commanded by Captain Walker) followed " C " Company, and took up its position on the tape in the same formation. " A " Company (Captain Greenhill) followed " B " and took up a position on the left, but in a different formation—one platoon being in front to form first and second waves ; two platoons close in rear of the left flank to deal with any hostile posts ; one platoon as reserve in artillery formation. " D " Company (under Lieutenant Harris), with two platoons close up in rear of the right flank of " C " Company to deal with enemy posts and two platoons as Battalion Reserve.

The Battalion was in position by 7.30 p.m. on a frontage of 350 yards, while the Headquarters was established at Frankfort Post.

At zero hour (8.30 p.m.) the artillery barrage opened, when the Battalion moved forward from its position—a line running from a point S. of Frankfort Post to Kyle Trench—and followed closely behind the creeping barrage towards the objective.

The first message came back at 9.30 from the Reserve Company, " D," reporting that all objectives had been captured and that consolidation had commenced, and the first batch of 35 prisoners soon followed. Colonel Girdwood, commanding the Battalion, moved his Headquarters forward, and then examined the ground won and the dispositions of the troops, sending two platoons of the Reserve Company across to the exposed left flank, while posts were established in front of the captured line—Gunpit Trench—and this was at once put in a state of defence.

Two officers and approximately 100 other ranks were captured and sent to the rear by the Battalion, but one dug-out, from which the enemy had refused to emerge, was bombed and unfortunately caught fire, the inmates perishing. Patrols were now pushed out to the front and others sent to establish communication with the 2nd K.O.Y.L.I. on the left ; and a strongly held enemy post being discovered on the Battalion left, some Stokes mortars, under Second-Lieutenant Simcocks, were sent in that direction and opened with effect on the enemy post.

At 4.30 a.m., on the 11th, the enemy delivered a counter-attack from a N.E.

direction, but on rapid rifle fire in conjunction with Lewis- and Vickers-gun fire being opened, the German attack wavered and was held up, except on the left, where, under cover of the smoke from the burning dug-out, the enemy managed to get close up ; here a bomb-fight ensued and the attackers were repulsed. The area concealed by the smoke was swept by rifle and Lewis-gun fire and barraged with all available rifle grenades ; the S.O.S. signal was sent up for artillery support, and on our guns opening, the enemy attack was completely broken and the German infantry retired into the valley and up the slope beyond.

Observation had been much hampered by a thick, low-lying mist, but at daybreak a patrol was sent out, and on return reported that the enemy was still in strength on the left and was holding a post with 3 machine guns. But the rest of the day passed quietly, except for sniping and occasional outbursts of shell fire.

When it became dark two attempts were made by the company on the left to capture the enemy post above-mentioned, but these were unsuccessful.

At 8.30 p.m. orders were received that the Battalion was to act, in conjunction with the Naval Division on the right, in another advance to be made along the Puisieux Ridge ; and " C " Company (under Captain Ross) with two platoons of " D " Company having been detailed, these took up a position on the left of the Naval Division, and, on the barrage opening at 9 o'clock, the advance commenced on a frontage of 300 yards, the direction being at right angles to the line held by the Battalion, and a fresh line of posts was now established connecting up with the Naval Division.

On the night of the 12th the Lonsdales were relieved and withdrew to dug-outs near Beaumont Hamel, and on the 62nd Division taking the place of the 32nd in this sector, several further moves took place, until by the end of February the Battalion was stationed in Le Quesnel for training.

When, however, the German retreat to the Hindenburg Line commenced about the 14th March, the 11th Border Regiment moved forward with the Division in pursuit, and on the 17th was at Rouvroy ; next day it occupied the old German front line S. of Fouquescourt, being employed thereabouts in improving the roads and bridging the trenches so as to allow guns and transport to move forward. From here the Battalion moved on again and was for some days in Nesle, doing much the same work and finding villages, orchards, etc., completely destroyed by the retiring enemy. Then on the 28th March the Battalion marched in an easterly direction, leaving Nesle at noon and passing through Voyennes and Toulle to ground N. of Germaine, where all began at once to dig trenches on a frontage of 700 yards facing W., two companies providing outposts during the night—the one at Vaux, the other at Etreillers. On the 30th March orders arrived detailing the Lonsdales to participate in an attack upon the village of Savy.

In accordance with these orders the Battalion moved forward, on the night of the 31st March–1st April, from Proseste on to the Roupy–Etreillers Road, where a brief halt was made ; and then at 3.30 a.m. moved some distance on to a position 500 yards S. of the village of Savy, where it deployed into attack formation and took up a position on a tape-line previously laid down. At 5 o'clock the artillery barrage opened and the attack on Savy commenced. The advance in rear of the barrage was very rapidly conducted, and the enemy was driven through and out of the village ; and while one company remained behind in Savy to " mop up," the remainder of the Battalion dug in on its further side. By 6.30 a.m. consolidation had been practically completed and the village put in a state of defence. For the space of an hour during the afternoon the position was heavily shelled by the enemy, but the Battalion held on to the village and its vicinity until the evening of the 7th April, working hard at the defences, and then withdrew to Holnon, where shelters had to be dug and the position improved. Here the 11th Border Regiment remained until the 11th, when it was once more in the front line, and the 32nd Division was now called upon, with the 35th Division co-operating on the left, to attack the village of Fayet, the object of this attack being to support the left of the French in an assault they were making upon St. Quentin, which was, however, unsuccessful.

The attack on Fayet was entrusted to the 97th Brigade, the assaulting battalions being the 2nd K.O.Y.L.I. and the 16th H.L.I., The Border Regiment remaining in the line ready to concentrate if ordered. The village with some 100 prisoners was captured at the first rush, but it was found to be more difficult to get possession of a wood called the Twin Copses beyond Fayet, and at 1 p.m. the Battalion was ordered to make an attack upon it. Some twenty minutes later it had reached a terraced road, and here the left flank of the leading company came under the fire of a machine gun which inflicted several casualties. Two platoons of the reserve company were ordered up to deal with it and they succeeded in capturing it. A wire was now run out to the Battalion and telephone communication established. By 2 p.m. all the companies of the Battalion were consolidating their line, while touch was established with the H.L.I. in Gricourt, and except for a slight shelling the situation was, and remained, tolerably quiet.

On the night of the 15th April the Battalion was relieved, and these particular operations having come to an end, it moved back to Hombleux, and thence, after some days, to Offoy, where a draft of 91 other ranks joined and where the remainder of the month of April was spent.

Thus ended the two first of the eight series of operations which marked the campaign of 1917, and preparations had already been some time in train for the Arras offensive. Much railway work had been done, new lines laid and existing ones added to, roads had been improved and material provided for carrying them rapidly forward as the advance progressed ; huge stocks of munitions and stores had been collected as near the front as possible, reservoirs were constructed and many miles of water mains laid ; while every advantage was taken of the existence of the large system of quarries and cellars in Arras and its suburbs to provide safe quarters near the front line for a large body of troops. These places were lit by electric light, were linked together by tunnels and the whole connected by subways with the trench system E. of the town.

" The new German lines of defence on the British front," to quote Sir Douglas Haig's despatch, " ran in a general N.W. direction from St. Quentin to the village of Tilloy-les-Mofflaines, immediately S.E. of Arras. Thence the German original trench system continued N. across the valley of the Scarpe River to the dominating Vimy Ridge, which, rising to a height of some 475 feet, commands a wide view to the S.E., E. and N.   Thereafter the opposing lines left the high ground, and, skirting the W. suburbs of Lens, stretched N. to the Channel across a flat country of rivers, dykes and canals, the dead level of which is broken by the line of hills stretching from Wytschaete N.E. to Passchendaele and Staden.   The front attacked by the Third and First Armies on the morning of the 9th April extended from just N. of the village of Croisilles, S.E. of Arras, to just S. of Givenchy-en-Gohelle at the N. foot of Vimy Ridge, a distance of nearly 15 miles.   It included between 4 and 5 miles of the N. end of the Hindenburg Line, which had been built to meet the experience of the Somme Battle.

" Further N. the original German defences in this sector were arranged on the same principle as those which we had already captured further S.   They comprised three separate trench systems, connected by a powerful switch line running from the Scarpe at Fampoux to Lièvin, and formed a highly organized defensive belt some 2 to 5 miles in depth.   In addition, from 3 to 6 miles further E. a new line of resistance was just approaching completion.   This system, known as the Drocourt–Quéant Line, formed a northern extension of the Hindenburg Line, with which it linked up at Quéant."

The main attack was to be carried out by the Third Army, commanded by General Sir E. Allenby, and the First Army under General Sir H. Horne.   Four Army Corps—the VIIth, VIth, XVIIth and XVIIIth, and the Headquarters of the XIXth—were placed at General Allenby's disposal, while the Cavalry Corps was also brought up into the Third Army area to be employed should opportunity arise for the use of the mounted arm on any considerable scale.   The disposition of our troops for the attack was as follows, taking them in order from S. to N— that is, from the right of Allenby's Third Army where it joined on to the left of Gough's Fifth Army :—

> Third Army.—VIIth Corps ; 21st, 30th, 56th and 14th Divisions.
> VIth Corps ; 3rd, 12th, 15th and 37th Divisions.
> XVIIIth Corps ; 9th, 4th, 34th and 51st Divisions.
> Third Army Reserve ; IXth Corps ; 17th, 29th, 33rd and 50th Divisions.
> First Army.—Canadian Corps ; 1st, 2nd, 5th, 3rd and 4th Divisions.
> Ist Corps ; 24th, 46th and 6th Divisions.
> First Army Reserve ; XIIIth Corps ; 2nd, 5th, 31st and 63rd Divisions.

It will be seen from the above that three battalions of The Border Regiment were to take part, practically from the outset, in the operations about to take place, viz. the 1st, 5th and 7th forming part of the 29th, 50th and 17th Divisions respectively ; but later on the 7th Division, containing the 2nd Battalion of the Regiment, was brought into action with the 58th and 62nd Divisions which formed part of Gough's Fifth Army, posted, as already above stated, on the right of Allenby's Third Army.

The entry into action of these different battalions took place within a very few days of each other, so that it may on the whole be most convenient to deal with them in order of seniority.

The Arras offensive commenced officially on the 9th April, and on that date the 1st Battalion of The Border Regiment was in huts at Bavincourt, not far from

1st Battalion. Grand Rullecourt; an unpleasant day—" hail, snow, rain and wind "—when all ranks must have been glad to find themselves in huts. On the 10th news of the opening of the attack began to come back from the front—" captures, 10,000 prisoners and about 10 guns "—and on the 12th the Battalion marched by way of Arras to Maison Rouge, there relieving the 7th Norfolks of the 9th Brigade, and so on to old German trenches near Orange Hill, about 2 miles E. of Monchy and between that place and Guémappe, where, as the entry in the Diary puts it in language expressive if unofficial, " we saw where the Cavalry had taken it in the neck "—in allusion, no doubt, to the charge on the 11th April of the 8th Cavalry Brigade near Monchy, where these suffered many casualties and had their Brigadier killed. The Battalion right was here about 400 yards S. of the main Arras–Cambrai Road.

On the 17th the 1st Border Regiment moved up to the firing line and on the following day Second-Lieutenant G. C. M. Cox, with a platoon of " B " Company, attempted the capture of a German strong point situated about 250 yards from the British front line; but the attempt was unsuccessful, as the position of the post was not accurately known, and when reached it was found to be strongly held with machine guns; Second-Lieutenant Cox and 5 of his party were wounded.

The 17th and 29th Divisions were now covering the wide area from the N. of the Cojeul River to the S. of the Scarpe.

On the 19th the Battalion moved back to the security of the caves in Arras, but the losses during the last tour in the trenches had not been wholly negligible, 9 men had been killed or had died of wounds, while 22 had been wounded, including 4 officers—Lieutenant C. Mills, Second-Lieutenants G. C. M. Cox, H. M. Woolf and H. Coward. The respite was but a very brief one, for on the 22nd orders were received to stand by ready to move out and take up a position in the line preparatory to an attack on the following morning; and in accordance with these the Battalion marched out from Arras that night and moved to a point on the Arras–Cambrai Road, 600 yards W. of Feuchy Chapel cross-roads. Here the companies were met by guides and conducted, at ten-minute intervals, to the N.W. entrance of the village of Monchy-le-Preux, whence the platoons were marched off to their " jumping-off " place, a line about 30 yards W. of the front-line fire trench up to the Sunken Road. The companies were here formed up in the order " D," " A," " B," " C " in practically one continuous line, while Battalion Headquarters was at the outset established in a shallow trench in rear. All was in readiness by 2.30 a.m. on the 23rd, but the task of getting the companies through the village of Monchy-le-Preux and into position was a difficult and hazardous one, as the village was being heavily shelled the whole time; while, owing to the relief of other battalions proceeding at the same time, Monchy-le-Preux was greatly congested with troops and transport animals. Casualties were, however, few, only 1 officer (Second-Lieutenant V. Blomfield) and 6 men being wounded.

In the meantime the adjutant, Lieutenant R. G. Cullis, had been sent forward to find a more suitable place than the shallow trench above mentioned for Battalion

Headquarters, and he returned about 3 a.m. reporting the discovery of a deep hollow in the Château Wood where the Battalion Aid Post had already been established, and where the E. slope of the hill afforded tolerable cover from direct shell fire; the Battalion Headquarters was accordingly moved thither.

At 4.45 " C " and " D " Companies of the 1st Border Regiment moved forward in rear of the attacking lines of the South Wales Borderers, " A " and " B " occupying the old firing line; but as they went on these companies suffered greatly from our barrage, which was falling very short, while no sooner had the attack started than the enemy put down a barrage on a line just W. of Arrowhead Copse, and a second following the line of the E. edge of Monchy-le-Preux. At this time the smoke from the barrage was so dense that the exact situation could not be clearly defined.

About 6.45 a report came back from Captain Ewbank, commanding " B " Company, to the effect that from information obtained from wounded men, orderlies and others, the South Wales Borderers had gained their objective and were making strong points on it, and that the Battalion losses from the British and the German barrages were said to be severe; and a little later the same officer sent word that " C " and " D " Companies had established themselves in the enemy front line. S.O.S. flares had been sent up on the left and considerable machine-gun fire was coming from that flank, and Captain Ewbank had accordingly pushed out a Lewis-gun section in that direction. Later again the O.C. South Wales Borderers sent in a message stating that a gap on the left of his line had been occupied by the enemy, who was sniping our men rather heavily, and instructions were now issued by the G.O.C. Brigade to place a company of The Border Regiment at the disposal of the South Wales Borderers in the event of the enemy endeavouring to turn his left flank, and Captain Ewbank was ordered to send a bombing party to Arrowhead Copse to work up the German trench to the Sunken Road and to clear it of the enemy.

At 9 o'clock that night a message came in from the 87th Brigade stating that the 17th Division had been unable to advance, and that the left flank of the South Wales Borderers was in the air, and that consequently, should the advance of the 29th Division be proceeded with, The Border Regiment was not to attempt to enter the Bois du Sart, but was to dig in on the W. side of it. Then about 11.20 the O.C. " B " Company reported that the bombing party sent to Arrowhead Copse under Second-Lieutenant Layard had returned bearing the following information, viz. that the supposed enemy trench up to the Sunken Road did not exist, but that the party had made its way up to this road and there found the enemy entrenched, some 80 in number. On discovering this, Second-Lieutenant Layard returned to Arrowhead Copse, secured a Lewis gun, and, returning with it towards the Sunken Road, got it into a position whence he could enfilade the enemy trench, and opening fire he succeeded in causing many casualties among the hostile party before his presence was located. He then came under heavy machine-gun fire and had four men hit, upon which he withdrew his gun.

Definite orders were now received that for the present at any rate no further advance was to be attempted.

Just about this time Lieutenant Johnson, commanding "D" Company, reported that he was dug in on the right rear of the South Wales Borderers and for a distance of 200 yards S. of this point, with "C" Company prolonging his left in a N. direction towards the Sunken Road, the King's Own Scottish Borderers and Royal Inniskilling Fusiliers being on his right; he also reported that Second-Lieutenant R. S. Pooley (attached from the 3rd Royal Scots Fusiliers) had been killed by shell fire. The hostile shelling now became both continuous and heavy on the Arrowhead Copse line and on the edge of the village of Monchy-le-Preux. Battalion Headquarters was taken in enfilade by a German battery apparently firing from somewhere in the Pelves Valley, and two heavy shells landed within a short space of time, one killing the Regimental Sergeant-Major, the Scout Sergeant, 2 scouts and a signaller, and wounding the adjutant, Lieutenant Cullis, and several men; while the second landed full on the roof of the dug-out in which the Commanding Officer and other Headquarter officers were sitting, burying them all completely and wounding a runner. Battalion Headquarters was then moved to a trench on the E. edge of the hollow, while Captain Ewbank was sent for from the firing line to take over temporary command, as the C.O. was knocked out. During the whole of this period—it was now midday on the 23rd—there was no appreciable change in the situation, but the intensity of the enemy's barrage now somewhat slackened.

About 1 p.m. Battalion Headquarters was moved back to the Château dug-out, and after dusk to another big dug-out, and now, as the situation on the left flank seemed by no means clear or satisfactory, orders were sent to the company commander there to move forward at dusk and establish a defensive flank parallel to the Sunken Road. This was done with two platoons, leaving the rest of the company in the old front line as a reserve. When night came on an attempt was made to relieve the Battalion, but as the C.O. of the Battalion detailed for relief only reached Battalion Headquarters at about 3.30 on the morning of the 24th, relief then was out of the question and it was put off for another twenty-four hours. The night of the 23rd–24th passed fairly quietly and only intermittent shelling went on, while there was no change in the situation on the Battalion front. The next day, too, the 24th, the gun-fire died down, but the ground between the firing line and Monchy-le-Preux was thoroughly well sniped all day, and movement by any but a single man at once drew machine-gun fire from the N. side of the Sunken Road.

Three of the Battalion companies were relieved early on the morning of the 25th, but owing to the commencement of operations on the left flank at the same time, when the enemy at once put down his barrages, "D" Company had to remain for a further twenty-four hours in the front line, eventually rejoining the rest of the Battalion at Duisans early on the 26th April; here the companies were accommodated in Nissen huts. From Duisans the 1st Border Regiment went to Saulty, where the rest of the month was passed. Throughout the action inter-communication was distinctly good. It had to be carried out almost entirely by runners, the telephone line to the Brigade Headquarters, although repaired three times, only remaining intact for about ten minutes each time. The devotion to duty displayed by the men carrying messages was magnificent, and though casualties among them were heavy, there was never any delay or hesitation whatever on the part of the survivors in going out repeatedly with fresh messages.

The casualties among all ranks of the Battalion totalled 156 ; 2 officers (Second-Lieutenants G. F. Kemp and R. S. Pooley) and 22 non-commissioned officers and men were killed, Captains B. H. Spear-Morgan and W. B. Wamsley (the medical officer), Lieutenant R. G. Cullis (the adjutant), and Second-Lieutenant V. Blomfield and 107 other ranks were wounded, while 21 men were missing.

During the course of the next few days there were many " alarms and excursions "—orders to stand by, to be ready to move up to the front—all in turn amended or cancelled, and it was actually not until the 13th—what is described in the Battalion Diary as the " stunt by 1st, 3rd and 5th Armies, in the central area, i.e. Monchy-le-Preux," having commenced at 3.45 a.m. on the 3rd— that the Battalion marched in the afternoon to Arras, when all the arrangements preliminary to an attack were made. In the evening of the 14th a further move was made, into the so-called " Brown Line " near Feuchy cross-roads, being part of the German line captured on the 9th and part of the Hindenburg Switch. The whole of the 15th was taken up in improving the trenches, while a patrol, consisting of Lieutenant Crane and 6 men, was sent up the line after dark to reconnoitre Devil's Trench, which was to be one of the objectives in the forthcoming attack.

On the 17th the Battalion took over the front line from the Monchy–Pelves Road to the Twin Copses inclusive, the order from N. to S. being as follows : one company of the South Wales Borderers (attached), " B " and " C " Companies of The Border Regiment in Snaffle Trench, " A " Company in Twin Trench, " D " in support in Shrapnel Trench, while Battalion Headquarters was in a Red House at Monchy-le-Preux. The companies were all in position just as dawn was breaking on the 18th, and that evening an assembly trench was dug through Twin Copse behind the front line, which was to be evacuated prior to the barrage opening.

The situation calling for the employment of the 1st Border Regiment in the ensuing action E. of Monchy-le-Preux on the evening of the 19th May was briefly as follows : after the 29th Division had fought itself to a standstill on the night of April 23rd, the date of the First Battle of Monchy-le-Preux, the remnants of the 87th Brigade had dug themselves in where their advance had halted, and on their relief this line had been more or less consolidated. The position, however, was anything but ideal from the point of view of observation, while that of the enemy was very good, and it was hoped to improve matters by turning out the enemy and occupying his line. The British line from which the assault was to be delivered had no properly organized trench system suitable for either defensive or offensive action ; the front line was disjointed, there being no connection whatever from N. to S. between the line passing between the two Twin Copses ; then, the soil being either clay or clay and chalk, the trenches in the low ground were wet and muddy, in some places were very shallow, in others deep and narrow, making passage very difficult. Further, there was no communication through to the front line by day under cover, and the companies in the fire trenches could only be reached by long and roundabout routes.

In conjunction with an attack to be made at the same time on the right, the 87th Brigade was to capture (a) Infantry Hill, and (b) the Bois des Aubepines, and to establish a line of strong points running along Devil's Trench—E. edge of Cigar Copse—Bois des Aubepines—May Trench—Long Trench—Tool Trench. The following were the objectives allotted to the different companies of the 1st Battalion :—

"A" Company (Captain Bunting, M.C.) was to attack and capture the positions in front, push through and establish a platoon (under Lieutenant New) as a strong point at a spot noted on the map, with two other platoons (under Second-Lieutenants Armstrong and Dunlop) forming a second strong point on the E. side of the Bois des Aubepines.

"B" Company (Second-Lieutenant Layard, M.C.) was to capture the enemy position in front and establish strong points, each of a platoon, the one (under Second-Lieutenant Middleton) near the E. edge of the Cigar Copse, the other (under Second-Lieutenant Rae) near the S. edge of Devil's Trench.

"C" Company (Lieutenant Thorburn-Brown, K.O.S.B. attached) on the assault commencing, was to extend to the left and occupy the ground vacated by "B" Company.

"D" Company (Captain Palmer) was to advance over the open from Shrapnel Trench to the line vacated by "A" Company.

Carrying and wiring parties were also arranged.

The company attached from the South Wales Borderers was given objectives in Devil's Trench with orders to dig strong points in this trench about 50 yards N. and S. of Bit Lane.

By dawn on the 19th all the very many preparations to be made were practically completed—so far as the infantry was concerned—the men were in position, the required battle stores were all either issued or at hand, and the ground in front had been very carefully examined. The day broke clear and cloudless, hot and dry with little or no wind, and so remained during the whole of this day and the night which followed. The attack was not to commence until 9 p.m., so final orders were issued during the evening. When the bombardment opened very many of the shells from the British guns fell short, causing no inconsiderable number of casualties among the troops waiting for zero hour in the trenches.

Punctually to the second the barrage fell at 9 p.m. and the attack commenced ; for some little time nothing came through of how it was progressing, but it was seen that the enemy had sent up S.O.S. signals asking for his barrage to open. Soon after 10 o'clock Private Crook, an orderly, who had been sent with a message to the company of the South Wales Borderers, returned to Battalion Headquarters stating that just as he arrived at the front the attack started and the waves went "over the top," while the rear parties picked up their wire and trestles and carried them forward. But shortly after it was reported from the artillery that the attack was held up between Cigar Copse and the Bois des Aubepines—the very place which the O.C. 1st Border Regiment, anticipating opposition, had specially asked that our guns might deal with. As, however, no reports had up to this come in from the assaulting companies, Colonel Ellis sent the adjutant (Captain Sutcliffe) up to the front to find out and report upon the situation ; he accordingly moved off with two orderlies.

Just after midnight Captain Bunting came back to Headquarters wounded in the eye, and made the following statement : that our barrage had failed to do the necessary damage to the enemy defences or material, that many shells had fallen among the attackers, but that the assaulting companies had still pushed on and had practically arrived at their objectives when they were met by a line of enemy bombers, who rained bombs on them. Captain Bunting was just organizing flanking attacks when he was wounded and temporarily blinded by an enemy bomb, but just previously he had noticed Second-Lieutenant Dunlop standing close to the enemy trench, picking off the enemy one by one with a rifle, regardless of the fact that they were hurling bombs at him in reply. This very gallant young officer was here killed, while Captains Palmer and Davies (of the S.W.B. Company) and Lieutenant Durham were also known to have become casualties.

Lieutenant Danielli now sent word that he was carrying on as O.C. " D " Company, which was in position and in touch with " C " on his left, but that there appeared to be no troops on his right, front or rear.

Since at 1.30 a.m. the general situation seemed clearly to indicate that the attack had failed, the Battalion Commander sent a message to the senior officer in the firing line—Lieutenant Thorburn-Brown, who, though wounded some hours previously, was still carrying on as O.C. " C " Company—to make every effort before dawn to get all the troops back to the original front line and there reorganize for defence in case of any counter-attack.

At 3.10 a.m. the adjutant returned from the front line and gave the following detailed information : " A " Company had been held up at the edge of the Bois des Aubepines by a strong bombing party in the strong point there ; " B " Company's attack had failed, having met with very heavy machine-gun fire from between Cigar Copse and the Bois des Aubepines, and that Second-Lieutenant Rae, the senior officer remaining, had withdrawn all available men to the original front line and was there reorganizing ; of the right portion of " A " Company very little was known, Lieutenant Dunlop and most of those with him were casualties, while Lieutenant New had been seen leading on his platoon, but as they also came under very severe machine-gun fire, it was feared the same fate had befallen him and his party ; " C " Company had extended to fill up the vacated line as far as possible, but the platoon supporting " A " Company's advance had been badly cut up ; " D " Company had been under a heavy fire while in the trenches, and came under the barrage on moving over the open to occupy the vacated front line, and Lieutenant Danielli, now in command of what remained of the company in the front line, was busy reorganizing and taking all defensive measures ; while as regards the South Wales Borderers Company attached, this had come under very heavy machine-gun fire from Devil's Trench and Bit Lane, the attack had been broken up, and while a few men had gained and were holding out in Arrow Trench, a general retirement to the old line had been ordered and was now being carried out.

About 4 a.m. the line was re-established as strongly as the paucity of troops permitted, two Vickers guns being in the front line.

Patrols were busy from the moment retirement was ordered while the stretcher-bearers worked unceasingly to clear casualties, with the result that by dawn the majority of the wounded had been brought in, and throughout the day the evacuation of stretcher cases was continued. During the night the 1st Border Regiment was relieved as a result of the very heavy casualties sustained and moved back to Arras. Ten officers were killed or wounded : the killed were Lieutenants L. W. Armstrong and P. New, Second-Lieutenants E. B. Dunlop and T. S. Middleton ; wounded were Captains H. Palmer and H. Bunting, M.C., Lieutenant T. E. Thorburn-Brown, Second-Lieutenants A. H. Crane and A. J. Durham ; Second-Lieutenant F. S. Layard, M.C., was wounded and missing.

The 2nd Battalion The Border Regiment was not called upon this year to take further part in any serious operations until May, remaining at Ervillers **2nd Battalion.** until the 5th April on return from the fighting about Carnoy, moving then to Ablainzeville, where the usual casualties inseparable to trench warfare were incurred, and where the service companies were joined by some trifling drafts totalling 34 only, as against 51 sick evacuated during the month, and by the following 11 officers : Captain H. L. Chatfield ; Lieutenants A. T. R. Hamilton and G. Neil ; Second-Lieutenants J. A. Stephen, J. S. Greenwood, W. Carr, S. T. Stevens, R. Paynter, J. Coulthwaite, J. R. Bartlett and A. R. Barnes. As a result, at the end of the month of April the Battalion was very strong in officers and comparatively weak in other ranks, there being 41 of the former and no more than 685 non-commissioned officers and men.

On the 3rd May the Battalion moved back again to Ervillers " to a position of readiness in support to the 62nd Division in an attack on Bullecourt." Of the operations that ensued General Sir Douglas Haig wrote in terms of high praise in his despatch. This runs : " to secure the footing gained by the Australians in the Hindenburg Line on the 3rd May it was advisable that Bullecourt should be captured without loss of time. During the fortnight following our attack, fighting for the possession of this village went on unceasingly ; while the Australian troops in the sector of the Hindenburg Line to the E. beat off counter-attack after counter-attack. The defence of this 1,000 yards of double trench, exposed to counter-attack on every side, through two weeks of almost constant fighting, deserves to be remembered as a most gallant feat of arms. On the morning of the 7th May, English troops (7th Division, Major-General T. H. Shoubridge) gained a footing in the S.E. corner of Bullecourt. Thereafter gradual progress was made in the face of the most obstinate resistance."

The account of those operations as contained in the Battalion Diary is, unfortunately, rather meagre. The 2nd Battalion was at first about Ecoust St. Mein in dug-outs and cellars there, and in shelters in the Sunken Road ; but on moving up to the front line the companies were employed in trench digging and consolidation, all under a tolerably continuous shelling by day and night ; and on the 9th a shell landed full on the Battalion Headquarters, wounding Major G. E. Beaty-Pownall and Second-Lieutenant B. L. Cumpston, the latter mortally, and 3 other ranks. A few days later the Battalion was withdrawn, but on the 15th a " Special Company," composed of 3 officers and 100 other ranks, was formed under Captain J. Moore and left camp for Bullecourt to assist the 22nd Infantry Brigade in the capture of a strong point in that village, known under the, no doubt, highly appropriate name of " the Red Patch," and was employed during the operations in carrying water and stores for the 58th Division.

In the meantime word having been received that the enemy was heavily counter-attacking in the proximity of Bullecourt, the rest of the Battalion, made up into two companies, left camp at 11 in the morning and took up a position in the defence line near the Sunken Road. Neither of these parties appears, however, to have been seriously engaged, and the Battalion was again concentrated at Ablainzeville by the 16th May, remaining here in training until well into June.

During the above operations the 2nd Battalion had 1 officer mortally wounded, 13 other ranks killed, 5 officers and 61 non-commissioned officers and men wounded ; the three British Divisions of the Fifth Army here engaged had been opposed by the picked regiments of the German Guards, and had pushed them from their carefully prepared and stoutly defended position.

The 5th Battalion also saw something of the fighting of this period of the year, for after several moves in the months of January, February and March, it was

5th Battalion. sent on the 11th April from the Somme area to the neighbourhood of Arras and marched, on the day following, to a position 1,000 yards N. of Neuville Vitasse, whence it proceeded early on the 14th to the bed of the Cojeul River to support an attack by the 6th Durham Light Infantry, but does not appear to have been called upon to act.

Then on the 23rd, the 5th Border Regiment was very early in the morning in occupation of Nepal Trench when the 150th Brigade of the Division attacked and captured a portion of the enemy line 1,000 yards E. of Wancourt Tower. But on this Brigade being driven back at midday by a strong counter-attack, the 5th Battalion and 9th Durhams attacked the Germans again at 6 p.m. and re-took the objective, capturing 5 machine guns, several trench mortars and 200 prisoners ; while they also succeeded in recovering and bringing back many of the wounded of the 150th Brigade who had been left behind when the enemy counter-attacked. On this occasion " A " Company remained in echelon to secure the flank, as the division on the right did not reach its objective. A platoon of " D " Company of the 5th Battalion got well forward and managed to occupy part of an old German trench, and thereafter came under the orders of the O.C. 9th Battalion Durham Light Infantry, with which corps the company remained until relief was effected.

At 4 p.m. on the next day—the 24th April—the 5th Border Regiment again attacked but was held up by enemy shell and machine-gun fire ; nothing daunted, they came on again at dusk and were this time successful, gaining their objective and digging in on, and consolidating, the line captured.

During these several attacks the Battalion had 6 officers and 45 non-commissioned officers and men killed, 4 officers and 131 other ranks wounded, while 23 men were missing, believed to be killed.

Photo

Imperial War Museum

HÔTEL DE VILLE, ARRAS

On the 26th April the Battalion was in billets at Rouville, whence it was moved next day to Arras and in the evening to a rest area at Coullemont. From this date on there was a succession of moves, but at the end of May the 5th Border Regiment was in or about the town of St. Amand.

The 7th Battalion of The Border Regiment spent the greater part of the earlier portion of the year 1917 in the Combles area, doing much useful trench work, but just before it left for the La Neuville training centre Lieutenant-Colonel Alexander, D.S.O., joined and assumed command. On the 2nd March the 17th Division was transferred from the XIVth Corps of the Fourth Army to the IInd Corps of the Fifth Army, the 51st Brigade moving into the Rubempre area for some days' training, and then to the neighbourhood of Gezain-court, where the Division left the IInd Corps of the Fifth Army for the XIXth Corps of the Third Army, and on the 9th March the Division began to move to Arras in very rough and snowy weather. On arrival the 17th Division joined yet another corps—the VIth—and relieved the 15th Division N. of Monchy. Here the 51st Brigade was placed in Divisional Reserve and remained in billets ready to move out at one hour's notice.

7th Battalion.

At this date the Monchy-le-Preux–Guémappe front was held by two divisions only, and by two, moreover, which had only just come up to the front line—the 17th in the N. which had relieved the 15th, and the 29th in the S. which had taken the place of the 12th Division. Early on the morning of the 14th April these two divisions advanced in order to push back the enemy further from Monchy, and it had been arranged that while two brigades of the 29th Division attacked, the 17th Division should protect the left flank. But as stated in the diary of the 7th Border Regiment, " the 88th Brigade, 29th Division, attacked on the morning of the 14th and obtained their objective, but the enemy made a strong counter-attack on the 88th Brigade, which was holding the ground gained E. of Monchy-le-Preux, and the 88th Brigade retired to its original position. The enemy attempted a further attack from the Bois du Sart about 4.30 p.m. but this was broken by our barrage, and the 51st Brigade was ordered to take over the line held by the 88th Brigade of the 29th Division if required, the 7th Border Regiment relieving the 4th Worcesters." The situation about Monchy was not cleared up, the relief was postponed and the Battalion remained in the Railway Triangle, and was busily employed during the next few days on the Monchy defences and in digging trenches on the Orange Hill–Chapel Hill line.

On the 22nd April, however, the Battalion was in the support line and late that evening moved up to the assembly trench S. of Lone Copse, " A " Company going forward at daylight to take the place of the 9th Northumberland Fusiliers in the front line. The relief was carried out with only two casualties and the night which followed was fairly quiet. Next morning the attack on the enemy position was commenced on the whole corps front, the 29th Division attacking on the right from in front of Monchy-le-Preux, the 51st Brigade on the N. side of the Scarpe River on the left of the 17th Division ; the objective assigned to the 51st Brigade was a line running from the E. edge of Pelves Village, along the road, thence along the E. side of the Bois du Sart.

The formation of the 7th Battalion for the attack was: " A " Company on the left and " D " on the right of the front line, supported by " B " and " C " Companies respectively—100 yards between waves, and 200 yards between attacking and support lines, the men being extended to ten paces.

At zero hour on the 23rd—4.45 a.m.—a standing barrage was put down on Bayonet Trench, while a creeping barrage began 200 yards W. of it, moving forward at the rate of three minutes per 100 yards. Both barrages lifted at " plus 10 " and then crept E. at the rate of four minutes per 100 yards as far as the Blue Line. Two tanks were told off to assist the attack on Pelves.

On the advance commencing the right leading company of the Battalion— " D "—lost direction, moving too much to the right, struck the old German trench, and then moving left crossed Bayonet Trench, where an intense machine-gun fire was met from Rifle Trench. The survivors of this company swung up to the left towards Rifle Trench and entered a German strong point, which they enlarged and consolidated, and where they were joined by some men of " C," the right support company, which had also crossed Bayonet Trench and had advanced E. The left leading company, " A," struck Bayonet Trench with its centre about the junction of Bayonet and Rifle Trenches, and was then met by heavy machine-gun fire from Rifle Trench and from the other side of the Scarpe. " B " Company (left support) followed and was also mown down by this fire, and the survivors of " A " and " B " fell back with some of the companies of the South Staffords to the assembly trenches N.E. of Lone Copse, by which time there were no officers of either company surviving.

After their retirement, some of the enemy in Bayonet Trench held up their hands, when the men of The Border Regiment again advanced, but they had once more to fall back before the machine-gun fire which was at once reopened.

The survivors of " C " and " D " Companies remained out in shell holes until dark, when they found their way back to our lines, many being wounded *en route* by machine-gun fire, and Lieutenant Saunders and about 50 wounded and unwounded men made their way back up to 2 a.m. on the 24th; the 10th Sherwood Foresters, who were occupying the S. portion of Bayonet Trench, sent out a party which brought in Second-Lieutenant Sanger and about 100 wounded and unwounded men.

On relief the 51st Brigade marched to Arras at 6 a.m. on the 25th April, and proceeded thence by train to Grand Rullecourt, where the 7th Border Regiment was accommodated in the Château or in huts in the grounds.

The Battalion had suffered very serious losses in the above-recorded action : 2 officers and 17 other ranks had been killed or had died of wounds, 3 officers and 183 non-commissioned officers and men had been wounded, while 10 officers and 204 men were missing. The names of the officers who were killed were Second-Lieutenants E. H. Belchamber and T. H. Lowe ; the wounded were Second-Lieutenants E. Sanger, H. F. Gascoigne-Roy and R. R. Boyd ; while the missing were Captains A. P. Nasmith, D.S.O., and L. Birch, Lieutenant (acting Captain) R. M. B. Welsh, Second-Lieutenants J. Kennedy, F. Andrew, E. G. Clarke, S. S. Heath, E. E. Brett, W. C. Campbell and C. Turner.

The retirement of the 7th Border Regiment to Grand Rullecourt after the hard fighting in April was no more than a very temporary one, a mere respite, and already on the 3rd May the reports coming back from the front must have prepared all ranks of the Battalion for a very early return to the neighbourhood of the recent operations. In the diary of the above date we read : '' offensive on the front of the First, Third and Fifth Armies : 4th and 9th Divisions attacked from the Scarpe River northward, 50th and 52nd Brigades at disposal of 4th and 9th Divisions respectively in case of emergency. The scheme was for the 17th Division, in the event of a successful attack, to be pushed forward and hold posts after dark. The 51st Brigade in reserve marched from camp at 6.47 a.m. to a bivouac camp E. of St. Nicholas under two hours' notice to leave. . . . Attack on XVIIth Corps front only successful at points.'' The emergency then passed, training and working parties were resumed, but on the 16th May the Battalion moved up nearer to the front, and that morning the 17th Division was ordered, in conjunction with the 5th Division, to attack and regain certain trenches which the enemy had captured that morning. The 7th Border Regiment then advanced and moved S. along Green Lane, which was reached about midday, and here the Battalion was held in reserve.

The attack which in the meantime the 17th and 51st Divisions had made N. of the Railway had been only partially successful, and at 5.30 in the afternoon the Battalion was detailed to take part in a fresh counter-attack and capture Curly Trench. Zero hour was 7.30 p.m., with a barrage of four minutes on Curly Trench.

At 6.30 the Battalion proceeded down Hopeful, Humid and Huddle Trenches to their junction with Cadiz Trench to the point of assembly, whence the attack was to be made by half-companies, the other halves remaining in Calabar and Clover Trenches. Unfortunately, it was impossible to get the Battalion into position in time, the distance to be covered being too great—no less than between 3,000 and 4,000 yards—and consequently the companies did not assault but took up the line Crook–Seaforth–Cash and Cuba Trenches to the junction of Cut Trench, there relieving the 8th South Staffords, who fell back. There was considerable shelling during the night which, however, grew less before dawn. The attack by the 51st Division failed.

The 17th passed in comparative quiet, though there was some heavy shelling by both sides, and early on the morning of the next day an enemy aeroplane was brought down near Cuba Trench by the rifle fire of a company of the Battalion. The Battalion remained up in the front line until the 21st, when it was relieved and went back to camp at St. Nicholas. During the remainder of the time that the operations in this sector lasted, the Battalion was constantly up in the line, enduring heavy shelling, but taking part in no attacks upon the enemy's positions ; and then when at the end of May the serious fighting hereabouts lapsed into the ordinary bickering of trench warfare, the Battalion was withdrawn to Arras and went from there by train to Mondicourt, being accommodated here in a disused internment camp.

Heavy losses and few drafts had reduced the Battalion very considerably, and at the end of May the strength was only 13 officers and 450 non-commissioned officers and men ; the losses in the recent fighting amounted to 9 killed or died of wounds—one of these being an officer, Second-Lieutenant F. P. Joyce—and 61 other ranks wounded.

The Arras Battle had lasted a month and during that time the British had captured nearly 20,000 prisoners, had taken 257 guns, 464 machine guns and 227 trench mortars, with huge quantities of war material of all kinds ; while the British line had been advanced to a depth exceeding 5 miles on a total front of over 20 miles, representing a gain of some 60 square miles of territory. The operations which immediately followed about Bullecourt had secured effective occupation of the ground lying between that village and the British front W. of Fontaines-les-Croisilles. Best of all were the actual losses inflicted upon the enemy, which reached the high total of 350,000 ; he had used 104 divisions in the several actions of the Arras Battle alone, and by the end of May had found himself obliged to withdraw 74 of these to refit.

CHAPTER IX

1917

THE 6TH, 8TH AND IITH BATTALIONS IN THE BATTLE OF MESSINES.

THE IST, 2ND, 5TH, 6TH, 7TH AND 8TH BATTALIONS IN THE THIRD BATTLE
OF YPRES.

THE Arras Battle had scarcely come to an end when General Sir Douglas Haig was able to turn his full attention and divert the bulk of his resources to the development of his northern plan of operations, and as stated in the despatch already several times quoted in the last chapter: " immediate instructions were given by me to General Sir Herbert Plumer, commanding the Second Army, to be prepared to deliver an attack on the 7th June against the Messines–Wytschaete Ridge, the capture of which, owing to the observation from it over our positions further north in the Ypres Salient, was an essential preliminary to the completion of the preparations for my principal offensive E. and N. of Ypres."

The preparations necessary for the successful carrying out of this attack were at least as elaborate and of much the same nature as those demanded for the Arras operations, while a special feature of the intended attack upon the Messines–Wytschaete Ridge was the explosion of no fewer than nineteen deep mines at the moment of assault, entailing the driving of 8,000 yards of galleries and the employment of more than one million pounds weight of explosive.

"The group of hills known as the Messines–Wytschaete Ridge lies about midway between the towns of Armentières and Ypres. Situated at the E. end of the range of abrupt, isolated hills which divides the valleys of the River Lys and the River Yser, it links up that range with the line of rising ground which from Wytschaete stretches N.E. to the Ypres–Menin Road and then N. past Passchendaele to Staden. The village of Messines, situated on the S. spur of the ridge, commands a wide view of the valley of the Lys and enfiladed the British lines to the S. North-east of Messines the village of Wytschaete, situated at the point of the salient and on the highest part of the ridge, from its height of about 260 feet commands even more completely the town of Ypres and the whole of the old British positions in the Ypres Salient.

" The German front line skirted the W. foot of the ridge in a deep curve from the River Lys, opposite Frelinghien, to a point just short of the Menin Road. The line of trenches then turned N.W. past Hooge and Wieltje, following the slight rise known as the Pilckem Ridge to the Yser Canal at Boesinghe. The enemy's second-line system followed the crest of the Messines–Wytschaete Ridge, forming an inner curve. In addition to these defences of the ridge itself, two chord positions had been constructed across the base of the salient from S. to N. The first lay slightly to the E. of the hamlet of Oosttaverne and was known as the Oosttaverne line. The second chord position, known as the Warneton line, crossed the Lys at Warneton, and ran roughly parallel to the Oosttaverne line a little more than a mile to the E. of it."

The Second Army (General Plumer) had been moved down the line so as to cover all the front to be attacked, while General Gough's Fifth Army had been brought up from the S. and put in on General Plumer's left in order to occupy the actual salient, and the arrangement of the British troops taking part in the Messines Battle was then as follows, reading from S. to N. :—

IInd Anzac Corps.—Lieutenant-General Sir A. Godley :
   3rd Australian Division, New Zealand Division.
   25th Division, with the 4th Australian Division in support.
IXth Corps.—Lieutenant-General Hamilton Gordon :
   36th, 16th and 19th Divisions, with the 11th Division in support.
Xth Corps.—Lieutenant-General Sir T. Morland :
   41st, 47th and 23rd Divisions, with the 24th Division in support.
On the left of the Xth Corps were the 30th and 8th Divisions of General Jacob's IInd Corps of the Fifth Army.

From the above it will be apparent that two battalions of The Border Regiment, the 6th and 8th, were destined to take part in the Battle of Messines, in the 11th and 25th Divisions respectively, while, as we shall see, another battalion, the 11th, was engaged in the operations subsidiary to this battle which took place on the coast and which are described in General Haig's despatch under the heading of " the Lombartzyde Attack."

Battle of Messines.

During the month of May the 6th Battalion The Border Regiment was stationed first at Fremicourt, later at Beaumetz and in the middle of the month at Le Transloy, and of this period the diary records that " this tour of duty in the line was most peaceful, the total casualties in the Battalion being 2 other ranks killed and 4 wounded. The moral effect on the men of the wanton destruction of trees and houses, roads and wells by the retreating Germans will, it is confidently anticipated, bear fruit in the next operations undertaken by the Battalion. Their feelings have undoubtedly turned to anger, and the local grindstones have been busy : the men, entirely on their own initiative, have sharpened their bayonets."

6th Battalion.

On the 15th the 6th Battalion marched through the area of the old Somme battle-fields to huts at Montauban and on the next day to Fricourt, when a halt of twenty-four hours was called, and then on again by Albert and Abbeville to a camp at Caestre.

During May two officers joined for duty, Second-Lieutenants A. D. F. Torrance and R. Pugh.

On the night of the 6th June the Battalion marched from the camp, where for some days past all ranks had been busily engaged in the practice of the attack upon flagged trenches, to Westhoutre and thence by a track to the place of assembly which was reached at 2 a.m. on the 7th, and here all lay down to get what sleep they might. This was not for long, however, for zero hour was announced at 3.10 by the simultaneous blowing up of several mines containing 600 tons of explosive, and the immediate opening of a tremendous bombardment from a very large number of guns arrayed along an unusually narrow front ; under this fire the German front line seemed, with its defenders, wholly to crumble and vanish.

While waiting for the opening of the bombardment every man had been provided with an extra water-bottle to carry on him, bombs, tools, flares and Very lights had been issued, and in all this preparatory work R.Q.M.S. Farra was of the greatest possible assistance, so that by 6 a.m. the Battalion, 23 officers and 607 other ranks, was completed in every particular and ready for the next move. Orders for this did not arrive until noon, and these were to march to Vierstraat Switch, where by 12.55 all was in readiness for a further advance ; the first and second waves were composed of " A " Company, Captain Ridley, M.C., on the right, and " B," Lieutenant Gandolfo, on the left ; the third and fourth of " D " Company, Captain Williams and " C," Captain Carr, M.C.

Pushing forward to the Chinese Wall, a brief halt was made while the Battalion objective—Van Hove Farm—was pointed out ; the advance, in artillery formation, was then resumed, Wytschaete Ridge was crossed and all went well until the companies had reached the eastern slopes of the ridge where they came under a heavy shell fire and began to lose men.   No pause, however, was made, though the advance to the Odonto Line was a long and trying one owing to the great heat, but it was carried out in perfect order, thanks in large measure to the admirable leading of the platoon and section commanders.

About 6.30 p.m. the rear Company, " C," was ordered to halt, and take up a position covering the valley of the Wambeke, but the others continued moving forward towards Polka Estaminet, where the Battalion Headquarters was now established, and to the Odonto Line, a company being sent forward under Captain Hood with orders to capture and consolidate Van Hove Farm, which was successfully done in face of considerable opposition from machine guns and snipers, but two very gallant young officers, Second-Lieutenants Roberts and Farmer, were here killed and several non-commissioned officers and men were killed and wounded ; the enemy was driven off suffering much from our rifle fire.   The capture of the farm was greatly assisted by two Vickers guns of the 33rd Machine Gun Company.

Patrols were now sent out to the right and left with orders to get into touch with other troops on the flanks, but were unsuccessful, and everything possible was done to make the line secure for the night, the Anzacs and the remaining two Vickers guns guarding the right while Second-Lieutenant Adams with two platoons of The Border Regiment looked after the left. Snipers were very active on the left front and the men were all dead beat, but there is no doubt the position could have been held had it not been for the very heavy shelling which began about 9 p.m. and which forced the companies to fall back to a line in rear, which was reached in good order and was at once consolidated. Here touch was established with the Royal Irish Rifles on the left and with the Anzacs and 25th Division on the right.

By midnight things quieted down, water was discovered close at hand, and the morning of the 8th showed no counter-attack imminent, so work was re-commenced, and, as the soil was easy, the men had soon linked up the many shell holes to form a tolerably strong defensive position. At 3 in the afternoon, however, things began to move ; the enemy guns commenced registering on the position and machine guns opened on it from the ridge in front, while half an hour later small hostile groups were seen moving forward, taking advantage of the cover afforded by hedges and banks, to the right front near Joye Farm. A message was at once sent back to the British guns and within a minute and a quarter a shrapnel barrage was playing on the enemy position, when large numbers of Germans were seen retiring. " Our men and the Vickers and Lewis gunners," says the Battalion diary joyously, " then had the time of their lives ! "

Just before darkness fell a heavy shell fire developed on both sides, and by 9 p.m. was continuous along the whole front, and the 7th South Staffords, who were due to relieve the 6th Border Regiment, had a difficult and hazardous time of it. The relief was, however, effected in due course and the companies rendezvoused at the Chinese Wall, where all lay down to get some sleep after the two last very strenuous days ; the casualties totalled 102, made up as follows :—

Killed, 3 officers, Second-Lieutenants G. E. Roberts, E. A. Barry and A. W. Farmer, and 15 non-commissioned officers and men ; wounded, Lieutenant-Colonel D. Mathers, D.S.O., Major K. M. Chance, D.S.O., Captains N. D. Williams, T. E. Bjerre, J. W. Hood, M.C. (adjutant), and A. J. McCreadie, R.A.M.C., Second-Lieutenants W. Constantine and A. D. F. Torrance, and 76 other ranks.

The Battalion now had an eight-days' march by way of Shaexken, Strazeele, Hondeghem, Renescure and through St. Omer to billets in the Fifth Army training area at Westrove, where reorganization was taken in hand and training schemes were sedulously carried out ; here the following message was received from Major-General W. B. Hickie, C.B., commanding 16th Division, and was read out to all ranks on parade :—

" I want to express my thanks to the officers, non-commissioned officers and men of the 33rd Brigade, not only for the manner in which they attacked and carried the Oosttaverne Line and held it under heavy fire until relieved, but also for the way they accepted and overcame the great difficulties thrust upon them by the change of plan which was made at 12 noon. I beg you to convey to your commanding officers the great appreciation of the 16th Division at the manner in which the troops under their command carried out their task and our regret at the casualties which they suffered."

The second of the Battalions of the Regiment to take part in the Battle of Messines was the 8th, which since the end of the year 1916 had been having, comparatively speaking, a more or less inactive time, so far as the word " inactive " can be applied to service in the Ploegsteert area, where the greater part of January 1917 was passed. On the 24th February, however, the 25th Division was withdrawn from the line and moved back to the

8th Battalion.

Photo

MESSINES RIDGE, 11th JUNE, 1917

Imperial War Museum

Photo

YPRES, 1st OCTOBER, 1917

Imperial War Museum

excellent training area in the neighbourhood of St. Omer, where every advantage was taken of the opportunity for musketry and field-firing practices.

On the 21st March the Division was transferred to the Second Anzac Corps and moved up into corps reserve in the Merris and Caestre area with the Divisional Headquarters at the first-named of these places, and a week later relieved the New Zealand Division in the Wulverghem sector, where work was at once commenced in view of the coming offensive. Large working parties were supplied by units of the Division for road-making, cable burying and the construction of dug-outs and shelters of all kinds. From the 30th April until the 11th May the 25th Division was away from the front line in corps reserve, and then once more relieved the New Zealand Division in the Wulverghem sector, the Divisional Headquarters being at Revelsburg, 1½ miles E. of Bailleul. In this sector the Division had the good fortune to hold the actual line allotted to it in the approaching Battle of the Messines–Wytschaete Ridge, and was thus able to reap the fruits of the hard work of the technical troops, pioneers and working parties of the units of the Division in the general preparations for the attack.

During the greater part of the middle of May the 8th Battalion The Border Regiment was at La Crèche, but on the 29th it marched to Revelsburg, and on the day following to Neuve Eglise, on this march a German shell bursting over " C " Company, killing 4 men and wonding 6 others.

On the 1st June Lieutenant-Colonel C. E. Bond, C.M.G., D.S.O., left the Battalion on appointment to command the 51st Brigade.

On the 7th the Second Army attacked, with three Army Corps, the German defences along the line of hills from Messines to Wytschaete, the capture of this line being necessary before any attack could be developed further N. and to the E. of Ypres. The front of attack allotted to the 25th Division extended from the Wulverghem–Wytschaete Road, and the New Zealand and 36th Divisions were on the right and left respectively of the 25th.

" The objective of the 25th Division lay in front of the village of Wulverghem and comprised the strip of ground with a front of about 1,200 yards on the German front line to a depth of about 3,000 yards, but narrowing towards the top of the Messines Ridge to about 700 yards. A short forward slope followed by a descent into the Steenebeek Valley. The stream, about 4 feet wide, ran through ground marshy in winter but fairly dry in summer except for occasional pools, and presenting no natural obstacles unless stiffened by the aid of military science. From this point the ground rises steeply, flanked on either side by Hell Farm and Sloping Roof Farm, with Four Huns Farm, Chest Farm and Middle Farm on the crest of the ridge, and Lumms Farm a little further on to our left front. These farms, both naturally and tactically strong points, had been converted by military art into positions of immense strength and importance, impregnable to all but overwhelming heavy artillery.

" Along this line of advance, which was considerably deeper than the ground to be covered by the New Zealand Division on our right flank, there lay nine distinct lines of enemy trenches to be stormed and captured." [1]

[1] *The 25th Division in France and Flanders*, pp. 50–51.

The Battalion moved up to the assembly position in Newcastle Trench on the night of the 6th June preparatory to the attack on the following morning.

At 1.30 a.m. on the 7th June the Division was assembled in order of battle, the 74th Infantry Brigade on the right, the 7th on the left and the 75th Brigade in reserve, the last named being now commanded by Brigadier-General H. B. D. Baird, D.S.O., and the 8th Battalion The Border Regiment by Major C. W. H. Birt. The Battalion was in brigade reserve and did not leave its assembly position until 7 a.m. the attack having commenced at 3.10, when it advanced in the following order : " C " Company on the left, " D " on the right, with " A " and " B " Companies in support, commanded by Captain Dawson, Lieutenant Johnson, Lieutenant Healy and Captain Coxon respectively, the task of these being the consolidation of the Black Line just E. of the Messines–Wytschaete Road, and the clearing of several " pockets " of the enemy left behind by the advanced troops. The Black Line was reached about 8.30 a.m. and the consolidation began, while two communication trenches were also dug from October Trench on the left and right of the position. A small but pugnacious party of Germans in a strong point was captured by two platoons of the 8th Border Regiment, while on the left Captain Dawson's company did good work in organizing and consolidating the new line, and a small party of " D," assisted by two tanks, helped to capture a gun and take several prisoners.

At 8.30 a.m. the 11th Cheshires, extended to form a line of skirmishers, reached their objective, a line running N. from Despagne Farm, and the construction of posts was at once commenced, a platoon of the 8th Border Regiment being sent up to establish posts on either flank of the Cheshires. Messines and the ridge had thus fallen into the hands of the British at the end of an hour and forty minutes, although, to quote the Commander-in-Chief's despatch : " The position assaulted was one of very great natural strength, on the defence of which the enemy had laboured incessantly for nearly three years. Its possession, overlooking the Ypres Salient, was of the greatest tactical and strategical value to the enemy. The excellent observation he had from this position added enormously to the difficulty of our preparation for the attack and ensured to him ample warning of our preparations."

The enemy shelled the new British line at intervals during the day and there was heavy shelling again at night, but the Battalion was relieved at midnight on the 7th–8th and went back into Brigade Reserve near Neuve Eglise.

The casualties this day were Second-Lieutenant Healy and 13 other ranks killed; Second-Lieutenants G. G. R. Bott and J. H. Johnson, and 15 non-commissioned officers and men wounded.

Two men of the Battalion especially distinguished themselves in the action of the 7th—No. 16232 Corporal H. Carter and No. 12893 Private F. Brown. These men had reached their objective and were hard at work consolidating when they noted an enemy battery in action, and, seeing one of our tanks going across the front in an E. direction, they ran across and called the Tank Officer's attention to the German guns, and on the tank moving off to attack them these two men followed close in rear. On getting up to the position the tank fired a broadside and Corporal Carter and Private Brown then charged the guns by themselves. By this time the German gunners had retired to their dug-out, but on Private Brown firing two rounds into it, the gun team—7 in number, 2 of them wounded—came out and surrendered to the two men of the 8th Battalion ; these then took possession of the gun and of a helio, marking the former with their names. This done the two men went on to another gun-pit immediately N. of the first. Here the Corporal was knocked senseless by a stick bomb and Private Brown then went on alone and took the 6 men of the second gun team prisoners. Thinking he might do more good work in this direction, Private Brown endeavoured to mount a stray Anzac cavalry horse, but the animal being wounded he was unable to manage it and returned to his company. Corporal Carter soon recovered and also returned.

It had been decided to carry out a further attack on the 14th and extend the line about 800 yards beyond that then held by the Second Anzac Corps, and to the 25th Division was allotted a front of attack of about 1,500 yards between the Blauweportbeek to the N. and La Douve River to the S. In accordance with the above the 75th Infantry Brigade moved up from camp near Neuve Eglise on the evening of the 12th June and before daybreak on the 13th had relieved the 14th Australian Infantry in the front line, the 8th Border Regiment taking the left and the 2nd South Lancashire the right. During the afternoon of the 13th Major Birt, commanding the 8th Battalion, not being altogether satisfied with the information sent in by his patrols, proceeded to make a personal reconnaissance of the front, accompanied by Lieutenant W. H. Anderson and 3 men, and established the fact that the enemy was holding Les Quatre Rois Cabaret, Steignast Farm and the Puits. Coming suddenly on a small party of Germans in a trench behind some trees, Lieutenant Anderson was unfortunately killed, but the remainder of the hostile party was disposed of by Lance-Corporal Robinson and Privates Bell and Livesay.

During the night of the 13th much good work was done in the preparation of communication trenches and the improvement of the existing trench, but it was considerably interfered with by the heavy barrage which was put down by the enemy, probably in anticipation of a further attack.

The assembly of the two battalions for the attack was completed by 6.30 p.m., the 8th Border Regiment in the new Switch Trench. Carried out in broad daylight, the men being dribbled up in twos and threes behind hedges, this operation showed good leading by company officers and the excellent discipline of other ranks. Snipers caused casualties among the men assembled behind the hedges, but the real significance of the movement was not detected by the enemy.

At 7.30 p.m. the line moved forward under a creeping barrage in conjunction with the New Zealand Division on the right ; on the left was the 8th Battalion The Border Regiment with "A" Company, Lieutenant Strong, on the right, "B," Captain Coxon, in the centre and " D," Lieutenant Duggan, on the left, in the front line, and " C " Company under Captain Dawson in support, and the 2nd South Lancashire Regiment on the right. Owing to our standing barrage falling on to the objective practically simultaneously with our advance, the enemy was unable to retreat, and in twenty-five minutes all the line of the Brigade objective—

Ferme de la Croix, Les Quatre Rois Cabaret, Gapaerde, Deconinck Farm—had been gained. The enemy was mostly discovered lying in shell holes and improvised trenches, which were soon cleared; one or two strong wired points gave some trouble but were quickly outflanked, leaving several machine guns and some prisoners in our hands. Five minutes after the line moved forward to the attack, the enemy barrage of 4.2's and 5.9's came down on our old front line in rear, and again about 9 p.m. the enemy's barrage fell with great intensity and lasted for about half an hour in rear of our front line, causing some casualties, but during the night the battalions energetically consolidated and wired the line against any counter-attack.

Four officers of the Battalion were hit during this attack, Second-Lieutenant W. A. Bell being killed and Major Birt, Captains Stewart and Dawson wounded.

On the night of the 15th June the 8th Border Regiment was relieved and moved back into support, and then on the 22nd the Division was finally withdrawn from this sector of the line and on the 24th moved back for a well-earned rest to the Bomy area, south of St. Omer.

The 11th Lonsdale Battalion after the action at Fayet in April remained for some little time training about Offoy, and then about the middle of May marched

11th Battalion. by way of Nesle, Corchy, Puzeaux and Caix to Domart-sur-la-Luce; here more training was undergone until quite the end of the month, when the Battalion marched to Villers Bretonneux and there took over billets. Leaving here again by train early on the morning of the 1st June the " Lonsdales " proceeded by train to Steenbecque via Abbeville, Etaples, Boulogne, Calais and Hazebrouck and detrained again at 4 in the afternoon, marching then to Neuf Berquin by Merville, not getting under shelter until 11 o'clock at night. Here a fresh training scheme was inaugurated and continued for the best part of a fortnight, when the Battalion moved off again by march and bus by way of Caestre and Godwaerswelde to the neighbourhood of Dunkirk, and after some further trifling movements the Battalion found itself at the end of June in occupation of what was known as " the ' C ' subsector " of the Nieuport–Lombartzyde Sector.

Something must now be said as to the reasons which had brought British troops into the coastal area of the Allied front. For the new offensive which was now about to be undertaken by the western forces a complete redistribution of the armies had been found necessary. The front of the Third Army, now commanded by General Byng, had been considerably extended and covered all the ground between Arras and the point of junction with the French, and consequently the Fifth and Fourth British Armies had become available for service further N. The French troops, which earlier in the year had held the Yser front, had been withdrawn and Rawlinson's Fourth Army had taken their place; on his right was the First French Army, with the Fifth, Second, and First British Armies following in succession from left to right or N. to S.

" The appearance of British troops on the coast," so runs General Haig's despatch, " seems to have alarmed the enemy and caused him to launch a small counter-attack. The positions which we had taken over from the French in this area included a narrow strip of polder and dune, lying on the right bank of the canalized Yser between the Plasschendaele Canal, S. of Lombartzyde, and the coast. Midway between the Plasschendaele Canal and the sea these positions were divided into two parts by the dyke known as the Geleide Creek, which flows into the Yser S.W. of Lombartzyde. If the enemy could succeed in driving us back across the Canal and river on the whole of this front, he could render the defence of the sector much easier for him."

The Allied line here, which from Dixmude northward lay on the W. bank of the Yser, crossed to the E. bank S. of Nieuport, thus giving the British a bridge-end about 2 miles long, and from 600 to 1,200 yards deep, from the Plasschendaele Canal S. of Lombartzyde to the sea.

The position here was held by the 1st Division under Major-General Strickland and the 32nd commanded by Major-General Shute.

During the first few days of July the 11th Battalion Diary describes the enemy as "very inactive except for shelling," and on the 4th the British appear to have taken the initiative, the Battalion launching a raid at 11.24 p.m. on the enemy line; the raiding party was made up of Second-Lieutenants Sykes, M.C., Fernie and Pigott and 35 other ranks, and the advance was preceded by the discharge of a Bangalore torpedo. But on the raiding party moving forward it was met by a heavy barrage of bombs from the enemy and being weakened by casualties— Second-Lieutenant Sykes was wounded and 2 men were killed—and the German trench being too strongly held, the party withdrew.

After this the German activity increased, their artillery fire became very much heavier and their aeroplanes were busy; on the night of the 6th–7th Second-Lieutenant W. Bishop was killed by indirect machine-gun fire when on a working party; and when on the 8th the Battalion was again in the front line several casualties had been incurred by the German bombardment.

On the morning of the 10th July the composition of the Battalion was as follows: Lieutenant-Colonel A. C. Girdwood, D.S.O., in command; Captain J. B. Lowthian, M.C., second in command; Lieutenant T. N. Hodgkinson, adjutant; Second-Lieutenant J. Cook-Gray, assistant adjutant; Second-Lieutenant J. Malley-Martin, M.C., intelligence officer; Second-Lieutenant O. Gillespie, bombing officer; Second-Lieutenant J. M. Jamie, M.C., signalling officer; Captain Anderson, R.A.M.C., in medical charge; the Rev. C. Langdon, chaplain.

> "A" Company.—Captain A. E. Greenhill, M.C., Second-Lieutenants H. C. H. Lane, R. E. Pigott and F. E. Brandon.
> "B" Company.—Captain C. H. Walker, M.C., Second-Lieutenants M. Smyth, A. G. Sharp and J. R. McDonald.
> "C" Company.—Captain J. Ross, M.C., Second-Lieutenants S. W. R. Rowsell, J. Cherry and I. Benson.
> "D" Company,—Second-Lieutenants J. B. Albon-Hope, R. M. Martin, W. J. Fernie and J. Malley-Martin, M.C.

Very early on the morning of the 10th July a heavy bombardment of the sector commenced and the first and second lines were heavily shelled, while a strong gale was blowing which prevented any counter-shelling from the British ships off the coast. In this water-logged country trenches were impossible, and the defences were merely breastworks built in the sand. These were very quickly flattened out, all the bridges across the Yser N. of the Geleide Dyke were destroyed, as well as the bridges over the dyke itself.

At 7.40 a.m. the following message was sent from the O.C. 11th Battalion to the 97th Brigade Headquarters : "Casualties last night 3 wounded. This morning 1 killed. Communication broken with both companies in front line. When bombardment ceases will send further information."

At 8 a.m. a message was received from the O.C. "C" Company (Captain Ross), which was holding the first and second lines on the right half of the Battalion front, to the effect that he had been endeavouring to get a message through since 6.5 a.m., that the wires were down and the signallers were using the lamp, but that so far there had been no reply from the British artillery ; that the company had been steadily shelled since before 6 that morning with heavy stuff of all kinds, and that retaliation was asked for. In consequence of the above Second-Lieutenant Cook-Gray was ordered to make his way to the two front-line companies, "C" and "D," in order to ascertain the exact state of affairs and the condition of the line ; at this time the enemy shelling was gradually becoming heavier, and it was not until 10 o'clock that the following message came back to Battalion Headquarters from Second-Lieutenant Cook-Gray :—

"I have reached and examined the second line. On the right the trench is somewhat bashed about, but is not in really bad condition. There has been a continuous bombardment, particularly with heavy T.M.B.'s, since 6 this morning ; 5 casualties are reported at present. Our 18-lb. shells are dropping short. I don't think there is any doubt of that fact this time. P.S.—18-pounders have just smashed in a machine-gun dug-out in our second line."

The bombardment increased in intensity about this period, and all communication with both front and rear was broken and could not be reopened.

An hour later, a message got through from the Brigade asking whether the first and second lines were intact, and for a report on the situation generally and with special reference to Putney and Vauxhall Bridges; but no information could be afforded on these points at the time, though later reports coming in from the companies of the Battalion seemed to show that though the shelling had been and was still very severe the casualties so far were by no means abnormal.

About 1 o'clock the enemy fire seemed for a time to slacken and a hostile aeroplane sailed over flying very low, evidently with the object of ascertaining the extent of the damage caused by the bombardment, while the enemy guns seemed to be employing a new kind of gas shell causing violent sneezing among all who came in contact with its fumes, also affecting the eyes and in some cases causing great sickness. Then the bombardment increased again to its original intensity and at 2.30 p.m. the O.C. "C" Company reported, "The whole three lines are under a deadly barrage. The last word I had from my front line was satisfactory, but that is some time ago. At first lull I shall endeavour to get news of that line. Owing to smoke of shells lamp signal is useless. Mr. Cook-Gray will explain situation fully. My support and reserve platoons have had a rough barrage, but communication is impossible. Can you let me have any fresh orders or news ? "

The O.C. " B " Company's report received much about the same time was that the second and first lines, held with about 15 and 22 men respectively, were knocked almost flat, that Lieutenant Sharp had been hit in two places and several other casualties had been incurred in No. 5 Platoon, and asking whether he was to take the company on to the second or stay in the third line."

The orders from the Brigade were unmistakably clear—" *that the front line must be held whether demolished or not !* "

Again about 3.30 in the afternoon was there a pause or slackening in the shell fire, but this soon grew again and the report received shortly after 4 from " C " Company read very ominously : " Front line very badly smashed now, right half completely wiped out. Second line very badly knocked about ; parts non-existent. Third line receiving particular attention and badly knocked about. Communication trenches, many blown in and always shelled. Approximate casualties 40. The shelling is very heavy throughout and continuous on first, second and third lines and communication trenches. I have 2 officers in the line now and have arranged with Rowsell to signal from first to second line where I have my signaller on the look-out. My signal lamp is still O.K. and I shall keep in touch with your O.P. Cook-Gray and 2 of my runners left for B.H.Q. about 3 p.m. I shall be glad to get any news. The shelling is the ' bally limit ' and I do not like it. We are lying low and I hope all will be well. I hope it will finish soon. I understand that ' D ' is still there as Ridgway has just turned up from there. Martin is slightly wounded."

By about 5 p.m. of two platoons which had been sent forward under Second-Lieutenant Smyth only some 15 men remained ; Lieutenant Rowsell had no more than 30 men with him, including 2 N.C.O.'s, Sergeant Hill and Lance-Corporal Lyons, and both his Lewis guns were out of action ; and half an hour later Smyth's 15 men had been reduced to 4. But still both these young officers, like all the other brave leaders in the front line, deprecated the sending up of reinforcements, as the trenches gave wholly insufficient cover even for the few men who were still holding them.

" At 6.30 p.m. the enemy's infantry attacked, and the isolated garrison of our position N. of the Geleide Creek, consisting of the 1st Battalion Northampton Regiment and 2nd Battalion K.R.R.C. of the 1st Division, were overwhelmed after an obstinate and gallant resistance. . . . On the S. half of the point attacked, opposite Lombartzyde, the enemy also broke into our lines ; but here, where our positions had greater depth and communication across the Yser was still possible, his troops were ejected by our counter-attack." [1]

From 7.30 p.m. onwards the reports coming in from the front showed how far the enemy attack was succeeding, that he was holding Nose Trench, with men of the 11th Battalion The Border Regiment in Nose Support, where, however, there were but 2 officers and 5 men ; later that the Germans had gained a footing in the second and in part of the third line ; and now orders were issued for every available rifle

[1] Despatch of 25th December, 1917.

to be used for defence while preparations were made for local and general counter-attacks. These went on all through the night and by early morning of the 11th the enemy had been finally driven back, and then at 4 a.m. the Battalion was relieved and fell back to the support dug-outs and later to Coxyde and Ghyvelde, having incurred casualties estimated at 8 officers and 350 non-commissioned officers and men.

The Third Battle of Ypres, which was now about to commence, was the final portion of a scheme of an offensive in Flanders which had been conceived during the previous winter. The preparations needed for its carrying out had been interfered with in various ways, and the actual attack had been postponed until very much later in the year than had been intended when the plan had originally been drawn up. The actual date for the opening of the attack had at least twice been changed ; arranged in the first instance for the 25th, it was postponed for three days, but subsequently a succession of days of bad visibility, combined with the difficulties experienced by our Allies in getting their guns into position in their new area, caused a further postponement until the 31st July, though a number of raids and certain preliminary operations in connection with the general attack took place during the week immediately preceding that date.

Third Battle of Ypres.

"The front of the Allied attack extended from the River Lys opposite Deulemont northwards to beyond Steenstraate, a distance of over 15 miles, but the main blow was to be delivered by the Fifth Army on a front of about $7\frac{1}{2}$ miles, from the Zillebeke–Zandvoorde Road to Boesinghe inclusive. Covering the right of the Fifth Army, the task of the Second was to advance a short distance only. Its principal object at this stage was to increase the area threatened by the attack and so force the enemy to distribute the fire of his artillery. On the left of the Fifth Army the First French Army was to advance its right in close touch with the British forces and secure them from counter-attack from the N. . . . The plan of attack on the Fifth Army front was to advance in a series of bounds, with which the right of the First French Army was to keep step. . . . It was hoped that in the first attack our troops would succeed in establishing themselves on the crest of the high ground E. of Ypres, on which a strong flank could be formed for subsequent operations, and would also secure the crossings of the Steenbeek." [1]

Four Army Corps had been placed at the disposal of the G.O.C. Fifth Army, and their composition and order from S. to N. were as follows :—

IInd Corps.—General Jacob :
    24th, 30th, 18th (one brigade of), and 8th Divisions.
XIXth Corps.—General Watts :
    15th and 55th Divisions.
XVIIIth Corps.—General Maxse :
    39th and 51st Divisions.
XIVth Corps.—General Lord Cavan :
    38th and Guards Divisions.

[1] Despatch of 25th December, 1917.

Immediately to the S. of General Jacob's IInd Corps was the Xth, General Morland's, of General Plumer's Second Army, and containing the 21st, 41st and 47th Divisions ; but as the battle progressed there were many changes in the above dispositions, as some of the divisions were drawn out of the line to rest and refit while others came up and took their places.

No fewer than six out of the seven battalions of The Border Regiment now in France and Flanders appear to have taken part, at different times and to a less or greater extent, in the operations which endured from the 31st July to the 10th November and which are known as the Third Battle of Ypres ; these were the 1st 2nd, 5th, 6th, 7th and 8th Battalions, and it may on the whole be best to deal with these in order of seniority, for though some may have entered the battle at a somewhat earlier date than did others, the difference of time is after all not a matter of very great moment.

The 1st Border Regiment had spent the greater part of May and June at Candas, described in the diary as a " comfortable, clean little village, beautifully situated,"

1st Battalion. but on the 26th of June it entrained at Doullens and railed to Proven, from where the Battalion moved by bus and by march route to support trenches in the bank of the Yser Canal. Here it almost at once went into the front line and active patrolling was commenced, a service accompanied by the usual casualties. On the 1st July Second-Lieutenant D. Macleod, M.C., was killed on this duty and 3 men were wounded ; young Macleod's body could not at the time be brought in although its whereabouts was known, owing to the activity of the German snipers, but on the 5th Private Williamson succeeded in recovering it.

On the 7th the Battalion was out of the line, training at Crombeke, when His Majesty the King, accompanied by H.R.H. the Prince of Wales, motored through the camp.

During the greater part of July the 1st Battalion was at Proven again, moving up on the 31st nearer to the front line and being employed on working parties making roads in the Guards Division area, from Clarges Street to the Canal at Boesinghe and then across the Canal to Artillery Wood : during this period C.S.M. Randolph and 8 other ranks were killed, Captain A. V. H. Wood and 13 non-commissioned officers and men were wounded, while 3 men were missing. At this time the weather was appalling; it poured with rain incessantly, but all the same, the field guns were all got safely across the Canal ready to continue the advance.

" The 2nd August," says the diary, " was another fearfully wet day, fighting practically impossible. St. Julien was lost during the night and retaken this morning."

When on the 12th August the Battalion moved up to the front line it came under very heavy shelling and within the next twenty-four hours had over 50 casualties, including 2 officers, Second-Lieutenant G. F. Hamlett being killed and Captain A. Fulton wounded ; then on the night of the 15th the companies began to move off at intervals to the place of assembly E. of the Steenbeek in preparation for the second phase of the Third Battle of Ypres, marching from bivouacs at Bluet

Farm via Bridge Street, Saules Farm, Captain's Farm, Signal Farm, the Battalion Headquarters being established at the last-named place.

For the projected attack the 87th and 88th Brigades of the 29th Division, now in the XIVth Corps, formed the front line, the 86th Brigade being in support, while on the right of the 29th Division was the 20th, these two forming the front of the XIVth Corps.

The 1st Battalion The Border Regiment was formed up E. of the Steenbeek in rear of the 1st Battalion K.O.S.B.'s on a two-company frontage, " B " and " D " Companies in the front line forming the first waves and " A " and " C " in support forming the second two waves.

The companies were this day commanded and officered as under :—

" A," Captain W. F. H. Chambers and Second-Lieutenant M. C. Nicholson.

" B," Captain J. W. Ewbank, M.C., and Second-Lieutenants H. R. C. Lucas and W. D. C. Thompson.

" C," Captain R. E. S. Johnson and Second-Lieutenants J. L. P. Gamon, W. S. M. Ruxton and Watson.

" D," Captain W. B. Butler and Second-Lieutenants A. J. F. Danielli and C. Helm.

During the approach march the Battalion was shelled intermittently, but owing, no doubt, to the gas shells which the British guns were sending over in a continuous stream, the Germans seemed unable to put down their usual heavy barrage. Just before the attack commenced Captain Butler was slightly wounded, but after being treated at the aid-post returned to his company, while Second-Lieutenant Danielli was blown up by a shell and rendered unconscious, but recovering consciousness on the way down he got off his stretcher and rejoined his company just in time to lead his men !

The British barrage fell with great precision and the advance began, the enemy putting down his barrage on the lines Captain's Farm–Fourche Farm and Signal Farm–Ruisseau Farm, but nothing beyond an occasional shell on the line of the Steenbeek.

Briefly stated, the result of the attack by the 29th Division was that, starting from the general line of the Steenbeek, Passerelles Farm was carried as was also Martin's Mill on the right, then crossing the abandoned railway line, the village of Wijdendrift was reached and a line established well to the N.E. of that place.

The first message sent back from the front and received at 6.40 came from Passerelles Farm and stated that the so-called " Blue Line " had been taken, but less than an hour later it was reported that the advance was held up on the Blue Line by machine-gun fire, and later still a message from Captain Ewbank confirmed this, saying that the K.O.S.B.'s were stopped by machine-gun fire from a " pill-box " near what appeared to be Montmirail Farm.

The Stokes mortar, which had been sent forward to Passerelles Farm on the Blue Line being reached, was accordingly brought up to engage this obstacle.

Reassuring news from all the advanced companies was now received that the objectives had been reached, that the advance was continuing and that many captures in men and machine guns had been made, and Battalion Headquarters was now moved forward to Wijdendrift from Signal Farm.   The work of consolidation went on smoothly all the morning, and so far the casualties had been light, though considerable sniping was kept up by the enemy from the other side of the Broembeek. The enemy's guns were also tolerably active and their fire was at times concentrated on Wijdendrift itself, but their observers did not seem able to locate the Battalion's front line, though German aeroplanes were coming over all the morning, flying low and firing on the trenches with machine guns.

At 1 p.m. a report came from O.C. " B " Company of the Battalion that 300–400 of the enemy could be seen massing in Ney Wood, and our guns were turned on with excellent effect, scattering the enemy, while further loss was inflicted upon them by the rifle fire of the front line garrisons, many of the men whose rifles were clogged with mud using captured rifles and ammunition.

During the late afternoon patrols were sent out and reconnoitred the line of the Broembeek and reported on its crossings ; no enemy was found W. of the stream, but the patrols were fired upon by Germans who appeared to be in occupation of a shell-hole line about 200 yards E. of the stream.

The enemy's activity now for a space died down, and the Battalion was relieved during the night of the 16th and early morning of the 17th and fell back to a camp in the neighbourhood of Elverdinghe.

The advance had been a very difficult one owing to the swampy nature of the ground, and was carried out diagonally across the front from Cannes Farm to the Broembeek. Touch and direction were admirably kept throughout and the endurance displayed by all ranks was beyond all praise, as the " going " was in an appalling state, and during the previous three days the Battalion had held the firing line for forty-eight hours and carried out two difficult reliefs under shell fire.

The casualties for the week ending on the 17th August amounted to : killed, 1 officer (Second-Lieutenant G. F. Hamlett) and 25 other ranks ; wounded, 3 officers (Captain A. Fulton, Second-Lieutenants J. B. Trotter and M. C. Nicholson) and 105 other ranks, while Second-Lieutenant H. T. Thompson and 22 non-commissioned officers and men were missing.

On the 24th the Battalion was up again in the line opposite Cannes Farm, special patrols being sent out to explore the passages of the Broembeek with a view to the establishing of posts on the far side ; some prisoners were taken by the Battalion patrols, one a Feldwebel of the Prussian Guard being captured by Private Corran of " C " Company, who killed 3 and wounded 1 of an enemy patrol of 5 men with his Lewis gun.

The 1st Battalion now proceeded for several weeks to a rest area, and when towards the middle of November it was again called upon to take part in the major operations which marked the close of this year on the Western Front, it had been for some time past in a training area about Bailleulmont.

On coming out of the Arras Battle in May the 2nd Battalion of The Border Regiment remained for some time near Albainzeville, moving in June to near

2nd Battalion. Mory ; in this month 6 officers joined but only 41 other ranks ; the officers were Second-Lieutenants F. Argles, F. Mahoney, G. W. B. Shepherd, H. A. Hislop, H. Haynes and W. S. Warren. In August the Battalion was very fortunate in the number of drafts which came out from home or up from the base, these amounting to no fewer than 390. At the end of this month the 2nd Battalion marched to Saulty and there entrained for Proven, and on arrival here proceeded by march route to a camp near Linde Goed Farm.

At the beginning of September an historical event took place ; on the 1st the Battalion marched to Oudezeele, arriving there next day, and later lorries came in bearing representatives of all ranks of the 1st Battalion, this being the first occasion on which in all their long association the two Battalions of The Border Regiment had met.

At the beginning of October the 2nd Battalion, after several minor moves, found itself in camp near Dickebusch, and from here on the 2nd it marched to dug-outs on the W. side of Zillebeke Lake, remaining there until 10.30 p.m., when it moved up to the place of assembly in order to take its share in the Third Battle of Ypres which had now been in progress for the greater part of three months.

The attack was now to be made against the main line of the ridge E. of Zonne-beke, the front of the main attack extending from the Menin Road to the Ypres–Staden Railway, and was carried out by six corps, containing twelve divisions, of the Second and Fourth Armies. These divisions taken in order from S. to N. were the 37th of the IXth Corps, the 5th, 21st and 7th of the Xth, the four divisions of the two Anzac Corps, the 48th and 11th of the XVIIIth and the 4th and 29th of the XIVth. The three divisions of General Morland's Xth Corps had in front of them the villages of Polderhoek, Reutel and Noordhemhoek. In the advance by the 7th Division the front line was formed by the 20th and 91st Brigades on the left and right respectively.

The war diary states that the rôle of the 2nd Battalion The Border Regiment was to " leap-frog " the 8th Devons on the Red Line, to take the portions of the Blue Line indicated on the map, and then, covered by the front companies, to " mop up " the ground between the two lines. " A " and " B " Companies were the attacking companies, " C " the moppers-up, while " D " was in reserve.

By 3 a.m. on the 4th October the Battalion was in position on the tape, while the enemy, whose suspicions appear to have been aroused, or, as appears more probable, was himself intending an attack, rained shells on the area occupied by the Battalion, which then closed up immediately in rear of the 8th Devons who were formed up some 200 yards in front. The ground to be advanced over was little better than a bog, while there was a belt of barbed wire on the further side of it.

Zero hour was at 6 a.m. when the Battalion went forward with the 2nd Gordons and 22nd Manchesters on the flanks, and the intention was that, having assumed normal formation, the battalions attacking the second objective should halt 400 yards inside No Man's Land. This plan, however, miscarried, for the battalions became completely mixed up, and the whole line, composed of all ranks of four battalions—Gordons, Devons, Manchesters and Border Regiment—went forward to the first objective, as it was found hopeless to try and withdraw troops from the advancing line.

On reaching the first objective, officers withdrew men of the Battalion, reorganized them into platoons and then led them forward again close in rear of the barrage ; this last was so accurate and the line so well defined that the men got up to it quite comfortably. At 9.40 the final objective was reported taken and consolidation in progress, and the Battalion at this time held the whole brigade frontage except for a space of 100 yards on the right where was the Manchester Battalion, and this very extended frontage made consolidation in depth rather difficult. The line here was practically divided into three subsectors, commanded from left to right by Second-Lieutenants Little, Abrams and Argles.

During the night of the 4th–5th reorganization continued, but when day broke the enemy got the range of the British front line and his snipers became very active, so that inter-company communication became practically impossible.

The Battalion remained on in the line until the night of the 7th–8th October, and then moved back to dug-outs near Zillebeke Lake and from there on the 10th to camp in the Westoutre area. On the 24th, however, the 2nd Border Regiment was up in the front line again in the area S. of the Menin Road opposite Lewis House ; and from here was ordered on the 26th to attack and hold a line in part of the village of Gheluvelt known as the Red Line, the attack being included in an operation to be carried out by the 20th Infantry Brigade, the 8th Devons and the 2nd Queens attacking simultaneously on the left and right respectively of the 2nd Border Regiment ; while on the objective being taken the 2nd Gordons were to leap-frog and establish a Blue Line parallel to the Red Line and about 500 yards in advance of it, the attack being carried out under a creeping barrage timed to start at 5.40 a.m., and to reach the objective at 6.36.

The 2nd Battalion advanced in normal formation, " C " Company on the right, " D " on the left, " B " Company moppers up, while " A " was in support, the Battalion forming up on two parallel tapes at 60 yards distance.

At 5.40 a.m. the advance commenced over very marshy ground through which the attackers were only just able to move, while " C " Company's line of advance took them into the valley where the men got stuck in the mud up to their waists, and were almost entirely wiped out by the machine-gun fire which opened from Lewis House on the right and from the " pepper boxes " on the left as soon as the barrage opened ; here Captain Dempster was killed and Second-Lieutenant Stephen wounded. " D " Company on the left, finding advance to their immediate front impossible owing to the state of the ground, moved over towards the Menin Road. Practically the whole of this company fell in an attempt to take some enemy pepper boxes, and what was left of them reformed in a crater near the road. The rear platoons of " B " Company, which had also moved to the left, were the next to come up against the pepper boxes with the same result as the others.

An attack was then attempted from the crater but met with no better success, there being many casualties in " B " and " D " Companies, and Captain Moore and Second-Lieutenant Inkpen were killed. " A " Company of the Battalion then came up and made an attack upon the same posts, and one of them was taken and a machine gun captured, but the remaining three pepper boxes, covered by fire from Lewis House, defied all attempts at their capture. Captain Little now collected what remained of " B " and " D " Companies and a few men of the Devon Regiment, and advanced along the line of the road, leaving the survivors of " A " to attempt to capture the pepper boxes or at least to keep down the fire from them, and, leading his party forward, he reached to withn 150 yards of Gheluvelt and then occupied a line of shell holes. Of the battalions on the flanks of the 2nd Border Regiment, the Devons on the left seemed to have got well forward, while on the right the 2nd Queens had so far failed to capture Lewis House.

By 10 a.m. it was clearly apparent that the objective could not be reached with the small and diminishing number of men left ; on the right the Queens were establishing a line on the original tape ; on the left the situation of the Devons was not clear, but they appeared to be in occupation of the railway. There were, however, many and serious gaps in the general brigade line, and it was therefore decided to collect as many of The Border Regiment as possible and put out posts along the original line to connect up between the defensive flank and the right. By this time, however, only some 40 men were left of the attacking companies, the remainder being either killed, wounded or missing, or mingled with the Devons.

At 11.15 p.m. on the 26th the Battalion was relieved and was sent at first to tent shelters near Zillebeke Lake, moving later by motor transport to billets between Blarringhem and Renescure, where reorganization was proceeded with.

The month of October had been one of very heavy losses to the 2nd Battalion, the majority of these being incurred between the 4th and 7th and on the 26th ; they amounted to 7 officers and 46 other ranks killed, 14 officers and 370 non-commissioned officers and men wounded, while 2 officers and 144 other ranks were missing. The officers killed were : Captains E. R. Chetham-Strode, D. B. Dempster, J. Moore and R. Abrams, Second-Lieutenants F. Mahoney, M.C., W. Inkpen, N. C. Seymour-Isaacs ; wounded : Captains A. Wright, E. W. Green and G. W. O'Brien, Lieutenant G. E. Coningham, Second-Lieutenants D. D. Low, J. R. Bartlett, M.C., E. Hallam, S. T. Stevens, W. Carr, W. A. Hislop, J. W. Harrison, W. A. Herbert, W. G. Grahame and J. A. Stephen ; while missing were Second-Lieutenants J. Harding and R. Paynter.

We left the 5th Battalion at the end of June of this year in the forward area near Wancourt Tower, but on the 1st July it was moved to a camp in the neighbour-hood of Boisleux-au-Mont, where on the 14th the Battalion suffered a grievous loss in the sudden death from heart failure of Lieutenant-Colonel J. R. Hedley, D.S.O., who had commanded since the 11th November, 1915.

5th Battalion.

On the 1st August the 5th Border Regiment was in camp near Henin, and on the 8th a very successful raid was carried out by volunteers from " C " and " D " Companies ; the raid was planned by Major Crouch and was executed by Captain J. L. Henderson, Second-Lieutenants J. C. Laidlaw and S. Hall. The operation was unsuccessful as regards captures for the reason that the enemy fled, and the party returned, after bombing the enemy dug-outs, having suffered one casualty, but the effect as regards the German *morale* was undoubtedly good.

The 50th Division was now in the VIth Corps and during the remainder of August the Battalion was in turn in divisional reserve at Mercatel, in the trenches about Guémappe, and in brigade reserve at Neuville Vitasse. During the month of September a draft, 196 strong, joined the Battalion, of which later Major W. B. Little, D.S.O., M.C., assumed command.

Between the 3rd and 12th October the 50th Division, on relief by the 51st, left the VIth Corps, and on the 16th the Battalion marched to Bapaume and there took the train for Esquelbecq, marching from there to billets near Eringhem; leaving here once more by rail and road the 5th Border Regiment proceeded via Rubrouck and Wormhoudt to Proven, and on the 22nd marched thence to Swindon Camp in Divisional Reserve to support an attack to be carried out on the 26th by the 149th Brigade, but in the operations which ensued the Battalion does not appear to have been employed. None the less the casualties this month were by no means negligible, 4 officers being killed: Captains J. Thomson, by bomb from enemy aircraft, J. C. Laidlaw and E. J. Pursglove, and Second-Lieutenant M. A. Burke; while two officers and 18 non-commissioned officers and men were wounded; the wounded officers were Captain J. L. Henderson and Second-Lieutenant C. H. Corbett.

At the end of October the Battalion was in camp near Watten where the following officers joined for duty: Second-Lieutenants R. A. Barrowman, E. R. Frew, H. J. Martin, W. D. Chisholme, J. S. Turnbull and M. R. McClennan, with Second-Lieutenants W. D. Brown, A. G. Croll, T. M. Ellis, A. S. Robertson, and F. Robertson, of the Durham Light Infantry, and Second-Lieutenant C. H. Bickley, of the West Riding Regiment.

During the greater part of July the 6th Battalion The Border Regiment was in the neighbourhood of Poperinghe, suffering many casualties when up in the front **6th Battalion.** and doing much good work when nominally "at rest" in rear. On the 26th July Lieutenant-Colonel D. Mathers left the Battalion owing to ill-health, handing over command to Major A. E. Scothern. Then on the 30th the 6th Border Regiment marched through Poperinghe to a camp near St. Jean-ter-Biezen, having lost during the month 1 officer and 21 other ranks killed, 1 officer and 43 men wounded, while 1 officer and 78 non-commissioned officers and men had been gassed. To replace this wastage a draft of 1 officer and 31 other ranks joined from the Base.

After a week at this camp there were two moves, the Battalion marching on the 8th to Dirty Bucket Camp and on the 15th to Siege Camp, where preparations were at once put in hand for going into action, and early next morning the companies marched to the Canal Bank by platoons at 100 yards interval, rested here for half an hour and then moved on to reserve trenches near St. Julien, Battalion Headquarters being established at Lancashire Farm. From these trenches at 6.15 that evening "C" and "D" Companies went further forward to a line 200 yards W. of François Farm, while some three hours later Headquarters and the remaining two companies came up nearer the front line as support and Headquarters occupied Goumier Farm.

On the 19th the 6th Border Regiment relieved the 9th Sherwood Foresters, and that night "C" and "D" Companies were directed to advance their line 300 yards in connection with certain operations which were to be undertaken on the right on the 22nd.

The barrage came down at 4.45 on the morning of this day, and on its lifting rather less than an hour later "C" and "D" Companies of the Battalion moved their front posts forward in rear of the barrage towards the objective. No enemy infantry was met, though the shell and machine-gun fire was heavy, but the objective was reached and consolidation began and by 7.45 all ranks were under very tolerable cover. During this advance Second-Lieutenant Hogg showed great gallantry and devotion to duty; he was commanding the right flank of his company and though wounded three times, once severely in the abdomen, refused to leave his men and remained with them till nightfall. Owing to the heavy shelling all telephonic communication was cut, but the Battalion runners did splendid work throughout. During the 23rd many patrols went out to try and discover the enemy dispositions.

During the next few days the Battalion spent most of the time up in the front, and when on the 29th it went back for rest to Brake Camp it had suffered some 75 casualties, 16 men being killed, 2 officers and 53 other ranks were wounded, 3 men died of wounds and 1 man was missing: against these losses must be set reinforcements amounting to 5 officers and 153 other ranks which came out this month.

During the whole of September the Battalion was training at Brake and Clyde Camps and in the neighbourhood of Houtkerque, where Second-Lieutenants R. G. Bird, A. B. Paterson and J. G. Jameson and 100 other ranks joined for duty.

On the 2nd October the 6th Border Regiment returned to Siege Camp and marched thence next day to dug-outs at Canal Bank preparatory to again going into action. Here at 1 a.m. on the 4th a hot meal was served out and then Battalion Headquarters, followed, at 50 yards intervals between platoons, by the four companies, moved forward towards the line. Headquarters occupied Varna Farm, while " A " and " B " Companies moved up and dug in between the Steenbeek and the Langemarck–Winnipeg Road, " C " and " D " digging in in the area about Varna Farm; all were in position and well under cover by 5 a.m. The attack opened at 6, the duty of the 6th Battalion The Border Regiment being to support the other battalions of the Brigade and re-counter any successful enemy counter-attack; it was *not* to be used to reinforce.

At 7 a.m. " A " and " B " Companies moved to the front and dug in 150 yards in front of Pheasant Farm, while half an hour later the remainder of the Battalion also advanced, Headquarters to Snipe House, the other two companies entrenching themselves in rear of Pheasant Farm, which was heavily shelled all the morning, many casualties being incurred. At night on the 5th the Battalion took over the whole Brigade front, and during the 6th and 7th much useful patrol work was done, Second-Lieutenants Bell and Knight, Corporal Douthwaite and Private Black specially distinguishing themselves.

Relieved on the night of the 7th–8th the Battalion thereafter had many moves —to Siege Camp, Watten, Bayenghem, Lillers, Nedon and Houchin-les-Bains, and then at the end of October moved by Grenay to Noeux-les-Mines, where it was accommodated in hutments; during October 37 were killed, 136 wounded, while 1 man was missing.

During the months of June and July the 7th Battalion The Border Regiment was in the St. Nicholas Camp area not far from Arras, doing much good work behind the line and when up in the front taking part in many raids on the German trenches ; at this time the Battalion seems to have become greatly reduced in strength despite the fact that the casualties during this period were not heavy ; on the 23rd July there were only 13 officers and 335 other ranks available for duty, although 7 officers had joined during the previous month—Captain E. P. B. Morrall and Second-Lieutenants Swan, Hirst, Jarvis, Hudson and Good, with Lieutenant Green of the Cumberland and Westmorland Yeomanry. In the last days of July the small officer corps of the 7th Battalion was further depleted by the loss of two senior officers, Captain Morrall being killed and Captain H. J. H. Hamilton mortally wounded.

7th Battalion.

August and September went by in much the same manner and the Battalion occupied the same positions when in the line or when withdrawn, but on the 22nd of this last month a considerable change was made in the composition of the 7th Battalion The Border Regiment, when it was announced that for the future it was to be known as the 7th (Westmorland and Cumberland Yeomanry) Battalion The Border Regiment, and about this date two drafts of 239 and 103 other ranks, with 19 officers, joined from the 1st/1st Westmorland and Cumberland Yeomanry.

On the 24th the Battalion left the neighbourhood of Arras and marched to Ivergny.

The Battalion had a change of commanding officers towards the end of this month, Lieutenant-Colonel W. N. S. Alexander, D.S.O., proceeding to the United Kingdom and Major W. E. W. Elkington, 1st Battalion Lincolnshire Regiment, assuming temporary command. About the same time a further Yeomanry reinforcement joined, Second-Lieutenant D. C. Day and 86 other ranks.

On the 10th October the Battalion was sent by train to Elverdinghe and marched thence to dug-outs at the Yser Canal, and here on the afternoon of the 11th orders were received that an attack was to be made on the Green and Red Lines on the following morning, the Battalion being detailed as a supporting and counter-attacking battalion. Zero hour was fixed at 5.25 a.m. and it was arranged that the Battalion should move forward as close up to the barrage as possible, " A," " B " and " C " Companies forming up 50 yards in rear of the respective supporting companies of the battalions they were themselves supporting, while " D " advanced and took the place of " B " Company.

The attack commenced at the appointed hour and proceeded " according to plan " as far as the Blue Line, when at 6.40 a message came back from Captain Hayes commanding " B " Company that a gap existed between the right of the Foresters and the left of the 4th Division, and that he had filled this with two platoons with two others in close support ; and on learning of this " D " Company was sent up to take the place of " B " on the Blue Line, about 200 yards N.E. of Senegal Farm, while " A " established itself at Taube Farm after assisting the Lincoln Regiment to clear it of the enemy, of whom some 130 were here captured. " C " on the left after reaching the Blue Line took up a line running from the railway, 200 yards from where it cuts the Poelcapelle–Les Cinq Chemins road to within 150 yards E. of the Brickfield ; but this company was later moved and joined " A " at Taube Farm.

At 10.30 p.m. on the 13th half " A " Company was ordered to assist the 7th Lincolns in clearing Aden House and in filling a gap between the 8th South Staffords and the Guards Division on the left of the Brigade front ; but this enterprise failed by reason of the casualties incurred while moving to the attack and also by reason of the very exhausted state of the men.

The Battalion was relieved on the night of the 13th–14th and withdrawn to Elverdinghe, whence it was sent to Poodle Camp in the Proven area.

The end of the month found the 7th Border Regiment at Persia Camp, where the Brigade was for a short time attached to the 35th Division.

During October the casualties were not inconsiderable : 34 men had been killed or had died of wounds, 3 officers (Captain W. F. Gaddum, Second-Lieutenants F. MacWilliam and W. A. R. Longstaff) and 102 other ranks were wounded, while 1 man was missing.

We left the 8th Battalion resting with the 25th Division about Bomy after taking part in the Ypres offensive of July, but during the first week in July the
8th Battalion. Division, less the 74th Brigade which remained for a further fortnight in the training area, proceeded by march and bus to Ypres to the forward area of the IInd Corps, and here for some days the 25th Division alternated with the 8th in taking the duty in the front line. Preparations for an attack on a large scale had been here going forward for some time, but it was not actually until 3.50 a.m. on the 31st July that the Fifth Army delivered its assault on the German main-line defences with the IInd, XIXth, XIVth and XVIIIth Corps, while on the right and left respectively of the Fifth Army the Xth Corps of the Second Army and the First French Army made subsidiary attacks. The front of the Fifth Army attack extended from the Zillebeke–Zandvoorde Road to Boesinghe inclusive, a distance of some $7\frac{1}{2}$ miles ; and the IInd Corps attacked with the 24th, 30th and 8th Divisions, with the 18th in support in the centre and the 25th on the left in Corps Reserve.

The two brigades present of the 25th Division moved up from their place of assembly at the Belgian Château at 8.30 a.m. on the 31st July and were held in readiness about 2,000 yards in rear of the attacking troops, it having been intended that they should pass through the 8th Division and carry on the advance ; but as the attack was unexpectedly held up on the right the 25th Division was not required to act, but none the less the 8th Battalion suffered a few casualties, Lieutenant King and 9 other ranks being wounded.

On the 1st August the 25th Division was holding Westhoek Ridge and Bellewaard Ridge, the 74th Brigade in the front line, the 75th in support at Ypres and the 7th in reserve W. of Ypres. The weather was terribly wet and cold and the men suffered a good deal from exposure in the trenches. The companies of the Battalion were now commanded as follows : " A " Company, Captain Smith ; " B," Lieutenant Birnie, M.C. ; " C," Captain King and " D " Company, Captain Duggan.

The Battalion was not now employed for some time in any offensive operations, but was exposed to much shelling and lost two promising young officers, Second-Lieutenant W. F. J. Lait being killed on the 3rd August, while Second-Lieutenant R. Smith died of wounds received on the 9th.

On the 17th and following days the 25th Division was relieved in the front line and withdrew to the Steenwoorde and Eecke area, but on the 1st September the Division moved up again to Ypres and took over on the 2nd the portions of the front comprising Westhoek Ridge and the trenches in front of Glencorse Wood and Stirling Castle. The divisional front was now held by two brigades with one in support, and much work was done in consolidation and improvement of the existing defences until, on the 9th September, the 47th finally relieved the 25th Division, which then moved to the First Army area in the neighbourhood of Béthune, where some three weeks were spent in reorganization and training.

At the beginning of October, however, the artillery of the Division and the 75th Infantry Brigade were lent for a few days to the 11th Division for an offensive intended to take place to the S.W. of Lens, but the proposed arrangements were cancelled, and on the 4th October the 25th Division took over the Givenchy Sector in the XIth Corps area with Divisional Headquarters at Locon, 2½ miles N. of Béthune, the line held being some 8,000 yards in length with the La Bassée Canal running almost through the centre of the 75th Brigade Sector. Givenchy itself was now about a mile inside the British line. Here the Division remained for some time, with a Portuguese division on the left, and for many weeks Portuguese battalions were attached for instruction to the different brigades of the 25th Division. When on the 10th November the long-drawn-out Third Battle of Ypres came officially to an end, the 8th Battalion The Border Regiment was at La Préol in the La Bassée Canal Sector.

So ended, so far as concerns the battalions of The Border Regiment, the Third Battle of Ypres; all that was hoped of it had not been achieved, due mainly to the continuance of very unfavourable weather; but our new armies had proved themselves, the enemy's *morale* had suffered enormously and we had taken, since the end of July, over 24,000 prisoners and nearly 1,200 guns of varying calibres.

CHAPTER X

1917

THE IST AND 7TH BATTALIONS IN THE BATTLE OF CAMBRAI.

THE 2ND BATTALION IN ITALY.

THE 9TH BATTALION IN SALONIKA.

WHILE the Allied Armies operating upon the Western Front had been engaged in obtaining certain solid successes against the common enemy, victory had been gained against the Turk both in Palestine and Mesopotamia, but elsewhere there were happenings which exerted a very great and an unfortunate influence on the course of the great struggle.

In March, 1917, a revolution broke out in Russia, the Czar abdicated, and although at first the Russian armies continued their offensive, particularly in Galicia, the new Government decided upon peace during the last week of October. Negotiations were at once opened for a cessation of hostilities, and the preliminaries of peace were actually signed on the 5th December, Roumania being practically forced to follow suit a few days later. Then at the end of October treasonable propaganda was found to have undermined the *morale* of the Italian Army, and the troops holding the centre of the line suddenly collapsed, the enemy pushed through the gap, capturing 200,000 men and 2,000 guns, and drove the Italians from the positions on the Isonzo and Tagliamento, until a stand was at last made on the line of the Piave. Despite the fact that the coming of the peace between Russia and the Central Powers at once set many divisions free to reinforce the German line in the West, reinforcements in British and French troops were sent to Italy so soon as the collapse there commenced, and by mid-winter two French and two English Army corps had arrived at or near the line of the Piave.

The British reinforcements were the XIIIth and XIVth Corps, forming an army under General Plumer, and containing the 5th, 7th, 23rd, 41st and 48th Divisions.

Against these unfortunate happenings may, however, be set one piece of good fortune for the Allies; Germany's announced intention of prosecuting unrestricted submarine warfare brought the United States into the field against her; in April America declared war against Germany and by the end of October of this year the vanguard of her army was actually in action, though naturally some considerable time had to elapse before her full strength could make itself felt.

The object of the Cambrai operations, which brought the fighting in 1917 to a close on the Western Front, was "to gain a local success by a sudden attack at a point where the enemy did not expect it." The many and repeated attacks in Flanders made by the Allies in the spring, summer and autumn of this year had produced here and there certain "weakened sectors." The Cambrai front was one of these, the ground was very suitable for the employment of tanks and the necessary preparations for an attack could easily be concealed. It was hoped as a result of such an attack to secure Bourlon to the N., while establishing a good flank position to the E. in the direction of Cambrai, and so be well placed to exploit the situation locally between Bourlon and the Sensée River and to the N.W.

The execution of the proposed operations was entrusted to General Sir Julian Byng. The enemy defences on this front comprised three main systems of resistance; the first, part of the Hindenburg Line proper, "ran in a general N.W. direction for a distance of 6 miles from the Scheldt Canal at Banteux to Havrincourt. There it turned abruptly N. along the line of the Canal du Nord for a distance of 4 miles to Moeuvres, thus forming a pronounced salient in the German front. In advance of the Hindenburg Line the enemy had constructed a series of strong forward positions, including La Vacquerie and the N.E. corner of Havrincourt Wood. Behind it, and at distances respectively varying from a little less to rather more than a mile, and from $3\frac{1}{2}$ to $4\frac{1}{2}$ miles, lay the second and third main German systems, known as the Hindenburg Reserve Line, and the Beaurevoir, Masnières and Marquion Lines." [1]

The two Battalions of The Border Regiment which gained for the Regiment the battle honour of "Cambrai," for the operations which commenced on the **Battle of Cambrai.** 20th November, 1917, and nominally came to an end on the 12th December, marking the close of all the hard and continuous fighting of this year, were the First and Seventh.

After withdrawal from the Ypres Battle the 1st Battalion spent some time in the training area about Bailleulmont, where Captain Sutcliffe, M.C., was **1st Battalion.** temporarily in command, but on the 16th November the Battalion left Bailleulmont, marched to Boisleux-au-Mont and there entrained for Peronne; arriving here about 4 p.m., it proceeded thence by road to Nissen huts at Haut Allaines, where all turned in at dawn on the 17th. At 6 o'clock on the following evening the 1st Battalion moved into tents in Dessart Wood, arriving there—"everyone very tired"—at 1 on the morning of the 18th, and resting all through the following day while battle stores were issued and all arrangements were made in anticipation of the approaching action.

In accordance with orders received, the Battalion left Dessart Wood very early on the 20th for the concentration area about Borderer Ridge, Gouzeaucourt, where some two hours later it was formed up in close column of companies facing N., and all then lay down to wait for zero hour—fixed for 6.20 a.m. The night, though fine, was bitterly cold and the troops obtained but little sleep.

For the forthcoming operations four corps had been placed at General Byng's disposal; these, reckoned from right to left or S. to N., were the VIIth,

_____
[1] Despatch of the 20th February, 1918.

IIIrd, IVth and VIth. The last-named, containing the 3rd and 16th Divisions, was to deliver a subsidiary attack in the neighbourhood of Bullecourt, while the remaining divisions to be employed were, on the 20th November, disposed as follows from S. to N.—12th, 20th, 29th; opposite Masnières—6th, 51st, 62nd and 36th.

At the hour appointed the British barrage fell with a crash, and at 7 a.m. the Battalion moved forward in rear of the K.O.S.B.'s to the "jumping-off place" on the W. of the Gouzeaucourt–Marcoing Railway—a sunken road running N. from the N. outskirts of Villerspluich, arriving there about 8 a.m. and waiting for further orders, which did not, however, arrive until 10.5 on news being received that the Hindenburg Support Line had fallen. During this halt several casualties were incurred by the Battalion, chiefly in the S. portion of the line and mainly from shrapnel; here Captain J. C. Clarke, M.C., the medical officer, was wounded, but he refused to go to hospital until his relief arrived.

The advance now commenced in diamond formation of companies, "A" Company the leading point under Captain Chambers, M.C., "B" the right flank company under Second-Lieutenant Johnston, D.C.M., "C" left flank company under Captain Johnson, and the rear point, Battalion Headquarters, under Lieutenant-Colonel Ellis, D.S.O., and "D" Company under Captain Butler, M.C., an interval of about 400 yards being maintained between the Battalion and the K.O.S.B.'s in front.

The first and second objectives were reached and passed, the enemy guns being silent and no infantry opposition being met; then on reaching the out-skirts of Marcoing a brief halt was made to give time for the Battalion in front to get into the place—it was followed about noon by the 1st Border Regiment, and "A" and "D" Companies crossed the railway bridge to the further side of the Canal, while "C" got over a little later at another spot. A hostile machine gun was now found to be in action in the open on the railway station platform, but the gun detachment was shot down, the gun captured and the advance continued, "A" and "D" Companies moving by the E. and "C" by the W. of the railway line. "B" Company had in the meantime been taking part with the Royal Inniskilling Fusiliers in the capture of Marcoing Copse.

It was for the capture of the above-mentioned machine gun that Sergeant Spackman was awarded the second of the Victoria Crosses won by the 1st Battalion in the war. He attacked the gun single-handed from a distance of some 200 yards, picking off the gunner with his first shot, then advancing some distance and shooting the second gunner who had taken the place of the first, finally bayoneting a third member of the detachment and capturing the gun.

The march went on, a platoon of "C" under Second-Lieutenant Denereaz capturing 2 machine guns *en route*, and the first serious opposition experienced being by "A" Company on the right when reaching some ammunition pits near a sunken road; these were very strongly held with machine guns and half a battalion of infantry, and the advance had now to be stayed as the battalion on the right was not yet up in line; a defensive flank was formed facing W. by "D" Company as "A" was in some danger of being outflanked. "B" Company had by this crossed the Canal and was placed in Battalion Reserve under the W. embankment of the railway station.

Shortly after this an attack by " A " Company and some of the Royal Inniskilling Fusiliers succeeded in clearing the ammunition pits, and the flank battalions having now come up in line, orders were issued that a further attack would shortly be launched.

The O.C. Royal Inniskilling Fusiliers now arrived at The Border Regiment Headquarters, stating that his right was being heavily fired upon by machine guns from the N. outskirts of Masnières, and the O.C. Tanks attached to the 87th Brigade sent 4 tanks to assist in silencing these guns ; but on arrival, the Colonel of the Fusiliers decided that it was then too dark to attack and so informed the right and centre companies of the 1st Border Regiment. In the meantime, however, about 4 p.m., The Border Regiment had been ordered to attack, but on the O.C. " A " and " D " Companies coming back to Battalion Headquarters to report personally, it was decided, in view of their information, to postpone any attack. Unfortunately this information did not reach Captain Johnson ("C" Company) on the left in time to stop his advance, and he attacked the third objective in rear of a tank which was advancing in his sector, and actually penetrated the German line just S. of Flot Farm, capturing 19 prisoners and 2 machine guns. His exposed right flank was, however, assailed by machine-gun fire, while parties of the enemy were noticed working round his flank. He was accordingly ordered to fall back to his original line, and succeeded in doing so, bringing back his guns and prisoners.

Consolidation of the line held was now carried out during the night of the 20th–21st, three companies holding the line of posts just N.E. of the Sunken Road, with the fourth in support along the road itself.

The night and the early part of the morning of the 21st passed quietly, except for some indifferent sniping and occasional bursts of machine-gun fire, and two battalions of the Brigade were to have attacked the third objective at 11. This did not, however, begin from the railway station till nearly noon, when their appearance over the rise was the signal for a tremendous outburst of fire from the enemy's position between the N. end of Masnières and Flot Farm —a fire so intense that it was clear the Germans there had been strongly reinforced, and the operations then came to an end for the day.

One of the tanks employed was stranded near Flot Farm, and though all the others got back, they were all badly damaged by armour-piercing bullets, and their crews had suffered many casualties. During the night, which passed quietly, many patrols were sent out.

During the early morning of the 22nd a very daring reconnaissance was made by Lieutenant J. W. Johnston, D.C.M., and from information brought back by him it was decided to push the line further forward to one affording a better field of fire and already marked by a German cable-trench dug to a depth of some 18 inches. Great progress in deepening and improving this line was made during the night, and it was ready for occupation on the 23rd ; this day was uneventful except that the enemy sniping was more pronounced, there was a certain amount of field-gun and trench-mortar registration, while enemy aeroplanes flew low over the position. During the night of the 23rd–24th the position was fully wired, a communication trench was dug, while patrols sent out came back reporting that the enemy was hard at work consolidating the Flot Farm–Roumilly Line.

The work in the line was all done with enemy tools, even the wire being drawn from an enemy dump in the railway station.

On the night of the 25th the Battalion was at last relieved, having with a trench strength of about 400 dug 1,500 yards of trench to an average depth of 4 feet 6 inches and wired a front of about 900 yards with a double belt of wire and knife-rest entanglements.

On the 26th the 1st Battalion The Border Regiment moved into Marcoing and lived very comfortably in concreted and boarded cellars ; the village, so far practically undamaged, was full of German stores of all kinds—weapons, clothing and rations, and the men quite enjoyed their stay there. On the 28th, however, the Battalion went back to its former sector of the front line, three companies in the firing line and one in support. Next day the enemy showed increased artillery activity, registering on the front line and communication trenches, and Battalion Headquarters in particular, near Marcoing Station and village. During the night the trenches were further improved and strengthened.

The 29th passed tolerably quietly, but on the next day the enemy broke through beyond the right of the 29th Division and got right round Marcoing Copse and as far as the outskirts of the village, when he was counter-attacked by a party of cooks, orderlies and others, collected by Captain Ewbank, M.C., from Brigade Headquarters, and the enemy was finally, with the assistance of other battalions, driven back to his original line.

The casualties from the 20th to the 30th November inclusive were as under :—

Killed, 30 non-commissioned officers and men ; wounded, 4 officers (Captain Clarke, M.C., R.A.M.C.; Lieutenants W. D. C. Thompson and L. Machell and Second-Lieutenant M. Elrington) and 130 other ranks, while 2 men were missing.

Of the 1st December the Battalion war diary informs us that " the situation was most precarious and indefinite this morning, heavy gun-fire could be heard on our immediate flanks but not very heavy in our own front. Received word from Brigade that the enemy broke through yesterday and captured Gouzeaucourt, also La Vacquerie and Les Rues Vertes, but large reinforcements had come up to counter-attack and the Guards retook Gouzeaucourt. Received message that the 86th Brigade will probably evacuate Masnières this evening and the Royal Inniskilling Fusiliers consequently refuse their right flank to conform to this. O.C. ' B ' Company (Lieutenant Johnston) therefore was ordered to carry out a reconnaissance of a possible support defensive line behind the Fusiliers, and this he did with great success. At 4 p.m. a message was received from the Brigadier that the enemy was in possession of the E. side of Les Rues Vertes and that he (the Brigadier) was holding the bridges, but was in a very bad way and would probably be driven back. Lieutenant Johnston was therefore directed to be ready to at once occupy his defensive flank through the Ammunition Pits. At 6.30 a message came from the Brigade giving details of the arrangements for the withdrawal of the 86th Brigade from Masnières, and this withdrawal was successfully accomplished during the night, without interference by the enemy, to the trenches at Marcoing."

During the 30th November and 1st December the German aircraft had shown much activity, as many as 37 enemy aeroplanes had been counted at one time flying as low as 150 feet from the ground, and these were but little opposed by our machines. About 12.30 on the morning of the 3rd December the 1st Battalion The Border Regiment was relieved by a battalion from the 16th Brigade of the 6th Division and marched through Marcoing into the Hindenburg Support Line at Ribécourt, the officers and men being greatly exhausted on arrival by reason of the strain of the last fortnight, during the greater part of which they had been in fighting order without greatcoats or blankets in very severe weather.

The Battalion "stood to" during the greater part of the 4th December ready to move to whatever part of the hard-pressed British line reinforcement might be needed, but that night the 29th Division was finally relieved by the 36th and was then retired via Sorrel, Etricourt and Mondicourt to Grand Rullecourt, "where all had comfortable billets and thoroughly appreciated them." During this last phase of the Cambrai Battle, Captain J. W. Ewbank, M.C., and 1 man had been killed—the officer in leading the attack to clear Marcoing Copse, Second-Lieutenant W. D. C. Thompson and 18 other ranks had been wounded, and 3 men were missing.

At Grand Rullecourt many messages of congratulation were received by the G.O.C. 29th Division, from Sir Douglas Haig downwards, on the magnificent services rendered in the Battle of Cambrai.

On the 1st November the 7th Battalion left the camp to which it had been withdrawn on the conclusion of the Battle of Ypres and, marching by Houtkerque and Herzeele, reached billets at Wemaers Cappel the same
7th Battalion.   evening; here the night was spent and next day the Battalion went on by road and rail to White Mill Camp in the Langemarck area, and was at once employed in working parties with the 93rd Field Company R.E. in the improvement of Claw and Candle Trenches. Then on the 19th it marched to the Canal Bank and relieved the battalion holding the front line in Eagle and Candle Trenches, while Headquarters was at places like Taube Farm and Millers Houses, of which we have already heard something in connection with the 1st Battalion of the Regiment.

At the end of the month of November the Battalion was taken out of the line and, entraining at Boesinghe at 5.30 a.m. on the 26th, proceeded to International Corner and marched from there to Dublin Camp, where it remained for some forty-eight hours only.

There is but little to be gleaned from the Battalion Diary as to how during this period casualties occurred, but they numbered 40—7 men being killed, while 2 died of wounds, and Lieutenant A. W. Bonome and 30 other ranks were wounded.

Although the 7th Battalion was repeatedly up in the front line in the Proven area during the remainder of the time that the Cambrai operations continued, and was more than once under orders for employment in an attack, nothing transpired, and when the battle came to an end at the close of the first week of December, it was in Penton Camp near Couthove.

Of the results of the three weeks' fighting, General Sir Douglas Haig wrote as follows in his despatch of the 20th February, 1918, published in the *London Gazette* of the 1st March : " We had captured and retained in our possession over 12,000 yards of the former German front line from La Vacquerie to a point opposite Boursies, together with between 10,000 and 11,000 yards of the Hindenburg Line and Hindenburg Reserve Line and the villages of Ribécourt, Flesquières and Havrincourt. A total of 145 German guns were taken or destroyed by us in the course of the operations and 11,100 German prisoners were captured. On the other hand, the enemy had occupied an unimportant section of our front line between Vendhuille and Gonnelieu.

" There is little doubt that our operations were of considerable indirect assistance to the Allied forces in Italy. Large demands were made upon the available German reserves at a time when a great concentration of German divisions was still being maintained in Flanders. There is evidence that German divisions intended for the Italian theatre were diverted to the Cambrai front, and it is probable that the further concentration of German forces against Italy was suspended for at least two weeks at a most critical period, when our Allies were making their first stand on the Piave Line."

In view of the foregoing remarks this seems to be a good time to take up the story of the operations of the 2nd Battalion The Border Regiment in the Italian theatre of the war.

At the beginning of November the 2nd Battalion The Border Regiment was engaged in training in the Blarringhem area, and here, on the 1st, two privates **2nd Battalion.** of the Battalion—No. 33088 Private Hulbert and No. 10154 Private Peacock—returned to the Battalion, having been found by a patrol of the Royal Welch Fusiliers inside the German lines on the Menin Road. All they wanted to know was when they might expect to be relieved, for, as they pointed out, they had been on their post for two nights at a stretch !

On the 8th the Battalion took part in an inspection of the 7th Division by H.M. the King of the Belgians at Ebblinghem, when 2 officers—Major (Acting Lieutenant-Colonel) W. Kerr, D.S.O., M.C., and Captain and Quartermaster F. W. Mitchell—and 76 other ranks of the original 7th Division landing in Belgium in October, 1914, were present.

On the 26th October the War Cabinet had approved of the transfer of several British Divisions from the Western Front to Italy, and early in November the 7th Division must have learnt that it was one of those selected to move thither, for on the 17th the 2nd Battalion The Border Regiment was stationed at Hunières engaged in refitting for campaigning in a very different climate.

Next day the following message was received from Lieutenant-General

Morland, commanding Xth Corps, addressed to the G.O.C. and all ranks of the 7th Division :—

" *On your departure from the Xth Corps I wish to thank you for all your good and gallant work whilst under my command. In bidding you good-bye, which I do with regret, I wish you all success and good fortune wherever you may find yourselves in the future.*"

The following is the number of casualties sustained by the 7th Division from its landing in Belgium on the 7th October, 1914, to its entraining for Italy on the 18th November, 1917 :—

Officers	2,327
Other Ranks	53,091

On the 19th the 2nd Battalion marched to Wavrans and there boarded two trains ; the first, containing Lieutenant-Colonel W. Kerr, 15 other officers and 408 non-commissioned officers and men, of " C " and " D " Companies, left at 9.12 a.m., while the second did not start until 1.12 p.m. ; in this were Major G. O. Ramsbottom, D.S.O., 14 other officers and 359 other ranks of " A " and " B " Companies, the strength of the Battalion thus being 31 officers and 767 non-commissioned officers and men. The route followed was St. Pol, Courcelle, Albert, Longuereau, Boves, Crepy, Château Thierry, Epernay, Chalons-sur-Marne, and the troops, one train now closely following the other, crossed the Italian frontier via the Mont Cenis Tunnel between 9 p.m. and 1 a.m. on the night of the 21st–22nd.

The following officers, warrant officers and staff-sergeants accompanied the Battalion : Lieutenant-Colonel W. Kerr, D.S.O., M.C. ; Major G. O. Ramsbottom, D.S.O. ; Captain S. J. C. Russell, M.C. ; Lieutenant R. K. Ehrenborg ; Second-Lieutenants E. J. H. Mettam and E. J. Peacock ; Captain and Quartermaster F. W. Mitchell ; No. 9479 R.S.M. R. L. Booth, and No. 7884 Acting R.Q.M.S. G. W. Cluley.

> " A " Company.—Captain C. Dand ; Lieutenant G. M. F. Prynne ; Second-Lieutenants J. H. Graham, E. H. Johnson, J. Rendall, R. K. Longmire and W. I. Atkinson ; No. 7890 C.S.M. J. Streeter, M.C., and 6607 C.Q.M.S. W. Lee.
>
> " B " Company.—Captain J. W. Little, M.C. ; Second-Lieutenants H. T. Haynes, M. Tomlinson, T. Bald, A. Elmslie and H. Davidson ; No. 6403 C.S.M. T. Fletcher and 7102 Acting C.Q.M.S. J. Sales.
>
> " C " Company.—Captain F. Argles ; Lieutenant C. A. Hill ; Second-Lieutenants S. F. Hawkins, A. E. Wilson and S. Forbes-Robertson ; No. 20961 Acting C.S.M. F. Larkin and 6445 Sergeant H. Loughman.
>
> " D " Company.—Captain J. G. Campbell ; Second-Lieutenants M. J. Melville, R. Kirk, F. S. Samut and R. Adey ; No. 7882 Acting C.S.M. W. Millard and 7744 C.Q.M.S. W. Fraser.

Captain R. M. Burmann, acting brigade-major, and Lieutenant W. E. Kelly accompanied Brigade Headquarters.

After crossing into Italy the halts were very irregular, and nobody knew when or where they would occur, no hot water was provided for preparing the constant libations of hot tea beloved of the British soldier, but the weather was bright and sunny, and the Italians gave the troops a great reception as the trains passed through their districts. Railhead at Minerbe was reached by the second of the two trains at 4.45 p.m. on the 23rd November, and here a whole day was spent preparing for the onward march, which commenced on the 25th and was a long one of between 22 and 24 miles via Albettone to Barbarano at the foot of the Berici Mountains.

Here an interesting discovery appears to have been made and is duly recorded in the Battalion War Diary. "The country wine," so the entry runs, "was found to be more potent than the thin French beer or light wine!"

The sound of distant gun-fire was now heard for the first time in Italy.

Moving on again on the 28th, the Battalion crossed the River Bacchiglione to Montegalda; on the 30th it marched to San Giorgio in Bosco, 4 miles S. of Cittadella, crossing the Brenta River by a pontoon bridge and seeing an enemy aeroplane about midday; on the 3rd December to Monastiero, passing *en route* through Cittadella and San Martino di Lupari, where Monte Grappa and other mountains came in sight; and so on the 4th to billets at Campigo, where the 20th Brigade found itself in Divisional Reserve, the 23rd and 41st divisions holding the Montello–Piave Line.

Here steady training commenced, while officers went forward every day to reconnoitre the routes to Monte Belluna and Selva.

On the 11th the Battalion marched from Campigo via Salvat Ronda and Valla to Riese, 5 miles S. of Asolo, as the 7th Division was now to form a reserve to the Italian and French forces, which were being heavily attacked between the Rivers Brenta and Piave, and the enemy shells could clearly be seen falling on the Grappa and Tomba mountains about 8 miles to the N.

Riese was found to be full of French guns and gunners and much fraternizing resulted. Here officers again went constantly to the front, to reconnoitre a Brigade position N. of Asolo to be taken up should it become necessary to support the French on Monte Tomba, and also to study concentration routes N., E. and W.

The British reinforcements arrived under General Sir H. Plumer had now taken over the Montello Sector with the French on their left, and this, as stated by the Commander in his despatch of the 9th March, 1918, "is a feature by itself and an important one. It acts as a hinge to the whole Italian line, joining as it does that portion facing N. from Monte Tomba to Lake Garda, with the defensive line of the Piave covering Venice, which was held by the Third Italian Army."

On the 21st December there is a pardonable note of exultation in the Battalion Diary: "First Military Cross in the B.E.F., Italy, awarded to Second-

Lieutenant Davies, a Border officer, attached to the Durham Light Infantry, for work on the Piave."

Here, then, at Riese the closing days of the year 1917 were passed. "December," wrote the Commander of the British Forces in Italy, "was an anxious month. Local attacks grew more frequent and severe, and though the progress made was not great and Italian counter-attacks were constantly made, yet the danger of a break through into the plains undoubtedly increased. . . . Rear lines of defence were constructed under our supervision, and as time passed and preparations became more forward the general atmosphere of security improved"; and finally on the 30th December the French, assisted by British guns, carried out a very successful attack in the Monte Tomba Sector, the course of which was visible from Riese, while the material results were seen in some 1,500 Austrian prisoners who were passed back from the front through the village.

On Christmas Day Major-General Shoubridge, commanding the 7th Division, sent the following message to Lieutenant-Colonel Kerr and The Border Regiment :—

"*My most sincere wishes to you and all ranks for a Merry Christmas and a Victorious and Happy New Year.*"

From the Commander of the British Forces in Italy came :—

"*Sir Herbert Plumer wishes all ranks every good wish for Christmas and every success in the New Year.*"

It is now time to return to the Macedonian theatre of war and the doings of the 9th Battalion.

In his despatch, dated the 1st October, 1917, in which General Milne reviewed the events of the previous twelve months in Salonika, he wrote : "since the 29th November, 1916, when, in accordance with General Sarrail's request, I took over the sector then held by the Italian troops, the army under my command has occupied the front covering Salonika from the E. and N., and extending from the mouth of the River Struma along the Tahinos–Butkova–Doiran Lakes to the River Vardar, a distance of approximately 90 miles. . . . At the commencement of the period under review, the rôle allotted to the British troops had for its object the engaging of the enemy along the front during the operations which culminated in the capture of Monastir on the 19th November. From that date onwards the advent of the winter season, accompanied as it was by heavy falls of snow and rain, made operations, except on a small scale, a matter of considerable difficulty owing to the paucity of metalled roads and the heavy nature of the soil in the valleys."

During January 1917 the 9th Battalion The Border Regiment remained about Spancovo, engaged in working upon the roads, making dug-outs and bridging
9th Battalion. the many streams and causeways across the marshes. February passed in like manner, and then in the middle of March the Head-quarter Wing of the Battalion moved to Cugunci, where work of much the same nature was engaged in. The weather, which up to this had been unusually inclement, reducing the Seres Road to such a state of mud as to render motor transport practically impossible, now began to get warmer and drier, and it was

hoped shortly to commence the active operations which the Commander-in-Chief was contemplating.

Of this attack General Milne's despatch tells us the following : " By the 10th March the Corps on the left had pushed forward for a distance of 1,000 yards on a front of 3,500 yards, extending in a S.W. direction from Horseshoe Hill, on the ridge which forms the watershed between the Doiran Lake and the Vardar Valley. This ridge, commonly called the ' P ' Ridge, running N. into the left centre of the enemy's position, rises to a height of about 500 feet above Horseshoe Hill, and dominates the whole country between Doiran Lake and the Vardar. On both flanks in front of Doiran and opposite Macukovo, the Bulgarian trenches are pushed forward, forming strong bastions, with flanks resting on Doiran Lake and the Vardar River respectively. . . . Situated some 800 yards in front of the Horseshoe Hill, which formed the apex of the salient between these two bastions, and about 11,000 yards N.E. of Krastali village, a hostile advanced work called ' P.$4\frac{1}{2}$ ' formed a valuable observation station to the enemy and its capture was essential to any further advance. The front, therefore, selected for the initial attack, with a view to threatening the approaches to Doiran town, extended from the W. shore of Doiran Lake, along the enemy's salient in front of the town, to the crest of ' P ' Ridge."

The arrangements for the attack were completed by the 8th April, but for one cause after another it was postponed until the 24th, being preceded by a very violent bombardment of the enemy position of several days' duration ; one effect of this fire was to elicit the fact that the strength of the opposing heavy artillery had lately been considerably increased.

On the 24th we read in the 9th Battalion war diary : " during the day the bombardment was terrific, ceasing almost entirely about 1800 hours and re-commencing about half an hour before X hours with renewed force and energy. The object of the attack on our portion of the front was to advance the line on about 1,800 yards frontage by about 600 yards on W. and 1,000 yards on E. in depth and take ' Point $4\frac{1}{2}$ ' on the W. and Hill 380 on the E., and this was most successfully carried out, the divisions on left and right co-operating. In the 60th Territorial Division on the left we took particular interest, because formerly we held a portion of the line and could realize the difficulties to be faced. It encountered a very heavy barrage, but, with a counter-barrage of guns, machine guns and trench mortars, attacked at three different points and found the trenches deserted and full of barbed wire. However, it attained its object by retaining the fire of many batteries on its front. The 26th Division on the right was thought to have much the most difficult task at this period of the advance, and so it proved. Though fighting with great gallantry, the 79th Brigade in the attacking line encountered such a heavy H.E., shrapnel and machine-gun barrage as to be unable to retain any position gained, and in the end had to return to the starting-point. This Brigade had an especially bad time when formed up in the Jumeaux Ravine waiting orders to go forward.

" The task allotted to the 9th Border Regiment (Pioneers) was to assist in consolidation of the new front line when taken, by putting up a wire entanglement on a front of 2,800 yards on a line of about 200–400 yards N. of the captured Bulgar trenches, and for this purpose 'B' Company (Captain C. Woodall-Smith) and 'D' Company (Lieutenant M. D. Stott) had been trained in rapid wiring by day and night. For better supervision and independence of action each company was divided into two half-companies and given its own portion of about 700 yards to work on, while these half-companies were again told off into seven wiring sections of 9 men, each man being allotted to and trained in his own definite task in the general wiring scheme and instructed what to carry forward from the R.E. dump to the wiring position. Thus each wiring section had a frontage of about 100 yards, and, it was anticipated, about four hours before dawn in which to erect a complete line of trench wire, with 6-feet stakes driven at five paces interval to a height of 4 feet 6 inches through the back of it. A 4-strand barbed wire fence and a double W barbed-wire apron fastened to short pickets with a trip wire running between them at about 9 inches from the ground."

The half-companies were commanded, those of " D " by Second-Lieutenants Moore and Warden, and of " B " Company by Lieutenant Kirk and Second-Lieutenant Brownlie. While carrying out this work Second-Lieutenant Moore and 55 other ranks were wounded.

On the following day, the 25th, the companies of the Battalion were moved further to the front to do similar work, and on this occasion 4 men were hit.

A small party of " C " Company, consisting of Lance-Sergeant Chadwick and 16 other ranks, was left in the position on the withdrawal of the company to look after stores, and during the evening of the 26th this detachment was called upon to help repulse an enemy attack on Hill 380, and was reported as having done excellent work in bringing up ammunition and bombs to the front line through a heavy enemy barrage.

It had been hoped to take advantage of the commanding position now gained on the ridge by advancing the line on the western slopes, but General Milne was directed to postpone further action until the 8th May, as it had been found impossible to effect all that had been hoped on the right bank of the Vardar River and in the neighbourhood of Monastir. In the operations which ultimately took place and which were only moderately successful, the 9th Battalion The Border Regiment had no share beyond preparing positions and improving roads ; and then on the 24th May definite instructions were received from General Sarrail that offensive operations were to cease for the summer months all along the front ; and in view of the above, and having regard to the fact that malaria and dysentery were very prevalent at this season in the low-lying areas, General Milne decided to abandon the forward positions on the right and centre of the British line and to withdraw to the foothills on the right bank of the Struma River and to the S. of the Butkova Valley. The bridgeheads were all, however, garrisoned and the vacated area was regularly patrolled. By the 14th June the retirement had been carried out without any interference by the enemy.

During the hot weather months the 9th Battalion remained on in the vicinity of Cugunci, in the British or eastern sector of the Balkan front. Our line during this period ran N.W. from the mouth of the Struma River, past Lake Tahinos and its marshes, up the broad valley to the junction of the Butkova and Struma Rivers. Here it turned W. along the slopes of the Krusha Balkans to Lake Doiran, and then near Doiran town swept S.E. to the Vardar Valley. The whole sector was some 100 miles long and distant between 50 and 60 miles from the town of Salonika. On the N.E. it barred the way against an advance from Seres and the Rupel Pass; on the N.W. it both guarded and threatened the Vardar Valley, the enemy's main line of communication and his shortest and easiest road to Salonika.

During the summer of 1917 the strength of the British Army in Macedonia had been very considerably reduced; originally containing five infantry divisions —the 10th, 22nd, 26th, 27th and 28th—it had been augmented in January of this year by a sixth, the 60th; but at the beginning of June this division was transferred to the Egyptian theatre of war and was followed thither at the end of August by the 10th Division. Two cavalry brigades were also taken out of the British Salonika force and sent to another theatre of war.

This reduction of strength brought the question of communications into greater prominence, it being very evident that with fewer troops it was necessary that means should exist for moving them with increased rapidity from one point to another; further, the line of defence had to be not only strengthened but shortened, and in all these works the services of a Pioneer Battalion were especially called for and the 9th Border Regiment was found particularly useful. With its help, and with the assistance of units similarly trained, good metalled roads were constructed to Seres, Doiran and to Karasuli on the Vardar River; light railways as well as roads led to Neohori, at the mouth of the Struma River, and to Snevce and Rajanova, at the foot of the Krusha Balkans; while lateral communications were constructed behind the first and second zones of defence. Then early in September 1917 an entrenched position was begun "running from Berovo on the E. via Lahana, the high ground to the E. of Kurkut and the hills round Janes to the Vardar River at Vardino. This position took several months to prepare, but, when finally completed, formed a strong and shorter line of defence, at a distance varying from 5 to 15 miles behind the front line, and covering all lines of advance from the N.E. and N."

And so the autumn passed away and the winter came round again, when the heavy rains, followed by snow and frosts, considerably hampered operations on all the fronts. The end of the year found the 9th Battalion The Border Regiment still at Cugunci, winning golden opinions for the good work cheerfully done by all ranks. In December a draft of 7 officers and 116 other ranks joined, and on the 31st the strength of the Battalion was 30 officers and 944 non-commissioned officers and men.

Towards the end of the year General Sarrail was succeeded in the command of the Allied Armies by General Guillaumat, under whose orders the existing defences of the town and district of Salonika were enlarged and improved and made into a third line of defence.

At Christmas time the following telegrams from Their Majesties the King and Queen—ever mindful of their fighting men on all fronts and all the Seven Seas—were published in the theatres of war for the information of all ranks ; the first from His Majesty runs :—

" *I send to all ranks of the Navy and Army my hearty good wishes for Christmas and the New Year. I realize your hardships patiently and cheerfully borne and rejoice in the successes you have won so nobly. The Nation stands faithful to its pledges, resolute to fulfil them. May God bless your efforts and give us victory.*"

The second message was from Their Majesties the King and Queen, and was as under :—

" *Our Christmas thoughts are with the sick and wounded sailors and soldiers. We know by personal experience with what patience and cheerfulness their suffering is borne. We wish all a speedy restoration to health, a restful Christmastide and brighter days to come.*"

CHAPTER XI

1918

THE 5TH, 7TH, 8TH AND 11TH BATTALIONS IN THE BATTLES OF THE SOMME.

THE 1ST AND 8TH BATTALIONS IN THE BATTLES OF THE LYS.

WHEN the year 1918 opened the general situation on the Western Front had undergone some considerable change. The extent of ground held by the British had been increased by some 28 miles, and Sir Douglas Haig's troops had now relieved the French on their right as far as the vicinity of the village of Barisis, immediately S. of the river Oise, the relief being completed by the end of January. The defection of Russia permitted of the transfer of many German and Austrian divisions from the Eastern to the Western Front, and it was increasingly evident at the end of 1917 and the opening of 1918, that the Western Powers must now adopt a defensive policy in view of the strong and sustained offensive which they might expect shortly to have to meet.

Towards the middle of February these signs of a big German offensive became more marked; it was known that the Central Powers had by this transferred 28 infantry divisions from the eastern and 6 from the Italian theatre; while not only were further reinforcements on their way to the West, but the enemy had also greatly increased his heavy artillery in that theatre of war, and by the end of the third week in March the number of German divisions here had risen to 192, an increase of 46 since the beginning of the previous November. Further, air reconnaissances over the German lines showed that rail and road communications were being improved and that ammunition and supply dumps had increased in number along the whole front from Flanders to the Oise. By the end of February these preparations had become very marked opposite the front held by the Third and Fifth Armies, and General Haig came to the conclusion that the enemy would probably attack from the Sensée River southwards. The Third Army, it may here be stated, held a front of 27 miles from N. of Gouzeaucourt to S. of Gavrelle with the Vth, IVth, VIth and XVIIth Corps, while the front of the Fifth Army extended from our junction with the French just S. of Barisis to N. of Gouzeaucourt, a distance of about 42 miles, and was held by the IIIrd, XVIIIth, XIXth and VIIth Corps.

For some little time past the heavy and increasing drain on the man power of the nation had been causing the military authorities very considerable anxiety, and it was finally reluctantly decided to carry out a reorganization of the divisional composition of the British Army in France; this measure was completed during the month of February, 1918, when the number of battalions in each brigade was reduced from four to three, and the number in a division from thirteen to ten. "Apart from the reduction in fighting strength involved by this reorganization, the fighting efficiency of units was to some extent affected. An unfamiliar grouping of units was introduced thereby, necessitating new methods of tactical handling of the troops and the discarding of old methods to which subordinate commanders had been accustomed." [1]

Before proceeding to narrate the events of the early months of this year and the share which the different battalions of The Border Regiment took in them, we must briefly state what each of the six battalions now in France was doing during January, February and the first weeks of March, and what particular sections of the long line each was occupying when the German offensive commenced.

At the beginning of January the 1st Battalion was in a camp in the Proven area, but towards the end of the month it moved, first by march to Brandhoek and then by rail to Wieltje, where it supplied parties for work in the Army Defence Zone. In February the Battalion was at Passchendaele and took its turn in the front line of the Brigade sector and suffered some few casualties, then moved back to Watou for training, and on the 26th marched to Poperinghe and there provided working parties in the Army Battle Zone; the 1st Battalion The Border Regiment was still in these parts when in March the great German offensive commenced.

1st Battalion.

The 5th Battalion was in the line at Passchendaele at the beginning of February, and on the 13th of this month, consequent on the reduction of the strength of infantry brigades from four to three battalions, it was taken out of the 50th Division then at Brandhoek and joined the 66th Division at Villers Bretonneux on the 18th February as a Pioneer Battalion. Here the 5th Border Regiment remained for about a fortnight, during which time it received special training in Pioneer work and was completely fitted out with equipment, extra transport, etc.

5th Battalion.

On the 2nd March the 66th Division relieved the 24th in the line, and on the 12th we find it stated in the divisional narrative that "evidence has been steadily accumulating that a German offensive will shortly take place. Work on defences is being pushed on with all possible labour; artillery harassing fire is being increased about dawn and special patrol activity has been ordered." But as late as the 18th there seems to have been no anxiety as to the situation, for we find it recorded that "except for increased aerial activity there has been no indication of any enemy offensive in the near future."

Only three days later the storm broke!

When the Third Battle of Ypres came officially to an end fighting did not automatically cease, and the 6th Battalion of the Regiment continued to suffer casualties during the two closing months of the year while holding the line in the neighbourhood of Cité St. Pierre. The beginning of 1918 found the Battalion at Fouquières, and here while in Brigade Reserve orders were received that the 6th Battalion was to be disbanded. It had for some weeks

6th Battalion.

[1] Despatch of the 20th July, 1918.

past been at a comparatively low strength, but it is only in the diary of the 1st February that this very disquieting decision is announced.

On the afternoon of the 2nd the Divisional General inspected and addressed the Battalion, thanking officers, non-commissioned officers and men for the good work all had done while serving with the Division, and expressing his deep regret that a battalion which had rendered such splendid services should meet with such an untimely end.

On the next day 7 officers and 150 other ranks of " D " Company and 5 officers and 100 other ranks of " B " Company proceeded to join the 7th and 8th Battalions The Border Regiment respectively; these were followed on the 4th by parties of 7 officers and 150 other ranks of " C " and 5 officers and 100 non-commissioned officers and men of " A " Company who left to join, the one party the 11th and the other the 1st Battalion. What was now left of the 6th Border Regiment remained at Malingarbe until the 9th when it marched to Allouagne and on arrival came under the orders of the Officer Commanding the First Army reinforcement camp, thus completing the disbandment of the 6th (Service) Battalion The Border Regiment.

During January the 7th Battalion was at Bertincourt and later at Moeuvres; in February it was about Hermies supplying many working parties for the improve-

7th Battalion. ment of the defences in case of an enemy attack which was now almost daily expected to take place, and when early on the morning of the 21st March the enemy bombardment opened, the Battalion, then in camp behind the front, " stood to " and was then ordered to move to battle positions in the Havrincourt defences.

At the end of November, 1917, the 8th Battalion in the 25th Division had left Bethune for the Somme area and inclusion in the IVth Corps and arrived at Achiet-

8th Battalion. le-Grand, 3 miles N.W. of Bapaume, during a spell of bitter winter weather, the 25th relieving the 3rd Division in the Quéant Sector due S. of Bullecourt. Here the right sector of the IVth Corps was held by the 51st Division, while on the left of the 25th was the 59th Division of the VIth Corps. The front line here consisted of a series of disconnected posts with very few communication trenches, and the Division now devoted all its energies to digging a continuous front system, with several strong belts of wire, communication trenches and reserve lines, all in very unfavourable weather—frost, during which digging was practically impossible, and sudden thaws, when the trenches collapsed and became impassable.

In the second week in February, owing to the reorganization to which allusion has already been made, the 8th Loyal North Lancashire Regiment was taken out of the 75th Infantry Brigade and disbanded, the *personnel* being distributed among other battalions of the same regiment.

On the 13th February the 25th Division was relieved in the line by the 6th and withdrew to Achiet-le-Petit, about 4 miles N.W. of Bapaume, and when the German attack began on the 21st March the 8th Battalion was in Savoy Camp in this area.

After taking part in the operations about Nieuport in July, 1917, the 11th

Battalion spent some time in the neighbourhood of Coxyde, and then in the latter part of August and beginning of September was at Oost Dunkerque, where the **11th Battalion.** camp was heavily shelled by a long-range high-velocity gun, the transport lines being hit and 4 officers' chargers killed. After this the enemy shelling became more regular and hardly a day passed without casualties, 1 officer (Second-Lieutenant A. Armer) and 8 other ranks being killed, Second-Lieutenant D. Walker and 18 non-commissioned officers and men being wounded during September. On the 6th October the Battalion went by barge and road to Teteghem, where nearly three weeks were passed, after which there was a further change to Zegers Cappel in the Roubrouck area.

At the end of November the "Lonsdales" were in the Bellevue area, where on the 25th they incurred several casualties during relief in the trenches, 12 men being killed, Captain Benson, Second-Lieutenants McDonald and Duncan and 35 other ranks being wounded, while 7 men were missing. Then on the 2nd December the Battalion had a smart little action ; moving up from Wurst Farm in the West-roose Beek area to the front line, the Battalion made a night attack on the German positions S. of Westroose Beek in conjunction with the other units of the 97th Brigade and two battalions of the 96th Infantry Brigade, the zero hour being 1.55 a.m. The "Lonsdales" took their objectives and held them all through the day until the enemy launched a counter-attack at 4.30 p.m., when the Battalion had to fall back to the old line. In this action Captains J. Benson, A. E. Sandeman and P. H. Martin, Second-Lieutenants Richardson and Macduff were killed, Captain McConnan, Second-Lieutenants J. M. Jamie, Fell, Hotchkiss and Maltby were wounded and Second-Lieutenant Ridgeway was missing.

The end of the year and the greater part of January, 1918, were spent in camp at Tournehem carrying out defensive training, but the Battalion left here again on the 20th and went by train and march route to Caribou Camp near Elverdinghe.

In his despatch from which in this chapter extracts have been made, Sir Douglas Haig makes special mention of the many raids carried out by both sides in the weeks immediately preceding the commencement of the German offensive ; one of these was conducted by Captain Ross, Second-Lieutenants Macrae and McDonald and 60 other ranks of " C " Company of the Battalion on the night of the 18th February. The raid was carried out by three parties, two of which, those on the flanks, reached their objectives and penetrated 150 yards behind the enemy's front system ; the centre party unfortunately came upon a machine gun which the barrage had not touched and had two casualties, Second-Lieutenant Macrae being killed and 1 sergeant wounded. As a result of the raid 12 of the enemy were killed, 1 machine gun was bombed and put out of action and one wounded prisoner was brought in. Captain Ross made several unavailing attempts to find and bring in Second-Lieutenant Macrae's body.

Another similar raid was carried out on the night of the 20th March by Second-Lieutenants Hunt, Oliver and Goodwin and 60 other ranks, who went forward under a heavy barrage, but meeting with stubborn machine-gun resistance had to fall back after getting within bombing distance of the enemy, a few of whom were accounted for. One man of the party was killed, while Second-Lieutenant

Oliver and 7 other ranks were missing.   The Battalion next day was back in Brigade Reserve at the Canal Bank.

The following was the order of the divisions of the two British armies which were destined to meet the full force of the German attack on the 21st March, reading from S. to N. :—

> Gough's Fifth Army.—58th, 18th, 14th, 36th, 30th, 61st, 24th, 66th, 16th, 21st and 9th Divisions, with in reserve the 20th, 50th and 39th, and the 1st, 2nd and 3rd Cavalry Divisions.
> Byng's Third Army.—47th, 63rd, 17th, 51st, 6th, 59th, 3rd, 15th and 4th Divisions, with in reserve the 2nd, 41st, 19th, 25th, 40th and Guards Divisions.

On the left of the Third Army, and involved later in the battle, was the 56th Division of the First Army, with the 31st in reserve.

" Launched on a front of about 54 miles on the 21st March, the area of the German offensive spread northwards on the 28th March, until from La Fère to beyond Gavrelle some 63 miles of our former line were involved.   On this front a total of 73 German divisions were engaged during March against the Third and Fifth Armies and the right of the First Army, and were opposed in the first place by 22 British infantry divisions in line, with 12 infantry divisions and 3 cavalry divisions in close reserve. . . .   Before the end of March, by which date the principal German effort had been broken, a further force of 8 British divisions was brought S. and sent into the fight.   Prior to the 9th April 4 other British divisions were engaged, making a total of 46 British infantry divisions and 3 cavalry divisions employed on the Somme Battle front."

It is very greatly to be regretted that no war diaries are forthcoming for the 5th Battalion The Border Regiment for the months of February, March and April, 1918 ; there are none at the Record Office at Preston, or even in

Battle of the Somme.

5th Battalion.

possession of the Historical Section, Military Branch, Committee of Imperial Defence.   Had the Battalion formed part of one of the brigades of the 66th Division, these omissions might to some extent have been made good from the brigade diaries for those months ; but, as has been stated, the 5th Border Regiment had been reorganized in the first part of February as a Pioneer Battalion, so that during the greater part of those epoch-making months it formed part of the divisional troops.   The result is that the record of the doings of the Battalion during the great retreat has had to be put together from such scraps of information as have been provided by surviving individuals and from the G.S. papers of the Division.

During the first three weeks of March, 1918, the 66th Division was holding the sector Le Verguier–Ronssoy, the 24th Division on the right, the 66th in the centre and the 16th, of the VIIth Corps, on the left ; the 24th and 66th composed the XIXth Corps of the Fifth Army.   The frontage occupied was one of some 4,500 yards divided into three brigade sectors, and this front was divided again in depth into a forward zone which was lightly held, a battle zone to be held at all costs, and a rear zone.

The 5th Border Regiment had its headquarters at Roisel and was employed in making roads and tramways, while two companies were in the quarries at Templeux engaged in the construction of huge dug-outs.

It seems to have been confidently expected at the headquarters of the Army Corps and Division that the weight of the enemy attack, should such come, would fall on the Third Army, and that only the merest fringe of it would extend sufficiently S. to involve the 66th Division.

The initial German onset was, of course, met by the infantry brigades of the 66th Division, which held its ground throughout the 21st, but Le Verguier had fallen by 10 a.m. on the 22nd, so that both Roisel and Epéhy were threatened from the rear, and when about 2.30 p.m. Roisel had to be evacuated the few men of the 5th Battalion then there remaining were the last to leave the village.

The retreat of the 66th Division may be traced by the different lines taken up :—

On the 22nd March the position was along the W. edge of the Templeux, Trinket, Trinity and Triple Redoubts.

On the 23rd to 25th the line of the Somme River was held.

On the 26th it was holding the line Estrées–Assevillers.

On the 28th it was in the line Wiencourt–Guillaucourt.

On the 29th it was holding the Ignaucourt–Marcelcave line.

On the 30th it was in position on the line W. of Aubercourt–Hangard Wood.

Finally on April 1st, when so far as the 66th Division was concerned, the retreat came to an end, the Division was at Pissy engaged in reorganizing.

The itinerary of the 5th Battalion The Border Regiment was approximately to Cartigny on the 22nd March, thence by way of Doingt through Peronne on the night of the 22nd, halting at Biaches where there had been some intention of making a stand, an intention which had to be abandoned as the enemy was closing in on the Somme N. of Peronné and the position became untenable ; thence by Flancourt, Harbonnières and Marcelcave to Pissy where the Battalion, strength 8 officers and 201 non-commissioned officers and men, arrived on the 1st April.

The casualties during these ten days of hard marching and fighting had naturally been very heavy ; 3 officers and 17 other ranks had been killed or had died of wounds, 7 officers and 102 non-commissioned officers and men had been wounded, while 13 officers and 345 other ranks were missing, a total all ranks of 487.

The officers killed in action or died of wounds were : Second-Lieutenants I. G. Jennings, W. R. McLennan and W. D. Chisholm ; wounded, were Lieutenants J. Huntingdon, M.C., and J. E. H. Coombes, Second-Lieutenants T. E. Bell, J. M. Stout, F. C. Price, A. S. Robertson and S. V. Campbell ; while the following were missing : Captain (acting Major) S. Rigg (wounded), Captain J. N. Franks, M.C., Lieutenants O. J. Feetham, N. Graham, E. L. Fleming, and A. T. Potter ; Second-Lieutenants A. G. Croll, F. Robertson,[1] J. S. Turnbull, W. D. Brown and J. H. Arnott ; Lieutenant H. R. Beaumont, attached to 66th Division M.G. Corps and Captain D. E H. Roberts, R.A.M.C., the medical officer.

[1] Died on the 3rd December in German hands.

On the 3rd April the G.O.C. XIXth Corps sent the following telegram to the Commander of the 66th Division :—

"*Please accept and convey to all ranks my warmest congratulations and thanks for your splendid efforts during the last ten days. The fighting spirit and powers of endurance shown are beyond all praise and have been of vital importance in maintaining the front of the XIXth Corps.*"

At the end of another week or so each battalion in the Division was formed into a cadre of some 10 officers and 45 other ranks, the surplus *personnel* being sent to the base—in the case of the 5th Battalion to the 11th Battalion of The Border Regiment—these cadres being intended to be used to train battalions of American troops. The Division went during April from Pissy to the Longa, then to the Buigny–St. Riquier, and finally to the Tilquier areas, to the Second Army ; but the 5th Battalion spent the greater part of this month trying to find Americans to train and finally training them near St. Omer.

At the opening of the German offensive the 7th Battalion The Border Regiment was serving in the 51st Brigade of the 17th Division and was included in General

7th Battalion. Fanshawe's Vth Corps, which covered with its three divisions the whole Cambrai Salient from Flesquières in the N. to the point near Gouzeaucourt Wood where the Third Army met the left flank of the Fifth. The line made a considerable bend at this point, marking the ground gained in the Cambrai Battle. The 17th Division was on the left of the Corps front, the 63rd was in the centre and the 47th on the right ; the 17th Division was placed astride the Canal du Nord with the village of Hermies in its rear and that of Moeuvres in its front.

During the 21st March the 7th Battalion remained in the Havrincourt defences whither, as already stated, it had moved on the opening of the enemy bombardment, but was withdrawn in the evening into Divisional Reserve ; the respite was, however, but a brief one, for at midday on the 22nd " A " Company was ordered to relieve a company of the York and Lancaster Regiment in the front line, the remainder of the Battalion being sent under Major Page to reinforce the 10th Sherwood Foresters in the Hermies defences. It had now, however, been decided that the Vth Corps must be withdrawn from its dangerous position in the Cambrai Salient, but it was not until after midday on the 23rd that the 51st Brigade began to fall back, the withdrawal beginning with the 10th Foresters, and the retirement being by Villers-en-Flos to Martinplouich. Here it was rumoured that enemy cavalry patrols had broken through and the 7th Border Regiment then manned the ridge overlooking Martinplouich, remaining out all the night of the 24th–25th, which passed quietly ; the Battalion then moved to a position on the ridge in front of Bazentin-le-Grand. Of the fighting on the 22nd Sir Douglas Haig writes in his despatch : " Shortly after noon the enemy attacked Hermies strongly from the N.W., and repeated his attacks at intervals during the remainder of the day. These attacks were completely repulsed by the 17th Division. Heavy losses were inflicted on the German infantry in the fighting in this area, the leading wave of a strong attack launched between Hermies and Beaumetz-lez-Cambrai being destroyed by our fire."

On the afternoon of the 25th the Brigade was holding a position on the high ground round Fricourt Wood, and the events of the next two or three days may, perhaps, best be given in the words of the 7th Battalion diary :—

" 26th March, 3.45 a.m.—Division evacuated position, being covered by Major Cobham's force and concentrated at Henencourt as corps reserve. The Battalion withdrew and marched to Henencourt via Dernancourt and Millencourt, was met by the transport and received hot food. Owing to a threatened attack on Hébuterne, the Battalion moved to Senlis and then to Millencourt and took up a position outside the village. The night passed uneventfully.

" 27th.—The Battalion remained in this position all day ; Millencourt was shelled regularly during the day. At 10.45 p.m. the Battalion took over the line from the Suffolk Regiment, relief being completed by the early morning of the 28th.

" 28th.—Artillery active ; otherwise things normal during the day.

" 29th.—Early this morning the enemy raided and occupied two forward posts held by ' C ' Company, but was immediately dislodged by our counter-attack in which 1 officer and about 50 other ranks were accounted for, 2 prisoners being taken. The Battalion was relieved by the Manchester Regiment about 10 p.m. and marched to billets in Henencourt.

" 30th.—Battalion in divisional reserve.

" 31st.—Battalion relieved 6th Dorset Regiment in right front sector, left Brigade ; dispositions as follows : ' D ' Company, right front, ' B ' centre, ' C ' left front, and ' A ' Company in support."

The casualties to date since the commencement of the German attack had been heavy, they amounted to 2 officers and 16 other ranks killed or died of wounds, 7 officers and 112 non-commissioned officers and men wounded, 1 officer and 11 men gassed, while missing were 1 officer (also wounded) and 64 other ranks. The officers killed were : Second-Lieutenants J. J. Halstead and A. P. Jay ; wounded were Temporary Major C. G. Page, M.C., Captains E. W. Hasell, N. M. Saunders, and the Hon. C. W. Vane, Second-Lieutenants C. S. Allison, D. McInnis and D. J. Hirst ; Captain C. A. C. Hazlehurst was gassed, while Second-Lieutenant R. G. Bird was wounded and missing.

Continuing to fall back, the Battalion marched on the 2nd April via Bouzincourt and Senlis to Warloy, rested on the 3rd, a day which, *more Britannico*, the men of the Battalion devoted to " bathing," then on the 4th by way of Contay, Beaucourt and Moulliens-au-Bois to Pierrecot, and when on the 5th April the German advance was for a time stayed and the Battle of the Somme ended, the 7th Battalion The Border Regiment was at Flesselles where it was joined by drafts of 45 and 149 other ranks from the Royal Welch Fusiliers and West Yorkshire Regiment.

We now return to the 8th Battalion The Border Regiment, which we left occupying Savoy Camp near Achiet-le-Petit. The 25th Division was now in the IVth Corps, the front of which was held by the 51st and 6th Divisions, the 25th being in reserve. The front allotted to the IVth Corps was some 12,000 yards in length, the battalions holding the front line being disposed in depth along a line lightly held with small posts and Lewis guns, with a support and main

8th Battalion. battle defence line in rear. At a distance of 3,000 yards from the first system was a second or Corps line of defence, and about 3,000 yards in rear of this again was a third or Army line of defence. Both of these lines were fairly well protected with wire defences, but were unprovided with communication trenches to connect the different systems.

In front of the 6th Division on the left was Lagnicourt, while in front of the 51st Division was the village of Demicourt.

When in the early days of March it seemed tolerably certain that a German offensive was imminent, the 74th Brigade of the 25th Division was moved up into close support of the 51st Division, just N.W. of Fremicourt, while the 75th Brigade marched forward to Biefvillers, N.W. of Bapaume ; the two were thus conveniently placed to deliver counter-attacks on prominent points should the enemy succeed in penetrating the British lines ; such points were the spurs at Demicourt, Doignies, Louvaval, Lagnicourt on the right of the IVth Corps, with Hermies ridge and the Longatte-Noreuil spurs on the left. As matters turned out, however, such counter-attacks were found to be impossible, and the brigades and even battalions of the 25th Division had to be used piecemeal to reinforce the divisions in front as the exigencies of the moment demanded.

At 5 a.m. on March 21st a heavy artillery fire opened on the whole of the IVth Corps front, and the German heavy guns bombarded the railheads, supply depots, dumps and camps in rear ; and soon after 8 o'clock the 75th Brigade was ordered to move forward from camp at Biefvillers to the Favreuil area, and by 11.30 a.m. it was in position in close support of the 6th Division ; at the same time the 74th Brigade moved up to the support of the 51st Division, while the 7th went into Corps Reserve near Fremicourt.

While marching up Captain Dove of the 8th Battalion was killed.

The Battalion was placed at the disposal of the G.O.C. 16th Brigade, and was thus disposed in readiness to counter-attack N. of Vaulx Wood in the Vaulx–Morchies Line ; " A " Company, Captain Birnie, on right, then " B," Lieutenant Reed, " C," Lieutenant Allan, with " D," Lieutenant Duggan, in reserve. The counter-attack was duly delivered and reached its objective by 3.10 p.m., but was unable to get any further, as the enemy wire was uncut ; Lieutenant Reed was mortally wounded in this attack. The enemy in this sector of the front was now driven back and the position of the Corps line seemed to be secured ; but later the Germans appeared to be getting round the left flank from the direction of Noreuil, and " D " Company of the Battalion was ordered up to the sugar factory at Vraucourt to form a defensive flank to the left. Here Lieutenant Bell, Sergeant Bowman and Private Stewart did excellent work when sent forward to reconnoitre ; later in the day Lieutenant Bell was wounded and Private Stewart was killed.

The Corps position up to the evening of the 21st March was very favourable. The Corps line of defence was intact except in places at Vaulx Wood and Maricourt Wood, where the enemy had effected a lodgment, and the casualties, all things considered, had not been unduly heavy ; the night was passed in reorganizing and in preparing for the attack expected next morning. This came about 7.30 a.m. on the 22nd when the Germans got into Vaulx Wood on the right of the 8th Border Regiment, which was then surrounded on three sides, but for four hours " B," " A " and " C " Companies of the Battalion maintained their position against heavy odds, only falling back when their right was in the air, the division on the left had retired, and communication with the Brigade and the guns had been broken ; the withdrawal was then carried out to the Vaulx–Fremicourt road and the remnants of the Battalion was reorganized in the Army line. Some of these gallant souls never returned, for Second-Lieutenants Oakden and Fentiman and 24 other ranks refused to fall back and so remained—to the end.

This day Second-Lieutenants Dowdall, McTavish and Warwick were killed, Captain Birnie, Lieutenant Gandolfo, Second-Lieutenants Lightfoot and Sandwell were wounded, and Second-Lieutenant Fryer was missing.

" Good work," so it is recorded in the Divisional History, " was done by Sergeant Macdonald, Lance-Corporal Stee, Privates Varty and Westbrooke with the Lewis guns. Sergeant Taylor, when all the officers of ' B ' Company had become casualties, took command of ' B ' Company, reorganized them, and during lulls in the battle produced a piccolo on which he played popular tunes to put new life into the weary men ! Sergeant Ives took charge of ' A ' Company later on, and with Corporal Pickup did splendid work in reorganizing and encouraging the men. Sergeant Crayson, Corporals Wise, Carr, Sewell and Burkin did excellent work in bombing attacks, and Privates Lawless and Porter as battalion runners never once failed in their duty. The former displayed the greatest courage in carrying an urgent message over ground swept by machine-gun fire, though 5 other runners had already become casualties in former attempts to do the journey. Privates Jones, Langley, Routledge, Crone, Bailey, Todkill, Wright and Singleton as stretcher-bearers were conspicuous for their disregard of danger in bringing in the wounded. Lance-Corporal Duckworth, in charge of carrying parties, kept up a steady supply of ammunition."

On the 23rd March the Battalion was relieved and went back for a very brief rest to Savoy Camp, and was then ordered to move to the ridge E. of Béhagnies–Sapignies and dig in.

When on the 21st March the German attack commenced against the Third and Fifth British Armies, the 11th Battalion The Border Regiment was training in **11th Battalion.** the neighbourhood of Boesinghe, but on the 26th it entrained at Elverdinghe for Aubigny, N.W. of Arras, which was reached at 9 o'clock that night, marching thence some 9 miles during an aerial bombardment to Wanquetin and then on by night on the 27th to Ransart, where it appears to have taken up, with the 32nd Division, a position in reserve behind the Guards and the 40th Divisions, the Battalion by the early morning of the 28th being accommodated in some old trenches about Adinfer Wood. On the 30th the " Lonsdales " were moved forward to an advanced position in the Scots Guards line in front of Moyenneville and Ayette, " D," " B " and " C " Companies being in front and " A " Company in reserve. Here the enemy was tolerably quiet except for sniping and machine-gun fire.

On the 1st April the Battalion, according to a statement in the war diary of this date, was "No. 2 Battalion of No. 3 Brigade, holding the line in front of Moyenne-ville and Courcelles," each company in the front line holding 300 yards of ground, furnishing from three to five posts each, and having in rear a length of old German trench for the accommodation of supports : "A," the reserve company, occupied a sunken road 300 yards behind, while Battalion Headquarters was in the embankment. Here some few wounded prisoners were taken and several identifications secured from dead Germans lying in the front.

On the 2nd April there was a good deal of shelling, "C" Company sustaining a few casualties, and on both sides snipers and aircraft were busy, while the enemy appeared to be massing in front of "B" Company ; but this was taken rather as security against a British attack than as an indication that the enemy himself proposed to make any serious advance.

The enemy had captured Ayette on the 27th March, and in the Field-Marshal's despatch he states that on the night of the 2nd–3rd April "the 32nd Division, under command of Major-General C. D. Shute, retook Ayette with 192 prioners," but as there is no mention of this in the 11th Battalion Diary, it would seem that the "Lonsdales" took no part in this operation ; when the Battle of the Somme came to an end the Battalion was still about Adinfer Wood.

Before, however, the enemy attacked again at another point of the Allied Line the 11th Battalion of the Regiment had undergone a very great change in its com-position. On the 10th May the 5th and 11th Battalions were amalgamated, and after amalgamation a Training Cadre of 10 officers and 51 other ranks was formed and designated the 11th Battalion The Border Regiment. This Cadre then left the 32nd Division and proceeded by train to Feuquières to join the 66th Division in the 199th Infantry Brigade, and on arrival here was employed in the training of units of the United States Army now reaching the war area. This good work was continued until well on into July when, while stationed at Abancourt, orders were received on the 24th for the disbandment of the 11th Battalion The Border Regiment.

This order was cancelled the very next day and training was resumed, but on the 29th fresh instructions were issued directing all warrant and non-commissioned officers and men of the 11th Battalion Cadre to proceed to join the 5th Battalion, the 11th being thereupon disbanded.

These orders were carried into effect, the *personnel* of the Battalion leaving on the 31st July by train to join the 5th Battalion, the 11th then ceasing to exist from that date.

While the fighting had been in progress, the pressing danger of a separation of the French and British armies made imperative the appointment of a Generalissimo, and on the 26th March, the Governments of Great Britain and France decided to place the supreme control of the operations of the Allies in France and Belgium in the hands of General Foch, who accordingly assumed command.

The retreat to and behind the Somme was now at an end, the Allied front was re-established, and Amiens was tolerably safe, though the enemy held several posi-tions on the high ground W. of the River Avre and about Villers-Bretonneux, from which his attack might be resumed. Much ground had been lost in the fighting of the past fortnight; on the 21st March the British Line ran from La Fère, W. of St. Quentin, W. of Bellenglise, through Villaret, Lempère, Epéhy, Gouzeaucourt, La Vacquerie, Ribécourt, Flesquières, Lagnicourt, Bullecourt and Monchy to Fampoux, E. of Arras; on the 5th April the line had been drawn back W. of the Avre, through Villers-Bretonneux, Sailly-le-Sec, Dernancourt, Martinsart, Auchonvillers, Beaumont Hamel, Hébuterne, W. of Ablainzeville, through Ayette, Mercatel, Tilloy-les-Mofflaines and Feuchy to W. of Athies. The enemy had certainly gained a qualified victory but at a great cost, while the splendour of the British defence cannot be gainsaid; with 46 infantry and 3 cavalry divisions the British had withstood the onslaught of 80 German divisions!

At home the crisis was courageously met; on the 10th April the House of Commons by a large majority passed a Bill raising the limit of military age to 50, and giving the Government power to abolish the ordinary exemptions and to extend conscription to Ireland; while before the end of that month 355,000 men were sent to join our armies in France.

The Germans having been brought to a halt on the Somme now prepared to attack the British front in Flanders, N. of the La Bassée Canal, and for this they had for some time been making ready. Such an attack offered many advantages; in the prolonged fighting in the S. Sir Douglas Haig had not only drawn upon the whole of his reserves, but he had brought some ten divisions from the northern to the southern area, replacing them in Flanders by divisions which had become depleted or exhausted in the Somme Battles. In the N. the British front was, in a normal spring, secured to some extent by the very marshy nature of the ground, but the early months of 1918 had been exceptionally dry and this front was in April almost everywhere readily passable. In this quarter again the British communications were bad, there being but the one line of railway from St. Pol by Béthune and Hazebrouck to Calais and Dunkirk, some portions of it consisting of a single line of railway only, while the German communications were particularly good, there being a great double line from Ostend to Douai and Cambrai with many feeders and auxiliary routes.

The Germans intended to make here a limited offensive, pushing through between La Bassée and Armentières with the object of capturing Béthune, thereafter arriving at the capture of Hazebrouck and the occupation of the hills N. of Bailleul. Then, when the British had been forced to retreat and the French had moved every man they could spare to the help of their Allies, the advance against Amiens was to be renewed. The initial attack was to be made by nine German divisions, and to meet these, reckoning from the La Bassée Canal northwards, were the following British divisions, all greatly exhausted and weakened by the recent fighting in the S.: 55th, 2nd Portuguese Division, 40th, 34th, 25th, 19th and 9th, seven in all, while behind these in reserve were from S. to N. the 51st, 50th, 49th and 29th.

When the Battle of the Lys opened, the 25th Division, containing the 8th Battalion of The Border Regiment, was occupying the Ploegsteert Sector, while the 29th, with the 1st Battalion, was in reserve behind Poperinghe.

As the 8th Battalion was serving in the front line with the 25th Division when the Battle of the Lys commenced, it seems best first to record the events in which this unit of The Border Regiment took part.

Battle of the Lys.
8th Battalion.

The line held by the 25th Division was some 7,000 yards in length and was in front of Ploegsteert Wood, in touch on the left with the 19th Division on the River Douve, then following the River Lys round to the N.W. of Armentières, where the line linked up with the 34th Division. On the right of the divisional sector for about 6,000 yards the German trenches lay on the far side of the River Lys; in front of Deulemont and Warneton they crossed to the British side of the river and then curved round the lower ground in front of Messines and Wytschaete, held by troops of the 19th Division. The river here was about 20 feet wide. The sector between the Lys and the Douve was held with the 75th Brigade on the right and the 7th on the left, the 74th being in Divisional Reserve, and on the morning of the 9th April the Brigade line had the 8th Border Regiment on the right, the 11th Cheshires on the left and the 2nd South Lancashire Regiment in support.

At 11 in the morning it was learnt that the enemy had opened a vigorous attack at daybreak on the divisions holding the right near Armentières, and that he had occupied the British defence line nearly as far south as Givenchy, and upon this the 74th Brigade was sent at midday to Steenwerck and placed at the disposal of the 34th Division. There was, however, no sign of any impending attack on the 25th Division front, and it was not until 5 o'clock on the morning of the 10th that a bombardment of the front was commenced with high explosive and gas, and then some forty minutes later, covered by a very heavy mist, the Germans crossed the river and attacked.

The Companies of the 8th Battalion were this day commanded as follows: "A" Company Second-Lieutenant Allan, "B" Captain Coxon, "C" Captain Bentley and "D" Captain Dawson.

On the right sector of the 75th Brigade front small parties of the enemy managed to get through the very thinly held line on each flank of the 8th Border Regiment; these parties were speedily reinforced in the mist and extended behind the Battalion and also in rear of the 11th Cheshires, "A" Company of the former being practically cut off, but the remaining three were able to effect a retirement to the reserve line. This also, however, was soon enveloped and at about midday the Battalion withdrew with other troops to a N. and S. line W. of Lebizet. A further withdrawal was necessitated during the afternoon to the road Clef de la Belgique–Oosthove, while late at night the flank was swung back to the line Courte Rue–Oosthove–Doudou, two companies of the Cheshires being on the right of the Battalion at Courte Rue and two at Oosthove.

At about 8 a.m. on the 11th April German troops were seen massing opposite Grey Farm and the reserve line, and at 11 a strong enemy attack developed W. of Ploegsteert Wood on the front of the 7th and 75th Brigades, the line held by the latter being broken near Romarin. This necessitated a withdrawal to the Trench Line about Le Rossignol which was held till night, Lieutenant Strong and 40 men of the 8th Battalion capturing a German machine gun and filling a temporary gap in the line about Brune Gaye during the afternoon. Orders to evacuate the

Nieppe Salient then being received, the Battalion fell back at dusk to Connaught Road where it dug in in support to the 75th Brigade Group. During the early half of the 11th there was no especial enemy activity on the Battalion front, but about 2 p.m. a general retirement was noticed on the right calling for a further retirement to Korte Pyp, where the line was reorganized.

Of this the Divisional History states: " the line now ran roughly N. and S. in front of Neuve Eglise, with the 75th Brigade on the right, the 100th (of the 33rd Division) in the centre, and the 148th Brigade on the left, the 7th Brigade being in support W. of the village. The batteries of motor machine guns were supporting the centre in Korte Pyp. . . . Lieutenant-Colonel Birt, D.S.O., 8th Border Regiment, won a bar to his D.S.O. for his fine leadership and great personal courage when in command of his Battalion. Captain Bentley, Lieutenants Duggan and Strong all received the M.C. for their services during the battle. Company Sergeant-Major Gent, when his officers had become casualties, took command of his company, which he led with great ability, and he and also Sergeant Grayston received decorations. The two cooks, Privates McGuinness and Stafford, and Private George of the Sanitary Squad won Military Medals for their capture of a German aeroplane and its pilot, which was forced to descend and would have got away again had it not been for the enterprise of these three men. Privates Jones and Todkill were conspicuous throughout for their courage as stretcher-bearers, and both received a bar to their Military Medals."

The night of the 12th–13th passed quietly, but the day broke in a very heavy mist. To quote the Battalion diary: " about 6 a.m. a battalion on the right was seen to be retiring along the Neuve Eglise Road and soon after, under cover of the mist and a heavy bombardment, the enemy attacked in great strength and forced us back to the line Neuve Eglise–Trois Rois Cabaret, where elements of the 75th Brigade group and the 9th H.L.I. had already dug in and where a stand was made. Captain Coxon and Lieutenant Bott were both killed while making a counter-attack on the enemy's flank during the morning. Meanwhile, a position was being prepared from Crucifix Corner along the ridge in a N.E. direction."

" During the attack and subsequent retirement," we read in the Divisional History, " Corporal O'Connell, 8th Border Regiment, did excellent work with the Trench Mortar Battery, while Sergeant Graham, Lance-Corporal Bray and Private Hewitt distinguished themselves with their Lewis guns. All these were decorated with the Military Medal as well as Private W. D. Jones for his gallantry as a runner."

On this day, the evening of the 13th, the Army line of defence, which was in front of Dranoutre, linking up with the Kemmel defences, was now held by a hastily organized composite force, while the 75th Brigade was established on the rising ground S.W. of Neuve Eglise; and later the 71st Brigade of the 6th Division was rushed up by bus to help hold the line and to afford much-needed relief to the sorely tried and greatly weakened battalions of the 25th Division. The 8th Battalion The Border Regiment was not, however, relieved in the line until 2.30 on the morning of the 15th, when it fell back on its brigade, and the whole then marched by way of Berthen to Boeschope on the slopes of the Mont des Cats, which was reached at 7 o'clock at night.

The troops of the whole Division were greatly in need of rest, while the fighting strength of the 7th and 75th Brigades together amounted roughly to some 600 men, the 75th Brigade—what remained of it—being formed into a composite battalion under Lieutenant-Colonel J. B. Allsopp.

While in huts near Mont des Cats the Battalion was badly shelled, one shell bursting in a hut occupied by " C " Company of the Battalion, killing 5 and wounding 26 men.   Here a draft of young soldiers joined, for the most part boys of 19, also Lieutenant Turnbull and Second-Lieutenant Mackie.

On the 25th warning orders for a move were received and early in the afternoon the Battalion marched to Hougraae Cabaret, where the Division had been ordered to concentrate in readiness to support the XXIInd Corps, and by 5 p.m. it had arrived in the Reninghelst area.   Information was rather vague, it was known that the French had been attacked on Kemmel Hill, but there was no definite news as to what, if any, success, had been achieved ; later, however, it became apparent that the enemy had possessed himself both of Kemmel Hill and of Kemmel Village, and at 11 at night the 25th Division was ordered to counter-attack in conjunction with the 39th French Division.   The 7th and 74th Brigades were to be in front with the 75th in support.

The attack met with a large measure of success, though the flooded state of the Kemmel brook proved a serious obstacle to the advance and made it difficult for the troops to keep up with the barrage ; but the division on the left failed to capture Le Rossignol Wood, while on the right little progress at all was made, and by 9 a.m. on the 26th it was clear that the front reached formed a dangerous salient and the 25th Division was consequently withdrawn to the line of the Kemmel Beek. During the afternoon the whole line was consolidated and the battalions were reorganized.

Later on the following message was received from the Commander in Chief :—

" *Please congratulate the 25th Division upon their very gallant counter-attack at Kemmel Village on the morning of the 26th inst.   The courage, enterprise and resolution shown on this occasion after so many days of heavy fighting both on the Lys front and south of Arras reflect the highest credit upon all ranks.*"

The Battalion remained up in the front until the night of the 29th–30th, when it was at last relieved and moved back to a position on the La Clytte–Reninghelst Road, 800 yards W. of La Clytte, where Major H. G. Fraser joined and assumed command.

Of this last fighting on the defensive the Divisional History reports that " the 8th Borders were especially successful in repulsing all attempts to get near their line. . . . Of the 8th Borders Lieutenant Williams beat off four attacks with his platoon and Second-Lieutenant Darwell gained most valuable information with a patrol.   Private Bell did useful work in bringing up ammunition during the attack ; Privates Roberts as a runner and Gelling and Hird as stretcher-bearers were all conspicuous for their gallantry."

The casualties were naturally very heavy particularly in officers, these totalling 26 in all during the operations commencing on the 9th April and lasting nearly three weeks ;   Captain P. H. Coxon, M.C., Lieutenant G. G. R. Bott, M.C., Second-

Lieutenants F. C. Corley and W. J. Crookson were killed; Lieutenant-Colonel C. W. H. Birt, D.S.O., Major T. S. Wilkinson, Captains J. Dawson, M.C., and H. E. Williams, R.A.M.C., Lieutenants M. C. Clodd, A. K. Lister and R. Strong, M.C., Second-Lieutenants C. A. Watts, J. Grellis, M.C., T. C. Vaughan, H. T. Lay, T. F. Middleton, J. W. Rogers, J. Gibson, J. H. Mackie and J. T. R. Varel were wounded; Captain W. J. Isbister, R.A.M.C., Second-Lieutenants A. Cameron, M.M. (also wounded), J. W. A. Allan, C. F. Hook and W. C. Preston were missing, while Captain C. W. McConnan was gassed.

The 1st Battalion of The Border Regiment, as already stated earlier in this chapter, was in rear of Poperinghe—the Battalion actually in camp at St. Jean-

1st Battalion. ter-Biezen—when the German offensive began, but it was not until the 9th April that orders were received warning the 1st Border Regiment to prepare to entrain for the St. Pol area, and accordingly at 8.30 that evening all ranks boarded buses at the cross-roads Proven–Poperinghe–Watou, leaving the 10 per cent. details behind in camp. On the morning of the 10th all ranks found themselves at Neuf Berquin and marched into close billets in the village, putting out outposts to cover the Brigade. But later in the morning the Battalion appears to have been placed at the disposal of the 50th Division and was then directed to take up a position across the Estaires–Neuf Berquin Road from the Lys Canal to the Meteren stream, the outpost line in front of Neuf Berquin being taken over by the 1st K.O.S.B.'s. The Battalion was itself relieved in the late afternoon and came back into brigade reserve, forming a support line to the 50th Division then in the firing line.

The companies of the 1st Battalion were this day commanded as follows: "A," Captain Chambers, M.C.; "B," Captain Ridley; "C," Lieutenant Ruxton, M.C., and "D," Second-Lieutenant Yates.

In the evening of the 10th April the enemy, after repeated attacks, forced his way into Estaires and the 50th Division fell back to a prepared position to the N. and W. of the town, where the arrival of reinforcements for a time held up the German advance. Early on the 11th, however, the situation seemed to change for the worse; at 10 it was reported that the 40th Division on the left was being driven in, soon after midday some of the troops of the 50th Division were also forced back; and by 3 p.m. this retirement becoming more pronounced, Captain Chambers was ordered to hold "A" Company in readiness to advance E. and counter-attack, while every endeavour was made to stay the men falling back and build up a line with them. Both "A" and "D" Companies of the Battalion were now engaged, and it being noticed that the flank of the latter was very much in the air, while its commander, Second-Lieutenant Yates, had been brought back wounded, orders were given for its retirement, but two of its platoons could not be extricated and when last seen were surrounded by the enemy, but were still fighting. The counter-attack made by "A" Company had held up the enemy advance for some two hours, but heavy trench mortars being now brought against this company, its position and that of "B" became untenable with both flanks in the air, and they were ordered about 5 p.m. to retire to a new line in rear, upon which two serious enemy attacks were repulsed and the assailants heavily punished. This line was held up to 11 on the night of the 11th by some six battalions of which the 1st Border Regiment was one, and the enemy had not succeeded in making here any impression ; but at the hour named it appearing that he had made good progress on both flanks, orders were received from the Brigade to withdraw, and the retirement to a fresh line was completed without interference by the enemy just as day was breaking.

This line was held as follows : the 86th Brigade the line to the left of the 87th as far as Doulieu, the 92nd Brigade was on the left of the 86th, the 149th on the right of the 87th in the northern portion of Neuf Berquin ; the 86th and 87th Headquarters were at Bleu.

At 7 a.m. on the 12th the Germans began attacking along the whole line, which they penetrated in several places, and the Battalion fell back to Bleu, where " A " Company gained touch with the K.O.Y.L.I. battalion of the 31st Division which in turn connected up with the Guards Division about La Couronne, while " B," " C " and " D " Companies of the Battalion held the line to the S. of Bleu ; later two platoons of " C," under Second-Lieutenant Chicken, at the urgent request of the 1st Lancashire Fusiliers and 2nd Royal Fusiliers, were sent up to fill a gap in their line.

The situation at 4 in the afternoon was obscure but disquieting, the German attack had been made in great strength on a front extending from S. of the Estaires– Vieux Berquin Road to the neighbourhood of Steenwerck, and the enemy seemed now to be overcoming all resistance about Doulieu and La Becque, forcing the British back in a N.W. direction and forming a gap in our line S.W. of Bailleul.

At 5 p.m. the officers commanding 1st Lancashire Fusiliers and 2nd Royal Fusiliers came to the headquarters of the Battalion bringing with them the remains of their respective corps, 30 men of the one and 20 of the other, also Second-Lieutenant Chicken, who was wounded and who had with him 3 men, all that was left of " C " Company's two platoons.   These reported that the brigade on their left had retired, and the residue of these three battalions now also fell back further. In doing so, however, they came under the close-range fire of enemy machine guns on the road N. of Bleu, besides light guns, and many casualties were caused during the withdrawal to a new line in a railway cutting under construction.

This line was held by men and officers of several battalions of the 29th, 31st and 50th Divisions, the strength of the 86th and 87th Brigades being 11 officers and 352 other ranks, with 12 Lewis and 2 Vickers guns, the detail of the 86th Brigade being : 1st Border Regiment, 8 officers, 195 other ranks and 11 Lewis guns ; South Wales Borderers, 24 other ranks; King's Own Scottish Borderers 47 other ranks ; but fortunately the enemy did not pursue his advantage here, the night passed quietly, rations were sent up and the line was consolidated, a barricade being built across the railway cutting.   The following were the dispositions made :   " B," " C " and " D " Companies of the Battalion occupied the railway cutting, while " A " Company was in a trench in front ; on the left the 92nd Brigade prolonged the line northwards towards Merris, while on the right the K.O.Y.L.I. connected with the Guards Brigade.

It was during the operations of April 11th and 12th that the 1st Battalion won its third Victoria Cross.   The recipient was Captain (acting Lieutenant-Colonel)

J. R. Forbes-Robertson, D.S.O., M.C., and the official account of the reasons for which this much-prized decoration was awarded is as follows :—

" For most conspicuous bravery while commanding his Battalion during the heavy fighting. Through his quick judgment, resource, untiring energy and magnificent example, Lieutenant-Colonel Forbes-Robertson on four separate occasions saved the line from breaking and averted a situation which might have had the most serious and far-reaching results.

" On the first occasion when troops in front were falling back, he made a rapid reconnaissance on horseback, in full view of the enemy, under heavy machine-gun and close-range shell fire. He then organized and, still mounted, led a counterattack, which was completely successful in re-establishing our line. When his horse was shot under him he continued on foot. Later in the same day, when troops to the left of his line were giving way, he went to that flank and checked and steadied the line, inspiring confidence by his splendid coolness and disregard of personal danger. His horse was wounded three times and he was thrown five times.

" The following day when the troops on both his flanks were forced to retire, he formed a post at Battalion Headquarters, and with his Battalion still held his ground, thereby covering the retreat of troops on his flanks.

" Under the heaviest fire this gallant officer fearlessly exposed himself when collecting parties, organizing and encouraging.

" On a subsequent occasion, when troops were retiring on his left and the condition of things on his right was obscure, he again saved the situation by his magnificent example and cool judgment. Losing a second horse, he continued alone on foot until he had established a line to which his own troops could withdraw and so conformed to the general situation."

At 9.30 on the 13th the enemy attacked persistently and with great vigour ; during the earlier hours of the day he was repulsed with heavy loss, but early in the afternoon the K.O.Y.L.I. were trench-mortared out of their posts and withdrew some 300 yards, while the Lancashire Fusiliers were shelled out of Vieux Berquin ; but " A " Company of the Battalion pushed out posts to the right and right rear to connect up with some men of the Lancashire Fusiliers who were seen to be still holding their ground.

" The troops of the 29th and 31st Divisions, now greatly reduced in strength by the severe fighting already experienced, and strung out over a front of nearly 10,000 yards E. of the Forest of Nieppe, were once more tried to the utmost. Behind them the 1st Australian Division was in process of detraining, and the troops were told that the line was to be held at all costs, until the detrainment could be completed. . . . Everywhere, except at Vieux Berquin, the enemy's advance was held up all day by desperate fighting, in which our advanced posts displayed the greatest gallantry, maintaining their ground when entirely surrounded, men standing back to back in the trenches and shooting in front and in rear. In the afternoon the enemy made a further determined effort, and by sheer weight of numbers forced his way through the gaps in our depleted line, the surviving garrisons of our posts fighting where they stood to the last with bullet and bayonet. The heroic resistance of these troops, however, had given the leading brigades of the 1st Australian

Division time to reach and organize their appointed line E. of the Forest of Nieppe. These now took up the fight and the way to Hazebrouck was definitely closed. The performance of all the troops engaged in this most gallant stand is worthy of the highest praise. No more brilliant exploit has taken place since the opening of the enemy's offensive, though gallant actions have been without number." [1]

At 10 p.m. on the 13th the remnants of the two brigades withdrew. Orders for this had been issued some time before but had not come to hand, and they marched back unmolested through the new line of defence now being dug in rear by the reinforcing Australians, and so right back to the St. Sylvestre area, where they found comfortable billets in barns. Here the Battalion was formed into two companies under command of Captain Cowburn, M.C., and made up a composite battalion composed of the various units of the Brigade under Lieutenant-Colonel Murray of the 1st K.O.S.B.'s.

During the operations above recorded the Battalion had 1 officer and 42 other ranks killed, 7 officers and 160 non-commissioned officers and men wounded, while 3 officers and 185 other ranks were missing.

But little rest was, however, yet obtainable, for on the 16th the composite battalion was ordered forward into close billets near Le Peuplier, where it arrived in the evening and took up a position in support of an impending attack by the French on Meteren. This did not come to anything, though the Battalion stood by till early morning on the 17th when, in response to an urgent request by the French commander, it moved to another position near Courte Farm. Things were tolerably quiet until 8 a.m. when there was a good deal of aerial activity, followed at 9 by a very heavy enemy bombardment which was kept up until after midday, and by which casualties amounting to 3 officers and 31 other ranks were caused in the 1st Border Regiment.

That night the composite battalion was relieved and went back by march route and in motor-lorries to La Bréarde, where it remained during such time as the Battle of the Lys still endured.

[1] Despatch of the 20th July, 1918.

CHAPTER XII

1918

THE 8TH BATTALION AT THE BATTLE OF THE AISNE.

THE 5TH AND 7TH BATTALIONS AT THE BATTLE OF AMIENS AND SECOND BATTLE
OF THE SOMME.

WHEN the 8th Battalion The Border Regiment was withdrawn from the Battle
of the Lys it was stationed in the Poperinghe area, and here, on the 2nd May,
8th Battalion. the following officers joined the Battalion : Lieutenants A. L. M.
Sheehan and W. Becket, D.C.M. ; Second-Lieutenants E. H.
Jackson, H. R. Shawe, H. G. Machell, G. A. Sutcliffe, A. S. Pearson and
G. E. H. Slater, while a few days afterwards, a move in the meantime having
been made to Wylder, the following additional officers reported themselves for
duty : Second-Lieutenants R. Scott, J. K. Mackenzie, A. Herborn, W. T. Thornton,
A. A. K. Dallas, D. Philip. J. Brown, J. D. Deas, L. Ritchie and L. Gordon.

On the 9th May the 25th Division entrained at various places N.W. of
Poperinghe—the 8th Battalion The Border Regiment at Heidebecke—and commenced its long journey of nearly thirty hours to the district near Fismes, about
20 miles S.E. of Soissons, in Champagne, where the Division was once again
included in the IXth Corps. The Battalion was accommodated in billets in
Courville. Here Lieutenant-Colonel J. N. de la Perrelle arrived and took over
command of the Battalion, and several minor appointments were made in the
Battalion Staff, Lieutenant Bloomfield being appointed Lewis gun officer,
Lieutenant Sheehan signalling officer, Second-Lieutenant Darvell intelligence
officer, while Lieutenant Turnbull became assistant adjutant.

The reasons for the transfer of the 25th Division to a portion of the Allied
line outside British control must now be as briefly as possible stated. To quote
Sir Douglas Haig's despatch of the 21st December, 1918 : " At the end of
April and early in May, the 8th, 21st, 25th and 50th Divisions, subsequently
reinforced by the 19th Division and constituting the IXth British Corps, under
command of Lieutenant-General Sir A. Hamilton Gordon, had been placed at
Marshal Foch's disposal. These divisions had been despatched by him to the
Sixth French Army to take the place of certain French divisions concentrated
behind Amiens. Of those divisions the 19th, 21st, 25th and 50th had taken part
in both the Somme Battle and the Battle of the Lys. The 8th Division had
been involved S. of the Somme in some of the heaviest fighting of the year, and
had behaved with distinguished gallantry. All these divisions had but lately

been filled up with young drafts, and, despite their high spirit and gallant record, were in no condition to take part in major operations until they had had several days' rest. During the first fortnight in May three of these divisions —the 21st, 8th and 50th—were put into line on a front of about 15 miles between Bermicourt and Bouconville, N. of Rheims."

Marshal Foch had himself described this particular sector allotted to those British divisions as " a quiet place on the Aisne " ; he had been assured by his local commanders that the position here was impregnable ; but he was also himself apparently persuaded that under no circumstances would the enemy attack on this portion of the Allied front, but rather between Arras and Montdidier. In the event of an attack, the position along the so-called Chemin des Dames, formed by the watershed between the Rivers Aisne and Ailette from Craonne westward to the Soissons–Laon Road, was a bad one, for it was too narrow, and should in fact never have been held as a line of resistance, which should rather have been on the south bank of the Aisne.

The 25th was the last of the British divisions to reach the Champagne area, and on arrival found that the other three were already gradually relieving the French divisions of the Sixth French Army in the sector E. of the Chemin des Dames, on both banks of the Aisne. The front here now held by the IXth British Corps ran along the high ground about 4 miles N. of the Aisne for the first 16,000 yards, gradually bending back S.E. on its right to the important point of Berry-au-Bac, where the line crossed the river and continued on S.E. in the direction of Rheims for another 8,000 yards. The right sector, S. of the Aisne, was held by the 21st Division, in touch with the 36th French Division on the right, the 8th Division was in the centre, and the 50th on the left, joining up with the 22nd French Division N. of Craonne. From this point the French front lay along the commanding ridge known as the Chemin des Dames, captured by the French in 1917. The 25th Division on arrival in this area was placed in reserve to the other three about midway between the Aisne and the Marne, with headquarters at Arcis-le-Ponsart, the 7th, 74th and 75th Brigades being respectively at Arcis, Coulonges and Vandeuil respectively.

Fortified by the assurance that they had now reached a real " rest area," all ranks settled down comfortably in hutted camps, anticipating a good three weeks' steady training, with opportunity for assimilating and instructing the boys under 20 and the " combed-out " men of over 35, who had lately been arriving in increasing numbers to take the places of the more than 10,000 casualties incurred by the 25th Division during the past two months. A divisional school was opened at Coulonges, and classes of instruction in musketry, Lewis guns, trench mortars, bombing, etc., were all duly started.

About the middle of May all the intelligence and other reports received tended to make it tolerably certain that the enemy was preparing to attack ; **Battle of the Aisne.** there were, it is true, no signs of any great concentration of troops, but there seemed no doubt that huge ammunition dumps had been formed behind the German front and gun emplacements prepared, and as a precautionary measure the 25th Division was moved across the River Vesle, the Headquarters to Montigny, and the 75th Brigade to a camp at Romain; here Second-Lieutenant H. Lansley joined the 8th Battalion.

On the morning of the 26th May definite information was received and published to all concerned that the enemy intended to attack both the Allied fronts on the day following, and at 1.45 p.m. the Battalion received orders to prepare to move in an hour's time. It was not, however, until 9.30 p.m. that the brigades of the 25th Division moved up in close support of the other three British divisions, the 8th Battalion The Border Regiment taking up a position S. of the Ventelay–Bouvancourt Road, about 800 yards E. of Ventelay.

The 8th Battalion Diary states that "at 1 a.m. on the 27th the enemy bombardment opened and a few H.E. and gas shells fell on our right," but this seems to give no idea of the intensity of the fire which now opened and which came from upwards of one thousand guns of all calibres, deluging the front and support lines and the villages in the back areas as far as Fismes, while all that the Allies could muster for reply were 310 guns, field, heavy, medium and howitzers. This bombardment continued until 4 a.m. when the infantry attack commenced, 8 German divisions assailing the front held by the IXth British Corps, while 21 German divisions in all attacked on the French front of 30 miles.

While the bombardment was still in progress the Battalion scouts were sent out to reconnoitre the roads and approaches to Concevreux, Roucy and Guyencourt, and then at 6.35 a.m. one platoon per company was sent to take up a position astride the Ventelay–Roucy Road in front of La Peite Farm, preparatory to the Battalion moving thither; but rather less than an hour later orders were received for the 8th Border Regiment to move forward and occupy a position to defend the Bridge-head to Pontavert, and "C" and "D" Companies at once marched thither with "A" and "B" in support; almost immediately after this the order was expanded to include *all* the bridge-heads between Pontavert and Concevreux, of which there were eight, so that each company had to be responsible for the defence of two.

While moving off, and when between Ventelay and Roucy, information was received that the Germans were already approaching the river and canal, and the C.O. was now directed to at once send forward two companies to reinforce the 2nd Battalion South Lancashire Regiment on a line 100 yards N. of the village of Roucy to the E. of the Roucy–Pontavert Road. "A" and "B" accordingly pushed on while "C" and "D" remained in support close to Roucy. On reaching the line indicated, "B" Company was sent on to reinforce the 11th Cheshires on the left of the 2nd South Lancashire, while "D" Company was placed in close support of the Cheshires to the W. of Roucy. At 12.30 p.m. messages came in from the O.C. "D" Company stating that he was in position 150 yards S. of the railway N. of Roucy, and from the O.C. "A" Company reporting that he had placed himself under the orders of the Colonel of the South Lancashire Regiment and was occupying the northern slope of the Butte de Marchanne.

Under instructions from the Brigadier, "B" and "D" Companies were now withdrawn into reserve to the top of the hill in the southern outskirts of

Roucy, but almost at once " D " was ordered forward again to the line W. of Bouffingereux ; the machine-gun fire met with was, however, very severe, and the Brigade-Major, coming up, directed its retirement to its original position. Then at 3 in the afternoon the Battalion was instructed to fall back to a position astride the Ventelay–Roucy Road ; this was accordingly done, " D " Company being on the right and " B " on the left of the road, while details of the 8th and 50th Divisions were collected and placed in the line with a certain number of machine guns intended to assist in the defence of the position. Several attacks were made by the enemy during the next two hours, but these were repulsed, and patrols were sent out to the flanks to try and get touch with other troops ; it was, however, now apparent that there were no troops on either flank and the situation was duly reported, the reply being " to hang on and ammunition would be sent up." This unfortunately did not arrive.

At 5.30 it was clear that the enemy was gradually encircling the position ; he brought up heavy trench mortars and inflicted numerous casualties, while his snipers crawled out from the woods in front and opened fire, and other bodies advanced from the cover on the flanks and began to enfilade the position with machine guns.

Of the remaining events of the day and night the Divisional History records :—

" The 8th Borders by 10.30 p.m. were practically surrounded. The road through Ventelay was blocked by the enemy, who were also established in small bodies on either flank. At 1.30 a.m. on the 28th the remainder of the Battalion determined to fight its way back in the dark, and started off with advance and flank guards along the spur running S. between Ventelay and Romain. The flank guard became engaged with the enemy in the outskirts of Ventelay, but the remainder of the Battalion were enabled to get through to Romain, which they found occupied by the 21st French Infantry Regiment. From this time on the 8th Borders remained with the 3rd Battalion 21st French Regiment, and took up successive positions with the French troops along the aerodrome to the N. of Courville, then to the N. and finally to the S. of Crugny. The morning of the 30th the Battalion, now commanded by Major Fraser, finally joined up with the 74th Brigade near Romigny."

The above may now be elaborated from the 8th Battalion war diary.

During the night of the 27th–28th, finding that the position was practically surrounded, arrangements were made to break through before dawn and endeavour to rejoin the Brigade. Forming up at 1.30 a.m. on the 28th on the road running through La Peite Farm, advance, flank and rear guards were told off and the retirement began along the spur running S. between Ventelay and Romain. The left-flank guard became engaged on the outskirts of Ventelay, but, thus covered, the remainder got through to Romain, where the 21st French Infantry Regiment was found, and the Battalion marched on through Breuil to Les Venteaux, from where runners were sent out to try and find the Brigade ; but this could not then be located, so the C.O. placed his Battalion at the disposal of the French Commander, who ordered that it should report to the O.C.

Photo

Imperial War Museum

MENIN ROAD, 1918

Photo

Imperial War Museum

TROOPS RESTING IN RESERVE TRENCHES

3rd Battalion of that corps at the farm Bonne Maison on the hills to the N.E. of Courville.

(It seems incorrect here to speak of the 8th Border Regiment as a *battalion*, since on arrival at the farm the remaining British troops made up but 2 companies, one formed from Border men, the other from details of several battalions of the 8th and 50th Divisions.)

Driven from the position taken up on the high ground near Courville, the Allied infantry fell back to another astride the spur to the N. of Crugny, and, the enemy pressing on, to a third to the S. of this village. But by 5 p.m. on the 28th the British detachment ran short of ammunition and was without rations, and, the French being unable to supply either, the details were ordered to withdraw and endeavour to rejoin their own troops. They marched therefore by Broullet, coming under heavy enemy shell fire, and arrived at Lagery, where rations were found but no ammunition. From here they marched on to Aougny, where a few hours' greatly needed rest was obtained.

Early on the morning of the 29th, Romigny, where was the Headquarters of the 8th Division, was reached, and here a position was occupied on the W. side of the Lhery–Romigny Road, about half a mile from Romigny, the remnants of the Battalion coming under the orders of the 74th Infantry Brigade ; this was a position of reserve against any possible enemy break-through from the direction of Lhery, and here the day passed fairly quietly except for some spasmodic shelling.

" About 4 a.m. on the 30th," we read in the Battalion diary, " the enemy were seen advancing down the slope towards the farm N.W. of Aougny ; they continued to work down the valley and, owing to the French withdrawing, our left flank was in the air and the village of Romigny was undefended from the S.W. By this time our position had come under heavy enemy machine-gun and light field-gun fire from the ridge. The troops on our right withdrew, and as our position had become untenable we withdrew in a S.W. direction over the Ville-en-Tardenois–Romigny Road into the Bois de Bonval, and, coming round in a W. direction, took up a position in the front edge of the wood facing N., the position running along the front of the wood from the road 800 yards S.W. of Romigny to where the track runs N. to the Romigny–Jonquery Road. By this time the enemy were in Romigny, but were driven out again by a counter-attack by the Northumberland Fusiliers."

This position, too, had shortly to be evacuated by reason of the enemy gun-fire and another was taken up 200 yards in rear ; and so the retreat went on from one line to another, from a position on either side of the Ville-en-Tardenois–Jonquery Road to one near Nappes, from there to another near Boujacourt, and again to another near the S.W. corner of the Bois de l'Eglise.

It was now the 1st June, and here near Nappes orders were received that a composite Battalion was to be formed called " the 1st/25th Divisional Composite Battalion," commanded by Major Traill, Worcester Regiment, and for this the 8th Border Regiment was called upon to supply 4 officers—Lieutenants C. A. Scott and V. Bloomfield, Second-Lieutenants J. D. Deas and R. Scott—and

14

104 other ranks, forming one company known as " No. 2 Company (Border Company)," and during the 2nd and 3rd June this Composite Battalion was held in support to the French. It remained in or near the front line until the middle of the month, usually under shell fire, but by this time reinforcements were arriving—mainly composed of Italian and American troops, and on the 18th the Composite Battalion was relieved and the Border Company proceeded via Germaine and Fère Champenoise to St. Loup and rejoined the remainder of the 8th Border Regiment.

The end of the retreat came actually on the 6th June, culminating in two desperate attacks made on the Montagne de Bligny, which were repulsed. The Commander of the Sixth French Army wrote a letter to Lieutenant-General Hamilton Gordon congratulating him on the endurance and fine fighting powers shown by his troops, and concluding :—

" *With a tenacity, permit me to say, wholly British, you have reformed in the remnants of your divisions, submerged in the hostile flood, the new reinforcements which you have thrown into the fight, and which have finally allowed us to build a dam against which the German flood has beaten itself in vain. All this, no French witness can ever forget.*"

This was the last action in which the 8th Battalion The Border Regiment was to be engaged as a unit. To the regret of all ranks it was now learnt that the infantry of the 25th Division was to be broken up and the Service battalions used as reinforcements for other battalions. On the 17th and 18th the various Composite Battalions were withdrawn from the line, the Regular battalions of the 25th Division were distributed amongst the 19th, 21st and 30th Divisions, while a Composite Brigade was made up from the remainder of the infantry battalions for service with the 50th Division until disbanded a few weeks later.

In accordance with the above arrangements the 8th Border Regiment now contributed 12 officers and 306 other ranks to form, with the 9th Loyal North Lancashire Regiment, No. 2 Battalion of the 50th Divisional Composite Brigade, while the rest—16 officers and 86 non-commissioned officers and men—proceeded by road and rail to Embry, from where arrangements for final disbandment of the Battalion were eventually carried out.

During this Second Battle of the Aisne the losses incurred by the Battalion had been very heavy, amounting to 3 officers and 9 other ranks killed, 2 officers and 75 other ranks wounded, while no fewer than 8 officers and 203 non-commissioned officers and men were missing—the majority, no doubt, killed or wounded. The officers' names are : killed—Second-Lieutenants H. G. Machell, J. Bell, and J. K. Mackenzie ; wounded—Second-Lieutenants H. W. S. Young and E. W. Jackson ; missing—Captain A. Miscampell, Lieutenant H. Lansley, Second-Lieutenants W. T. Thornton, J. Brown, D. Philip, C. Spence, F. H. Darvell and G. A. Sutcliffe.

It was at this stage that Marshal Foch decided to take the offensive.

The organization of the 5th Battalion of the Regiment as a Pioneer Battalion does not appear to have lasted for any very great length of time, since there is an entry in the diary of the 9th May—when the Battalion had left the 66th to join the 32nd Division, thus taking the place of the 11th Battalion—to the effect that " the Battalion once more takes its place amongst the fighting units after working for a short time as a Pioneer Battalion " ; but none the less the Battalion was not very actively engaged during the months of May, June and July, took no part in the Battles of the Aisne and Marne, which were fought during these months of 1918, and was not again called into the field until the advance in Picardy commenced early in August.

5th Battalion.

On the 6th August the 97th Brigade, in which the 5th Battalion was now serving, was inspected by H.M. the King, and early the following morning all left Proven and proceeded by train and bus to Domart, marching thence up the line to bivouacs in a field near Beaucourt. From here at 4 a.m. on the 10th the Battalion marched to Warvillers and deployed for attack, passing through the Canadians, who were holding the line, and the objective being that portion of the railway between Hattencourt and Fresnoy. On reaching the slopes of the ridge the enemy opened a very heavy machine-gun fire and the platoons were forced to deploy into sections and advance in snake formation, and the old line of trenches on the top of the ridge was reached ; but uncut wire and machine-gun fire in front of Fouquescourt and Parvillers held up the advance, while the troops who were to have attacked on the flank were not yet up in line.

Here occurred several casualties among the officers : Lieutenant Huntingdon, M.C., was killed, and Lieutenant-Colonel Bradley-Williams, Captain Williams and Second-Lieutenants Jones and Jackson were wounded.

The night of the 10th–11th was quiet and no further advance was made ; and during the early morning of the 12th the Battalion was relieved and marched back to Berteaucourt, where the Divisional General came and thanked all ranks for their services. The losses had amounted to 12 killed and 99 wounded among the other ranks, while Captain Harrison had also been mortally wounded while arranging about the relief.

On the 17th the 5th Battalion was sent to the neighbourhood of Harbonnières and took part on the 22nd in an attack on Herleville, where the casualties among the other ranks were slight, but 4 officers were wounded—Lieutenant Calvert, Second-Lieutenants Morton, McNab and Drummond.

On the 27th the Battalion—now temporarily with the 96th Brigade—was concerned in an attack on Ablaincourt, the attack starting at 5 a.m., the 5th Border Regiment in the centre, with the 2nd Manchesters and 1st Dorsets on right and left respectively. The Battalion reached the top of the ridge and occupied trenches S. of Starry Wood, but now and later the forward companies were badly shelled by high explosive and gas shells and suffered some casualties. The advance was continued next day, and by 8 a.m. Ablaincourt was in our hands ; the move forward was then made on Mazancourt and that also had been captured by 5 p.m., and now a defensive position was taken up for the night, " A " and " C " Companies being in trenches N. and S. of the village with supports and reserves in rear.

On the 29th the advance was again successfully pressed and Misery was reached and held, touch established on the flanks, patrols sent out and trenches occupied.   On this day the Battalion was re-transferred to the 97th Brigade and went back into brigade reserve.

The following letters testify to the high opinion entertained of the value of the services of the Battalion in the action by those who fought with them, and at all times by their own Brigadier; Lieutenant-Colonel Lamotte, 2nd K.O.Y.L.I., wrote to the C.O. :—

" I should like to take this opportunity of thanking your Regiment for the very great assistance given me by your " A " Company in our recent fight.   Your Company Commander was most willing and carried out his orders in a very thorough and most conscientious manner, giving me every assistance and very greatly aided me and my Regiment.   Will you please thank him and his company from me and my Regiment."

Brigadier-General Minshull Ford wrote as follows :—

" We are all very proud of what the Borders have been and are doing.   Please give them all our best wishes and congratulations.   I am so sorry that you are away from us, but I hope that you will be back with us very soon.   I very much regret your casualties, of which we only know bare facts at present.

" The very best of luck."

In his despatch of the 21st December, 1918, the Field-Marshal wrote as follows of the operations just described : " The results of the Battle of Amiens may be summarized as follows.   Within the space of five days the town of Amiens and the railway centring upon it had been disengaged.   Twenty German divisions had been heavily defeated by thirteen British infantry divisions and three cavalry divisions, assisted by a regiment of the 33rd American Division and supported by some 400 tanks.   Nearly 20,000 prisoners and over 400 guns had been taken by us and our line had been pushed forward to a depth of some 12 miles in a vital sector.   Further, our deep advance, combined with the attacks of the French armies on our right, had compelled the enemy to evacuate hurriedly a wide extent of territory to the S. of us.

" The effect of this victory, following so closely after the Allied victory on the Marne, upon the *morale* of the German and British troops was very great. Buoyed by the hope of immediate and decisive victory, to be followed by an early and favourable peace, constantly assured that the Allied reserves were exhausted, the German soldiery suddenly found themselves attacked on two fronts and thrown back with heavy losses from large and important portions of their earlier gains.   The reaction was inevitable and of a deep and lasting character."

Ludendorff describes the 8th August as " the black day of the German Army in the history of this war."   He ascribes directly to it the defection of Bulgaria and the general discouragement of Germany's allies.

On the 3rd September orders were issued for the Brigade front to be divided into two sectors, when the 5th Border Regiment took the left, the 2nd K.O.Y.L.I. the right, " B " and " D " Companies of the former holding the line with two platoons each, the remaining platoons being in some quarries in rear, while " A " and " C " Companies were in reserve. At 10.30 on the morning of the 5th the Brigade was directed to effect the crossing of the Somme at Brie, and " A " and " C " Companies of the 5th Battalion The Border Regiment were over about 12.45 and then worked their way forward in a S. direction, "mopping up" the woods and other lurking places of the enemy, while seeking to get in touch with the 2nd K.O.Y.L.I., who were to cross the river at St. Christ. " A " Company captured René Wood with some 25 prisoners, while " C " took the quarry in front with 25 more, supporting at the same time the passage of the river by the K.O.Y.L.I. and assisting in the surrender of 80 Germans, who were sheltering in dug-outs from our fire.

" B " and " D " Companies now passed through the line the other two companies had taken up and moved on towards Athies and were in position by 6.30 p.m. In the evening orders came in to renew the advance next morning to the Green, Red and Blue Lines in succession, and this commenced soon after daylight on the 6th, the Dorset Regiment being on the left and the K.O.Y.L.I. on the right with the Omignon River as the boundary. Some opposition was met with from enemy machine guns on the right, but the Green Line was reached at 7, and the advance pressed on ; resistance was of small account until the troops reached the neighbourhood of the Red Line, when a heavy fire opened on them from Valley Woods, but this was overcome and the Red Line was arrived at by 10.45 a.m., when " B " and " D " Companies of the 5th Border Regiment established themselves in a line along the Tertry–Peronne Road with outposts on the high ground to the front ; " C " Company was in support and " A " in reserve. There was some shelling of the line, which increased in severity during the afternoon and evening.

Advancing again early on the 7th September, " A " and " C " passed through " B " and " D " Companies, and with these following in support the Blue Line was reached at 9.15, the advance being held up for a time by fire from machine and field guns, but this was soon crushed, the line was established and touch gained by 11 o'clock with the troops on either flank.

The 8th was occupied in consolidation and in patrolling—the reports sent in stating that Vermaud was clear of the enemy, but that Marteville and Atilly were still held.

By noon on the 9th the K.O.Y.L.I. had established outposts in front, and " C " Company of the Battalion moved up and occupied a line about Bocquet Copse, with a strong post in the S.W. corner of the Cemetery. At last, at midnight on the 10th, the 5th Battalion The Border Regiment was relieved and went back into Brigade Reserve at Monchy Lagache ; two days later the 1st Division took the place of the 32nd, which then moved to Villers Bretonneux, there to enjoy a very brief respite until again called upon to help in the final discomfiture and pursuit of the enemy.

At the termination of the First Battle of the Somme of 1918 we left the 7th Battalion The Border Regiment occupying Flesselles during the first few days of April, but a week later it was moved to Engelbelmer, where the strength of the Battalion is given as "about 20 officers and 740 men," and where it remained until the last day of the month, marching then to Forceville. Leaving

7th Battalion. here again on the 20th May, a move was made by way of La Vicogne and Le Vert Galon to Beauquesne, which appears to have been something of the nature of a rest area, and where, while steady training went on, sport and recreation were also not overlooked

During June the Battalion, now about Auchonvillers, suffered a good deal from Spanish influenza, which then was everywhere very prevalent ; at the end of this month the 7th Border Regiment was at Herissart and was employed on the Senlis defences. While up here in the line about the middle of July an amusing incident occurred. The Americans were now arriving at the front in small parties but in ever-increasing numbers, and one day " B " Company of the Battalion sent back to Battalion Headquarters under escort an American private whom they had found wandering about. His excuse seems under the circumstances to have been accepted as a perfectly natural one—as excusable if idle curiosity, as something which time no doubt would remedy ; he said he " had only come up for a look ra-ound ! "

The Battalion war diary for the 31st July contains the entry : " Nothing of importance to record," but if the last three months had been comparatively uneventful, August was to prove full of sufficient excitement, and the 7th Battalion The Border Regiment, though denied participation in the Second Battles of the Aisne and Marne, was at least to share in the hard fighting of the Second Somme Battle of 1918.

The weather turned very rainy towards the end of July and so continued during the early days of August, and the activities of the troops were consequently somewhat restricted ; but at the 2nd of the month a reconnaissance, carried out by Second-Lieutenant Stewart of the Battalion, disclosed the fact that the enemy had evacuated his front system, and a general forward move was consequently made in the direction of the Ancre, a new line being established about 500 yards from the river with standing patrols on the Aveluy–Authuille road. Here the following message was found left behind by one of the late occupants of a German dug-out : " Dear Tommy. When you are coming we are gone, hoping you have many pleasures in our cottages. Why you send so many iron postcards, eat some yourself. Make peace next time, have you not enough ? "

After this the Battalion had a few days in rear at Vaux-sur-Somme, and then on the 12th August moved to Mericourt and there relieved the support companies of the 11th Infantry Brigade of the 3rd Australian Division, being in support now to the 7th Lincolns and 10th Foresters—" everything very quiet and the weather beautiful." But this peaceful condition of affairs was not to last, for on the very next day the enemy put over clouds of gas, which appear to have come upon portions of the Battalion before they had time to adjust their gas-masks, with the unfortunate result that over 200 casualties resulted, including 8 officers, " C " and " D " Companies suffering the most severely and having to be amalgamated temporarily into one company under command of

Lieutenant Rennie, M.C. The other units of the Brigade also were affected, and the whole day was taken up in salving the rifles and equipment of the gassed cases, of whom upwards of 700 passed through the Regimental Aid Post.

The Division was now withdrawn on relief by the Australians and the Battalion marched away towards the N., leaving Rawlinson's Fourth Army to join the Vth Corps of Byng's Third Army, and, proceeding by Fouilloy, Vecquemont, Herissart, Toutencourt and Hedauville, arrived on the 24th at Thiepval and was at once sent forward into positions of readiness for an attack upon Courcelette.

When the Second Battle of the Somme opened on the 21st August the Vth Corps had attacked with the 21st and 38th Divisions in the front line and the 17th in support in rear, inadequately supported by artillery **Second Battle of the Somme.** and over ground that was too marshy for the action of tanks, while from the heights on the E. of the Ancre the ground to be advanced over was completely overlooked. On this day Beaucourt was captured, small bodies of troops had effected in places the passage of the Ancre, and one brigade of the 17th Division had been brought up into the line ; on the 23rd the river was crossed and that night Thiepval Ridge was carried, and on the 24th the advantage was to be pressed and the enemy driven back and pursued, the whole of the 17th Division being now up in the line.

The story of the operations, so far as these concerned the 7th Border Regiment, is told in the Battalion Diary as follows :—

" *25th August.*—Attacked Courcelette with Lincolns on right and Sherwoods in support. ' C ' Company on right, ' A ' on left, ' B ' Company in support and ' D ' in reserve. Attack passed through Courcelette and on towards Martinpuich, held up on ridge W. of Martinpuich, no troops on left and Lancashire Fusiliers on right. Lincolns moved up on left and the attack went forward again to the ridge E. of Martinpuich, which was held. A very heavy rainstorm made these operations more difficult and Company Commanders did great work in getting their companies into position. Lieutenant Laing did particularly well in reconnoitring positions for ' B ' and ' D ' Companies. During the fighting on the ridge E. of Martinpuich, where the enemy put up a stiff resistance and attempted a counter-attack, Second-Lieutenants Scott and Burn were wounded by machine-gun fire.

" After two attempts ' B ' and ' D ' Companies advanced our line (on the 26th) 300 yards E. of Eaucourt l'Abbaye, taking up a position with the flanks protected ; during this advance Captain Moorsom was wounded. ' A ' and ' C ' Companies, missing their direction, attacked at the same time on the right of the village of Eaucourt l'Abbaye and advanced 1,200 yards towards Flers with the Lincolns, they then withdrew to the support of ' B ' and ' D ' Companies and took part in the third attack in which our line was advanced another 200 yards E. of Eaucourt l'Abbaye."

The resistance was now everywhere stiffening, and it was evident that the enemy was putting up a strong fight in order to gain time for the withdrawal of his guns and supplies.

" *27th August*.—Early in the morning the 7th East York of the 50th Brigade advanced through us and occupied a position about 300 yards further E.—' B ' and ' D ' Companies forming a flank guard as the troops on the left were not yet up in line. We remained in support for the remainder of the day. . . .

" *29th*.—The Battalion attacked Gueudecourt and captured the village and some prisoners, establishing ourselves on the ridge 500 yards E. of the village, ' D ' Company formed a defensive flank and ' C ' Company remained in support to ' A ' and ' B '; later in the day the troops came up on the left and drew level with us, and ' A ' and ' B ' Companies then advanced over 1,500 yards to the outskirts of Le Transloy and remained there until dark, when we were ordered to withdraw on account of having pushed too far ahead of both flanks; this move cost us 20 or 30 men wounded.

" *30th*.—Early this morning we again advanced 1,500 yards and established our line about 500 yards W. of Le Transloy—' B ' and ' C ' Companies in front, with ' D ' in close support, while ' A ' formed a defensive flank, the left again not having advanced with us. During the day, and especially in the afternoon, very plucky efforts were made by our men to gain the village of Le Transloy, but these failed owing to heavy sniping and machine-gun fire and to the fact that our flanks were quite unprotected. Second-Lieutenant White and a party of ' C ' Company gained the outskirts of the village, but had to retire late in the afternoon. The 10th Lancashire Fusiliers relieved the Battalion and we marched back to the Martinpuich–Eaucourt l'Abbaye road for a rest."

The casualties during the operations of this month, but mainly, of course, during the last week of it, had been serious, 1 officer and 30 other ranks had been killed or had died of wounds, 13 officers and 375 men had been wounded or gassed, while 20 men were missing; the names of the officers are: Killed or died of wounds—Second-Lieutenant A. G. Sharp; wounded—Captain R. S. Moorsom; Second-Lieutenants W. G. Brewen, E. N. Burn, D. McKinley and Scott; gassed—Captains H. C. Lloyd and R. R. Hayes, M.C.; Lieutenant E. Sanger, M.C.; Second-Lieutenants F. W. Hinde, M.C., A. J. W. Dunnett, W. J. Caird, J. B. Trotter and W. L. Cobban, D.C.M.

The rest afforded the 7th Battalion was but a brief one, for on the 2nd September it was pulled out again and sent into brigade support to Gueude-court and on the 4th to the sunken road S.E. of Bus; but in the afternoon it was brought back and distributed in depth, the rear company being about 600 yards E. of Rocquigny in some old trenches, moving forward again next morning to Lechelle in support to the 7th Lincoln Regiment in the line. From here the Battalion was ordered at very short notice to make a flank attack on the system of trenches on the ridge E. of Vallulart Wood, the Lincoln Regiment having suffered very severely and being held up. In a very heavy thunderstorm the Battalion moved up into position and at 8.30 p.m. " C " Company attacked, completely surprising the enemy, a number of whom were killed and 10 captured with 13 machine guns, the remainder running away, and the whole enemy system here being occupied as far as the outskirts of Equancourt. At the end of this operation the Battalion had three companies in line—" A," " B " and " C "—distributed in depth, one platoon of each forming a line of sentry groups, and two platoons holding the trench 500 yards E. of Mouette Farm as a defensive flank facing Equancourt. During this day especially good work was done by Lieutenant R. C. White.

Early on the morning of the 6th the Battalion improved its position and occupied several small trenches further to the front. During this morning Lieutenant Mackenrot was wounded by machine-gun fire, and in the course of the next twenty-four hours the Battalion was relieved and marched back first to Rocquigny and then two or three days later to Lechelle.

In all these operations, as a historian of the war has pointed out, the 17th Division had the supreme satisfaction of hurling the enemy out of a long series of villages which the British had themselves been forced to relinquish during the pressure of the great March advance.

The period now arrived at marks the close of the second stage of the British advance in Flanders and Picardy. "Having in the first stage freed Amiens by our brilliant success E. of that town, in the second stage the troops of the Third and Fourth Armies, comprising 23 British Divisions, by skilful leading, hard fighting and relentless and unremitting pursuit, in ten days had driven 35 German divisions from one side of the old Somme battle-field to the other, thereby turning the line of the River Somme. In so doing they had inflicted upon the enemy the heaviest losses in killed and wounded, and had taken from him over 34,000 prisoners and 270 guns.... In the obstinate fighting of the past few days the enemy had been pressed back to the line of the Somme River and the high ground about Rocquigny and Beugny, where he had shown an intention to stand for a time. Thereafter, his probable plan was to retire slowly, when forced to do so, from one intermediary position to another, until he could shelter his battered divisions behind the Hindenburg defences. The line of the Tortille River and the high Nurlu Plateau offered opportunities for an ordered withdrawal of this nature, which would allow him to secure his artillery as well as much of the material in his forward dumps.... In such circumstances, a sudden and successful blow, of weight sufficient to break through the northern hinge of the defences to which it was his design to fall back, might produce results of great importance. At this date our troops were already in position to deliver such a stroke." [1]

[1] Despatch of 21st December, 1918.

CHAPTER XIII

1918

THE 2ND BATTALION IN ITALY.

THE 9TH BATTALION IN SALONIKA.

THE 1ST/4TH AND 2ND/4TH BATTALIONS IN INDIA.

DURING the early months of the year 1918 the infantry of the British Expeditionary Force did not take part in any serious fighting on the Italian front, although, as General Plumer writes in his last despatch, " we can fairly claim to have had some share " in the general improvement in the situation. Early in the year the Italians had driven the Austrians from the W. bank of the Piave about Zenson, had achieved a measure of success in an attack on Monte Asolone, and had carried out certain operations of a generally satisfactory nature on the Asiago Plateau. In some of the above the British artillery assisted and an additional 3,000 prisoners in all were captured.

The 2nd Battalion The Border Regiment was still at Riese when the year commenced, but on the 11th it marched thence by way of St. Vito and Asolo to billets

2nd Battalion. in Cunial, the Battalion Headquarters being at Castelcucco, and was at once set to work on the reserve defensive positions between Costalunga and Cunial on the N. slopes of the hills opposite Monte Tomba. Here the Rev. E. W. Burnell joined the Battalion as chaplain.

On the 19th January the 2nd Border Regiment marched by way of Montebelluna and Volpago to billets in the Selva area, where the 7th Division relieved the 41st in the right sector of the Corps front, the 22nd and 91st Brigades holding the line with the 20th in Divisional Reserve. But under date of the 26th we read in the war diary that " the Battalion moved forward on to the Montello at 5.30 p.m. and relieved the 20th Manchesters as support battalion in the Brigade right sector. . . . 2nd Gordon Highlanders hold right of Brigade sector including Nervasa, 8th Devons left sector with left near St. Croce, and 9th Devons in reserve at Bavaria. The Battalion is scattered among dells and hollows among the hills, some of the men in good dug-outs, others in cubby holes or Italian bivouacs ; most of the positions are well camouflaged by brushwood. Battalion Headquarters in a deep hollow, originally the headquarters of the Umbria Brigade which held back the Germans and Austrians from crossing the Piave during the Italian retreat. An inscription in the Mess states their first visitor was H.R.H. the Prince of Wales on November 25th."

On the 27th the Divisional Guard supplied by the Drums of the Battalion had a very cheering little excitement, capturing 2 officers and a non-commissioned officer of an enemy bombing plane which had been forced to descend near St. Floriano, and who had eluded observation and were escaping to the mountains. The sentry, Drummer McGuinness, noticed their movements which aroused his suspicions, and he turned out the guard, who captured them, the prisoners wildly protesting that they were Italians !

The following is an account of the general line of the Battalion front now occupied : " the front companies each had two platoons below the cliff on the shore and islands, with their Company Headquarters at heads of Roads 2 and 3 respectively. Battalion Headquarters in a cottage on the extreme right of Road 2 with dug-outs in a neighbouring hollow. The troops below the cliff occupy fifteen posts by night along the water's edge and spend the time wiring and improving their positions. The ground occupied is covered with scrub and small trees which hide the day positions, shelters and dug-outs, 50 to 500 yards behind the posts. The river is divided into three to eight streams of varying width and depth, but all very swift. Except for scrub near the foreshore, the river bed is of shingle, gleaming white by day, with ribbons of blue water threading it. Posts can only be visited by night, with the exception of two Observation Posts on the cliff. ' D ' Company's Headquarters are in a big cave near the base of the cliff approached by the goat-track. The other ways to the foreshore are the mule-track and quarry steps."

While up in the line several attempts were made, notably by Lieutenant Gascoigne-Roy, Second-Lieutenants Tomlinson and Clifford, with patrols from their companies of the Battalion, to cross the Piave and reconnoitre the enemy bank, but the centre stream was too deep and swift, while the water was so cold that it turned to ice on the men's clothes and these attempts had therefore to be abandoned.

Towards the end of February rumours began to circulate that the 7th Division was likely to be recalled to France, and it was not until the 4th March, when part of the 20th Brigade had already entrained at Camposampiero, that it was announced that the recall was postponed, and thereupon several moves took place, the end of the month finding the Division on the Asiago Plateau, the Battalion crossing the valley of the Astico River at Caltrano and taking over billets from the Italians in Camisino, a small and practically deserted village, to the S. of which the ground dropped sharply to the Astico, 300 feet below, while on the N. the ground rose steeply for about 2 miles to Monte Sunio, 4,000 feet in height.

By this time, however, the very serious situation created on the Western Front by the success of the German offensive of this month had induced the recall of certain of the Allied divisions sent to Italy at the time of the Caporetto disaster, and by the 3rd April four French divisions and two British had returned to France ; the two British defections, the 5th and 41st, did not cause any difference in the *original* strength of the British contingent, for these had only arrived in Italy, the 5th early in December 1917, and the 41st on the 12th November of that year. This left in

Italy three British divisions only, the 7th, 23rd and 48th, and these were now commanded by Lieutenant-General the Earl of Cavan *vice* General Sir H. Plumer, who returned to France on the 10th March.

"During April," writes Lord Cavan in his despatch of the 14th September, 1918, "signs continued to accumulate that the enemy contemplated an offensive astride the Brenta, but it was not until the middle of May that it appeared probable that this operation would be combined with an attack across the Piave. By the end of May the general plan of the enemy for their forthcoming attack could be clearly foreseen. Subsequent events proved that the Italian High Command had made a forecast correct in nearly every detail."

After a pleasant three weeks spent in or near Camisino the 2nd Border Regiment marched on the 21st April by a mule-track via Monte Grumo and Monte Sunio to huts near Monte Brusabo in heavy rain, changing as the troops mounted higher to sleet and snow ; the camp here was some 4,000 feet above sea-level and must have provided a pleasant change from the devastated fields of France and Flanders, since we read in the war diary of the Battalion that "the ground was covered with crocuses, snowdrops, primroses and other flowers." Next day the Battalion moved to Casa Magnaboschi, a farm in a sheltered dip behind the support line, where the Battalion was at first in divisional reserve ; the front line was between Monte Lemerle and the Ghelpac Valley.

While here a great misfortune befell the Battalion ; on the 2nd May the enemy opened a barrage on the Battalion front, in retaliation no doubt for the raiding activities of the 2nd Border Regiment in general, and especially in retaliation for a raid then actually in progress by the 1st Royal Welch Fusiliers on the left. At 2.10 a.m. a shell entered the Battalion Headquarters hut, killing Lieutenant-Colonel W. Kerr, D.S.O., M.C., and wounding Captain Russell, M.C., Second-Lieutenant Bell and two other ranks. Next day the command of the 2nd Battalion The Border Regiment was taken over by Major H. A. Ross, D.S.O., of the Gordon Highlanders. This unhappy affair rather increased than checked the raiding and patrolling by the Battalion, in which Lieutenants Gascoigne-Roy and Davidson, Second-Lieutenants Craine, Wilson, Ashton and Bald were especially conspicuous, and in one of these several prisoners were taken and brought in.

The loss of Lieutenant-Colonel W. Kerr, D.S.O., M.C., cannot be passed over without a final tribute to this gallant officer, who, on the outbreak of the war, was a company sergeant-major in the 2nd Battalion. He was commissioned in the field in 1914 and rose step by step until at the end of 1917 he obtained command of the Battalion which he had so well served and which he continued to command until he was killed.

At the end of May the Battalion was in billets at Arzignano, but moved again during the first week in June by motor-lorries to St. Maria, and later in the month to a camp on Monte Serona.

On June 15th the Austrians attacked on two fronts of respectively 25 and 18 miles, from St. Dono di Piave to the Montello on the plains and from Grappa to Canove in the mountains, the whole of the British sector being involved and the 23rd and 48th Divisions being engaged. The 7th Division "stood to" all the

15th, but was not required to act. In this offensive the enemy obtained some initial success, but being counter-attacked the ground gained was recovered and a portion of the right bank of the Piave, which had been in Austrian hands since the previous November, was finally cleared of the enemy. On the 27th June there were indications that the Austrians intended to renew their offensive and the 7th Division was held in readiness, but nothing transpired and things for a time at least became quiet again.

During June drafts amounting to 152 other ranks joined the Battalion, and in the month following the 7th Division appears to have returned to the neighbourhood of Magnaboschi on the Asiago Plateau, and on the night of the 8th–9th August a very successful raid was carried out on Stella Fort. The party was composed of " B " and " D " Companies under the command of Captain Little with Captain Campbell in charge of the assaulting company. Twenty-one prisoners and 3 machine guns were captured, all of these being taken by a small party made up of Second-Lieutenant Samut, Company Sergeant-Major Loughman, Sergeants Creighton and Bell and Private Garside. The enemy put up a considerable resistance, making much use of his trench mortars, but any enemy barrage was practically non-existent owing to the excellent counter-battery work of our artillery. The hostile trench mortars, however, caused many casualties and the proportion of killed to wounded was high. A prisoner captured next day stated that all the garrison of Stella Fort was either killed or wounded.

During the month of September the 2nd Battalion The Border Regiment was training in the plains at Montecchio Maggiore, and now the question of a return to France seems again to have cropped up. In his despatch of the 15th November, 1918, General Lord Cavan writes :—

" Early in September, as it appeared unlikely that offensive operations would be undertaken in Italy in the near future, it was decided to assist France with some or all of the British troops in this country. . . . In accordance with this idea the 7th, 23rd and 48th Divisions were reduced from 13 to 10 battalions, and the 9 battalions [1] thus released were despatched to France on September 13th and 14th. The 7th Division was then at rest, and it was intended to dispatch this Division as soon as a battle-worn division should arrive from France to replace it. . . . As a result of the tactical situation in France and the subsequent demands on rolling stock, the proposed exchange of divisions was postponed from day to day. The situation in Italy also changed, and finally all three divisions remained in this country."

On the 25th October the 2nd Border Regiment marched with the 20th Brigade from Montecchio Maggiore to the Palazzo-Sforza della Torre, 1 kilometre N. of Vicenza, remained here until the 12th and then proceeded by train to Preganziol, S. of Treviso, and marched thence to St. Giuseppe W. of Treviso, and there took over billets from the 12th Cyclist Battalion of Bersaglieri ; here the passage of a river in boats was carefully practised. Finally, on the 23rd October, the Battalion moved to an assembly area S. of Maserada preparatory to an attack across the Piave.

[1] The 9th Devons was the battalion now taken out of the 20th Brigade.

The Commander of the Allied Forces in Italy, General Diaz, had an army made up of representatives of nearly every one of the Allied nations ; he had under him 57 divisions—51 Italian divisions, 3 British, 2 French, 1 Czecho-Slovak, and 1 American Regiment. On the Asiago Plateau was the Sixth Italian Army containing the 48th British Division ; in the Grappa sector was the Fourth Italian Army which included a French Division ; along the Piave and as far S. as the Montello was the Twelfth Italian Army with the remaining French Division ; at the Montello itself was the Eighth Italian Army ; to the S. of this was the Tenth Italian Army, commanded by Earl Cavan and containing 1 Italian and 1 British Corps, the XIVth, composed of the 7th and 23rd Divisions ; while between Cavan and the sea was the Third Italian Army.

The plan of attack which General Diaz now proposed to carry out was simple enough : a feint attack by the Fourth Army on the Grappa, while the Twelfth, Eighth and Tenth Armies struck at the two Austrian armies, drove a wedge between them and cut their communications ; the Twelfth Army was to fight its way up the Piave to Feltre, the Eighth to make good the Valmarino and Vittorio, driving the Sixth Austrian Army northward, while the Tenth Italian Army was to move due E. to the Livenza, protecting the flanks of the two other armies and driving back the rest of the Austrians on a different line of retreat.

" The problem that faced the Tenth Army was not an easy one. The breadth of the Piave on the front of attack was approximately 1½ miles, and consisted of numerous channels dotted with islands. The main island was the Grave di Papadopoli, which was some 3 miles long by 1 mile broad. The current varied according to the channels. In the main channel it ran at a rate exceeding 10 miles an hour in time of flood, and never dropped below 3 miles an hour at summer level. The enemy held the Grave di Papodopoli as an advanced post.

" On October 21st the XIVth British Corps took over the northern portion of the XIth Italian Corps front from Salletuol to Palazzon. Orders were issued that all troops visible to the enemy should wear Italian uniform, and that no British gun should fire a single shot previous to the general bombardment. By these means it was hoped to conceal the presence of British troops from the Austrians. On the date of relief the Piave was in full flood, which not only made reconnaissance of the river bed impossible, but also raised the probability of changes in the main channels. This added considerably to my anxieties as regards bridging requirements. Lieutenant-General Sir J. Babington, commanding the XIVth British Corps, at once suggested the advisability of occupying the island of Grave di Papadopoli previous to the general advance. With this opinion I concurred." [1]

The following extracts are taken from Battalion operation orders by Lieutenant-Colonel Darwell, M.C., commanding 2nd Border Regiment, dated the 24th October :—

" On the night of the 24th–25th the 7th Division is to force the passage of the Piave and advance rapidly to Livenza. The initial attack of the 7th Division against the enemy main line of defence will be made by the 20th Brigade on the

[1] Despatch of the 15th November, 1918.

right, the 91st Brigade on the left and the 22nd Brigade in reserve. The task of the 20th Brigade is being carried out in the following order :—

1. 2nd Gordon Highlanders.
2. 8th Devon Regiment.
3. 2nd Border Regiment.

"At an hour to be notified later, probably 21 hours, which will be called ' zero hour,' the passage of the river will be commenced. The hour of attack on the main enemy defences on the left bank of the river will be shortly after dawn, the exact hour being notified later : this hour will be called ' H ' hours. . . . The troops of the 20th Brigade will form up on the Grave di Papadopoli under cover of the troops already in occupation of that island. . . . The general bombardment of the defences will commence at 2330 hours. . . . In addition to the ferry boats it is hoped to throw across the following bridges :—

1. Two footbridges to the Grave di Papadopoli capable of taking infantry and pack animals.
2. Two medium pontoon bridges in the neighbourhood of Salletuol capable of taking wheeled traffic.

"The final line reached will be held as the line of resistance.

"The Battalion will be in brigade reserve, and will form up on the Grave di Papadopoli ready to advance to the attack at ' H ' hours in one line of companies in artillery formation, depth 500 yards, order of companies from the right : ' A,' ' B,' ' C,' ' D.' "

On the night of the 24th–25th October the island of Grave di Papadopoli was seized by units of the 22nd Infantry Brigade, but it poured with rain throughout the whole of the next day and consequently the attack on the left bank which was to have taken place on the 26th was postponed until the 27th, and during the night of the 26th–27th the 2nd Battalion The Border Regiment crossed over to the island by a footbridge in rear of the 2nd Queens, then forming up in line of four companies in artillery formation behind the 8th Devons with the 2nd Queens on the left.

The objectives allotted to the 20th Brigade were five in number and were as follows :—

1. The enemy front line of trenches on the further bank of the Piave.
2. The road joining St. Michele di Piave and Cimadolmo.
3. The road connecting Tezze and St. Paolo di Piave.
4. The Rezze and Rai road.
5. The Rai and Vazzola road.

The right boundary of the Brigade was a line joining Cimadolmo, Caminada, Rai and Fontanalette, inclusive ; the left a line joining Vendrame, Busca and Bonotto.

"The position to be stormed by the Division on the morning of October 27th, stretched, on the river bank from Zandonadi to Cimadolmo, a frontage of some 3,000 yards, and the line of attack gradually widened out until it reached about

4,000 yards, stretching along the Tezze–Rai road, which was fixed as the final objective for the first day. This road averaged a distance of some 5,000 yards from the starting point. Thus the whole terrain to be captured on the first day was an area of some ten square miles, which included three large villages, S. Michele di Piave, Cimadolmo, Tezze and several smaller ones. The whole country was quite flat and thickly overgrown with vines, with farm-houses scattered at intervals all over it. The main line of defence consisted of a high bank, known as the ' Bund,' which had been built in times of peace to contain the river when in flood. This Bund, which looked like a railway embankment, was about 10 feet high and 6 feet wide at the top. The banks of it were sloped at an angle of 60 degrees to the ground and were quite smooth and overgrown with grass. The whole was built of stones and gravel taken from the river bed, reinforced wherever there was a curve in it by concrete walls." [1]

The Battalion having formed up, " A " Company, Lieutenant Dowding, on the right, then " B " under Captain Little, " C " under Captain Argles and " D " on the left under Captain Gascoigne-Roy, all began to dig in as rapidly as possible, but at a depth of 3 feet water was met with, so there was nothing more to be done but to sit down at the bottom of the trenches and wait for zero hour. The Battalion was some 500 yards in rear of the forming-up line, so it was moved forward rather in advance of schedule time ; it was dark and raining hard, while after proceeding some 50 yards only a belt of uncut wire was encountered which had to be negotiated, and progress was slow. On the actual advance commencing—the 2nd Border Regiment in touch with the rear of the 8th Devons—the hostile shell fire became heavier and the companies were ordered to break up into platoon groups.

After moving forward some distance a halt was called as the situation seemed to be rather obscure and patrols were sent out under Second-Lieutenants Elmslie, Mettam and Graham to report on where the other branch or branches of the river could best be crossed, where was the left flank of the Italians and whether any gap existed between the 20th Brigade and the Allies. The runners sent back by these patrols with such information as had been gathered do not seem to have in all cases been able to find their way back, consequently about 12.30 Lieutenant-Colonel Darwell decided to move on and endeavour to reach the mainland, when the Battalion marched off in line of companies, forded the river and reached the bank near Vendrame ; but it now appearing that the Battalion was too far to the left, it moved S. and took up a position between Vendrame and Cimadolmo.

At 4.30 p.m. orders were received to take over the line then held by the Gordon Highlanders and Devons, and the 2nd Border Regiment then fell in on the bank and proceeded by companies independently—" C " to the right, " B " to the centre and " D " to the left, " A " Company being in support near Casa Angelina ; the enemy was sniping heavily from a line of houses N. of the Tezze–St. Paolo di Piave road, while he was also in strength along the hedges in front. Attempts were made to clear him out by parties from " C " and " A " Companies, but it was found this could not be done by rifle fire alone, and no guns, trench mortars or rifle grenades were here available. As it was thought that the Austrians would probably counter-

[1] Crosse, *The Defeat of Austria as seen by the 7th Division*, p. 54.

attack, attempts to dislodge them were given up and all set to work to consolidate the position. The troops again spent a very cold night in their trenches, but there was no enemy attack and orders were issued for the advance to be continued next day, the 28th, at 12.30 p.m.

All through the night of the 27th–28th the enemy kept up a continuous sniping ; Battalion Headquarters at Casa Altinia was freely spattered with machine-gun bullets, and while the orderly-room clerk, Corporal White, was barring the window, with an old door to prevent the light being seen, a bullet came through the window, wounding him in the back. On the left at Casa Busca a lively duel was kept up between our Lewis gunners firing from the windows of a top story of the farm and the enemy machine gunners at Casa Vital ; these had been largely instrumental in holding up the advance of the Brigade during the day, the man mainly responsible for the defence being a German sergeant-major who, on the farm being captured, was found dead in the yard behind it.

The Battalion advance on the 28th was to be supported by the 104th Battery R.F.A. and by an Italian Mountain Battery, and it was decided that the companies should go forward in echelon from the left—" D " Company to attack Casa Vital at 12.30 p.m., " A " to rush Casa Palladin, N. of the Tezze–St. Paolo di Piave road, at 1 o'clock, " B " to clear up the area round Casa Palladin S. of the Tezze–St. Paolo di Piave road at 1.15, while " C " was to clean up the area between " B " Company and Caminada. The 104th Battery was to support each company in turn, switching its fire from left to right along the front, while the Italian Mountain Battery was to have assisted " D " Company at Casa Vital, but unfortunately it did not get up in time. The tasks of " A " and " D " Companies were carried out according to plan, Casas Vital and Palladin were rushed and many prisoners and machine guns captured, while on the right the Austrians, seeing how things were going, mostly gave themselves up without waiting to be attacked, and consequently " B " and " C " Companies met with but little opposition. A whole Austrian company surrendered to 2 men of " A " Company of the Battalion armed with a Lewis gun. At 1.30 p.m. the Tezze–Rai road was reached and held and consolidation commenced, while as the night went on the line was advanced and patrols were sent out. One of these, consisting of two platoons under Captain Little, was ordered to go forward as far as the River Monticana, provided no opposition were met with. This patrol reached the bridge due N. of Visna without encountering any serious resistance and took up a position covering the bridge, which the enemy managed to blow up at dawn on the 29th, when his troops S. of the river collected at Visna and advanced. The patrol attempted to check them, but was surrounded by several hundreds of the enemy and suffered many casualties, the remainder being captured.

At 8.30 on the morning of the 29th the advance was resumed from the line of the Rai–Vazzola road, which had been reached during the night, to the Monticano River, " A " and " C " Companies moving along the Rai–Fontanelle road covered by an advance guard, while " D " and " B " followed the Rai–Visna road. Sniping was frequent from the farms along the whole line of advance and became heavier as the river was neared, its banks being held with artillery and machine guns. " No opposition to speak of was encountered on the left until the Monticano was reached, and Visna was occupied without resistance. On the right, where ' A ' and ' C ' Companies of the Borders were in front, considerable opposition was encountered in crossing the Piaveselle and in the neighbourhood of Fontanelette. Great difficulty was found in establishing touch with the Italians on the right. The E. bank of the Monticano being still held by the enemy, it was decided that ' D ' Company of the Borders should attack this at 9.30 p.m. under cover of a bombardment from our field guns and some Italian light guns which had taken up a position in Visna. As soon as these batteries opened fire the enemy replied from the neighbourhood of Fontanelle with a vigorous bombardment of the village. . . . Just before the attack on the river was timed to start Major Laurence, the G.S.O. 2, arrived from the Division to say that if severe casualties were anticipated the attack need not be undertaken. . . . The attack was accordingly cancelled and arrangements completed for handing the 20th Brigade front over to the Italians. The relief was carried out during the early hours of the 30th October, and the 20th Brigade was then withdrawn in readiness to pass over the Vazzola–Cimetta Bridge the following morning." [1]

The night of the 29th–30th the 2nd Border Regiment passed in billets at Casa Gircomini and next day marched with the Brigade, now in reserve, via Rai–Vazzola–Codogne–Garjarine to Casa Vianella, where the Battalion remained until the morning of the 2nd November.

During the operations above described the 2nd Battalion The Border Regiment had 10 non-commissioned officers and men killed or died of wounds, 26 other ranks were wounded, while 2 officers (Captain J. W. Little, M.C., and Second-Lieutenant A. Emslie) and 49 other ranks were missing.

Early on the morning of the 2nd November the Battalion marched with the main body of the 20th Brigade by Sacile, Fontanafreda and Pordenone to Cordenons, and in the last-named place three Austrian snipers were captured, for though the enemy had left the place twenty-four hours before, and it had been occupied during the night by Italian cavalry, while numbers of British troops had passed through, these men were still sniping when the Battalion entered. One of these gentry was captured by No. 23045 Private H. Batt of " D " Company, who, hearing some shots fired, refused to accept the usual explanation that Italian civilians were " loosing off " from sheer excitement, and discovered and took prisoner an Austrian with a loaded rifle and abundance of ammunition. The other two were captured by Headquarter runners, who were fired at on their way to " D " Company Headquarters with messages.

The advance was resumed on the 3rd November, first on the River Tagliamento and then on the line Pantianicco–Varazetto–Nogaredo–Coseano, but on reaching the river the advance guard was halted, as it was stated that the cavalry was in touch with the enemy, who reported that an armistice had already been signed. The 2nd Border Regiment was at the moment on the road just W. of St. Giorgio and was moved to a field near Pozzo ready to cross the Tagliamento if required, and the night was passed in billets in Cosa with " A " and " C " Companies holding an

---

[1] Crosse, *The Defeat of Austria as seen by the 7th Division*, pp. 81, 82.

outpost line along the river E. of the village. At the time it was thought probable that the enemy statement as to the signing of an armistice was merely a ruse to gain time to organize their defence, and a bombardment which was going on further down the river seemed to lend colour to this view. But when on the 4th the march was resumed, it was known that an armistice had actually been signed, was to come into effect at 3 p.m. this day, and that the Austrians were already surrendering by divisions.

" And so at 3 p.m. on November 4th by the waters of the Tagliamento, the part played by the 7th Division in the war came to an end. They ended, as their record deserved, in the front line of the advance, and the history of the last ten days made a fitting climax to their four years of toil. In these ten days the Division had advanced 92 kilometres, crossed five rivers, and captured prisoners far in excess of their own entire strength. . . . The 7th Division had been to all intents fought until exterminated on five separate occasions in the war ; first at Ypres in 1914, when they earned their laurel of immortality by holding the flower of the German Army at bay for three awful weeks ; secondly in the offensives in 1915, when, with a childlike faith by no means barren of results, we had hoped to break through the German line ; thirdly on the Somme in 1916, when after terrific fighting, the entire Division obtained its objective at every point both on the 1st and again on July 14th ; fourthly in 1917 in following up the German retirement to the Hindenburg Line, where they sacrificed themselves without stint in the bloody Battle of Bullecourt ; finally in the attack on the Passchendaele Ridge, when they captured Broodscinde and Reutel, and fought themselves to a standstill in the pitiless mud which alone baulked them of the capture of Gheluvelt. It was a record of which every man was justly proud, and light as had been the tasks they were called upon to bear in Italy, it is beyond question that if it had proved necessary in October 1918 to sacrifice themselves again, the Division would once more have done so with unhesitating loyalty." [1]

The British XIVth Corps in these operations captured 28,000 prisoners and took 219 guns.

It is full time now after a considerable interval to return to the 9th Battalion of the Border Regiment, which we left at the end of 1917 on the Macedonian front, where the events which early in 1918 occurred in France and

9th Battalion. Flanders were not without their effect upon the operations in Salonika and the forces with which they had to be conducted. During the winter of 1917–1918 both the French and the British forces here had received some welcome and much needed reinforcements, but with the opening and initial success of the German attack in the West both the British and the French military authorities began to examine into the possibility of withdrawing troops from other and less vitally important theatres of war, and it was decided to send to France from the armies under Generals Sarrail and Milne the equivalent of 24 battalions, 12 from each army. From the British contingent of 12 brigades each of 4 battalions, 1 battalion was taken per brigade, and though these as a whole did not provide any very important accretions on the Western Front where armies were counted in millions,

[1] Crosse, *The Defeat of Austria as seen by the 7th Division*, pp. 96 and 99.

they constituted anything but a negligible reduction of force in Macedonia.   Happily the Italians had found themselves in a position to make an increase in their forces in Albania, the Greek troops raised by Venizelos were more numerous than ever before, while the Serbian contingent was of the first quality.

During the first eight months of the year 1918 the 9th Battalion remained about Cugunci ; the strength of the Battalion was well maintained, for though the drafts were small and infrequent the men appear to have kept their health.

In January Second-Lieutenants V. R. McKay and J. R. Tunstall and 27 men joined ; in February two drafts came out amounting to 134 other ranks under Captain Holme-Parker and Second-Lieutenant Morgan ; in March a draft of 37 men came out ; in April 1 officer and 15 men arrived ; in May 4 officers and 5 men only ; June provided reinforcements to the number of 25 ; in July there were none, while in August there was a draft of 25 other ranks ; so that when September began, during which month the new French Commander-in-Chief, General Franchet d'Esperey, proposed commencing offensive operations, the 9th Battalion stood at a very useful strength of 30 officers and 928 other ranks.

" Towards the end of July," writes General Milne in his final despatch, " I received instructions from the Allied Commander-in-Chief to prepare for my share in a general offensive of the Allied Armies which was timed to take place during the first fortnight of September.   In this the British troops—provided the Allies on the front held by the Royal Serbian Army succeeded in piercing the enemy's centre— were to attack and take the heights to the W. and N.E. of Lake Doiran.   To reinforce my three divisions in this sector General Franchet d'Esperey placed at my disposal two divisions of the Corps of National Defence of the Hellenic Army, a regiment of Hellenic cavalry, and a group of Hellenic heavy artillery. . . . In the general instructions which I had previously received it was indicated that the main operations should be directed against ' P ' Ridge and the neighbouring heights W. of Lake Doiran, the scene of the battles in the spring of 1917.   I had decided to reinforce the British troops here by one of the Hellenic Divisions of the Corps of National Defence, which, as I have previously stated, had been placed at my disposal, and had selected the Seres Division for this purpose.   In addition, between Doiran Lake and the Vardar were the 22nd and 26th Divisions under Major-General J. Duncan, C.B., C.M.G., D.S.O., and Major-General A. W. Gay, C.B., C.M.G., D.S.O., respectively, and on the W. of the Vardar the 27th Division under Major-General G. T. Forestier-Walker, C.B. . . . The Allied Commander-in-Chief reinforced my command by a regiment of French infantry.   The whole of this composite force of British, Hellenic and French troops I entrusted to the command of Lieutenant-General Sir H. F. M. Wilson, K.C.B., K.C.M.G."

The Bulgarian front here was very strong, broken hills with deep ravines, dominated by the " P " Ridge and the Grand Couronné ; the enemy was strongly entrenched in three successive lines, with concrete gunpits and emplacements, and he held the position with his very best troops.

On the 15th September all detachments of the 9th Battalion The Border Regiment were called in to headquarters and next day instructions for the projected attack were issued ; it was therein stated that the 22nd Division had been ordered to attack the " P " Ridge and the neighbouring high ground, the main attack being divided into a left and a right attack, the former being carried out by the 22nd Division with the addition of one regiment of Greek troops, the objective being the " P " Ridge and Grand Couronné ; the boundary between the right and left attacks was to be roughly the line Grand Couronné–Mansion Ravine–Dagger Ravine–Hand Ravine–Christmas Ravine.   The Left, or 22nd Division, attack was to be carried out on a three-brigade front, the Greek Regiment being, for this purpose, regarded as a brigade.

On a date and at an hour to be notified later " A " and " C " Companies of the 9th Border Regiment were to move to Pillar Camp for work under the C.R.E., the rest of the Battalion proceeding to Oxford Camp and the whole Battalion being thereafter for tactical purposes directly under the orders of the Divisional Commander.

The following details were given for the employment of the Divisional Pioneers in company with the Royal Engineer Field Companies : " to prepare the Doldzeli–Volovec track, from the British lines to a point near the Tongue, where the track was then in use by the enemy, first for mule and then for wheeled traffic ; to search for and open up the water supply in the area captured by the right brigade ; continue the Doldzeli–Jackson Ravine mule-tracks and improving them where necessary along the slopes of ' P ' Ridge ; search for and open up the water supply in the area captured by the left brigade ; also assist in forming forward dumps of R.E. material in the captured areas."

The Battalion moved forward on the 17th September, " A " and " C " Companies to Pillar Camp, where they were attached to the 66th Infantry Brigade, and Headquarters, " B " and " D " Companies to Shrew Nullah, where they came under the command of the G.O.C. 67th Infantry Brigade ; during the morning of the following day the companies in Shrew Nullah were very heavily shelled, so withdrew towards evening to Senelle Camp.   It seems to have been here that the adjutant, Captain J. R. Brownlie, M.C., was wounded, his place being filled by Lieutenant J. Warrington.

On the 22nd the Battalion, which had been greatly dispersed by reason of the duties demanded of it, was concentrated in Senelle Camp.

In the meantime the Allies had everywhere won a certain amount of ground but not all their objectives ; the 66th Brigade reached the enemy third line of defences on " P " Ridge, but having lost 65 per cent. of its effectives was unable to hold on, while the British and Greek forces attacking between " P " Ridge and the Grand Couronné penetrated here about a mile and reached the lower slopes of the Grand Couronné.   The failure of the attack on " P " Ridge, however, made it impossible for these to hold their ground and they were forced to fall back.   On the E. of Lake Doiran the 28th British and the Cretan division had been no more successful, and on the 19th General Milne decided to hold and consolidate the line Petit Couronné–Teton Hill–Doiran Town.   Happily the Franco-Serbian troops had won ground and had turned the enemy's flank before General Milne, thus cutting the Bulgarian communications down the Vardar Valley, and by noon of the 21st it was plain that a hurried enemy retreat had commenced on the Doiran front.   He was seen to be blowing up his ammunition depots, our aircraft reported that the only good line of retreat open to the Bulgarian Army was congested with masses of men and transport moving northwards, and our airmen flying low bombed the hostile columns, causing heavy casualties and general panic.

By the evening of the 21st the enemy trenches on the British front were found to be vacated, before dawn next day the whole Allied Army was on the move forward, and by nightfall was pressing the pursuit of the Bulgarians in all directions.

On the 22nd the 9th Battalion The Border Regiment left Senelle Camp and moved by Volovec, Cerniste and Hasanli to Zeus Junction, and here on the 30th a telegram was received stating that " by reason of the Convention which had just been signed, hostilities with the Bulgarian Army were to cease at midday."

During the operations of this month the casualties of the Battalion had amounted to 3 non-commissioned officers and men died of wounds, 3 officers and 66 men wounded, and on this day when the campaign came to an end the strength of the Battalion is given as 29 officers—Lieutenant-Colonel C. G. Jones, D.S.O., in command—and 786 other ranks.

The rest may be very briefly stated.   On the 4th October King Ferdinand of Bulgaria abdicated in favour of the Crown Prince Boris, when the new King issued a proclamation announcing his respect for the constitution and that he was " imbued with the spirit of democracy."   The Allies advanced to the Danube, meeting little or no opposition, and, within scarcely more than three weeks after the opening of the offensive, had arrived on the Bulgarian shores of that river, while by the end of October the Balkan States S. of the Danube and Save were cleared of the enemy.

On the 4th October General Sir George Milne published the following Special Order :—

" *Thanks to your gallantry, determination and devotion to duty, the Bulgarian Army is now defeated and the Bulgarian nation has sued for peace.   This result has been obtained only by your extraordinary exertions after three summers spent in a malarious country and against obstacles of great natural and artificial strength.*

" *What appeared almost impossible has been accomplished.*

" *I gratefully thank you all, of every arm and of every rank, for your steadfast loyalty, your perfect discipline, and for the magnificent manner you have answered to every call made on you.   No one knows better the odds against which you have had to contend, and I am proud to have had the honour of commanding you.*"

The following message was received from the Secretary of the Army Council :—

" *The War Cabinet wish me to convey to you and all ranks under your command their heartiest congratulations on the decisive success which has at last crowned the operations of the British forces in Macedonia.   In common with their Allied comrades in arms they have for three years cheerfully sustained the burden of an arduous campaign in an unhealthy climate, without the stimulus of great offensive operations and with few opportunities for leave.   The endurance and devotion of the troops have now secured the most far-reaching results, which will profoundly influence the course of the war in favour of the Allied cause.*"

It is thought that this chapter, which describes how the war came to an end in two countries distant from the main theatre of operations, might reasonably conclude with a necessarily very brief account of how two other battalions of The Border Regiment saw the war-period through in the plains and on the borders of India.

On arrival in India in December, 1914, the 1st/4th Battalion relieved, as already stated, the 1st Battalion of the Regiment at Maymyo and provided a detachment **1st/4th Battalion.** at Mandalay. Some little trouble had for months past been simmering among the tribes who inhabit the Kachin Hills on the Burma frontier, and in January 1915 a wing of the Battalion formed part of a small punitive expeditionary force which during the next few weeks moved about the country.

In August of this year a detachment, under Lieutenant A. P. Wilson, was sent to Mesopotamia for service, and later in the year another provided a sea-patrol round the Burmese coast ; but the 1st/4th Battalion The Border Regiment remained in Burma until, early in 1918, it was relieved and transferred to India, being quartered at Jubbulpore in the Central Provinces. With the remainder of the service of the Battalion in the East, which did not come to an end until the winter of 1919, this record has no concern, but it should be mentioned that just after the Armistice was concluded with the Central Powers, Lieutenant-Colonel Waterlow was relieved in command of the Battalion by Lieutenant-Colonel Davidson.

In the preliminary reference which was made in an early chapter of this History to the 2nd/4th Battalion of the Border Regiment, it was stated that in December, **2nd/4th Battalion.** 1914, it was sent to Blackpool, and here in February of the year following officers and men were asked to volunteer for service in Burma. Practically all ranks volunteered to a man, but owing to a considerable percentage being too young for foreign service only 767 non-commissioned officers and men were eligible. Very soon after this the destination of the Battalion was changed from Burma to Poona, and on the 3rd March the 2nd/4th Border Regiment left Blackpool in two parties for Avonmouth, embarking next day at a strength of 28 officers and 767 other ranks in the *Dongola*, sailing the same evening. During the night, however, as the vessel, with all lights out and escorted by two torpedo boats, was proceeding down Channel, she collided after midnight with a steamer in the Bristol Channel off Barry, a mishap which necessitated the landing here of all on board and the docking of the *Dongola*, when the troops were transferred for further passage to the *Tunisian*.

The following letter from the Secretary to the Army Council followed the Battalion to India :—

"*I am commanded by the Army Council to request that your Excellency will be good enough to inform the Officer Commanding 2nd/4th Border Regiment that the Council have been glad to receive a good report of the discipline and conduct of the Battalion during the accident to H.M.T. " Dongola " on the 5th March last, and during its subsequent transfer to another ship.*"

During the voyage Second-Lieutenant G. H. McVittie died of meningitis and was buried at sea.

Bombay was reached on the 31st March, when the Battalion disembarked and left for Poona the same evening. The following officers appear to have landed with the Battalion : Lieutenant-Colonel J. F. Haswell, V.D. ; Major F. W. Halton, T.D. ; Captains J. E. C. Graham, V. S. Jones, P. S. Hamilton and W. C. S. Angus ; Lieutenants R. Hargreaves, J. Jackson, H. C. Grierson-Jackson, J. L. Strang, H. Thompson, adjutant, and M. G. Fisher ; Second-Lieutenants W. A. Sewell, R. I. Smith, N. E. Coates, E. P. Hardy, L. MacGlasson, A. W. Anderson, R. T. Bruckman, G. H. Topham, W. R. Walker, E. C. Kinghorn, J. Glasson, C. F. Ball, H. G. Marshall and P. M. Rheam ; Hon. Lieutenant J. Brooks was quartermaster and Lieutenant J. B. Burgess, M.D., R.A.M.C., was in medical charge.

During this year the Battalion provided many escorts, one of the most important of which was that under Captain Fisher which escorted 1,200 Turkish prisoners by sea from Bombay to Rangoon, then proceeding to Singapore to bring the mutineers from there to India. Detachments were also sent to Kirkee, and in August 2 non-commissioned officers and 13 privates left Poona to join the 1st Battalion Oxford and Bucks L.I. in Mesopotamia. This party served in General Townshend's Force, advanced on Baghdad, fought at Ctesiphon and was besieged in Kut ; of these 7 were wounded and 3 taken prisoners. Later, 3 officers, Captains Angus and Hargreaves and Lieutenant Kinghorn, served in Mesopotamia with various units.

In November, 1915, the Battalion left Poona for Kamptee, in the following March it was sent to Peshawar, whence it was sent by wings for the hot weather to the Murree Hills, and from February to May, 1917, was employed on the Mohmand Blockade Line ; when in November, 1918, the Armistice was announced the Battalion was quartered at the small hill station of Cherat near Peshawar.

It will not be altogether out of place to quote here the words with which General Sir Charles Monro, the Commander-in-Chief in India, bade farewell in the name of the Army to the Territorial soldiers who had volunteered for service in that country :—

" *On your departure from India, I desire to place on record my high appreciation of your services to the Empire during the period of the Great War.*

" *Many of you previous to the outbreak of war had, by joining the Territorial Force, already given proof of that patriotism and public spirit for which the Force has rendered itself so conspicuous. On the declaration of war your ranks were quickly filled by eager volunteers, animated by the same spirit of self-sacrifice ; when called upon to undertake the further obligation of service overseas your response was immediate and unanimous. By so doing you set free a large number of Regular units for service in the main theatres of war, at a time when every trained soldier was of the greatest value. I share with you the disappointment, which I know you all feel so keenly, that it has not been your luck to fight the enemy in Europe. Many of you, however, have seen service on the Indian frontier and by your conduct and bearing have added to the reputation of the famous regiments whose name you bear.*

" *For the greater portion of your service in India you have been engaged in the somewhat dull routine of garrison duty. The standard of efficiency which you attained, both in training for war and in discipline, reflects the highest credit on you all.*

" *Since the termination of active fighting in all the theatres of war you have been subjected to the further stress of waiting for your relief. That you have appreciated the difficulties which the authorities have had to face in this respect is clear from the patience with which you have borne this trying period.*

" You are now returning to your homes in the United Kingdom and I bid you good-bye, Godspeed and a happy homecoming. As an old commander of a Territorial Division at home, I am proud to have again been associated with this Force in India."

CHAPTER XIV

1918

THE 5TH AND 7TH BATTALIONS IN THE BREAKING OF THE HINDENBURG LINE.

THE 1ST, 5TH AND 7TH BATTALIONS IN THE FINAL ADVANCE.

" THE Hindenburg Line was selected and organized for defence in the latter end of 1916, and the work was continued during the spring of 1917. It was the direct result of the Battle of the Somme, as it was to this line that the Germans retired in March, 1917, in order to shorten their line and make good the losses suffered during their defeats of the preceding summer and autumn. It was first discovered and photographed by the Royal Air Force in February, 1917, thus confirming vague rumours of its existence received from refugees repatriated by the enemy through Switzerland. Since March, 1918, when the British Army had been driven back, the Hindenburg defences had been unoccupied and more or less neglected." [1]

The defences of the Hindenburg Line are thus described by Sir Douglas Haig : [2]

" Between St. Quentin and the village of Bantouzelle the principal defences of the Hindenburg system lie sometimes to the W. but more generally to the E. of the line of the Scheldt Canal. The canal itself does not appear to have been organized as the enemy's main line of resistance, but rather as an integral part of a deep defensive system, the outstanding characteristic of which was the skill with which it was sited so as to deny us effective artillery positions from which to attack it. The chief rôle of the canal was that of affording cover to resting troops and to the garrisons of the main defensive trench lines during a bombardment. To this end the canal lent itself admirably, and the fullest use was made by the enemy of its possibilities.

" The general configuration of the ground through which this sector of the canal runs produces deep cuttings of a depth in places of some 60 feet, while between Bellicourt and the neighbourhood of Vendhuille the canal passes through a tunnel for a distance of 6,000 yards. In the sides of the cutting the enemy had constructed numerous tunnelled dug-outs and concrete shelters. Along the top edge of them he had concealed well-sited concrete or armoured machine-gun emplacements. The tunnel itself was used to provide living accommodation for troops and was connected by shafts with the trenches above. S. of Bellicourt the canal cutting gradually becomes shallow, till at Bellenglise the canal lies almost at ground-level. S. of Bellenglise the canal is dry.

---

[1] *The Story of the Fourth Army in the Battle of the Hundred Days*, p. 147.
[2] Despatch of the 21st December, 1918.

" On the W. side of Bellicourt two thoroughly organized and extremely heavily wired lines of continuous trench run roughly parallel to the canal, at average distances from it of 2,000 and 1,000 yards respectively. Except in the tunnel sector, the double line of trenches known as the Hindenburg Line proper lies immediately E. of the canal, and is linked up by numerous communication trenches with the trench lines W. of it. Besides these main features, numerous other trench lines, switch trenches and communication trenches, for the most part heavily wired, had been constructed at various points to meet local weaknesses or to take advantage of local command of fire. At a distance of about 4,000 yards behind the most easterly of these trench lines lies a second double row of trenches known as the Beaurevoir–Fonsomme Line, very thoroughly wired and holding numerous concrete shelters and machine-gun emplacements. The whole series of defences, with the numerous defended villages contained in it, formed a belt of country varying from 7,000 to 10,000 yards in depth, organized by the employment of every available means into a most powerful system, well meriting the great reputation attached to it."

We left the 5th Battalion The Border Regiment at Villers Bretonneux on the 12th September, the 32nd Division of which it now formed part having been relieved **5th Battalion.** in the front by the 1st ; but on the 24th it marched by way of Framerville to Misery, thence via Tertry to Le Verguier, which was reached at 11 o'clock on the night of the 28th and where orders were issued for an advance on the following day.

The 32nd Division was now in the IXth Corps consisting of the 1st, 6th, 32nd and 46th Divisions and was included in the Fourth Army, which was on the extreme right of the British line next to the French.

The front on which on the 29th September the Fourth Army was to make its attack extended from Selency to Vendhuille, a distance of 12 miles, and on the right **Battle of the Hindenburg Line.** the IXth Corps was to attack from Selency to near Buisson Gaulaine Farm, a frontage of 10,000 yards. The main attack of this corps against Bellenglise and the canal N. of it was to be made by the 46th Division with the 32nd in support, while the 1st Division, operating between Gricourt and Bellenglise and keeping W. of the canal, was to maintain touch with the 46th Division and press forward towards Thorigny and Le Trouquoy ; S. of Gricourt the 46th Division was to try and gain ground to the E. It was hoped to reach the general line Masnières–Beaurevoir–Fonsomme on the first day.

The morning of the 29th September was fine but foggy, and though, owing to recent rain, the ground was soft and slippery, it was hard underneath, and offered little impediment to the advance of the 33 tanks allotted this day to the Fourth Army.

The attacking infantry moved forward about 6 a.m. and the 46th Division by 3 p.m. had captured Lehaucourt and Magny-la-Fosse, and had in fact secured the whole of the first objective on their front.

" Meanwhile, the 32nd Division had moved forward from its assembly area round Le Verguier, with the 14th and 97th Brigades leading on the right and left respectively "—of the 5th Border Regiment " A " and " D " Companies in front,

" B " and " C " in support and reserve—" and with the 96th Brigade in reserve. The leading brigades, with batteries of field artillery, began to cross the canal at 3 p.m."—the 5th Battalion near La Baraque—" the 96th Brigade remaining W. of the canal. At about 4 p.m. the attacking brigades leap-frogged the 46th Division on the first objective, but the tanks allotted to the 32nd Division to co-operate in the attack were unfortunately unable to reach their rendezvous in time to take part in the advance. They were therefore concentrated near Magny-la-Fosse ready for the next day's operations. Although the advance of the 32nd Division met with determined opposition, it made good progress and the village of Le Trouquoy was captured. The right of the 97th Brigade was held up in the valleys S.W. of Levergies, and its left, exposed to heavy fire from the enemy's machine guns posted S. of Joncourt and on the S. slopes of Mill Ridge, was temporarily checked N.E. of Magny-la-Fosse. . . . By nightfall all three brigades of the 32nd Division were E. of the canal; the 96th Brigade, which had moved forward during the afternoon, being in close support of the 14th and 97th Brigades." [1]

The war diary of the 5th Battalion The Border Regiment merely states under date of the 30th : " Consolidating. Counter-attack on left against " C " Company repulsed and left brought up in line " ; but General Montgomery in his book on the operations of the Fourth Army, gives a very much more detailed account of the doings of the 32nd Division on this day ; he says : " The 32nd Division continued to press forward with strong patrols of the 14th and 97th Brigades, while the 15th Lancashire Fusiliers of the 96th Brigade, which was in support, attacked Joncourt from the S.W. In spite of strong resistance the line was advanced to close to the S. outskirts of the village and connection was established with the 5th Australian Division. During the day the 14th Brigade completed the ' mopping-up ' of the Le Trouquoy tunnel defences, and at 7.30 p.m. in conjunction with troops of the 97th Brigade, attacked Levergies, capturing the village with 400 prisoners. During the night of September 30th preparation was made for the 14th Brigade to attack Sequehart ; for the 96th Brigade to operate against Joncourt in conjunction with the 5th Australian Division, and to gain the Beaurevoir–Fonsomme line round Chataignies Wood in co-operation with the 97th Brigade."

During the operations of the 29th–30th September the casualties incurred by the 5th Battalion The Border Regiment numbered 10 non-commissioned officers and men killed, with 70 wounded, including two officers—Lieutenant C. E. Renshaw and Second-Lieutenant A. S. Pearson.

" On the morning of 1st October the IXth Corps held its line thus : the 1st Division from Le Trouquoy to Levergies, with the 1st Brigade in the line. The 32nd Division held from Levergies to Joncourt with the 14th, 97th and 96th Brigades all in line from right to left, and with the 46th Division in support. The attack on Joncourt was launched at 8 a.m. on October 1st under cover of a barrage. . . . There was little resistance, as most of the enemy had retired to the Beaurevoir–Fonsomme line during the night and only 8 prisoners were captured.

" The attack by the 32nd Division on the Beaurevoir–Fonsomme line and Sequehart was not delivered until 4 p.m. This was a much more difficult operation,

---

[1] *The Fourth Army in the Battle of the Hundred Days*, pp. 160, 161.

Photo *Imperial War Museum*

TROOPS ADVANCING THROUGH RUINED TOWN

Photo *Imperial War Museum*

FROM TRENCHES TO THE OPEN

as the enemy's position on the high ground at Sequehart was one of great natural strength, and the Beaurevoir–Fonsomme line at this point was well wired and strongly held. The infantry, accompanied by 16 tanks, advanced under cover of a barrage. Sequehart was captured with great dash by the 5th/6th Royal Scots of the 14th Brigade with over 200 prisoners of the newly arrived 221st Division. The enemy, however, at once counter-attacked in strength, after shelling the village heavily, and drove the 5th/6th Royal Scots back to the W. of the village. Further N. the 1st/5th Border of the 97th Brigade encircled Chataignies Wood and entered Preselles, but the frontal and enfilade machine-gun fire, which was encountered from the Beaurevoir–Fonsomme line, rendered it impossible for our men to retain the ground gained, and they were finally withdrawn to the railway cutting 100 yards W. of the Wood." [1]

Of this attack the Battalion diary says: " advance continued. Orders to attack Chataignies Wood and the trench system to the E. in the Fonsomme line. ' A ' and ' D ' attacked, ' B ' and ' C ' in support. We pushed right through the wood, but could not get a footing in the trench owing to heavy machine-gun fire and consequent casualties and withdrawal was ordered to the railway embankment, which was held."

The line was held throughout the 2nd October, the enemy shelling the position at frequent intervals, and the 14th Brigade made another attempt to capture Sequehart, with the same result as on the previous occasion, the enemy being determined to retain possession, since the village commanded all the ground to the E., S. and W., while its capture by the British would widen the breach already made in the Masnières–Beaurevoir–Fonsomme line, his last prepared line of defence, and would facilitate the turning of his positions N. of St. Quentin.

" As a result of the determined fighting by the 32nd Division during the past three days," writes General Montgomery, " the IXth Corps had added materially to its previous success and had driven the wedge deeper into the enemy's position. On the evening of the 2nd the IXth Corps held a front of some 8,000 yards from Le Trouquoy to Swiss Cottage. This line ran along the high ridge to Sequehart, along the W. outskirts of that village, thence to a point 1,000 yards N.W. of Preselles, from which point to Swiss Cottage we held the Beaurevoir–Fonsomme line. The 1st Division held from Le Trouquoy to just S. of Sequehart, while the 32nd Division held thence to Swiss Cottage. With three British divisions the IXth Corps had defeated portions of four divisions in the line and of four divisions in reserve. Of the latter the enemy had hurried up reserve battalions belonging to both the 84th and 241st Divisions from the La Fère area, as well as the whole of the 221st Division from S. of St. Quentin, and the 25th Reserve Division from close support in the Lesdins area."

During the night of the 2nd–3rd October the 5th Battalion The Border Regiment appears to have been withdrawn to cellars in Levergies, but in the morning when the attack was resumed and the 32nd Division again advanced, the Battalion was attached for the day to the 14th Infantry Brigade which attacked, captured

[1] Montgomery, *The Fourth Army*, etc., p. 173.

and this time succeeded in holding Sequehart, the Battalion being in Brigade Reserve.

During the 4th, on which day the Battalion reverted to the 97th Brigade, there was no advance on the 32nd Division front, and next day the Battalion marched by Lehautcourt and Vendelles to huts at Le Catelet, remaining here nearly a fortnight and then going on the 18th by Pontruet, Levergies and Bohain to St. Souplet which was reached on the 31st and where the 5th Battalion entered upon a term of rest and recreation varied by training of all kinds.

Of the results of the fighting of these days the Field-Marshal wrote as follows in his Victory Despatch : " The enemy's defence in the last and strongest of his prepared positions had been shattered. The whole of the main Hindenburg Line passed into our possession, and a wide gap was driven through such rear trench systems as had existed behind them. The effect of the victory upon the subsequent course of the campaign was decisive. The threat to the enemy's communications was now direct and instant, for nothing but the natural obstacles of a wooded and well-watered countryside lay between our armies and Maubeuge. Great as were the material losses the enemy had suffered, the effect of so overwhelming a defeat upon a *morale* already deteriorated was of even larger importance."

These successes had not been bought without losses : in the 5th Battalion The Border Regiment Second-Lieutenants W. V. Matthews and K. E. G. Buy, and Sergeant-Major Moffat and 18 other ranks were killed or died of wounds, while Captain A. A. Stirling, M.C., Second-Lieutenants T. F. Beggan, T. A. Jackson, R. H. Stalker and H. P. Miller and 93 non-commissioned officers and men were wounded.

The losses in officers were made good while the Battalion was at Le Catelet, where the following officers joined : Lieutenants J. H. K. Hotchkiss and J. Burns-Albon, Second-Lieutenants V. Taylor, N. K. R. MacRae, H. T. Pearce, W. Fair, G. Carey, N. Miller, H. Thornton and J. Thompson.

The following appreciation of the work of the 97th Infantry Brigade was published :—

" *The Divisional Commander has asked the Brigade Commander to make known to all ranks his high appreciation of the fine work of the Brigade during the past few days. He quite realizes the extreme difficulty of the operations and would point out that though apparently costly—especially during the last two days—the casualties caused to us are small compared with those inflicted on the enemy, who has been forced to reinforce this sector several times—four new regiments were identified yesterday in one batch of eight prisoners. He heartily thanks all ranks for their splendid dash and tenacity which paved the way for the success of the IXth Corps this morning. The Brigadier wishes to add his thanks to those of the Divisional Commander.*"

The 7th Battalion The Border Regiment remained quietly at Lechelle until the 17th September spending the last day or two of its stay in this area training **7th Battalion.** for and rehearsing the part which it was to play on the 18th, on which date the Battalion moved off at 12.10 a.m. to the attack on Gauche Wood, " C " Company on the left, " D " on the right, " B " in support and " A " Company in reserve.

The 17th Division was now in the Vth Corps on the right of General Byng's Third Army. On approaching Gauche Wood, after passing through the 50th and 52nd Brigades, which had captured the first and second objectives allotted to them, the companies came under heavy machine-gun fire, and before the wood could be cleared it became necessary to bomb the enemy out of the trenches running through the wood ; this was successfully carried out by " C " Company of the Battalion, and the leading companies then took up their position in trenches just E. of Gauche Wood. The enemy counter-attacked at 2 p.m. and was able to bomb " C " and " D " Companies out of the trenches they were holding and they suffered some loss, but the other two companies moved at once up to their support and the lost ground was regained. The enemy here, however, was full of fight and attacked again at 5 and 7 p.m., but, being held, he then formed a bombing stop at the junction of two trenches, only to be ejected therefrom at 2 o'clock on the morning of the 19th.

During this fighting on the 18th the 7th Battalion lost : Captain W. Constantine, M.C., killed ; Lieutenant R. C. White, died of wounds ; while the following officers were wounded : Second-Lieutenants A. R. M. Tranter, A. Patterson, G. Slaughter, H. D. Barr, G. B. Barrow and T. Ashbridge.

On the 19th touch was established with the other battalions on the flanks ; then in the evening the enemy heavily bombarded the front line causing a number of casualties, and at night, on relief by troops from the 32nd and 50th Divisions, the Brigade was withdrawn and the 7th Battalion marched back to the shelter of a sunken road in rear, where it remained until the evening of the 20th, then moving forward to the area S.W. of Gouzeaucourt, being then in support to the 52nd Brigade in the event of any counter-attack being attempted by the enemy.

The next few days were passed up in the line, until on the 26th the Battalion was withdrawn to Etricourt, where Lieutenant-Colonel R. S. Irwin, D.S.O., relinquished the command and left for England, the command being temporarily assumed by Major A. D. Adams, M.C., pending the arrival of Major Thomas, East Yorkshire Regiment, who had been appointed and who arrived next day.

During this month the casualties in other ranks had amounted to 25 killed or died of wounds, 225 wounded and 33 missing.

The 7th Battalion remained some days training at Etricourt, and was actually thus occupied on the 5th October when at about 11 o'clock in the morning orders came for a move forward ; within little more than an hour all were on their way, and by that evening the Battalion was back in the sunken road S. of Gouzeaucourt where it remained throughout the 6th and 7th.

" The second and concluding phase of the British offensive now opened, in which the Fourth and Third Armies and the right of the First Army moved forward, with their left flank on the canal line which runs from Cambrai to Mons and their right covered by the French First Army. This advance, by the capture of Maubeuge and the disruption of the German main lateral system of communications, forced the enemy to fall back upon the line of the Meuse and realized the strategic plan of the Allied operations." [1]

[1] Despatch of the 21st December, 1918.

The position on the 7th October was roughly and very briefly as follows : the British Armies had crossed the Canal du Nord and the Scheldt Canal, they had broken through all the main Hindenburg, or Siegfrid, Line, and were pressing upon the last of the German defences—had in fact at one point actually passed them, so that nothing but the natural obstacles of the country lay between the British and Maubeuge.

At 4.30 a.m. and 5.10 a.m. respectively on the 8th October the Third and Fourth Armies attacked on a front of over 17 miles from Sequehart to S. of Cambrai.

On the 8th October the 21st Division had established themselves on a line 500 yards W. of Walincourt on which they were that evening relieved by the 17th, the 7th Border Regiment moving forward to the Hindenburg Support S.E. of Bantouzelle in the vicinity of the Bonne Enfance Farm. From here in the early hours of the 9th October the Battalion advanced to near Hurtebise Farm, moving off at 4.50 in artillery formation ; very little opposition was experienced and within a couple of hours of the start the first two objectives had been reached, the second being a sunken road near the cemetery E. of Selvigny. At this point the advance was checked for over half an hour by the fire of the British guns, the shells from which were falling upon our own men, some casualties resulting, but touch was established with the 7th Lincolns on the right and the 37th Division on the left ; and, the artillery fire ceasing, the advance was continued to the third objective, a point E. of Caullery, which was reached at 8 a.m., and the fourth objective only some twenty minutes later.

The enemy shell and machine-gun fire was now very heavy and no further advance was possible until our artillery were able to assist, and a position was taken up about the railway. Later, however, " A " and " C " Companies pushed on, and after overcoming considerable enemy opposition occupied Montigny ; " C " Company then took up a position in the Cemetery, while " A " worked along the line of the light railway and, after clearing the ground of enemy snipers, took post in support of " C " ; " B " and " D " Companies, moving on the left, came at the cross-roads under heavy artillery fire.

At 5.30 an advance was made towards Le Trouquoy, but on reaching the ridge severe German machine-gun fire was met, and finding it impossible to get on, a defensive flank was formed, the companies being thus disposed : 2 in front, 1 in support and 1 in reserve.

On the 10th the companies of the Battalion were withdrawn, first to Montigny and then to Inchy, where the Battalion was in brigade reserve.

The four Corps composing General Byng's Third Army had now after many weeks of fighting and pursuit reached the western bank of the River Selle, a small stream of no great width, but with high banks, which runs from the hilly ground about Bohain and Busigny northwards to Le Cateau and Solesmes to join the Scheldt ; and the objective of the Third Army was the river line N. of Le Cateau to Denain, 5 miles from Valenciennes, where the stream joins the Scheldt.

The Vth Corps of the Third Army attacked at 2 o'clock on the morning of the 20th with the 38th Division on the right and the 17th on the left. The 50th

Brigade had as its objective the village of Neuvilly, the 51st that of Amerval, and on arriving here the 7th Battalion The Border Regiment was suddenly counter-attacked and pushed out of the village. The Battalion then attacked a second time and regained Amerval just after dark, but the Commanding Officer, Lieutenant-Colonel W. E. Thomas, D.S.O., M.C., and Captain N. M. Saunders were both killed by German snipers. By this evening the whole of the objectives allotted to the Vth Corps had been secured after a very prolonged and stubborn fight in which the Corps captured 4 guns and 600 prisoners.

From the 21st to the 25th inclusive the Battalion was in billets at Inchy and Ovillers, and then on the 26th the 17th Division relieved the 21st in the line, the 51st Brigade being in divisional reserve in Vendegies where Lieutenant-Colonel P. Kirkup, D.S.O., M.C., of the Durham Light Infantry, took command of the Battalion.

During this month again the losses in the 7th Border Regiment had been considerable : 2 officers (Lieutenant-Colonel W. E. Thomas, D.S.O., M.C., and Captain N. M. Saunders) and 32 non-commissioned officers and men had been killed in action or had died of wounds ; 7 officers (Captains G. W. O'Brien and J. R. W. Taylor, Lieutenants J. Laing, M.C., and J. B. McNair, Second-Lieutenants T. B. Gibson, W. T. Wilkin and J. G. Fleming) and 131 other ranks were wounded, while missing were Lieutenant H. S. Tuckett (also wounded) and 4 men.

On the 2nd November the Battalion moved in the dark and by bad roads and by way of Neuvilly, Amerval, Ovillers and Vendegies to the neighbourhood of Poix du Nord, where just an hour after arrival the Headquarter Mess was wrecked by a shell ; and here on the 3rd all arrangements were perfected for an attack upon the enemy positions in the Forest of Mormal, an advance being made at 7.30 that night to an assembly position near Engelfontaine.

" By this time the rapid succession of heavy blows dealt by the British forces had had a cumulative effect, both moral and material, upon the German armies. The difficulty of replacing the enemy's enormous losses in guns, machine guns and ammunition had increased with every fresh attack, and his reserves of men were exhausted. In the Selle Battle the 24 British and 2 American divisions engaged had captured a further 20,000 prisoners and 475 guns from the 31 German divisions opposed to them, and had advanced to a great depth with certainty and precision. Though troops could still be found to offer resistance to our initial assault, the German infantry and machine gunners were no longer reliable, and cases were reported of their retiring without fighting in front of our artillery barrage.

" The capitulation of Turkey and Bulgaria, and the imminent collapse of Austria consequent upon Allied successes, which the desperate position of her own armies on the Western Front had rendered her powerless to prevent, had made Germany's military situation ultimately impossible." [1]

Immediately in front of the right of the Third Army was the Mormal Forest, its edge strongly held, but when once entered it presented no especially serious obstacle by reason of the very wide clearings contained therein ; it was hoped to gain a passage over the Sambre, though it was hardly expected to accomplish so

[1] Despatch of 21st December, 1918.

much in one day's fighting. In the front of the Vth Corps were the 38th and 17th Divisions on the right and left respectively, and of the two the former had the easier task, the 17th Division meeting a lively resistance in Locquignol and being for some time checked. It was arranged that each brigade should have its allotted objective : the 52nd the first, the 51st the second, and the 50th Brigade the third, each brigade succeeding and passing on through the other as objectives were arrived at. In the 51st Brigade the 7th Border Regiment was on the right and the 7th Lincolns on the left, the Brigade objective running along the Route Dunamol.

The 52nd Brigade moved forward at 5.30 a.m. on the 4th November under a creeping barrage, the front battalions of the 51st Brigade following about 500 yards in rear, the enemy putting down a protective barrage along the Engelfontaine–Louvignies–Le Quesnoy Road. During this advance, however, " B " Company found that a gap had been left between the 52nd Brigade and the 38th Division, this they filled up and succeeded in capturing 35 prisoners. The first objective having now been taken, the Battalion established itself thereon : " A," " B " and " C " Companies in front with " D " in reserve ; but at the hour arranged for moving forward to the next objective, the companies advanced under a creeping barrage and appear to have found it tolerably easy going until arrival within 100 yards of the line, when they came under a fairly heavy machine-gun and rifle fire, one German gun-team being especially troublesome ; 4 of the detachment were, however, killed and 1 wounded by a small party of men of the 7th Border Regiment who attacked with the bayonet.

Having seized the objective indicated, the Battalion now reorganized and awaited the arrival of the 50th Brigade, which had been told off to pass through and attack the " Brown Line " and the third objective, when, at 2.17 p.m. the Battalion was to follow on, occupy the " Brown Line " and there establish itself. This was done and the night was very quiet. During the operations the 7th Border Regiment had taken 127 prisoners and had captured 4 field guns, 8 machine guns and 1 trench mortar, at a cost, however, of 3 officers and 55 other ranks killed and wounded.

On the 5th November the 21st Division passed through the 17th and the men of the Battalion made themselves as comfortable as conditions generally and the rainy weather permitted ; then on the 6th an advance was made to La Tête Noire, and next day to Le Bouvist where they arrived at 2 p.m., whence at 5.30 they moved on to Eclaibes, being under orders to pass through the 9th K.O.Y.L.I.—the front line battalion of the 21st Division—and continue the advance, taking in succession three objectives which had been pointed out. Owing to various causes, insufficient artillery co-operation, exposure of the flanks and other matters, the advance could not then be pressed, though heroic efforts were made and considerable losses were experienced, and it was decided to wait until it was dark, withdrawing meanwhile to the original line. Later another attempt was made to get forward, but the conditions had in no way improved and the companies had to fall back. During the night, patrols discovered that the enemy in front had retired and his lines were then occupied. Finally on the 9th the Battalion was relieved by one from the

52nd Brigade, and moved back, all ranks greatly exhausted, to billets in Aulnoye, where two days later the news of the Armistice was received.

During these final operations of the four years' war the 7th Battalion The Border Regiment had 15 non-commissioned officers and men killed or died of wounds, 6 officers and 103 other ranks wounded, while 10 men were missing. The names of the wounded officers were: Lieutenant A. H. Watson, Second-Lieutenants H. Hutchins, H. C. Sykes, J. Gibson, N. Shaw and T. H. Grassby.

The 5th Battalion The Border Regiment in the 32nd Division seems to have remained out of the line until the beginning of November, when it marched to take

The Final Advance. 5th Battalion. up a position of assembly for the general attack which was to open on the 4th and which was to constitute the last phase of the war. The operations in which the Battalion was concerned are dismissed in a very few lines in the war diary, but they were none the less of great influence upon the final issue, and an attempt must therefore be made to elaborate the rather vague statements contained in the Battalion war diary by drawing upon other accounts which are available of the events of these days.

In his despatch of the 21st December, 1918, Field-Marshal Sir Douglas Haig wrote :—

" The front of the decisive attack delivered by the Fourth, Third and First Armies on the 4th November extended for a distance of about 30 miles from the Sambre, N. of Oisy, to Valenciennes. The nature of the country across which our advance was to be made was most difficult. In the S. the river had to be crossed almost at the outset. In the centre the great Forest of Mormal, though much depleted by German wood-cutting, still presented a formidable obstacle. In the N. the fortified town of Le Quesnoy, and several streams which ran parallel to the line of our advance, offered frequent opportunities for successful defence. On the other hand, our troops had never been so confident of victory or so assured of their own superiority."

General Montgomery [1] describes as follows the ground over which the Fourth Army was to advance : " On the right there was the obstacle of the Sambre and Oise Canal, which had to be crossed at the outset. This canal runs from La Fère by Mont d'Origny, Vadencourt and Etreux to Landrecies. From La Fère to Vadencourt it follows the course of the Oise, thence, swinging to the N. near Etreux, it enters the Sambre Valley near Oisy. At Landrecies the canal terminates and the canalized Sambre begins as a separate waterway. The canal is of the ordinary type to be met with in France and Belgium and forms a considerable obstacle, being some 70 feet wide from bank to bank and 35 to 40 feet wide at water-level, except at Lock No. 1 and at the locks at Catillon, Ors and Landrecies, where it is 17 feet wide. It contained at that time an average depth of 6 to 8 feet of water and was nowhere formidable except at the bridges, which had been either demolished or prepared for demolition. In addition to the obstacle offered by the canal itself, the low ground on both sides of the canal had been inundated by the Germans and much of it had been transformed into swamp. In some places the water was only ankle deep, but N. and S. of Ors there were small streams parallel to the canal

[1] *The Story of the Fourth Army in the Battle of the Hundred Days*, pp. 241 *et seq.*

swollen to a width of about 15 feet and a depth of 2 to 3 feet ; similar streams existed S. of Catillon. Along each side of the canal between Oisy and Lock No. 1 there are wide reservoirs ; at their N. end they are more than twice the width of the canal and at that time contained a fair depth of water, but they are narrower and shallower further S. South of Catillon the enemy had felled the trees along the W. bank of the canal for the double purpose of improving his field of fire and of forming an abattis."

The IXth Corps and the XIIIth on the left of it had been given two main objectives ; the first extended approximately due N. and S. from E. of Fesmy to E. of Lendrecies, and thence N. through the Mormal Forest about 3,000 yards from its W. edge. The second objective ran E. of Cartignies, Dompierre and St. Remy Chaussée. The preliminary objective for the IXth Corps was, first, a line running from the bridge at Petit Cambrésis along the road to Hautrève, thence to the E. outskirts of Catillon and, on the front of the 32nd Division, from Catillon through Petit Versaille to La Folie ; the second objective was a line which ran on the 1st Division front from the bridge at Petit Cambrésis to La Groise, excluding Fesmy and including Robelmetre, Grand Galop Farm and Petit Galop Farm, and, on the 32nd Division front, from E. of Mezières to Petit Versaille, including Locquignol Farm.

For the forcing of the passage of the canal the IXth Corps was disposed with the 1st Division on the right, the 32nd on the left and with the 46th in support ; this division was to follow close in rear of the right or 1st Division, relieving it on arrival at the first objective and then continuing, with the 32nd, the advance to the second objective.

Major-General Lambert, commanding the 32nd Division, had ordered the 14th Brigade to cross the canal just S. of Ors, the 96th immediately S. of the bend in the canal N. of Ors, the passage being covered by a powerful artillery barrage and smoke screen. After crossing, these two leading brigades were to reorganize before resuming the advance to the bridge-head line under a creeping barrage ; this barrage was to remain on the E. bank of the canal for five minutes ; it was then to be lifted 300 yards and remain for thirty minutes, after which pause it was to advance at the rate of 100 yards every six minutes.

At 5.45 a.m. on the 4th November the barrage came down in front of the IXth Corps on the E. bank of the canal, and the 14th and 96th Brigades, on the right and left respectively, moved forward, the 97th Brigade, less two companies of the 2nd K.O.Y.L.I., being for the present held back in reserve in the vicinity of St. Souplet.

The 14th Brigade managed to get across, but the 96th was beaten back again and again, eventually succeeding in crossing where the 14th had effected its passage, then cleared the area N.E. of Ors, and joined up with the 14th Brigade on the inter-mediate objective. The advance of the IXth and XIIIth Corps was resumed in heavy rain on the morning of the 5th November, the 97th Brigade having come up during the night and taken over the whole divisional front ; and although, owing to the state of the ground, progress was slow, by nightfall on the 5th the 32nd Division held the spur about 2,000 yards E. of Favril and was in touch with the

25th Division S. of Maroilles. Next morning a late start was made and there was not much fighting; the 32nd Division cleared Grand Fayt before noon, but found the Petite Helpe a difficult obstacle; however, the 97th Brigade forced its way across the river at the lock at Grand Fayt in spite of hostile machine-gun fire, and by 5 p.m. its leading infantry had passed Le Foyaux and established an outpost line astride the ridge some distance further E. The IXth Corps had thus gained the second objective assigned to it by the Fourth Army Commander in his orders for the attack, and was in touch with the French on the right S. of Cartignies, and on the left with the XIIIth Corps at the cross-roads 1,500 yards E. of Marbaix.

Advancing again at dawn on the 7th November, the 32nd Division was by evening in possession of Avesnes and Avesnelles with an outpost line 1,000 yards further E. For the infantry of the Fourth Army the advance now practically came to an end, while a mobile column was sent forward to keep in touch with the retreating enemy, for the rate of pursuit of the Germans had caused the British to outmarch their supplies, and as they moved forward roads and railways had to be repaired.

On the 11th came the sudden news of the signing of the Armistice, thus bringing to an end the fine work of the IXth Corps which in the last three weeks had marched 50 miles and had captured 17,000 prisoners and taken 318 German guns.

We must now go back several months and take up again the story of the doings of the 1st Battalion The Border Regiment which we left at Labréarde at the close

1st Battalion. of the Battle of the Lys. Labréarde can hardly, however, be considered as altogether a rest area, for the enemy repeatedly shelled the particular sector occupied by the Battalion, and on the 3rd May Second-Lieutenant Holt and 2 other ranks were wounded, while in retaliation every effort was made to raid the German lines and effect the capture of prisoners. On the night of the 4th–5th a raid on a rather elaborate scale was carried out and the following is the diary report of what happened :—

" Raid on the sunken road. The raiders consisted of 20 other ranks under Captain B. R. Durlacher, M.C., Lieutenant H. Hayman-Joyce and Second-Lieutenant R. Rae, the O.C. Raid being Second-Lieutenant S. M. Olden. Zero hour 1.5 a.m. Artillery barrage went down correctly to time with good density, advancing E. by 200 yards lifts every two minutes, forming a box barrage. No counter-barrage was put down by the enemy, but a few bursts of machine-gun fire were opened. Firing of red Very lights was used as a signal for the raiders to return. Enemy casualties : 1 man and a light machine gun were captured, 5 men were bayoneted and several who ran back into the barrage were seen to fall. Second-Lieutenant S. M. Olden was killed by shell fire, being hit by our own shrapnel, 2 other ranks were slightly wounded by machine-gun fire."

On the night of the 5th–6th May the Battalion was relieved and went back into Nissen huts at Le Grand Hasard, but coming out of the line a shell fell among a party of the Battalion, causing wounds among 10, one of whom was Second-Lieutenant L. A. Huddart. The rest of the month was passed tolerably quietly in and out of the line, though there was a good deal of hostile aerial activity.

During June there was also considerable raiding and patrolling in which activities the following showed much initiative and boldness : Lieutenants Towle and Pattinson, Second-Lieutenants Youdale, Little, Marshall, Hayman-Joyce and Chicken, Sergeant Moore and Corporal Ellis ; then on the 12th July the 29th Division commenced a move to Hazebrouck, where the Battalion at once began drawing battle stores of all kinds and on the 14th moved up to the trenches, " A," " B " and " C " Companies holding the front line, with " D " Company in reserve at Gotha Farm and Battalion Headquarters at Tiflis House. Here Second-Lieutenants Rae, Marshall and Smith—this last-named had only quite recently been commissioned—were very active in patrolling and harrying the Huns, but unfortunately on the 18th Second-Lieutenant A. R. Dick and 3 other ranks were killed and Regimental Sergeant-Major Malia, D.C.M., and 9 men were wounded. Later on this day the Battalion was sent, most of the way in motor-lorries, to the Blakinghem area where it was accommodated in very scattered billets. Only a very few days were spent here, however, for on the 22nd the Battalion moved N. to St. Marie Cappel, where intensive training began and where Lieutenant-Colonel H. E. Festing arrived and assumed command of the Battalion. Here also a very small draft of 23 other ranks arrived from the base with Second-Lieutenants E. R. Frew, T. Clayton and N. M. Clayton.

On the 14th August the Battalion moved into the support system of trenches in the Strazeele area and supplied many working parties for carrying up material to the forward dumps ; and on the 16th orders were received from the 97th Brigade that an attack was to be made on the 18th at 11 a.m. with the view of capturing the enemy's front-line system approximately on an E. and W. line between Garbedoen Farm and the Meteren Becque, and with the ultimate object of exploiting any success obtained and making good the Outtersteene Line.

In accordance with the above the 1st Battalion The Border Regiment was relieved on the night of the 17th–18th from its positions in the Strazeele defences, Court Croix Switch and Support Line by the 88th Brigade, and at 11 a.m. on the 18th the attack commenced, our artillery barrage falling one minute later on the enemy's line ; " B," " D " and " C " Companies moving forward in artillery formation, " B " passing through the original front line just to the N. of Scarpe Cottage, thence E., crossing the Becque by a bridge thrown by the R.E. and forming up in depth facing S. between the Becque and Belle Croix Farm. On arrival here " B " Company came under the orders of the O.C. 1st K.O.S. Borderers.

" D " Company took up a position in the old front line just S.W. of Scarpe Cottage, arriving there at noon ; while ten minutes later " C " Company occupied the trench vacated by " B " ; there were no casualties up to this in these companies.

At 12.55 p.m. the Blue Line was reported captured and a message was received by the Brigade that British patrols were moving towards Outtersteene, but that they appeared to be held up about half a mile N.W. of the village. On arrival in the assembly position between the Becque and Belle Croix Farm at 12.14 p.m. Captain Proctor, commanding " B " Company, went forward to get in touch with the K.O.S.B.'s and to reconnoitre the ground, being accompanied by Lieutenant Puddicombe, and touch was gained with " A " Company, K.O.S.B.'s, who were digging in on the Blue Line ; here Captain Proctor was informed that the enemy appeared to have vacated Outtersteene and that K.O.S.B. patrols were about to go forward and reconnoitre, and thereupon Captain Proctor decided to advance and take up a position S. of the village.   He sent No. 8 Platoon to the right of Outtersteene, No. 5 to the left, giving orders for Nos. 6 and 7, followed by Company Headquarters, to push through and " mop up."   Only slight opposition was encountered during this advance and by 1.15 p.m. the village was practically surrounded, patrols were sent forward, the house S. of Scandal Crossing was searched, a deserted machine-gun emplacement being there discovered, and the enemy was seen retiring; but fire could only be very sparingly opened upon him as the difficulty of renewing ammunition in the firing line was already causing anxiety.

Shortly after this the O.C. " B " Company established his headquarters in Outtersteene.

In the meantime, " A " Company had been sent forward to occupy a position in the old front line from the left of " D " Company to Scarpe Cottage, and was later directed to extend its left along the Red Line to the Becque, so getting in touch with the 9th Division ; while " C " Company was instructed to advance and take post in the old front line S. of " D " about Garbedoen Farm.

About 7.30 p.m. two enemy machine guns came into action on the railway line E. of Scandal Crossing and some few Germans crossed the line under cover of this fire, but their advance was easily stopped ; about dark, however, as there was considerable enemy movement S. of the railway, it appeared that a hostile counterattack was probably imminent, and an S.O.S. signal was sent up and machine-gun and rifle fire opened on the enemy.   The artillery barrage fell at once and the enemy machine guns E. of Scandal Crossing gave no further trouble.

At this time " B " Company, 1st Border Regiment, was in the front line S. of Outtersteene, the remaining three companies were in the old front line.

During the night of the 18th–19th patrols frequently went out, and early on the morning of the 19th " B " Company was relieved by a company of the K.O.S.B.'s, but at night the Battalion in turn relieved the 1st K.O.S.B.'s under considerable artillery fire, when " A " and " D " Companies were on the right and left of the firing line respectively, with " B " and " C " in left and right support ; but on the same night the 2nd Lincolns took the place of the 1st Border Regiment which was withdrawn to the " Z " Line, where it came temporarily under the orders of the G.O.C. 88th Brigade.   Here, however, early on the 20th the enemy opened a heavy artillery barrage with guns of all calibres on the position held by the Battalion, this continuing for 2½ hours, but the casualties were remarkably light.   This gunfire was continued at short intervals all through the day, while hostile aeroplanes flew low over the sector.

During these operations the Battalion had 1 officer (Second-Lieutenant J. McIntyre) and 15 other ranks killed ; while Lieutenant A. L. Puddicombe and 53 non-commissioned officers and men were wounded.

On the night of August 26th–27th the 1st Battalion The Border Regiment moved to the front-line trenches forward of Outtersteene Ridge, and twenty-four hours later the 29th Division side-stepped, when the Battalion relieved a battalion of the 31st Division in the Hoogenacker Mill sector. On the night of the 29th–30th the Battalion advanced its position without opposition, and early next morning a further forward movement was commenced, the objectives being Bailleul Station, Steenje Cemetery and Nooteboom. Again no opposition was met with, but the ground was very heavy and much difficulty was experienced in maintaining touch on the flanks. By 10 a.m. on the 30th all objectives had been carried with the exception of Nooteboom, which was very stubbornly defended, but within three hours the resistance here also was overcome, and " B " and " D " Companies of the Battalion sent back word that they were on the E. side of Steenje Cemetery and were there digging in. Unfortunately they had been noticed by the German airmen observing for the guns, and shortly after were heavily fired on with shrapnel, escaping, however, with but few casualties. At dusk the Battalion was relieved, and next day furnished outposts for the day, taking up a front of some 3,500 yards, covering the whole of the Xth Corps.

On the night of the 31st August–1st September orders were received from the Brigade for the Battalion to advance at 9 a.m. on the 1st September and to establish itself on a line, La Kirlem–Steenwercke–Mire Farm–the Station De Seule, to each of the four companies of the Battalion being allotted 1 field gun, 1 trench mortar, 2 machine guns and 2 platoons of cyclists, and the advance was made as follows :—

Right.—" A " Company, Captain Gemmell-Smith, moved forward at 11.15 a.m. on the 1st September, having for its objectives Steenwercke and La Kirlem. After advancing for 1,000 yards the centre and left platoons were held up at 1.15 p.m. by enemy machine-gun fire ; this resistance was, however, overcome by a flanking movement and the cyclists passed through Steenwercke an hour later, when the company established itself on the line it had then reached.

Centre.—" C " Company, Captain Durlacher, M.C., commenced its advance at 10 a.m., its objective being Mire Farm, but the movement had hardly begun when resistance was met with on the right from an enemy strong point and from Mutton Farm ; endeavours were unsuccessfully made to overcome this opposition with the field gun and trench mortar. Mutton Farm was eventually cleared by No. 9 Platoon with a section of rifle grenadiers and Lewis guns working up the ditches on either side of the road, while No. 9 Platoon moved along the Bailleul railway line, so turning both flanks of the enemy strong point, when the defenders surrendered, thus enabling the further advance to be carried on more quickly, and by 4.30 p.m. the company had gained all its objectives, a line was established and consolidation commenced.

Left.—" B " Company, Second-Lieutenant Davies, was ordered on the night of the 31st to move from the right of the outpost line and take up a position on the left ; the objectives assigned to it were De Seule, Jail House, the Station. A few rounds of H.E. having been fired at Pegasus Farm and one or two other places reported as being occupied as enemy machine-gun positions, the cyclists advanced at 10.30 a.m. on the 1st September and were soon in contact with the enemy. At 11 o'clock three platoons of " B " Company moved forward, but at 12.30 the right and centre were held up by machine guns in La Crêche, the resistance being very obstinate and causing some loss among the cyclists. " B " Company was now reinforced by two platoons of " D," the support company, and La Crêche was finally captured, when the company pushed forward and established itself on the line reached.

Support.—" D " Company, Lieutenant Slater, was called upon as above stated to assist " B," and La Crêche having fallen, the two platoons occupied the line taken up by " B."

The 1st Border Regiment had in this way carried out an advance of an average depth of 5,000 yards on a frontage of 3,500 yards, and had captured 14 prisoners and incurred itself 22 casualties. On the evening of September 1st the Battalion was relieved and withdrew to the reserve line about Steenje.

Of the success of these operations the Field-Marshal wrote as follows : " Thereafter the enemy's withdrawal continued rapidly. At certain points indeed his rearguards offered vigorous resistance, notably about Neuve Eglise and Hill 63, captured with a number of prisoners by the 36th and 29th Divisions ; but by the evening of September 6th the Lys Salient had disappeared. Kemmel Hill was once more in our hands, and our troops had reached the general line Givenchy, Neuve Chapelle, Nieppe, Ploegsteert and Voormezeele." [1]

On 8th September a warning order was issued for an early move from the Bailleul area, and, marching by road or proceeding by rail, the Battalion was in turn at Fletre, Wallon Cappel, St. Jan-ter-Biezen, Orvillers Camp, Road Camp and Poperinghe, which last was reached on the 26th, and entraining next day on the light railway it detrained at Machine Gun Farm, Ypres, moving on thence to assembly positions E. of Ypres.

The 29th Division had now left the XVth Corps with which it had lately been serving, and here formed part of the IInd Corps, commanded by Lieutenant-General Sir C. Jacob, in General Plumer's Second Army. This Second Army was now on the extreme left of the British line, on its right was Birdwood's Fifth Army, while on its left were the French and on their left again the Belgians. The Second Army contained four corps—the IInd covering Ypres, the XIXth opposite Hollebeke, the Xth facing Messines and the XVth to the S. of it. The IInd Corps was to attack down the Menin Road with two divisions in front, the 9th on the left, the 29th on the right, and the 36th in reserve.

The events of the next few days are wholly taken from the account contained in the Battalion Diary which is unfortunately very slight, but it must be said in excuse that the advance was exceptionally rapid during these days and the success achieved such as could hardly have been expected ; and all taking part in the epoch-making occurrences of those wonderful days were more concerned in the making of history than in the recording of it.

The British barrage began at 5.30 a.m. on the 28th September and the enemy made but a weak reply, and the infantry pushed off in a drizzling rain. By 7.30 the high ground about Jackdaw Tunnel was captured by " C " and " D " Companies, while an hour later the final objectives—Inverness Copse and Unknown Copse—had been reached by two platoons of " A " Company of the 1st Border Regiment, under Captain Hood, M.C., and " D " under Captain Duggan, M.C.,

[1] Despatch of 21st December, 1918.

D.C.M., with but little opposition, the enemy machine guns being easily overcome ; while about this time two platoons of " A " Company, commanded by Captain Chambers, M.C., and Battalion Headquarters, captured the Headquarters of the 12th Bavarian Regiment with the C.O., adjutant, medical officer and about 110 other ranks.

The 1st Battalion K.O.S.B.'s now " leap-frogged " the 1st Border Regiment and pushed on to Tower Hamlets, while the Battalion was ordered to hold the high ground at Stirling Castle for the night, assisted by 8 Vickers guns ; but about 6.30 these orders were cancelled and the Battalion was sent to Gheluvelt.

The Battalion's total " bag " for this very successful day was 200 prisoners, of whom 7 were officers, 2 field guns, 2 trench mortars and 15 machine guns ; the total captures of the Second Army were 10,000 prisoners with more than a hundred guns, and the Battalion's casualties on the 28th were 18 killed, 1 officer (Second-Lieutenant A. R. Pennington) and 53 non-commissioned officers and men wounded, with 1 man missing.

On the 30th September the 1st Battalion was in Kruiseik, where the 2nd Battalion of the Regiment had so greatly distinguished itself in the early days of the war, and the advance was pressed all the morning, the enemy falling back until, about 4.15 p.m., on reaching the high ground just E. of America Road, he began to stand once more and the fighting was severe, the defence by his machine gunners being very stubborn, but at dusk a line was taken up and held. The Battalion had outmarched its supplies and that night officers and men had to make good with their " iron rations."

On this day the 1st Border Regiment captured another machine gun and 3 more prisoners, at a cost to themselves of 6 men killed, 3 officers (Captain W. F. H. Chambers, M.C., Lieutenant H. D. Lees, M.C., and Second-Lieutenant J. W. Craig) and 44 other ranks wounded, and 4 men missing.

The Battalion was not relieved until the night of the 1st–2nd October, when it withdrew first to a hutment camp near Kruiseik, which was shelled on the 4th ; then on the 5th a move was made to the neighbourhood of Westhoek, on the 7th to billets in Ypres, on the 10th to Becelaere, and on the 11th October to the Support Battalion area at Potterijebrug, where it bivouacked. Here Lieutenant M. A. Ashley, Second-Lieutenants E. R. Raine, C. A. Watts and L. V. Little, Hon. Lieutenant and Quartermaster H. Browning and 42 other ranks joined from the Base.

Matters of diplomacy are naturally outside the scope of a purely regimental history of the war, but possibly it may assist to a clearer understanding of all the causes which helped to bring about the German surrender now imminent, if we break off for a moment the narrative of the operations in the field, and state very briefly what steps the German Government was taking to bring about a cessation of arms while securing the best possible terms.

At the end of September the Macedonian front had collapsed, Turkey was on the verge of defeat and Austria was ready to make peace on almost any terms. In the West the German great offensive had failed and it was becoming questionable whether the German troops were now capable of standing on the defensive. " For a time, on the British front at least, the German *morale* broke down, prisoners were taken from the German infantry in great numbers and without much resistance, and there were signs of confusion and disorder in the enemy ranks, though the German artillery retained much of its efficiency and the machine gunners continued to fight with their old devotion and skill."[1] But most important of all, the German reserves were exhausted, while the Allies had captured enormous numbers of guns and huge stocks of stores of all kinds, and these the output of the German munition factories was quite incapable of making good.

On the 2nd October Marshal von Hindenburg deputed one of his Staff to make a statement on the military situation in the German Reichstag, and from this it was clear that only by the immediate opening of peace negotiations could the German armies escape an overwhelming disaster. In a letter dated the 3rd, Hindenburg repeated his demands for peace even more insistently, and on the 5th the Imperial Chancellor sent a Note to President Wilson asking him to take in hand the restoration of peace and the conclusion of an immediate armistice. There was an exchange of letters, but for the moment the German offer came to nothing, for President Wilson insisted that the conclusion of anything of the nature of an armistice was a matter which must be left to the judgment of the military advisers of the Allied Governments ; while he (the President) for his Government could accept no arrangement which did not provide satisfactory safeguards and guarantees for the maintenance of the present military supremacy of the armies of the Western Powers and of the United States of America. This was final ; the war went on to its inevitable end.

At midnight on the 13th–14th October the 1st Battalion The Border Regiment left the Potterijebrug area and occupied the assembly positions which had been prepared during the day. The enemy was still in places inclined to be aggressive and early on the morning of the 14th put down a counter-preparation barrage on the Battalion front line and support, scoring two direct hits on the Battalion Headquarters, causing a few casualties and setting fire to four motor-ambulances.

Our barrage fell exactly at the appointed hour, drawing a reply from the enemy, and the 1st Border Regiment then advanced, " A " and " B " Companies from the assembly position past Hooley House by the old German track as far as Kanter Hoek, thence by the main road running E. through Ledgehem Station. " C " and " D " followed a more northerly route : by the cross-country track by Triumph House to Whitworth Junction and thence through Ledeghem Station ; while Battalion Headquarters proceeded with the Brigade Headquarters in advance of the leading company. On reaching a point about 600 yards E. of Ledeghem Station along the Ledeghem–Hemelhoek road, a very dense fog was encountered which made it impossible to see for a distance of more than 3 feet, and orderlies were accordingly sent back to bring the companies along the Ledeghem–Hemelhoek road, as it was impossible to move across country, while Headquarters pushed on to Iveson Farm. Here it was clearer, and it was found that the elements of the leading brigades were still about Barraken and fighting could be heard just in front.

[1] Maurice, *The Last Four Months*, p. 165.

The 87th Brigade therefore assembled near Barraken until the ground in front became clearer, while the Battalion was disposed along the hedges of the enclosure of Iveson Farm and picquets were put out to protect the right flank and front, patrols being sent forward to gain touch with the leading brigades. At midday the Battalion was ordered to move out in diamond artillery formation to cover the whole division front from the N. edge of Sovereign Wood to Olivia Farm, and was in position an hour later; but about 2.30 p.m. the Battalion was sent forward into closer support of the 86th and 88th Brigades: "A" and "B" Companies on the right and "C" and "D" on the left with scouts out in front. The Battalion now came under a certain amount of machine-gun fire and was directed by the Brigadier to fall back to the cover of two farms.

The night was passed tolerably quietly, and it was arranged that on the morning of the 15th October the 87th Brigade should attack under a barrage, the 1st Border Regiment and 2nd South Wales Borderers being on the right and left of the divisional front respectively. At 8.15 a.m. the two battalions moved forward simultaneously, both in diamond formation, the 1st Border Regiment having "A" and "D" Companies in front and "B" and "C" in support. The enemy appears to have at once noticed the movement and fired bursts from numerous machine guns, while his aeroplanes flying over in formation directed a certain amount of artillery fire on the assembly area, but happily very few casualties resulted.

Four minutes before zero hour the barrage fell on the front of the 36th Division, which was on the right of the 29th, whose barrage opened three minutes later, when the Battalion advanced to the assault, passing through the front line of the 86th and 88th Brigades.

The Battalion came at once under heavy fire of all kinds, but pressed on, and carried the enemy's first line of resistance; a second line in rear of a broad belt of wire gave more trouble, but this was overcome and this line carried by about 9.35 a.m., while ten minutes later "A" Company reported being in possession of the village of Salines. There was now a slight check owing to opposition from the enemy holding Gulleghem, but about 10.40 this village also was cleared, touch established with the 36th Division and the advance went on, the front line companies attacking the buildings and enclosures in Heule, where the left flank company managed to get a footing; but the Bois d'Heule had not yet been taken, and enfilade fire being experienced on the left, "C" Company under Captain Durlacher formed a defensive flank facing N. towards this wood, which was captured soon after noon, and some half-hour later the Courtrai–Inglemunster Railway was also in our possession.

The Battalion now halted for a time on the line reached and began to consolidate it, while the K.O.S.B.'s moved on to try and seize the crossings of the Heule stream, the 9th Division on the left of the Brigade pushing forward to the capture of Cuerne, and on the success of these operations being reported the Battalion went into billets in the houses near the line it was holding, putting out company picquets. The night passed very quietly and on the 16th the 1st Border Regiment on relief went back to Salines.

During this attack the Battalion captured 150 prisoners, 1 howitzer and 5 machine guns ; throughout, the enemy resisted with considerable vigour, causing a continuous running fight. His artillery fire was never very severe and was chiefly from " whizzbangs " and 4.5's, and for defence he relied mainly on a large number of heavy machine guns, which were very difficult to locate owing to the enclosed nature of the country and the number of farms and cottages ; the advance was across land traversed by many streams, the banks of which were sodden and spongy The 1st Battalion The Border Regiment had thus, in an action lasting for three hours, advanced 4,500 yards on a front of some 750 yards, capturing the village of Salines and the N. half of that of Heule.

During the action 14 non-commissioned officers and men were killed, Lieutenant G. E. H. Slater, Second-Lieutenants G. E. H. Blackburn, C. H. Davies and M. N. Clayton and 80 other ranks were wounded, and 10 men missing.

The officers who took part were Major A. W. Sutcliffe, M.C., in command ; Second-Lieutenant J. H. Smith, M.C. (adjutant) ; Lieutenant H. K. Clucas, M.C. (intelligence officer) ; and Lieutenant C. Helm, M.C. (signalling officer).

"A" Company, Captain F. J. Gemmell-Smith, Lieutenant W. H. Youdale, Second Lieutenants E. Oxley and M. N. Clayton.

"B" Company, Lieutenants G. E. H. Slater and R. Rae, Second-Lieutenant C. H. Davies.

"C" Company, Captain B. R. Durlacher, M.C. ; Second-Lieutenants T. Clayton, C. A. Watts and E. R. W. Raine.

"D" Company, Captain J. Duggan, M.C., D.C.M. ; Lieutenant M. A. Ashby, Second-Lieutenants G. E. H. Blackburn and L. V. Little.

While at Salines 2 officers (Captain R. E. S. Johnson, M.C., and Lieutenant T. R. Morris), with 81 other ranks, came up to the Battalion from the Reception Camp at Mendighem, but this did not go very far towards replacing wastage, especially as Lieutenant Morris was almost immediately wounded, thus becoming non-effective. The rest here was a very short one, for on the 20th the Battalion moved across the Lys River as advance guard to the Brigade, which was in divisional reserve, and was then again, and for the last time in the war, in action.

On the previous night the 88th Infantry Brigade had been detailed to endeavour to bridge the Lys between Courtrai and Cuerne and establish bridge-heads, when an attack would next day be made by the Division in a S.E. direction with the object of gaining approximately the line of the Scheldt River from Avelghem inclusive to Waermaerde inclusive. At 11.30 a.m. on the 20th the Battalion received orders to move at 2 p.m. to the area just W. of Cuerne, but en route was halted near Watermolen and ordered to remain here pending the receipt of further instructions. About an hour or more later the Brigadier told the O.C. 1st Border Regiment that as a result of its attack the 86th Brigade was roughly on a line running N. and S. through the village of Krote and W. of St. Louis, that the right of the Brigade was completely exposed, and that nothing was known of the situation on the further bank of the canal, and that the Battalion must get in touch with the 86th Brigade and form a defensive flank along the canal bank to deny the crossings to any enemy advance from the W.

Eight machine guns were placed at the disposal of the Battalion, and moving forward it was found that the 86th Brigade was on a line E. of St. Louis through Krote with a footing on Wolfsberg Hill, but was held up from Brandhout Bosch, which was strongly held by the enemy. The G.O.C. 86th Brigade was, however, satisfied as to his security, and as he needed no assistance at the time, the 1st Border Regiment withdrew into billets in an area which was subjected to a good deal of shelling during the night and again towards dawn.

It was arranged that next morning, the 21st, the 86th Brigade would attack, supported by the 87th. This did not, however, materialize until early in the afternoon when Brandhout Bosch was captured, and the Battalion was directed to get into touch with the Royal Fusiliers of the 86th Brigade with a view to attacking through their line on the 22nd; and very early on this morning full instructions as to boundaries, barrage, objectives, etc., were issued : that the 41st Division would be on the right, the 1st K.O.S.B.'s on the left, the 1st Border Regiment on the right of the Brigade front, and the 2nd S.W. Borderers in reserve.

The Battalion moved off at 6.30 a.m. on the 22nd, assembling in diamond formation of platoons in the area notified, " B " Company under Lieutenant Slater on the right, " C " on the left under Captain Johnson, M.C., " A " under Captain Gemmell-Smith and " D " under Captain Duggan, M.C., D.C.M. in support of " B " and " C " respectively. The assembly was noticed by the enemy, who opened fire from Hill 66 and from Kattestraate, causing some loss.

At 9 a.m. the British guns opened and the Battalion advanced, coming under heavy machine-gun fire from the above-named points, but pressing on, passed through the leading lines of the 86th Brigade, while " A " Company formed a defensive flank towards Hill 66 and helped much to keep down the fire from it. The very sodden nature of the ground made it difficult to keep up with the barrage, but moving forward by platoon and section rushes the houses of Kattestraate were gradually approached sufficiently closely to allow of the defenders being engaged by trench mortars and rifle grenades. Particularly good work was here done by Second-Lieutenant Chicken, commanding the trench-mortar section, and by Lieutenant McGregor with his machine guns. This officer, who had moved his guns forward on a limber to a sunken portion of the road, having recognized the situation, went back and galloped his limber up from the sunken road into the open, over the rise and into the cover of a small bank in front. He was subjected to heavy concentrated machine-gun fire, but succeeded in getting through, bringing his guns into action. Unhappily this very gallant officer was killed beside his guns about an hour later.

The situation now, at noon, was obscure, but could not be cleared up owing to the difficulty of communicating with the front-line troops, but it was evident that, though the N. end of Kattestraate had been cleared of the enemy, fighting was still going on there; the companies in front sent word that the enemy was counter-attacking but was being repulsed; and during a slight lull in the action the line occupied was consolidated, ammunition was brought up and touch gained with the flanks.

By 4 p.m. the companies of the Battalion had been greatly reduced, and shortly after dark the 1st Border Regiment was relieved and moved back to billets S. of Harlebeke, having sustained casualties totalling 6 killed, 3 officers and 90 other ranks wounded and 14 missing; the names of the officer casualties were: Captain R. E. S. Johnson, M.C., Lieutenant T. N. Morris and Second-Lieutenant L. V. Little.

The opposition encountered throughout the operations was of the strongest. It was established from observation and from the statements of prisoners that the defence controlled a very large number of heavy and light machine guns manned by 5 or 6 men and commanded in each case by an officer. These fought their guns gallantly and skilfully and could be seen directing operations. The position held was of great natural strength and was eminently suited to the defensive tactics employed by the enemy; it consisted of a series of spurs, the crests dotted with numerous farms and enclosures with low hedges. The ground below the crests was bare agricultural land, almost wholly devoid of cover; it was mainly plough and sodden by the recent rain, thus making the going very heavy.

For some ten days or more the 1st Battalion The Border Regiment remained in the neighbourhood of St. André and Tourcoing, and opportunity may here be taken of recounting the course of the negotiations which brought about the Great Surrender.

Germany now broke into revolution, the High Seas Fleet refused to move out of harbour and raised the Red Flag, and the German Emperor and his heir fled into Holland; finally, on the evening of Thursday, the 7th November, the German delegates entered the French lines authorized to make the best terms they could. Their childish proposals for a truce were at once brushed aside, and at 5 a.m. on the 11th November they accepted gratefully and in haste the terms laid down by Marshal Foch. These were that all Allied prisoners were to be forthwith released, the left bank of the Rhine was to be handed over, 5,000 guns, 3,000 machine guns and 2,000 aeroplanes were to be at once surrendered, and all submarines and a large portion of the German Fleet were provisionally to be given into the charge of the Allies.

" The military situation on the British front on the morning of the 11th November can be stated very briefly. In the fighting since 1st November our troops had broken the enemy's resistance beyond possibility of recovery, and had forced on him a disorderly retreat along the whole front of the British Armies. Thereafter the enemy was capable neither of accepting nor refusing battle. The utter confusion of his troops, the state of his railways, congested with abandoned trains, the capture of huge quantities of rolling stock and material, all showed that our attack had been decisive. . . . A continuance of hostilities could only have meant disaster to the German Armies and the assured invasion of Germany." [1]

And so it came to pass that, as the 1st Border Regiment moved forward again to take its place in the line of battle and help to add to the discomfiture of the

[1] Despatch of 21st December, 1918.

enemy, near Celles on the 11th November, to quote the words of the diary : " *At 08.30 news came through that hostilities were to cease at 11.00 as the enemy had accepted terms of Armistice.*"

No battalion diary, of the many that the writer has consulted, tells us how the news of the coming of peace was received by regimental officers and men ; some historians would have us believe that it was received with a great shouting, and that the cheering could be heard rolling along the whole length of the battle line ; others state that the announcement was received in silence by the men whose combined and loyal and sustained efforts had brought peace in our time—silence born of thankfulness and regret : thankfulness that the killing was at last over, regret for the splendid comrades who had fallen, who had helped to gain the victory and had not lived to reap its harvest.

Writing of the soldiers whom he had led, Sir Douglas Haig said : " We have been accustomed to be proud of the great and noble traditions handed down to us by the soldiers of bygone days. The men who form the Armies of the Empire to-day have created new traditions which are a challenge to the highest records of the past and will be an inspiration to the generations who come after us." While of the work of the infantry in particular he wrote : " Despite the enormous development of mechanical invention in every phase of warfare, the place which the infantryman has always held as the main substance and foundation of an army is as secure to-day as in any period of history. The infantryman remains the backbone of defence and the spearhead of the attack. At no time has the reputation of the British infantryman been higher, or his achievement more worthy of his renown.

" During the past three months, the same infantry divisions have advanced to the attack day after day and week after week with an untiring, irresistible valour which refused to be denied. No praise can be too high for the valour they have shown, no gratitude too deep for the work they have accomplished."

As might have been expected, His Majesty the King, who throughout the war had followed with so deep an interest the operations of his armies in every theatre of the World War, was not behindhand in offering his tribute to the results of their bravery :—

" *No words can express my feelings of admiration for the glorious British Army whose splendid bravery under your leadership has now achieved this magnificent success over the enemy. You have fought without ceasing for the past four years. My warmest congratulations to you and your undaunted Army, where all ranks with mutual confidence in each other have faced hardships and dangers with dogged resolution, and have fought on with an irresistible determination that has now resulted in this final and overwhelming victory.*"

APPENDIX A

THE 2ND/4TH BATTALION THE BORDER REGIMENT IN THE OPERATIONS AGAINST
AFGHANISTAN IN 1919.

" AFTER many years of peace there was a recrudescence of trouble in Afghanistan
and all along the border between that country and India.   On February 22nd the
Ameer Habib Ullah Khan, who had always been a loyal friend to Great Britain, was
murdered while camping in the Laghman Valley.   Thereupon ensued a competition
for the throne.   At Jelalabad a proclamation was issued that Nasr Ullah Khan
had assumed the throne, but in Kabul power was seized by Aman Ullah Khan, the
third son of the late Ameer.   Aman Ullah's mother was Habib Ullah's chief wife ;
but the late Ameer's eldest son was Inayat Ullah, who appears to have supported
the claims of Nasr Ullah.   Aman Ullah soon showed, however, that he had control
of the situation and the rival claimant withdrew.   There was more than a suspicion
that Nasr Ullah (who was a brother of the late Sovereign) had not been unduly
disturbed at Habib Ullah's assassination.

" The new Ameer, Aman Ullah, began his reign by announcing that he would
punish those who were guilty of the assassination of his father, that he would
institute reforms in the country—including the abolition of the virtual slavery
which existed in a disguised form—and that he would preserve the tradition of
friendship with India.   On April 13 a durbar was held at Kabul, at which the
assassination of the late Ameer was investigated.   A certain colonel, who was found
guilty of committing the murder, was executed, and the new Ameer's uncle,
Nasr Ullah, was found guilty of complicity in the crime and was sentenced to
imprisonment for life.   Possibly owing to the intrigues of the Russian Government,
the new Ameer did not long keep his promise of preserving friendship with Great
Britain.   Early in May a large Afghan army came pouring across the frontier
and proceeded to pillage far and wide in the north-west provinces." [1]

" The distribution of the Afghan army at the end of April is believed to have
been as follows : on the northern line, including Kabul, were stationed $7\frac{1}{2}$ regiments
of cavalry (2,800 sabres), 29 battalions (16,500 rifles), and 110 guns, of which about
200 rifles and 4 guns were located between Kunar and Asmar on the Chitral border.
On the central line, including Ghazni, were 3 cavalry regiments (1,100 sabres),
17 battalions (9,150 rifles) and 60 guns ; and on the southern line, 1 cavalry regiment (460 sabres), 10 battalions (5,250 rifles) and 24 guns.   The Afghan garrisons
of Herat, Farah and Mazar-i-Sharif, and in the Maimana and Badakshan Districts
are not included in the above and amounted to about 2,700 sabres, 11,100 rifles
and 70 guns.   The force at the Ameer's disposal thus comprised about 7,000 sabres,

[1] *Annual Register*, 1919, pp. 255, 256.

17

42,000 rifles and 260 guns, but it should be noted that at least half of his guns were either immobile or obsolete. But the Ameer's real strength lay, not in his regular army (which of itself is of small account), but in the potential fighting value of the frontier tribes on either side of the Border. Expert in all forms of guerilla warfare, and amounting in the aggregate to some 120,000 men, armed with modern rifles, many of which are provided from Kabul, these tribes are the outstanding factor in the Indian frontier problem, and it was on their co-operation that the Afghan plan of campaign was based. As far as can be judged, this plan contemplated operations on three fronts, viz. :—

(a) From Jelalabad on the Khaibar and Mohmand Sector ;
(b) From Gardez on the Kurram and Waziristan border, utilizing the Khost salient ;
(c) From Kandahar on the Chaman Border. . . .

" The general idea seems to have been to push forward in the first instance detachments of Afghan regular troops, whose function was to raise the tribes on both sides of the Border. . . . The formations at my disposal at the outbreak of war (excluding units allotted to area defence) comprised two divisions and two cavalry brigades on the Khaibar line, one brigade in the Kohat–Kurram area, two brigades in Waziristan, and one division and one cavalry brigade and two mixed brigades in central reserve. During the course of the operations seven additional brigades and one cavalry brigade were formed, increasing the total force employed at the signing of peace to the equivalent of about seven divisions and four cavalry brigades, with one cavalry and five infantry brigades in reserve." [1]

Towards the end of April, 1919, the Afghan Commander-in-Chief arrived at Dakka for the ostensible purpose of inspecting his frontier posts, and on May 3rd the usual convoy proceeding under militia escort through the Khaibar was confronted by Afghan picquets between Tor Kham and Landi Khana. Next day large numbers of copies of a *firman*, signed by the Ameer and containing an exhortation to *Jehad*, were distributed in the city of Peshawar through the agency of the Afghan post-office there, while the same day the Afghan postmaster arrived from Jelalabad with a motor-car load of leaflets, printed at Kabul, stating that the Germans had resumed war and that India and Egypt had risen.

On the 5th May orders were issued for the mobilization of the Field Army, which at first was organized in two forces, the North-West Frontier Force commanded by General Sir A. Barrett, and the Baluchistan Force commanded by Lieutenant-General R. Wapshare. Before the month was out, however, the troops allotted to the Bannu and Derajat areas were separated from the North-West Frontier Force and placed under the orders of Major-General Climo, being designated the Waziristan Force.

The plan of campaign was to take the offensive against Jelalabad with the main striking force, the object being to divide the Mohmands and Afridis, two of the most important of the frontier tribes, cutting them off from Afghan influence and support ; to strike at any Afghan concentration within reach ; and to induce

[1] General Monro's despatch of the 1st November, 1919.

the withdrawal of Afghan forces from our tribal borders elsewhere, for the purpose of covering Kabul.

During April the 2nd/4th Battalion The Border Regiment was in camp at Peshawar; it then formed part of the 1st Infantry Brigade, commanded by Brigadier-General G. D. Crocker, of the 1st Peshawar Division commanded by General Sir F. Campbell, K.C.B., D.S.O., in the Northern Command, of which General Sir A. Barrett, G.C.B., K.C.S.I., K.C.V.O., A.D.C., was then in charge.

It was on the 6th May that the Battalion was ordered to mobilize, the operation being completed next day, when the strength stood at 17 officers and 548 other ranks.

The *Indian Army List* for April, 1919, shows the following officers as then serving with the Battalion: Lieutenant-Colonel F. W. Halton, T.D., Major G. H. Heelis, Captains J. E. C. Graham and J. Jackson, Lieutenants H. C. Grierson-Jackson (acting captain), L. MacGlasson (acting captain), adjutant; A. W. Anderson (acting captain), R. T. Bruckman, J. Glasson, E. H. Barker, E. H. Ashburner and B. F. Chester, Second-Lieutenants G. H. Snow, D. G. Perry, H. Deuchars, W. Pepperell, J. B. Saint, P. V. Curtis and O. D. Gibbings; Captain J. Brooks was quartermaster.

General Campbell had seen much of the Battalion while it had been quartered on the North-West Frontier, and the good opinion which he had formed of it should be placed on record :—

" *The 2nd/4th Border Regiment joined the 10th (Peshawar) Division at Peshawar in March, 1916, at a time when the Buneyrwals, Swatis and Mohmands were simultaneously giving trouble. I was very much struck with the level appearance which the Battalion presented—all stuggy fellows, ruddy and fit. Both officers and men showed great keenness in all that fell to their lot. The rank and file were remarkably well-behaved and many of the officers filled staff appointments, showing great ability. There is no doubt that the arrival of the Battalion at a critical period proved a valuable asset. I am glad to say that the unit took some part in the active blockade of the Mohmands, which was an enlivening experience and their duties were most creditably performed.*"

Then another general officer under whom the Battalion served while in India, Major-General N. G. Woodyatt, C.B., C.I.E., in a lecture which he delivered on " The Infantry of the Territorial Army in India, 1914–1920," paid the 2nd/4th Border Regiment a very fine compliment. He said :—

" *The men of this unit were of fine physique and as keen as mustard. It was a great pleasure to deal with them, and to have a chat with individual N.C.O.'s and men in the blockhouses. On one occasion a picquet of this unit, put out to protect the Viceroy on his visit, was threatened and heavily sniped by the Mohmands. On withdrawal it was followed up by the enemy with some determination. I happened to be present as the picquet was approaching our nearest blockhouse, and noted the extreme reluctance with which the men withdrew under orders. I saw that their eyes were blazing, and that they were full of suppressed excitement. Quite the right fighting spirit. About a month later I added a hundred men of the 2nd/4th Border Regiment to a column I was taking out to destroy some villages. The start was at 4 a.m. and the men returned to camp at 7 p.m., having marched 26 miles and helped to destroy two villages. It is not exactly child's play, pushing over strong mud walls, blowing up towers and burning houses. I thought the day a good test of endurance and all ranks were very cheery at the finish."* [1]

It is evident that the 2nd/4th Battalion of The Border Regiment entered upon the Third Afghan War with a good reputation and in the enjoyment of an invaluable experience of frontier warfare.

By this time General Sir F. Campbell had left Peshawar, and Major-General C. A. Fowler, C.B., D.S.O., had assumed command of the 1st Division in his place.

It is very much to be regretted that the diary kept and preserved in the Battalion during the course of the Afghan War of 1919 is not very full, and that adequate justice cannot therefore be rendered in this account to the good work which was performed.

On the 7th May Brigadier–General L. W. Y. Campbell was appointed to command the Peshawar Internal Security Area with 6 battalions and 8 guns, among the former being the 1st/4th Royal West Surrey Regiment, the 2nd/4th Border Regiment, the 37th Dogras and the 3rd/2nd Gurkha Rifles. On the 8th a cordon was drawn by the troops round the city of Peshawar, whereupon the Afghan postmaster surrendered himself with his staff and escort and was deported to Burma. The city was subsequently picqueted and the Battalion provided signallers for communication with the fort, which overlooked the city, and also the garrison for it.

On the same day a detachment of 1 officer and 60 other ranks proceeded to Risalpur as guard for the local Royal Air Force aerodrome, and was there joined two days later by another officer and 26 more men.

During the course of the next few days the Battalion was required to find two more detached parties ; one, of an officer and 12 other ranks, was provided for the armoured train moving between Pabbi and Jamrud, while another, of a strength of an officer and 11 men, had to be found to protect the Bara aqueduct nightly. Then on the 26th May a large detachment was called for from the Battalion, when Captain A. W. Anderson, 2 other officers and 100 other ranks proceeded to Kohat to join the Thal Relief Force ; these arrived at Kohat early on the morning of the 29th and were at once sent down the Miranzai Valley in motor-lorries to Hangu, where they arrived on the 30th and joined the 45th Brigade there assembled under Brigadier-General R. E. H. Dyer, C.B., being attached to the 1st/25th Battalion The London Regiment.

The course of events which had led to this movement is described as follows in General Monro's despatch of the 1st November, 1919 : " On the evening of the 24th May information was received at Thal that General Nadir Khan, the Afghan Commander in Khost and ex-Commander-in-Chief of the Afghan Army, intended to advance either into the Tochi or the Kurram, and it was reported from Spinwam that Afghan troops were moving on that post. Major-General Eustace accordingly proceeded to Thal and ordered one more battalion and two more mountain guns to rail from Kohat to Thal. On the arrival of these units the garrison of Thal comprised 4 battalions, 4 mountain guns, one squadron

[1] See *Journal of the Royal United Service Institution* for November, 1922.

and one company of sappers and miners. On the 27th a considerable force of Afghan troops, with a large following of tribesmen, advanced on Thal city and the hills to the S.W. of the posts. The enemy's guns and the majority of his regular troops were on the S. bank of the Kurram River, which at this season, is liable to sudden floods. The fort and camp were subjected to considerable shelling, 2 of the guns used being German howitzers of 3.8 calibre. On the morning of the 28th General Sir A. Barrett ordered the immediate despatch to Kohat by rail from Peshawar of a field battery of the 2nd Division and a battalion of the 45th Infantry Brigade, to be followed by the remaining units of that brigade under the command of Brigadier-General R. E. H. Dyer, C.B. The Headquarters of the 16th Division were also ordered to proceed to Kohat from Lahore, instead of to Peshawar as previously ordered. These troops began to arrive at Kohat on the morning of the 29th, and were followed in quick succession by two additional battalions and the 46th Brigade from Ambala which I had also ordered to Kohat."

Captain Anderson's detachment of the Battalion marched out from Hangu with the 45th Brigade on the afternoon of the day of its arrival and reached Togh late the same night. Leaving Togh early on the 31st the force arrived at Doaba, a march of 18 miles, entering Thal on the 1st with but little opposition, the Border detachment being employed as escort to the artillery, which came into action near the aerodrome N.N.E. of Thal; the detachment bivouacked for the night of the 1st–2nd June on the artillery position. On the 2nd June General Dyer took steps for clearing the enemy from the hills to the S.E., when Captain Anderson and his men moved out and attacked the enemy occupying a small hill N. of Thal; but the Afghans were not prepared to make any real stand and withdrew hurriedly, leaving behind their camp equipment and a large amount of cordite ammunition.

On the 3rd June, and again on the 4th, the detachment of The Border Regiment marched 4 miles up the Parachinar road beyond Thal, forded the Kurram River and proceeded to the Afghan camp at Yusaf Khel, clearing the camp and the ammunition dump and bringing in 2 wounded Afghans found in the deserted camp.

" During the advance of General Dyer's column on Thal," so runs General Monro's despatch, " the extreme heat had made the long marches exceedingly arduous and exhausting ; but the march discipline and spirit of the men were excellent, and the commander and troops deserve great credit for the manner in which the operation was carried out. A flight of aeroplanes based on Thal co-operated throughout, and contributed largely to the enemy's hasty retreat."

On the 8th Captain Anderson and his party left by train for Kohat and all arrived safely at Peshawar on the following day.

While the detachment had been away the Headquarter Companies had experienced a certain amount of " scrapping," the armoured train being attacked and partly derailed on the 2nd June by certain of the tribesmen between Kacha Garhi and Jamrud, when Corporal Murray and Private Brown of " C " Company were wounded.

The Ameer of Afghanistan had now entered into tentative negotiations for peace with the Indian Government, but the fighting did not immediately cease, our aeroplanes bombed both Jelalabad and Kabul, and it was not until after prolonged procrastination that a peace conference was opened at Rawal Pindi on 26th July, a preliminary peace being finally signed on the 8th August and duly ratified a month later. The neighbourhood of Peshawar was, however, very unsettled, and on the 22nd June it had been necessary to send out a force to clear the Kajauri Plain of the many raiders who had been very active at Peshawar, Bara and Kacha Garhi ; the Battalion—strength, 15 officers and 282 other ranks— accompanied this force and 40 prisoners were taken during the operations.

The Afghan War was now at an end so far as the 2nd/4th Border Regiment was concerned, but it had been a very strenuous time, for in addition to finding the detachments for Thal, Risalpur and other places, the Battalion had provided the guard at Peshawar Fort and a very large number of the ordinary guards of the garrison. At the opening of war, owing to the absence of the regular battalions, the 2nd/4th had to find all the duties in the station, the men remaining on permanent guard from 10 to 14 days at a stretch until at last relieved by battalions from other divisions ; numerous escorts had also to be supplied to Dakka and Jamrud with the Northern Army Commander, with the Afghan peace envoys, or with convoys of prisoners, ammunition, etc.

When the 2nd/4th Battalion of The Border Regiment finally left Peshawar to return to England, it had been three years and eight months on the North-West Frontier of India, and during that time, when things were more than usually unsettled, it had not lost a single rifle or a round of ammunition.

By its services in the Afghan War of 1919 the Battalion added a Battle Honour to the Regiment's long roll.

APPENDIX B

SINCE the middle of the last century when, with the close of the Sikh Wars, the country on and beyond the North-West Frontier of India became our natural and troublous inheritance, the tribesmen of Waziristan have been the cause of very many wars and minor expeditions, of the loss of countless valuable lives and of an infinite expenditure of treasure.

Waziristan forms the connecting link on the Afghan frontier between the districts of Kurram and Zhob; on the N. and N.W. lie the Afghan districts of Birmal and Khost, while on the N.E. and E. Waziristan is coterminous with the districts of Kurram, Kohat, Bannu and Dera Ismail Khan; on the S. lies Zhob. In shape Waziristan resembles a rough parallelogram, with an average length of 110 miles from N. to S. and an average breadth of 60 miles from E. to W.; it is intersected from all sides by chains of mountains, ridges and ravines, and the rugged and mountainous character of the country becomes the more accentuated the further one advances into it from the east.

The country is inhabited by four main tribes of which by very far the largest and the most important are the Darwesh Khel Wazirs and the Mahsuds; and the chief highways of Waziristan are the Tochi and the Gumal Valleys, the former giving access from the Bannu District to the Afghan district of Birmal, while the latter connects the two British districts of Derajat and Zhob.

We first came into contact with the Wazirs in 1852 when John Nicholson led a force into their country; there was a second expedition in 1859–60; another in 1879; there was an expedition against the Mahsuds in 1881; another against the Darwesh Khel and Mahsuds in 1894; further trouble in 1897–98; there was a blockade of the Mahsuds in 1900–01; another expedition in 1902; and from 1914 onwards there was frequent trouble, and movable columns were constantly marching and fighting about the country. The diplomatic relations of the Indian Government with the people of Waziristan were not rendered the less delicate and difficult by the claims persistently put forward by the Ameer of Afghanistan, from 1884 even up to as late as 1920, that Waziristan belonged to him, while he has made more than one attempt to establish his supremacy over the Wazirs. These claims were for some time ignored and were not indeed formally repudiated until 1892, by which time the Afghans had occupied Wana, when the Ameer was informed that we did not admit his right to occupy that place; he was told that on no account was he to advance further into the country; and he was reminded that the Indian

Government had always insisted on the independence of the Wazirs and upon our right to deal directly with them.

" Early in September, 1922, the Government of India obtained sanction to a scheme for the permanent control of Waziristan. The salient features of this scheme included the completion of the mechanical transport road from Idak via Razmak, Dwa Toi and Sorarogha to Jandola ; the construction of a mechanical transport road from Jandola to Sarwakai, and the improvement of the cis-Border road from Draband to Ghazni Khel so as to make it fit for mechanical transport. A force, based on the Tochi, was to be located permanently at Razmak and Ladha was to be abandoned. When Razmak was occupied, all regular troops, with the exception of those at Razmak and on the Razmak–Tochi line of communications, were to be withdrawn, law and order being maintained by a system of scout and khassadar posts." [1]

At the end of February, 1922, the situation became easier and normal conditions began once more to prevail, the situation in Waziristan remaining good up to the middle of October.

The 1st Battalion The Border Regiment had arrived in India in November, 1919, and was at first stationed at Karachi with a detachment at Hyderabad in Sind ; from here it was moved two years later to Kohat and in the hot weather of 1922 it was quartered at Parachinar, 117 miles W. of Kohat and 16 from the Peiwar Kotal, and being situated in a plain only 3 miles from the southern slopes of the Sufed Koh, Parachinar possesses a temperate climate. Here the Battalion was in the Kohat District, temporarily commanded by Colonel-Commandant E. A. Fagan, C.S.I., C.M.G., D.S.O., and in the 5th Indian Infantry Brigade under Colonel F. E. Coningham, C.B., C.S.I., C.M.G., the Brigade being composed as follows :—

No. 28 Squadron, R.A.F.
Dett. No. 31 Squadron, R.A.F.
108th Lahore Pack Battery.
No. 20 Company 3rd Royal Sappers and Miners.
1st Battalion The Border Regiment.
1st/56th Rifles, Frontier Force.
1st/5th Royal Gurkha Rifles, Frontier Force.

The *Indian Army List* for October, 1922, shows the following officers then on the strength of the 1st Battalion The Border Regiment : Lieutenant-Colonel H. Nelson, D.S.O. ; Majors A. J. Ellis, D.S.O., G. Darwell, M.C., and H. E. Festing, D.S.O. ; Captains W. F. H. Chambers, M.C., C. W. O'Brien, M.C., H. J. Hayman-Joyce, J. H. B. Warren and P. D. W. Dunn, D.S.O., M.C. ; Lieutenants C. M. Craig-McFeely, D.S.O., M.C., J. S. Nichols, M.C., A. G. Wilkinson, M. A. E. Ashby, V. Blomfield, W. J. Murphy, M. Elrington and F. L. Samut ; Second-Lieutenants H. S. Cooper, C. C. Blackwell, E. C. Brewer and P. J. Kington-Blair-Oliphant ; Brevet Major W. O. Lay was adjutant, Captain E. O'B. White, M.C., D.C.M., was quartermaster and Lieutenant E. A. E. C. Hopkin was education officer. Three

---

[1] General Lord Rawlinson's despatch of the 25th July, 1923.

officers were attached from the 2nd Battalion Royal Dublin Fusiliers recently disbanded : Lieutenants D. C. A. Shepard, T. E. Flewitt and D. S. Norman.   On leave
out of India were Captain P. R. Dowding, Lieutenants H. T. Thompson, G. H. Bates
and A. J. Smith, D.S.O., D.C.M. ; while Lieutenant M. C. Nicholson was A.D.C. to
the General Officer Commanding the Sind and Rajputana District, and Lieutenant
(temporary captain) A. H. Craine, M.C., was officer in charge of the Clothing
Depot, Quetta.

By virtue of a regulation which seems to have taken effect from the beginning
of this year only, under which two Indian officers were attached to every British
Infantry battalion serving in India, the following Indian officers were at this time
attached to the 1st Battalion The Border Regiment, viz. Subadar Parmanand and
Jemadar Sujan Singh ; they were in charge of the Indian establishment (drivers)
of the machine guns.

Towards the end of October the Mahsud situation, which had been distinctly
promising in the early autumn, now began rapidly to deteriorate ; attacks on our
troops became very much more frequent, there was considerable opposition to the
establishment of khassadar posts in that country, and finally a British officer
was murdered by certain irreconcilables among the tribesmen.   The Indian Government then, late in November, ordered the discontinuance of work on the Sorarogha–
Razmak and Jandola–Sarwakai roads, and later directed that the survey of the
former should not be carried beyond Dwa Toi ; and these several decisions seem to
have given rise to the belief among the Mahsuds that no force would now advance
on Razmak and that the proposed occupation of that place had been abandoned.

The advance of the Force had, however, only been postponed from the 1st
to the 15th December, and for a month previous to the latter date all hostile sections
of the Mahsuds were heavily bombed.

The Razmak Force was placed under the command of Major-General A. Le G.
Jacob, C.M.G., C.I.E., D.S.O., and its composition is given in great detail in an
appendix to Lord Rawlinson's despatch to which reference has already been made ;
it will, however, be sufficient for our purpose briefly to enumerate the fighting units
of the Force and these were : 2 squadrons Royal Air Force, the 16th Light Cavalry,
1 Pack Artillery Brigade, 1 section of a Howitzer Battery, 2 Pioneer Battalions, 2
Sections of an Armoured Car Company, the 5th, 7th and 8th Indian Infantry
Brigades, and, in reserve, 2 Gurkha Battalions.

The 1st Border Regiment had by this been transferred from the 5th to the 7th
Indian Infantry Brigade, commanded by Colonel H. E. Herdon, C.I.E., and which
contained, besides themselves, the following infantry battalions :—

1st/3rd Madras Regiment.
2nd/3rd Gurkha Rifles.
1st/9th Gurkha Rifles.

In December the Headquarters of the 7th Brigade was at Dardoni, which is
thus described in an article in the *Journal of the United Service Institution* of India
for January, 1922 : " Dardoni is a hutted cantonment for a brigade, with electric
light and fans.   Although the Tochi line is not so very much further from Makin,

the centre of disaffection, than the Ladha line, the tribesmen seem less persistent. Possibly those actually on the spot have less initiative, possibly because wheeled transport is not so vulnerable as strings of slow-moving camels. Also the country is more open, cavalry action being possible in many places. As a result of these things life is less strenuous. Officers can reach the broad gauge at Mari Indus in a single day, whereas 4 to 6 are necessary from Ladha or Wana. The Tochi line, however, shares with other frontier posts the irksome restraint of the perimeter camp. Relaxations are few. Polo is played in Dardoni and tennis courts are being gradually built, but officers cannot stroll out in the evening with a gun for sand-grouse, the country is too unsafe and, incidentally, the sand-grouse are too few."

While the various units of the Razmak Force had been effecting their concentration, very much had been done for improving communications ; the main object of the Force, as stated in Lord Rawlinson's despatch, " was to establish a force of all arms on the Razmak plateau, and, as the force was dependent for its line of communication on the Isha–Razmak road, its movements were largely regulated by the progress made in the construction of that road. Work on the road was commenced on the 11th July, and progress was at first slow owing to the difficulty in obtaining civil labour and to the inadvisability, for political reasons, of employing technical troops. As time went on, however, the necessity of expediting the work was allowed to overrule other considerations, and by the middle of November five companies of Sappers and Miners and two battalions of Pioneers had been sent up to the Razmak Force and were engaged on the construction of the road at, and forward of, Tal " (in the Tochi). " By the 15th December Ford vans were running from Tal to Asad Khel ; by the 30th December the road was fit for heavy mechanical transport as far as Damdil ; and by the 5th January it was in use by Ford vans up to within a mile of Razani. . . . By the 12th December, 15 days' supplies for the whole Force had been collected at Tal. The 5th Infantry Brigade, which had concentrated at Idak on the 13th, moved to Tal on the 15th and to Asad Khel on the 16th, the 8th Infantry Brigade being responsible for the protection of the road from Bannu to Damdil. By the 31st the 5th Brigade had, without encountering any hostile opposition, established permanent picquets as far as the Tambre Oba camp. Meanwhile the 7th Brigade, with two pack batteries and a company of Sappers and Miners, had concentrated at Asad Khel on the 1st January, and on this day this Brigade marched through the 5th Brigade and encamped at Tambre Oba on the 3rd. On the 4th the advance was continued without incident to Razani."

We may now take up the story and fill in the details from the Battalion diary of the 1st Border Regiment.

Early on the morning of the 31st December, 1922, the Battalion left Dardoni for Tal in Tochi as part of " C " Echelon of the 7th Brigade, the echelon being under the command of Lieutenant-Colonel Nelson, D.S.O., of The Border Regiment ; the advance guard was composed of " A " and " B " Companies and the machine-gun platoon and was commanded by Major Ellis, D.S.O., while the rearguard under Major Festing, D.S.O., consisted of " D " Company. The Tochi River was crossed shortly after starting, and here the " Concessions " or " War Area " was entered. The camping ground, just below the fort at Tal, was reached at 1.30 p.m. and this was not very comfortable, being rather broken and cramped for the many units for which room had to be found, but the water supply was fortunately close at hand. The Battalion had here to find two night picquets—one by " A " Company on a hill some distance from the camp and a second by " B " Company close to the perimeter ; " C " Company also provided a guard of two platoons over the camel serai near the river and some distance from camp.

On the 1st January, 1923, " C " Echelon, to which a battalion of Sikh Pioneers had now been added, marched to Asad Khel, a distance of some 12 miles up and down hill ; camp was reached about 2.30 p.m. and was found to be not only comfortable but tolerably secure against enemy snipers, being in a re-entrant and below the crest of a ridge, on the top of which " B " and " C " Companies put out picquets at night. Here orders were received that the Battalion would move next day to Tambre Oba, and on the 2nd the 1st Border Regiment had formed up preparatory to starting, while the advance guard had already moved off, when orders were received from the G.O.C. 5th Infantry Brigade, who was here in command, that the 7th Brigade required the Battalion to remain at Asad Khel pending further orders, and it was not until 9 a.m. on the 3rd January that Asad Khel was left, the Battalion escorting a convoy of 1,000 camels with stores.

The first part of the march was along the bed of the Khaisora River and the column was sniped at *en route*, but reached Tambre Oba without any casualties, and here the Battalion rejoined the 7th Infantry Brigade and occupied the perimeter camp.

The Battalion marched on to Razani on the 4th, and here work was at once commenced to make the camp secure against attack, sangars being erected and wire put up ; three picquets were allotted to the Battalion, Nos. 5, 7 and 8, two of these requiring 2 N.C. officers and 12 men each, while the other was of the strength of a platoon under an officer. That night the camp was sniped from two sides, but the only casualty was one of the battery mules wounded.

The 5th was spent in improving the defences of the camp and in providing covering parties for men engaged in preparing positions for the more distant picquets.

On the 6th there was a reconnaissance in force by the 7th Brigade in the direction of Razmak ; there was no opposition whatever and nothing was seen of any enemy tribesmen, and the whole Brigade was back at Razani by the early afternoon ; it was a raw, cold day with a slight fall of snow.

During the next ten days the troops at Razani were busily employed in finding positions for permanent picquets on the Razmak Road, in making paths to all those in occupation and in clearing the ground which in some places was very thickly wooded ; and then on the 15th January a further reconnaissance in force was carried out by the 7th Infantry Brigade, the Brigadier being desirous of selecting a camping ground at Razmak for occupation when the move thither should be made. This was successfully carried out and the return to Razani effected without any encounter with the local firebrands.

The next few days were passed in much the same manner, and at last on the morning of the 23rd January the final advance to and occupation of the Razmak plateau was commenced. The advance guard of the 7th Brigade moved out under Major Ellis of the Battalion at 7.55, the Battalion marching with the main body and being allotted transport to the number of 124 camels and 140 mules *in addition* to the battalion mules. At the start the morning was mild, but snow soon began to fall, developing later into a heavy snowstorm which lasted all day. As there had been a hard frost during the previous night, the camel track by which the column marched to Razmak was especially difficult for the transport and particularly for the camels.

On reaching the top of the Narai, which was as far as the early reconnaissance had penetrated, the advance guard secured the Razmak plateau and advanced to a distance of 2 miles from the Narai and there occupied positions covering the construction of the camp. On arrival at the plateau the whole country was found to be deep in snow and the going was difficult, while as snow was still coming down and clouds were hanging about, observation was not easy. Under such conditions it was very hard to pick up the exact line of the various ranges of hills, and the selection of a secure camping ground near the water supply took time ; one was, however, finally chosen and the Battalion reached its allotted ground at 2 p.m., having taken five hours to traverse the 6 miles from Razani to Razmak.

Of this march Lord Rawlinson's despatch states : " the advance up the track, which had a gradient of 1 in 9 and a width of only 6 feet, took place in a blinding snowstorm, and the passage over the Narai of some 1,500 camels and 1,100 mules, which accompanied the column, was a fine performance. The march commenced at dawn, and, though the distance to be covered was only 6 miles, the last camel did not reach camp till 10.45 p.m."

The 7th Brigade now proceeded to make itself secure at Razmak, and the next few days were spent in establishing permanent picquets—of which two known as " Tauda " and " Borridge," the former some 1,500 yards from camp and the track thereto lying through deep snow, were allotted to the Battalion—in reconnoitring towards Makin, the Mahsud capital, and in building up a reserve of supplies. The distribution of the Razmak Force at this time was as follows :—

At Saidgi, 1 battalion ; at Shinki, 1 platoon ; at Khajuri, 1 platoon ; at Idak, 1 battalion, less 1 company ; at Isha, 1 platoon ; at Tal, 2 companies ; at Damdil, 1 battalion, less 1 company ; at Asad Khel, 5th Brigade Headquarters, 1 pack battery, 2 battalions, less 2 companies ; at Tambre Oba, 1 battalion, less 1 company ; from Razani to Kupiri Algad, 3 companies ; at Razmak, 7th Brigade.

During the next few days the troops at Razmak were strenuously engaged in the strengthening of the position, in escorting convoys and in cutting wood ; while preparations were perfected for dealing a heavy blow at the Mahsud stronghold at Makin by combined operations conducted by the 9th Brigade of the Waziristan Force and the 7th Brigade of the Razmak Force.

On the 30th January the strength of the 1st Battalion The Border Regiment was reduced by the departure of all short-service and time-expired men for the depot at Peshawar under Major Lay and Second-Lieutenant Sangster ; and on the

4th February the Battalion, strength 26 officers and 540 other ranks, marched S. towards Tauda China *en route* to Makin, leaving behind in the camp at Razmak, under Captain Dowding, all unfit men and excess tentage and baggage, the march being at first secured from molestation by the permanent Razmak picquets, and thereafter by others put out by the advance guard.

Early in the advance a few shots were fired at the column from the right flank, while on the left, immediately E. of the village of Shingi, a sniper was busy at short range.

At about 11.30 a.m. " A " and " D " Companies of the Battalion were ordered to attack and occupy the ridge overlooking the villages of Abbas and Azdi Khel; they started their advance from the S. of Shingi village and, covered by our guns, the ridge was successfully occupied. The Brigadier had ordered up the machine-gun platoon to support " A " and " D " Companies, and these all now remained on the ridge until 5 o'clock in the afternoon, covering the construction of a picquet post which was placed on this ridge and which proved an invaluable supporting point in the operations afterwards undertaken against the villages N. and E. of the Dara Toi. The remainder of the Battalion, after a long wait in the nullah near Shingi, proceeded to the camp at Sorarogha via the Tauda China nullah, and thence across the plateau. At Sorarogha was met the 9th Brigade, containing the 1st Royal Welch Fusiliers, the 4th and 6th Gurkhas and the 39th Garhwal Rifles, which had arrived by way of Marobi from Ladha, and the two brigades were now occupying one large camp on the same site as that tenanted by the column which in 1920 had carried out operations against Makin.

The 7th Infantry Brigade now came under the orders of Major-General Sir T. G. Matheson, K.C.B., C.M.G., of the Waziristan Force.

During the afternoon of this day, while engaged in superintending the building of sangars to the camp and the erection of picquet posts outside it, Captain P. D. W. Dunn, D.S.O., M.C., was wounded by one of the snipers who by this time were showing an increased activity. On the 5th February Captain Chambers, M.C., came in with the convoy from Razmak, having handed over command of the Battalion Depot at Peshawar to Captain O'Brien, M.C.

On the 6th February the 7th and 9th Brigades left the camp for the purpose of destroying the villages about Makin, the objectives of the former being Lali Khel—part of Makin proper, and of the 9th Brigade the villages of Dinour and Kut. In the 7th Brigade the operations were carried out as follows: the 1st/9th Gurkhas left camp early and occupied the highest points of a hill, known as Vantage Hill, to cover the destruction of Lali Khel, while the 1st Border Regiment, leaving " A " Company in camp, moved out behind the Gurkhas and on reaching Tree Picquet posted the three companies as under :—

" B " on Borbush Hill overlooking Vantage village.
" D " on Azdi Khel Ridge overlooking Abbas Khel and Azdi Khel villages.
" C " in reserve.

Both battalions, with the 2nd/3rd Gurkhas in brigade reserve, were in position by 10 a.m., at which hour parties of the 34th Pioneers and 13th Company Sappers and Miners entered the village and made all preparations for destroying it. On the left " B " with 2 machine guns had several good targets and fired on the enemy moving up the nullah to Makin, while " D " Company engaged small parties of the Mahsuds, and the remaining machine guns, on the ridge where was " C " Company in reserve, fired across the valley at hostile snipers who were busy from above Bozam. This sniping could not be wholly checked, and continued more or less all day, the 1st/9th Gurkhas having several casualties.

At 12.30 preparations for retirement to camp were initiated ; all mules except those with machine guns were ordered back, an hour later the advanced guns were directed to withdraw, and the retirement should thenceforward have proceeded " according to plan," when dense clouds of smoke arose from Lali Khel which had been rather prematurely set on fire, and visual communication was wholly interrupted between Brigade Headquarters and the 1st/9th Gurkhas, and also between the Battalion Headquarters and " B " and " D " Companies ; so that at the moment when orders for the withdrawal were on the point of being issued, messages could only be sent by hand.

These, however, were got through, though with some unavoidable delay, and the Gurkhas began falling back about 2.25, closely followed up by the enemy who, as so often happens on the frontier, appeared on Vantage Hill almost as soon as the Gurkhas left it. Happily " B " Company of the 1st Border Regiment in support caught this party of Mahsuds as they surmounted the ridge, and the Lewis-gun fire was so intense and accurate that the enemy was unable to follow up. The Gurkhas and " B " and " D " Companies fell back through each other by turns and camp was reached without the Battalion sustaining any casualties.

On return to camp the O.C. 1st/9th Gurkhas personally thanked the O.C. " B " Company, Lieutenant C. M. Craig-McFeely, D.S.O., M.C., for the invaluable supporting fire provided by the company during the retirement, stating that without it the Gurkhas could only have been extricated with serious loss.

The work of destruction was to have been resumed on the 7th, but the orders for this were cancelled as during the night rain fell very heavily, flooding the camp, soaking the men's kits and blankets and filling the trenches with 3 feet of water. On the 8th some snow fell and the operations were still in abeyance, but on the 9th the intended programme was carried out, the 7th Brigade being detailed to destroy Vantage and Azdi Khel villages, while its left flank was covered from molestation by the 9th Brigade.

The Battalion was in support of the Tochi Scouts, who, with the 1st/9th Gurkhas, formed the destruction party, while the 2nd/3rd Gurkhas operated on the right, and the 6th Gurkhas, from the 9th Brigade, formed the brigade reserve of the 7th. The Vickers guns of the 1st/9th Gurkhas were lent to the 1st Border Regiment to aid in the support of the covering troops. As usual there was not much opposition during the actual operations ; at 2 p.m. the villages were on fire, and when fifteen minutes later the withdrawal began, the scouts were followed up and had several casualties ; they fell back covered by " B " and " C " Companies, and this last in retiring in turn was worried by snipers on the right and had 2 men wounded.

On the 10th similar operations against other Mahsud villages were carried out in much the same manner, except that the work of destruction was entrusted to the 9th Brigade, while the 7th safeguarded its most exposed flank.

On the 11th the camp was sniped and Lieutenant J. S. Nichols, M.C., was wounded.

The next day the troops were given a rest while the guns bombarded hostile villages within reach. The only portion of Makin now remaining undestroyed lay within the difficult defile of the Dara Toi, an advance into which would probably have entailed severe casualties. It was therefore decided to deal with it by means of artillery fire and aerial bombing. This was successfully accomplished on the 12th, three pack batteries, the 6-inch howitzers and the squadron of heavy bombers all operating in conjunction, the whole operations being clearly visible from camp and providing, as the Battalion diary informs us, " a popular spectacle."

This completed the devastation of the Makin area, and, in addition to the material damage inflicted, the enemy was known to have suffered over 60 casualties in the course of the operations. The Mahsuds now expressed a desire to make peace and on the 22nd February met Major-General Matheson in *jirga* and accepted the terms offered. The work on the roads, however, was continued and reconnaissances were carried out all over the country.

On the 28th February Lieutenant-Colonel H. Nelson, D.S.O., left the Battalion prior to going on leave pending retirement, and Lieutenant Blomfield also left, having been nominated for duty at the Regimental Depot at Carlisle.

On the 12th March the 7th Brigade returned to Razmak, to a new camp, and so reverted to the command of the G.O.C. Razmak Force ; on the very next day Corporal Barnett of " B " Company was killed by a sniper.

The stay of the 1st Border Regiment in Waziristan was now coming to an end ; on the 15th March news was received that the Battalion would be shortly relieved by the 1st Battalion The Welch Regiment ; the relief was effected on the 21st and on the 23rd the Battalion marched to Razani, where it was met and thanked for all its good work by Major-General Jacob, and then, moving on by Asad Khel and Idak to Bannu, it there entrained and arrived on the 30th March at Peshawar, where it was accommodated in Roberts Lines.

Of the work done by the troops Lord Rawlinson reported as follows in his despatch :—

" The operations have been arduous in the extreme and the troops have throughout experienced great hardships from the rigours of the climate. The intense heat of a Waziristan summer was followed by a bitterly cold winter, while the frequent spates during the rainy season caused serious interruptions of communications by the destruction of the bridges, and a consequent scarcity of supplies at the front.

" The spirit of the infantry, on whom the greatest strain has always fallen, has been worthy of the highest praise, and they have at all times willingly responded to the calls made upon them."

APPENDIX C

1st Battalion. MOVED on 4th December, 1918, into Germany and was stationed at Hilgen till 27th March, 1919, having gradually been reduced to Cadre strength. It then proceeded to Mulheim and on the 30th March the Cadre left for Dunkirk, sailed from there on the 3rd April in the *Antrim* for Dover, going thence by train to Brookwood and by march route to Dettingen Barracks, Blackdown. The Battalion remained here until it embarked for India later in the year.

2nd Battalion. Was quartered at or near Lonigo until the end of February, 1919, and on the 17th March, having been reduced to Cadre strength, it entrained at Tavernelle for Havre *en route* to England. It arrived at Carlisle on the 24th March and was accorded a civic welcome, being entertained by the Mayor and Corporation. In July, 1919, the Battalion moved to Claremorris, County Mayo, Ireland, where the *personnel* of the 3rd Battalion, less permanent Staff, was absorbed into it.

3rd Battalion. On the declaration of the Armistice the Battalion was quartered at Crosby. In March, 1919, it moved to Blackdown and in the following May to Claremorris, where it was absorbed into the 2nd Battalion, the permanent Staff being sent to Carlisle to complete the establishment of the Regimental Depot.

1st/4th Battalion. Was mobilized for the Third Afghan War in May, 1919, but was not employed. It remained in India until December, 1919, when it returned to England.

2nd/4th Battalion. Remained in India until the end of 1919, having served in the Third Afghan War of that year. Left Peshawar on the 11th November and embarked in H.M.T. *Friedrichsruh* on 15th. Disembarked at Plymouth on the 9th December and proceeded thence to various dispersal stations. The Cadre was sent first to Kendal and then to Carlisle, being finally dispersed on the 31st January, 1920.

5th Battalion. Remained in Flanders till the 31st January, 1919, when it marched into Germany, being quartered in Cologne and neighbourhood till the end of March, when it moved to Bonn. Left Bonn on the 6th November by train via Cologne for Calais; arrived here on the 9th December, embarking next day for Dover and proceeded thence by train via London to Kendal, which was reached on the 11th. The Battalion finally arrived back at Workington on the 14th December, 1919.

6th Battalion. Was disbanded at Malingarbe on the 9th February, 1917, the officers and other ranks being absorbed into the 1st, 7th, 8th and 11th Battalions of The Border Regiment.

7th Battalion. Remained for some days at Troisvilles after the proclamation of the Armistice, and then moved to Liercourt in the Amiens area on the 14th December and was there gradually reduced to Cadre strength. The Cadre left Liercourt on the 16th April, 1919, and entrained at Longpré for Havre, which was reached on the 17th. Havre was left on the evening of the 19th, the Cadre arriving at Southampton early on the 20th and leaving again late the same night for Catterick, where it was eventually disbanded.

8th Battalion. Was disbanded at Embry in July, 1918, on the 25th Division being broken up and sent home.

9th Battalion. Moved on the 20th October, 1918, to Stavros, on the 28th to Dedeagatch and back to Stavros on the 13th November and following days. On the 16th January, 1919, the Battalion proceeded to Kukus and on the 7th March to Janes. On the 16th, greatly reduced in strength, it embarked in H.M.T. *Katonia* for Constantinople, where it remained until the 10th November, when all remaining officers and other ranks were posted as a draft to the 9th Battalion The King's Own Regiment.

11th Battalion. Was amalgamated with the 5th Battalion on the 10th May, 1918, and finally disbanded on the 31st July.

APPENDIX D

THEATRE OF WAR AND BATTLE HONOURS OF THE BORDER REGIMENT, SHOWING IN
EACH CASE THE BATTALIONS WHICH GAINED THESE HONOURS.

THEATRE OF WAR HONOURS.

Theatre of War.	*Battalion.*
FRANCE AND FLANDERS, 1914	2nd Battalion. 5th ,,
FRANCE AND FLANDERS, 1915	2nd ,, 5th ,, 7th ,, 11th ,,
FRANCE AND FLANDERS, 1916	1st ,, 2nd ,, 5th ,, 6th ,, 7th ,, 8th ,, 11th ,,
FRANCE AND FLANDERS, 1917	1st ,, 2nd ,, 5th ,, 6th ,, 7th ,, 8th ,, 11th ,,
FRANCE AND FLANDERS, 1918	1st ,, 5th ,, 6th ,, 7th ,, 8th ,, 11th ,,
ITALY, 1917, 1918	2nd ,,
MACEDONIA, 1915, 1916, 1917, 1918	9th ,,
GALLIPOLI, 1915, 1916	1st ,, 6th ,,
EGYPT, 1916	6th ,,
NORTH-WEST FRONTIER, 1916, 1917, 1918, 1919	2/4th ,,

BATTLE HONOURS.

Operations.	Battles.	Battalion.
FLANDERS, 1914	Ypres, 1914	2nd Battalion.
	Langemarck, 1914 ...	2nd ,,
	Gheluvelt	2nd ,,
SUMMER OPERATIONS, 1915 ...	Neuve Chapelle	2nd ,,
	Ypres, 1915	5th ,,
	Bellewaerde	5th ,,
	Aubers	2nd ,,
	Festubert, 1915 ...	2nd ,,
	Loos	2nd ,,
OPERATIONS ON THE SOMME, 1916	Somme, 1916	1st ,,
		2nd ,,
		5th ,,
		6th ,,
		7th ,,
		8th ,,
		11th ,,
	Albert, 1916	1st ,,
		2nd ,,
		7th ,,
		8th ,,
		11th ,,
	Bazentin	2nd ,,
	Delville Wood	7th ,,
	Pozières	8th ,,
	Guillemont	2nd ,,
	Flers-Courcelette ...	5th ,,
		6th ,,
	Morval	5th ,,
	Thiepval	6th ,,
	Transloy	5th ,,
	Ancre Heights	8th ,,
	Ancre, 1916	11th ,,
ARRAS OFFENSIVE, 1917	Arras, 1917	1st ,,
		5th ,,
		7th ,,
	Scarpe, 1917	1st ,,
		5th ,,
		7th ,,
	Bullecourt	2nd ,,
FLANDERS OFFENSIVE, 1917 ...	Messines, 1917	6th ,,
		8th ,,
	Ypres, 1917	1st ,,
		2nd ,,
		5th ,,
		6th ,,
		7th ,,
		8th ,,

BATTLE HONOURS—*continued*.

Operations.	Battles.	Battalion.
FLANDERS OFFENSIVE, 1917 ... (*continued*)	Pilckem ... ... Langemarck, 1917 ... Polygon Wood ... ... Broodseinde ... ... Poelcappelle ... ... Passchendaele	8th Battalion. 1st ,, 6th ,, 2nd ,, 2nd ,, 1st ,, 2nd ,, 6th ,, 2nd ,, 5th ,, 7th ,,
CAMBRAI OPERATIONS, 1917 ...	Cambrai, 1917	1st ,,
OFFENSIVE IN PICARDY, 1918 ...	Somme, 1918 ... ... St. Quentin ... ... Bapaume, 1918 ... ... Rosières ... ... Arras, 1918	5th ,, 7th ,, 8th ,, 11th ,, 5th ,, 7th ,, 8th ,, 7th ,, 8th ,, 5th ,, 11th ,,
OFFENSIVE IN FLANDERS, 1918 ...	Lys ... ... Estaires ... ... Messines, 1918 ... ... Hazebrouck ... ... Bailleul ... ... Kemmel ... ... Scherpenberg	1st ,, 8th ,, 1st ,, 8th ,, 1st ,, 8th ,, 8th ,, 8th ,,
OFFENSIVE IN CHAMPAGNE ...	Aisne, 1918	8th ,,
ADVANCE IN PICARDY, 1918 ...	Amiens ... ... Somme, 1918 ... ... Albert, 1918 ... ... Bapaume, 1918	5th ,, 7th ,. 5th ,, 7th ,, 5th ,, 7th ,, 5th ,, 7th ,,

BATTLE HONOURS—*continued.*

Operations.	Battles.	Battalion.
BREAKING OF HINDENBURG LINE, 1918	Hindenburg Line ...	5th Battalion.
		7th ,,
	Épéhy	7th ,,
	St. Quentin Canal ...	5th ,,
	Beaurevoir	5th ,,
	Cambrai, 1918	7th ,,
FINAL ADVANCE	Ypres, 1918	1st ,,
	Courtrai	1st ,,
	Selle	7th ,,
	Sambre	5th ,,
		7th ,,
AUSTRIAN OFFENSIVE, 1918 ...	Piave	2nd ,,
ITALIAN OFFENSIVE, 1918	Vittorio Veneto ...	2nd ,,
MACEDONIA OFFENSIVE, 1917 ...	Doiran, 1917	9th ,,
MACEDONIA OFFENSIVE, 1918 ...	Doiran, 1918	9th ,,
HELLES OPERATIONS	Helles	1st ,,
	Landing at Helles ...	1st ,,
	Krithia	1st ,,
ANZAC AND SUVLA OPERATIONS	Suvla	1st ,,
		6th ,,
	Scimitar Hill	1st ,,
		6th ,,

INDEX

Bishop, Capt. A. O., 85 ; wounded, 86
Bishop, 2/Lt. E. R. L., 114, 115
Bjerre, Capt. T. E., wounded, 136
Black, 2/Lt. G., wounded, 85
Black, Pte., 6th Bn., 152
Blackburn, 2/Lt. G. E. H., wounded, 237
Blackwood, Capt. A. P., 38
Blair, Capt. R. R., 25, 39, 68 ; killed, 93
Bloomfield, 2/Lt. V., wounded, 121, 124 ; Lt., 189, 193
Bond, Lt.-Col. C. E., assumes command of 8th Bn., 70 ; 137
Bonome, Lt. A. W., wounded, 161
Booth, Sergt. R. L., 11 ; R.S.M., 163
Borman, 2/Lt. J. R. S., wounded, 85
Bosanquet, Major J. T. I., 4 ; wounded, 12
Botham, C.Q.M.S. H., 1st Bn., 42 ; wounded, 48
Bott, 2/Lt. G. G. R., wounded, 138 ; Lt., killed, 183, 184
Bourne, 2/Lt. K. M., S. Lanc. R., 37
Bousfield, Major E., 23
Bowden, Sergt., 1st Bn., wounded, 49
Bowe, Capt. J. H., 69
Bowley, 2/Lt. T. H., Leinster R., killed, 12
Bowman, Sergt., 8th Bn., 178
Boyd, 2/Lt. R. R., wounded, 130
Bradley-Williams, Lt.-Col., 8th Bn., wounded, 195
Bradshaw, 2/Lt. B., 48 ; wounded, 49
Brady, 2/Lt. D. W., 103
Brander, Lt.-Col. H. R., 27, 70
Brandon, 2/Lt. F. E., 141
Bray, L./Cpl., 8th Bn., awarded M.M., 183
Bremner, Lt., 1st Bn., 87 ; wounded, 88
Brett, 2/Lt. E. E., missing, 130
Brewen, 2/Lt. W. G., wounded, 200
Brewer, L./Cpl., 2nd Bn., awarded D.C.M., 14
Broadley-Smith, Capt. A. F., 25 ; Major, killed, 39
Broadrick, Major G. F., 18, 19 ; Lt.-Col., 22, 25, 26, 53, 55, 56, 57, 58 ; killed, 89
Brooke, Lt.-Col. C. R. I., K.O.Y.L.I., 29
Brooke, Major G. C., 16, 18, 42 ; killed, 47
Brooks, Lt. J., 216
Brown, Capt. C., killed, 84
Brown, Sergt.-Cook C., 42
Brown, Lt. C. S., 71
Brown, Pte. F., 138, 139
Brown, Capt. & Qr.-Mr. F. W., 18
Brown, 2/Lt. J., 189 ; missing, 194
Brown, 2/Lt. W. D., D.L.I., 151; missing, 175
Browne, Major G., 28 ; Lt.-Col., 29
Brownlie, 2/Lt., 9th Bn., 167
Browning, Lt. & Qr.-Mr., 1st Bn., 234
Bruckman, 2/Lt. R. T., 216
Bunting, Capt. H., 125 ; wounded, 127
Burgess, Lt. J. B., R.A.M.C., 216
Burke, 2/Lt. M. A., killed, 151
Burkin, Cpl., 8th Bn., 179
Burmann, 2/Lt. R. M., 35, 36, 37, 38 ; Capt., 164
Burn, 2/Lt. E. N., wounded, 199, 200
Burnell, Rev. E. W., 202
Burns, 2/Lt. G., 62
Burns-Albon, Lt. J., 222
Butler, 2/Lt. W. B., 90 ; Capt., 146, 158
Buy, 2/Lt. K. E. G., killed, 222
Byng, 2/Lt. H. G., killed, 37
Byng, Gen. Sir J. 5, 6, 7, 77, 140, 157, 224

Caird, 2/Lt. W. J., gassed, 200
Calvert, Lt., 5th Bn., wounded, 195
Cambrai, Battle of, 157, et seq.
Cameron, 2/Lt. A., missing, 185
Campbell, 2/Lt. C., 64
Campbell, Rev. H. E., 24, 25
Campbell, Capt. J. G., 163, 205
Campbell, 2/Lt. S. V., wounded, 175
Campbell, 2/Lt. W. C., missing, 130
Capper, Major-Gen. T., 3, 5, 12 ; mortally wounded, 67
Carey, 2/Lt. G., 222
Cargill, 2/Lt. D., 62 ; wounded, 88
Carr, 2/Lt. R. N., 55 ; wounded, 58 ; Capt., wounded, 96 ; 135
Carr, 2/Lt. W., 127 ; wounded, 150
Carr, Cpl., 8th Bn., 179
Carter, Cpl. H., 138, 139
Cassels, Capt. W. G., killed, 86
Castle, 2/Lt. N., wounded, 14 ; 48 ; wounded, 50
Casualties in principal battles and actions : At Ypres, 11, 12, 13 ; at Sailly, 14 ; at Ypres, 37 ; at the Dardanelles, 45, 47, 48, 49, 51, 56, 57, 59, 62 ; at Loos, 67 ; at Bray, 74 ; on the Somme, 82, 84, 85, 86, 88, 97 ; at Guillemont, 116 ; at Arras, 130 ; at Messines, 136 ; at Ypres, 147, 150, 152, 154 ; at Cambrai, 160 ; on the Somme, 175, 177 ; on the Lys, 184, 186, 188 ; on the Aisne, 194 ; on the Somme, 200 ; on the Piave, 210 ; at the Hindenburg Line, 222
Caulfield, Major A. M., 26, 55 ; missing, 58
Cavan, Lt.-Gen. Earl of, 116, 144, 204, 205, 206
Cay, 2/Lt. C. S., 42, 48 ; wounded, 51
Chads, 2/Lt. H. F., 4
Chadwick, L./Sergt., 9th Bn., 167
Chamberlayne, Major, 1st Lancers, I. A., 84
Chambers, 2/Lt. W. H. F., 51 ; Lt., wounded, 62 ; Capt., 146, 158, 185 ; wounded, 234
Chance, Capt. F. S., 23
Chance, Capt. K. M., 55 ; Major, wounded, 136
Chatfield, 2/Lt. H. L., 4, 8 ; Capt., 23, 127
Cherry, 2/Lt. J., 141
Chetham-Strode, Lt. E. R., 38, 68 ; Capt., 114 ; killed, 150
Cheverton, 2/Lt. S. C., 62 ; Lt., killed, 116
Chicken, 2/Lt., 1st Bn., wounded, 186 ; 230, 238
Chisholme, 2/Lt. W. D., 151 ; killed, 175
Cholmeley, 2/Lt. H. L., 31 ; wounded, 32, 33 ; missing, 88
Cholmondeley, Capt. C. A. J., 4 ; killed, 12
Christmas Truce, 1914, 15, 30
Clague, 2/Lt. W., 18, 42 ; wounded, 47, 61
Clancey, 2/Lt. T. J., 4 ; killed, 12
Clark, 2/Lt. A. M., killed, 116
Clark, 2/Lt. F. L., wounded, 86
Clarke, 2/Lt. E. G., missing, 130
Clarke, Capt. J. C., R.A.M.C., wounded, 158, 160
Clarke, Pte., 2nd Bn., awarded D.C.M., 14
Clart, Capt. C. H., 71
Clayton, Lt. A. B., 18 ; Capt., 30 ; wounded, 32, 33
Clayton, 2/Lt. N. M., 230 ; wounded, 237
Clayton, 2/Lt. T., 230, 237
Clegg, Lt. E. C., 3rd Bn., 4 ; wounded, 12 ; Capt., 55 ; killed, 59
Clifford, 2/Lt., 2nd Bn., 203

3788218R00165

Printed in Great Britain
by Amazon.co.uk, Ltd.,
Marston Gate.